# GREAT LAKES
## Great
## Legacy?

# GREAT LAKES
# Great Legacy?

Theodora E. Colborn

Alex Davidson

Sharon N. Green

R. A. (Tony) Hodge

C. Ian Jackson

Richard A. Liroff

The Conservation
Foundation
Washington, D.C.

The Institute for
Research on Public Policy
Ottawa, Ontario

**Great Lakes, Great Legacy?**

Cover design by Meadows & Wiser Graphic Design, Washington, D.C.
Typeset and printed by Harper Graphics, Waldorf, Maryland

In the United States, orders should be directed to The Conservation Foundation, P.O. Box 4866, Hampden Post Office, Baltimore, Maryland 21211.
Telephone: (301) 338-6951.
In Canada, phone 1-800-565-0659 for order information.

**Library of Congress Cataloguing-in-Publication Data**
Great Lakes, great legacy? / Theodora E. Colborn . . . [et al.].    p.   cm.
  Includes bibliographical references.
  ISBN 0-89164-115-7
  1. Pollution—Great Lakes Region. 2. Environmental protection—Great Lakes Region. I. Colborn, Theo.
TD181.G73G73 1990                                              89-25238
363.73′94′0977—dc20                                                CIP

# Contents

viii

# BOXES

# FIGURES

## 4. Legacies and Challenges: Water

## 5. Legacies and Challenges: Air and Climate

# Foreword

Long abused by its human inhabitants, the Great Lakes basin became the focus of an intensive rehabilitative effort by the United States and Canada during the early 1970s. Since then, there have been marked improvements in environmental conditions—Lake Erie is no longer casually referred to as "dead" or "dying"—and the rate of degradation appears to have slowed. But, in many respects, environmental conditions remain unsatisfactory, and the health of the basin's inhabitants remains in jeopardy.

The Great Lakes basin faces complex environmental problems. Many identifiable stresses caused by humans—contamination by chemicals, harvesting of resources, and physical change of the landscape—are not unique to the basin. In that sense, the messages from the Great Lakes should be heeded globally. They serve as a reminder that humans must respect nature's limits and that human well-being and the health of natural ecosystems are intertwined.

The Great Lakes basin has been a laboratory for testing new approaches to protecting and enhancing environmental quality. Because it is the joint responsibility of two nations, the basin provides a model for managing other shared resources around the globe. Environmental problems do not respect national boundaries; those who care about shared resources elsewhere have much to learn from programs tested in the Great Lakes.

In 1987, The Conservation Foundation (CF) and The Institute for Research on Public Policy (IRPP) embarked on a two-year study of the Great Lakes basin to assess environmental conditions and trends and the adequacy of government programs. CF brought to the project its experience with *State of the Environment* reports. Foundation staff believed that data about environmental conditions in the Great Lakes basin were plentiful but needed to be better organized and made more accessible to decision makers and the public; a single, well-documented volume would promote public understanding of environmental trends and help identify needs for new policies and programs. CF also sought to focus on the Great Lakes because of an abiding interest in promoting greater integration of programs for controlling pollution of land, air, and water. Staff believed that, too often, pollution control programs simply shift risks among air, land, and water, rather than reducing them, and fail to take account of the cumulative effects posed by toxic contaminants in these media.

IRPP staff came to the study with a conviction that there is no necessary conflict between the economy and the environment—that the much-vaunted "trade-off" is a myth and, indeed, that in the long run there can be no successful economic structure built on continuing degradation of the environment and depletion of the renewable resource base. The path-breaking study by the World Commission on Environment and Development, now known as the Brundtland Commission, whose report *Our Common Future* was published in 1987, encapsulated that view in a simple phrase—"sustainable development"—which underlined the extent to which environmental and economic concerns can be mutually supportive. IRPP sought to explore these linkages between economic development and environmental quality in the Great Lakes basin, to identify the need for greater integration of environmental considerations with economic decisions affecting agriculture, energy, and other societal investments. IRPP emphasized the importance of institutional structures to assure widespread involvement and participation in community decisions and action to deal with these issues.

Despite the commitment of both institutions to reporting on environmental conditions, each brought to the project a wariness of environmental statistics. Environmental data are not as abundant or precise as economic data, so it is sometimes difficult to describe the state of the environment as objectively as, say, the economy. Also, there is little point in reproducing data for data's sake; the environmental data that do exist must be analyzed rather than merely reported. Further, the lack of data proving beyond doubt that environmental problems are caused by particular human actions should not be used as an excuse for inaction.

This report concludes that, although progress has been made in rehabilitating the Great Lakes ecosystem, much more must be done. A new agenda is needed. Future policies for the Great Lakes basin must emphasize anticipation and prevention along with rehabilitation. They must cope with the legacy of deterioration inherited from the past, while ensuring that undesirable environmental legacies are not created for future generations. Anticipatory programs must encompass and reduce the broad range of stresses on the Great Lakes ecosystem. More efficient use of energy, less chemically dependent agriculture, and changes in manufacturing processes to reduce dependence on toxic substances and limit their production are among the measures required. Implementing the new agenda will be a job for more than traditional pollution control and natural resource agencies. Transportation, energy, and agriculture agencies, and many others, must mount a searching reevaluation of their policies to assure that actions taken to satisfy short-term needs do not create long-term environmental problems.

This report was produced by a six-member project team: at CF, Dr. Richard A. Liroff (project director), Dr. Theodora Colborn, and Sharon Green; at IRPP, Alex Davidson (project director), R.A. (Tony) Hodge, and Dr. C. Ian Jackson. The team members differed in national perspectives and professional training, senses of optimism and pessimism, and penchants for advocacy. All of them, if they did not know before they started, learned to appreciate how challenging interdisciplinary research can be, let alone conducting such research across a national boundary. The final manuscript evolved out of a series of collective reviews of drafts, points debated, positions hammered out, and substantial consensus achieved.

At both organizations, additional guidance and support was provided by Bethany Brown, Edwin H. Clark II, Tabitha Cox, J. Clarence Davies III, Brian Day, Jeffrey Holmes, H. Jeffrey Leonard, James MacNeill, Robert McCoy, Rice Odell, German Reyes, Angela Rockall, Barbara Rodes, Bradley Rymph, David Runnalls, Timothy Sivia, Walter Stewart, Maureen Tamarit, and Marsha White.

A binational advisory panel, cochaired by Jim MacNeill of IRPP and Richard Liroff of CF, included Lee Botts, Fred Brown, Michael Cleland, J.D. (Doug) Cook, Michael Donahue, Carlos Fetterolf, Jr., Walter Giles, F. Kenneth Hare, Jean Hennessey, John Jackson, Nicholas

Kachman, Bonnie Koenig, David Miller, Jean Piette, and Maurice Yeates. Although panel members hold leadership positions in many organizations concerned about the Great Lakes, they were asked to serve as individuals rather than as representatives of institutions. The project team is indebted to them for their early advice that the report should be a thematic interpretation of data and not merely an encyclopedic compendium of figures. The final report is markedly different from the draft reviewed and commented on by many of the panelists. The opinions expressed herein are solely those of the project team and should not be attributed to panel members.

Assistance was also provided by consultants who gathered data on selected subjects or conducted institutional analyses. Thanks are due to Mimi Becker, Mara Cohen, Connie Gaudet, Leonard Gianessi, Robert Hoffman, Bertram McInnis, Susan MacKenzie, Robert Morris, David Rapport, Cathy Schaeff, and Phil Weller.

Outside reviewers who commented on drafts of this report included: David Bates, Mimi Becker, John Cairns Jr., Jack Christie, Elizabeth Dowdeswell, George Francis, Kent Fuller, Michael Gilbertson, Jim MacLaren, Paul Muldoon, Henry Regier, Blair Seaborn, Bill Steggles, and Frank Stone. Their comments prompted fundamental changes in the tone and structure of the report.

Many individuals attended roundtables on the project in Toronto and Ottawa; the wetlands and fisheries consultancy projects benefited from those who served on an advisory panel.

The project team is especially indebted to the more than 200 individuals in both government and the private sector who so generously gave of their time and information in personal interviews and notes, phone conversations, and other contacts with the project team. Without their willingness to share their knowledge, this project would not have been possible.

This experiment in binational cooperation also could not have been done without generous financial support given to The Conservation Foundation and The Institute for Research on Public Policy. It was provided by the Joyce Foundation, the Charles Stewart Mott Foundation, the George Gund Foundation, the Moriah Fund, the Prince Charitable Trust, the Gaylord Donnelley 1983 Gift Trust, the USX Foundation, the Laidlaw Foundation, Environment Canada, the Ontario Ministry of the Environment, Dofasco, Dow Chemical, Esso Petroleum, INCO, Manulife, Noranda Group, Ontario Hydro, Polysar, Shell Canada, Stelco, Suncor, Union Carbide, and donors of unre-

stricted funds to The Conservation Foundation. All of this support is
gratefully acknowledged.

Kathryn S. Fuller
President
The Conservation Foundation

Rod Dobell
President
The Institute for Research on Public Policy

# Overview

# An Ecosystem in Trouble

Despite regulatory vigilance to rein in polluters and significant government cleanup efforts over the last two decades, the environment of the Great Lakes basin is still in trouble. Dramatic evidence remains that the Great Lakes are imperiled by continuing habitat destruction and the long-term accumulation of toxic chemicals, which are increasingly pervasive throughout the ecosystem.

Many of the signs of environmental crisis are clearly evident to the 35 million people who reside within the Great Lakes region.

- Around the Great Lakes, 42 particularly degraded localities have been singled out by the International Joint Commission (IJC), as "Areas of Concern." A combination of human wastes, toxic industrial garbage, and relentless ecological destruction has left these areas with environmental crises that can only be relieved by expenditures of vast sums of money and decades of remedial attention.
- Some of the beaches in the Great Lakes region are permanently closed because they are not safe for bathing; many others are closed at periodic intervals because of fecal and chemical contamination.
- The most productive natural systems of the Great Lakes region are wetlands, but two-thirds of them have been filled, drained, or bulldozed out of existence.
- Many of the nearly 80,000 small lakes in the Great Lakes basin, like countless others in southern Canada and the northeastern United States, are dying slowly from the effects of acid rain.

- But acid rain is not the only air-related problem. Clear evidence is now available that large quantities of toxic chemicals find their way into the Great Lakes ecosystem after having been carried perhaps several thousand miles by air currents. Thus, long-range deposition accounts for more than 90 percent of the dangerous polychlorinated biphenyls (PCBs) found in Lake Superior and is the *only* significant source of chemicals such as DDT and toxaphene, which are restricted in the United States and Canada but still used in Mexico and Central America.
- Tests of underground water systems throughout the Great Lakes region indicate steadily mounting contamination from the leaching of chemicals dumped on the land.

The symptoms are evident everywhere, and are reflected in the minutiae of life as well as the grand sweep of nature. The plight of aquatic species, fish-eating birds, and some land animals that spend part or all of their lives in the Great Lakes region is ominous.

- Bald eagles along the shores of the lakes do not reproduce as well as those that reside inland; in some lake areas, bald eagles do not reproduce at all.
- Such problems are not unique to bald eagles; other fish-eating birds and animals at the top of the food web have suffered marked developmental abnormalities that have resulted in significant increases in birth defects and population declines in some species.
- Many species of fish no longer survive in the waters of the lakes, and many of the survivors can no longer reproduce *in situ*.
- New varieties of fish have been introduced to replace the species destroyed by human activities. However, authorities warn that these new species should be eaten only in small quantities because they are contaminated with poisonous chemicals.

Evidence is growing that the well-being of the region's human inhabitants cannot be divorced from the fate of the Great Lakes' wildlife.

- By the process called "biomagnification," which passes along toxic substances in higher and higher levels as they proceed upward through the food web, contaminants that are almost undetectable in lake water may be magnified hundreds of thousands of times within the flesh of a Great Lakes fish. That is why it is often not safe to eat the fish that swim in the same water that one can drink. Humans, too, are constantly accumulating toxic chemicals that may not be lethal but may be associated with long-term, adverse health, developmental, and reproductive effects.

- The suite of chemicals introduced into the Great Lakes environment over the past half-century has been shown in the laboratory to disrupt normal functioning in cells of animals. The clinical effects of residues on human health are not yet understood. It is known, however, that such chemicals are associated in animals with a number of reproductive, neurological, immunological, and carcinogenic effects and with abnormal sexual development. Stepped-up efforts to test for parallel effects in human beings are a clear priority.

Urgent action is needed by federal, state, provincial, and local governments in both Canada and the United States if the process of long-term environmental degradation in the Great Lakes region is to be reversed. Yet it is increasingly clear that simply augmenting what has been done—greater control of polluters, more resources for cleaning up crisis areas, piecemeal restrictions on physical development—is not going to be a sufficient response.

A far-reaching commitment to reduce the environmental assault on the Great Lakes from all sources is necessary. This will require attention not only to direct discharges of pollution but also to the long-range deposition of toxic chemicals from the air, as well as the indirect contamination caused by "nonpoint" sources such as runoff from agriculture and urban streets. Governments at all levels must develop programs designed to anticipate and prevent environmental problems from occurring in the first place. This will necessitate economic policies that encourage the private sector and government to design production processes and facilities that produce far less waste rather than policies that focus largely on cleaning up waste after it is produced. Local governments throughout the basin must develop new ways of assessing the total environmental impacts of physical development.

The long-term environmental health of the Great Lakes region cannot be secured until the cumulative adverse environmental effects of all human activities are reduced to levels that the total ecosystem—not just the water but the land, the air, and the wildlife as well—can tolerate. There are four reasons why this will be exceedingly difficult to accomplish.

*First*, huge residual problems from environmental contamination and past destructive development still must be confronted.

*Second*, greatly increased environmental protection efforts in both Canada and the United States have already succeeded in doing the "easy" things. The next generation of remedial steps will be both more complex and much more expensive.

*Third*, an action agenda will require unprecedented levels of international cooperation between Canada and the United States. Indeed, it may require a degree of coordinated and integrated response that has proved difficult to achieve even among different layers and agencies of government *within* each country.

*Finally*, it may be that even the most stringent conventional pollution control measures and restrictions on ecologically destructive development will not be enough. The challenge to restore the health of the Great Lakes ecosystem may require sweeping changes in life-style from societies increasingly dependent on the motor car for transportation, chemicals for agricultural production, fossil fuels for energy, and human-made environments for recreation. The environment must become a mainstream economic issue for both societies. This means that environmental quality must become a principal concern of cabinet members concerned with tax and fiscal policies and of the chief executive officers of major corporations, not just a fixation of those directly charged with environmental protection.

*Great Lakes, Great Legacy?*, from which these conclusions emerge, is a two-year, binational study of the Great Lakes basin undertaken by The Conservation Foundation in the United States and The Institute for Research on Public Policy in Canada. This report confirms that it is not possible merely to deal with one element in the environment— water, air quality, land, living organisms—and hope thereby to cure the whole. Work in the Great Lakes and elsewhere has shown that it is necessary to treat the elements of the entire ecosystem within a region as interconnected. Moreover, in the open system of the environment, noxious debris wafted into the air hundreds—even thousands—of miles away can become, within days, the source of waterborne contamination in the Great Lakes. Government responses to the environmental stress can succeed only if they thoroughly consider all of these factors.

This study also underscores the need for a dramatic break from the crisis management approach to environmental degradation that persists in the Great Lakes region. Time and again, environmental contamination has been allowed to continue to a point where it threatens human health and wildlife; the cumulative consequences of ill-planned, piecemeal development are not assessed until their damage is apparent. Today, the challenge is to move beyond the cycle of periodic environmental crises to anticipate and indeed prevent future legacies of environmental destruction.

One positive note is the fact that the institutional wherewithal already exists to integrate environmental quality efforts and eclipse the crisis management mode of environmental protection. A remarkable set of institutions and mechanisms on both sides of the border can support and coordinate the substantial actions that are necessary to reclaim the natural heritage and ecosystem health of the Great Lakes region. These include: the International Joint Commission—established by Canada and the United States in 1909—with its many boards and committees; the Council of Great Lakes Governors; diverse member organizations such as Great Lakes United, as well as many other nongovernmental and governmental institutions; and formal and informal links among scientists, academics, policy makers, other professionals, and concerned citizens. There is no reason to think that a new, single "super-agency" to manage the Great Lakes region would, in fact, offer an improved institutional framework.

What is needed to rescue the Great Lakes region from its continuing environmental decline is the will to act and the discipline to take a long-term perspective. It seems clear that this is an area in which public opinion in both countries is well ahead of politicians. Poll after poll in both the United States and Canada has confirmed the importance of the environment in the public mind and the willingness to take action to improve the situation.

Crucial ingredients to such action, however, are still missing. For the course to be reversed, there must be *understanding* of the severity of the environmental perils, *foresight* to anticipate crises before they hit, *political leadership* willing to stand tall for the environment, and an unflagging *public commitment* to provide the financial resources necessary to achieve environmental protection.

## A LEGACY OF DESTRUCTION AND CRISIS RESPONSE

The first settlers from Europe found in the Great Lakes region a vast area of rich soil, dense forests, and abundant fish, game, and fresh water. From the outset, the arrival of European civilization set off a pattern of uncontrolled development and assault on the natural environment that has continued largely unabated to this day.

Prosperity was wrung from a countryside increasingly tamed, conformed, and made comfortable. Swamplands turned into cities, forests became farms, lakes became millponds, and rivers became sewers. Transportation corridors slashed across the land, and harbors edged the lakes; industrial complexes were created, and vast areas of wilderness habitat eliminated. Of course, this kind of development process was not unique to the Great Lakes. But "these inland seas," as they were once called, seemed so incalculably huge, and became so central to the expanding nations on both sides of the border, that their visible distress, when at last it began to be noticed, came as a shock.

Late in the last century and early in this one, epidemics of cholera and typhoid swept the Great Lakes region, and hundreds of men, women, and children died. The epidemics were traced to supplies of drinking water that had been contaminated with raw sewage. This was the Great Lakes region's first recognizable, major public health and environmental crisis. Society reacted by chlorinating the water; the epidemics passed. Yet, in the late 1940s and early 1950s, tests showed that the level of harmful bacteria were triple those found earlier in the century.

The 1930s brought a second environmental crisis, one that continued for several decades. This crisis appeared to affect not people but fish. In pioneer days, salmon were caught in all the rivers that empty into Lake Ontario, and many farms were paid for by the salmon catch. At Newcastle, Ontario, salmon were so numerous in the late 18th century that women waded into the water to seine them with flannel petticoats. Sturgeon came up the large rivers every spring to spawn; there were so many that they were considered pests. Lake trout, whitefish, and the freshwater herring, or cisco, were common, along with muskellunge, northern pike, walleye, bass, and dozens of other species.

Fish populations were threatened simultaneously on three fronts: they were victims of new species introduced into the system, they were suffering from the degradation of water quality, and they were being overfished. The parasitic sea lamprey, an eel-like fish, reached Lakes Huron and Michigan when the Welland Canal provided a detour around Niagara Falls, and lake trout disappeared from these lakes soon after. Pollution, which led to the overproduction of algae, robbed lake water of much of its oxygen and devastated the fish population. At the same time, overfishing added to the problem. In Lake Erie alone, the walleye catch ran to an average 7 million pounds a year in the 1940s; it dropped to 328,411 pounds in 1968.

In 1955, in response to increasingly alarmed protests from lake fishermen, the Great Lakes Fishery Commission was created. In a natural experiment without precedent, a variety of innovative management initiatives has since led to a rebounding of the fishery and the creation of a multibillion dollar sport-fishing industry. Again, a crisis apparently was met and conquered.

But the "quality" of fish has not recovered. Several key species, including the lake trout, are no longer naturally self-sustaining and remain only because of expensive artificial stocking programs. New exotic organisms (with an unknown impact on the ecosystem) continue to find their way into the Great Lakes in the bilge water of ships. Advisories warn against high levels of fish consumption because of toxic contamination. Although fish have become readily catchable once again, whether they are fit for human consumption is questionable.

Moreover, by the 1960s, the degradation of Lake Erie was extreme. Nutrient enrichment, mainly phosphorus, had led to excessive eutrophication—that is the abundant growth of plant life, whose decay in turn depletes the water of life-supporting oxygen. Huge algal blooms piled up rotting on beaches. Lakes and rivers near numerous municipal and industrial areas in the region were devoid of visible aquatic life. The Cuyahoga River in Cleveland, Ohio, ran a chocolate brown or rust color and was choked with debris, oils, scum, and floating organic sludges. Even lower forms of life such as leeches were absent. On June 22, 1969, the Cuyahoga was carrying such high concentrations of oil and other flammable industrial wastes that it caught fire and burned two railway bridges beyond use. Some observers pronounced Lake Erie "dead." Perhaps the other Great Lakes were not far behind.

For the third time, society found itself reacting to an environmental crisis in the Great Lakes basin. Although the United States and Canada had commissioned studies of boundary waters' pollution through the IJC in 1912 and again in 1946, and loud warnings had been sounded, little action had resulted. In 1964, a third study was initiated. This time, the result was the Great Lakes Water Quality Agreement of 1972. Controls on phosphorus discharges to the lakes were introduced, and an extensive set of broad studies under the Pollution from Land Use Activities Research Group (PLUARG) was initiated.

Action brought results. Lake Erie and the other Great Lakes have, to varying degrees, visibly and invisibly improved in quality. So, too, have many urban waterfronts, where a burst of development is bringing a revival of economic activity.

Ambient concentrations of phosphorus have been reduced to levels that are allowing the recovery of much of the aquatic ecosystem. To date, more than U.S.$10 billion has been spent to upgrade municipal sewage treatment and to bring the problems of nutrient enrichment and excessive eutrophication under control. This recovery must be considered a significant success story.

However, the battle is far from won. The amounts of phosphorus discharged into the system and "ambient levels"—the total amount of phosphorus present in the system—have been reduced but still have not met target objectives set by the Great Lakes agreement. Oxygen depletion in the deep central basin of Lake Erie remains a concern. More than 30 local areas around the major lakes and many hinterland lakes, particularly on the U.S. side, still experience elevated levels of phosphorus and the associated problems of eutrophication. Furthermore, in the shadows, a second nutrient issue has become a nagging concern. While phosphorus levels have declined, nitrogen levels have grown, and the ratio between the two, an important factor for the balance of natural systems in the lakes, has changed. So far only minor shifts in the nature of the plankton in Lakes Michigan and Ontario have been found, but careful monitoring of long-term consequences is essential.

The fourth crisis registered on the public consciousness was the contamination of Great Lakes waters with persistent toxic chemicals. In the 1970s, the degraded condition of Cleveland's harbor could be seen repeated in many harbors around the Great Lakes. Analyses of bottom sediments tracked massive increases in the discharges of contaminants and clearly identified industrial and municipal sources. The levels of persistent toxic chemicals in the water itself grew alarmingly high. Waterfowl populations, fish, and wildlife dependent on the aquatic ecosystem were found laced with toxic contaminants, deformed, and dying. Was human health in jeopardy?

Again, society reacted. In 1978, a revised Great Lakes Water Quality Agreement was signed. The new document continued controls on phosphorus but shifted the emphasis to the issue of toxic contaminants. Furthermore, driven by the results of the PLUARG studies demonstrating the connection between the status of the lakes and human activities throughout the drainage area, an "ecosystem approach" was agreed on as a governing strategy for management of the Great Lakes basin. This binational recognition of the principle that all components of the ecosystem must be considered as an interconnected whole (air, land, water, and living organisms) represented a major step in international environmental cooperation.

There was another major advance. The new agreement adopted a philosophy of "zero discharge" of persistent toxic substances and a parallel policy of virtual elimination of such substances en route to zero discharge. In principle at least, there was no longer an "acceptable level" of contamination by these toxic substances. Again, action brought results; the reduction in loadings was mirrored in improved water quality throughout most of the region—until recently.

In the wake of the agreement, the critical movement of contaminants among different media—air, land, surface water, and groundwater— was increasingly recognized. Concern was voiced that regulation of one component of the system without regard for the others, and interactions among them, would inevitably limit success. Direct discharges to water could be controlled, but if, for example, the atmosphere was delivering chemicals from the local incinerator or from fertilizers, herbicides, and pesticides used hundreds and even thousands of miles away, the improvement achieved would be limited. Despite growing appreciation of these linkages, concrete action to address them has not been sufficient.

Beyond water quality, other water issues have also surfaced. Extreme high and low water levels have led to difficulties for many users of the lakes—shoreline residents, shippers and marina owners, and generators of hydroelectric power. High levels combined with storms have resulted in hundreds of millions of dollars in property damage along shorelines. Conversely, low levels have caused financial losses for shippers and energy producers.

Many of those affected by varying lake levels have blamed "nature" for their problems and want to see more human control. Yet human ability to manage lake levels is limited. It cannot, for example, eliminate the problems that stem from putting buildings in the wrong places along shorelines. In the case of high water levels, most of the difficulties have been a result of construction in vulnerable areas. In the case of low levels, builders' expectations have been dashed as natural variations in conditions occur and as lake-front properties have become beached hundreds of feet from the water. In both cases, it has been the lack of recognition and unwillingness to adapt to natural conditions on the part of human society that has caused the problem, not "nature."

## THE CUMULATION OF INSUFFICIENT RESPONSES

The pattern is clear. Since European settlers arrived in the Great Lakes region, development and economic expansion have pushed ahead with woefully inadequate consideration of the natural environment. As an environmental crisis has occurred that threatens human life or interferes with immediate human wants, a partial, bandage solution that alleviates concern is found and applied. Some success is achieved. The cycle is frequently repeated. As the problems become more complex, the actions that society takes with its narrow, reactive perspective become progressively less adequate. Hidden costs are simply passed on.

In fact, when a major breakthrough in protection of the environment occurred, it did not come as a result of anything as dramatic as an epidemic but in a rather dull, bureaucratic way. During the first few years of this century, a series of disagreements between Canada and the United States led to the Boundary Waters Treaty of 1909 and the subsequent establishment of the International Joint Commission, which was given the authority to deal with any matters affecting the use or diversion of boundary waters. A small clause slipped into the treaty committed each nation not to pollute the waters of the other. It is that clause that has led to the creation of one of the most innovative and successful mechanisms in the world for the binational resolution of environmental issues. The instrument is there. Unfortunately, it has not always been in use.

Moreover, as the 20th century has proceeded, humankind's capacity to alter and even destroy the environment has accelerated. This has placed a greater burden on fledgling efforts to protect the environment. One of the world's great industrial areas emerged in the Great Lakes basin, and a population of several million people scattered throughout the region became 35 million residents heavily clustered in large metropolitan areas. With this growth has come an equally dramatic shift in society's economic base, from subsistence resource extraction to the development of a scientific industrial complex. As part of this evolution, there has been an extraordinary increase, particularly in the four decades since the end of World War II, in the use of manufactured chemicals. Every facet of life has been touched; the increase in chemical use has been accompanied by a massive dumping into the environment of the by-products and leftovers of the process.

It has been 40 years since the dramatic growth in chemical use began, 25 years since scientists first recognized the crisis of toxic contaminants in the fish and wildlife of the Great Lakes, 20 years since the Cuyahoga River burst into flames, and a decade since the Great Lakes Water Quality Agreement was amended to focus on the issue of toxic contaminants. Environmental indicators point to the conclusion that the sum of all the crisis responses that have accumulated during this timespan is not sufficient to protect the Great lakes ecosystem from further deterioration, much less to restore it to a healthier condition in the long run. A review of the state of the Great Lakes environment shows that, despite all the gains made in recent years, the ecosystem is still, on balance, threatened.

## THE STATE OF THE GREAT LAKES ENVIRONMENT

What is the state of the environment in the Great Lakes basin today? Figure 1 lists 15 factors and summarizes the data presented in this study. In addition to presenting an overview of the current status and trend for each factor, the figure indicates a "response time" and a "spatial context." The response time provides a rough estimate of time during which the factor would "recover" should human-induced stresses be eliminated. The spatial context provides an indication of the geographic area in which the factor operates.

Notwithstanding the overview presented in figure 1, the actual status of the Great Lakes ecosystem is difficult to summarize because of the complex knowledge required about the interaction between all environmental factors. The Great Lakes aquatic system alone includes, in addition to transboundary waters of the Great Lakes and their connecting channels, over 80,000 inland lakes with a combined area greater than that of Lake Erie. The system also contains nearly half a million miles (750,000 kilometers) of inland streams and rivers, a groundwater system that provides drinking water for 7.5 million basin residents and serves to transmit contaminants both to those drinking-water supplies and to surface water, and the St. Lawrence River, which provides the final link to the ocean.

## A SEAMLESS WEB OF ENVIRONMENTAL PROBLEMS

Although a general recovery of Great Lakes water quality from pollution by toxic metals and organic contaminants has been under way since the 1970s, there are lingering problems with some extremely dangerous substances such as dioxins and furans. Furthermore, the

# Figure 1

## Indicators of Ecosystem Health in the Great Lakes Basin

### A. Contaminants in the Environment

| Element | Recovery Time | Spatial Context | Status |
|---|---|---|---|
| 1. Air quality | days to months | local to global | Air quality probably has improved over the last two decades because of declines in emissions of various pollutants. Quality still is unsatisfactory in many areas, principally because of high levels of ozone. The problem of airborne toxic pollutants is not yet well defined or addressed. Atmospheric deposition remains a problem for water quality, aquatic organisms, and vegetation. More reductions in emissions are needed. |
| 2. Surface water quality | months to years | basin | Substantial progress on excess nutrient problems has been made in the last two decades, by resolving crisis situations in Lakes Erie and Ontario, although trophic conditions still are not at targeted levels in some areas. Eutrophication and acidification remain serious problems in many inland lakes within the basin. Concentrations of nitrogen compounds have been rising at least over the last two decades in the Great Lakes, and their implications are not yet clear. Nonpoint pollution (urban and rural) remains a serious problem. Cumulative concentrations of metals in three Great Lakes are at elevated levels. Forty-two degraded Areas of Concern require a massive remedial effort. Although concentrations of some pollutants meet ambient water quality standards, concentrations are still high enough to cause serious contamination problems in fish and other wildlife. |

| | | | |
|---|---|---|---|
| 3. Contaminated sediments | decades | basin, river, and lake bottoms | Sediments contaminated with metals and organic compounds are a serious problem in 41 of 42 Areas of Concern. In many locations, sediments remain a continuing source of contaminants and excess nutrients for the food web. Concentrations of many contaminants in recent sediments are significantly less than in older sediments, with some exceptions. |
| 4. Groundwater | decades to centuries | basin | Water sources are contaminated in various locations throughout the region. Degraded conditions stemming from persistent toxic substances will last long into the future. Groundwater can be a major source of contaminants to surface water. Preventive activities are in their infancy, so groundwater quality is degenerating. |
| **B. Fish and Wildlife** | | | |
| 5. Body burdens of toxics | years to decades (generational effects) | local to continental | Contaminant levels in many organisms are substantially lower than they were in the early 1970s, but declines appear to have leveled off and present trends are difficult to interpret. For many substances, levels remain above objectives specified in the Water Quality Agreement or other guidelines and standards. Continued high levels for substances whose use has been restricted signals releases of contaminants previously deposited in the ecosystem, continued release from improper storage of remaining stocks, and remaining uses in remote areas. |
| 6. Population status | years to decades | local to continental | Populations of many bird species are recovering. Problems remain for specific species or populations in particular locations. Some key species, such as lake trout, still are unable to establish self-sustaining populations in several lakes. Biota are threatened in acidifying inland lakes. |
| 7. Habitat | days to centuries | basin | The pace of habitat destruction is substantially reduced from earlier eras, but protection of remaining habitat is still a concern. A coordinated basinwide effort is needed. |

| 8. Fisheries | years to decades | local to basin | A substantial reduction in the lamprey population during the past 20 years and heavy stocking of exotic salmonids and other species has permitted development of a robust sport fishery. The forage base for the fishery may be limited due to controls on phosphorus discharges. The artificially managed "fish ranch" in the lakes may be quite fragile, and the future of the commercial fishery still is uncertain. |
|---|---|---|---|

**C. Terrestrial Conditions**

| 9. Forests | decades | local to basin | Many forests are maturing after recovering from massive overcutting and fires during the late 19th and early 20th century. The future increasingly is seen in managing public lands to allow for multiple uses of forest resources. Forests are at risk from transported air pollutants, such as ozone and acid deposition, with a prospect of widespread stress in the coming decades from climate change. |
|---|---|---|---|
| 10. Wetlands | years to decades | local | Two-thirds of the original wetlands in the basin have been destroyed since the beginning of European settlement. The key role of wetlands in the Great Lakes ecosystem is now recognized. Public policies encouraging wetland destruction must be adjusted to make them consistent with wetland protection goals. |
| 11. Soil erosion | years to decades | local to basin | Available data indicate that erosion generally is below the threshold of concern for short-term, on-site productivity, but there is growing evidence of serious impacts on water quality due to transport of nutrients and pesticides from agricultural areas. |
| 12. Agricultural productivity | years to decades | local to basin | Yields of major crops have risen dramatically through use of fertilizers, pesticides, new varieties of crops, and other changes in farming practice. Economic and environmental doubts about long-term sustainability of chemically dependent agriculture are prompting growing interest in alternative farming practices. |

| | | | |
|---|---|---|---|
| 13. Shorelines | days to years | basin | Record high levels of the Great Lakes in the mid-1980s increased demand by riparian landowners for protection. There is continued public reluctance to accept that substantial year-to-year changes in levels are beyond cost-effective human control. Long-term declines are envisaged due to global warming. Greater emphasis is needed on shoreline management to prevent development in vulnerable areas, protect habitat, and allow multiple use. |

**D. Human Conditions**

| | | | |
|---|---|---|---|
| 14. Human health | days to years | local to global | Available public health data on birth defects and cancer incidence are inadequate as indicators of health effects that may arise from biomagnification and bioaccumulation of toxic substances in the Great Lakes food web. Subgroups at risk may be offspring of those who consume sizable amounts of fish and other predators. A special effort is needed to develop measures for and examine the incidence of subtle developmental problems in groups at risk. Other probable risks to human health occur in areas of contaminated air and groundwater. |
| 15. Economic conditions | months to years | local to global | The Great Lakes basin is the manufacturing heartland of the United States and Canada. The U.S. side was affected strongly by the recession of the early 1980s. A general recovery is under way, speeding the transition from manufacturing dominance towards a more service-oriented economy. Facility modernization has benefited the environment. |

swift progress in reducing toxic contaminants that took place in the late 1970s and early 1980s appears to have slowed or stopped.

Recently deposited bottom sediments in the Great Lakes proper are significantly less contaminated than those deposited in previous decades. But progress on this front is mitigated by the legacy of the past, when virtually every form of chemical, mineral, and organic waste known was deposited in the depths of the lakes. Inevitably, most of these buried contaminants are recirculated into the water, both by natural processes and when the removal of contaminated sediments is required—during dredging, for example, or for the construction of new facilities. This source of potentially dangerous contamination will be around for decades.

And there is much more than water to think about. Not too long ago the air of many urban centers was visibly degraded with smoke. As usual, society reacted long after creating the problem: regulations were passed to control the levels of particulate matter in the air. Yet unhealthy levels of air pollution continue. Although the political wrangling over acid rain has popularized concern about air, the larger issue of long-range transport of all airborne contaminants, which includes the precursors of acid rain as well as ozone and a range of conventional and toxic contaminants, has not received the attention it deserves. The presence of toxic contaminants carried by the air to humans and wildlife, to growing crops, and to water is worrisome. Hexachlorobenzene, for example, a pollutant resulting from incomplete combustion and the manufacture of chlorine-containing chemicals, is subsequently transferred to land, water, and living organisms. Anglers are warned by health departments about eating large lake trout caught in Lake Superior; the fish are contaminated by PCBs deposited into the lake from the atmosphere. When it comes to assessing the ecological health of the Great Lakes basin, government environmental protection programs have frequently underemphasized the relationship between air pollution and water quality.

Over the past two decades, both the emissions and ambient levels of sulfur dioxide—a major contributor to acid rain—have been significantly reduced. But acid rain continues to be a serious problem. One reason is that virtually no progress has been made in reducing emissions of nitrogen oxides, another of its precursors. Indeed, Ontario's emissions of nitrogen oxides were 29 percent higher in 1984 than in 1970. Some versions of proposed revisions of the Clean Air Act could permit U.S. utilities to emit up to one million additional tons of nitrogen oxides into the atmosphere annually by the year 2000. In addition, the transborder movement of ozone, carried from major urban areas of the midwestern United States, looms as a growing problem for Canada—recent studies show that about 50 percent of Ontario's ozone originates in the United States!

On land, new regulations and increased public scrutiny have helped to reduce many of the worst "point" sources of contaminants—factories, waste treatment plants, hazardous waste dumps. At the same time, however, nonpoint pollution, such as runoff from urban streets and agricultural areas, remains substantially unaddressed. And groundwater contaminated by existing land-based hazardous waste sites is now likely the single largest source of contaminants to the Niagara River—and may be for many decades.

Direct discharges from human activities, resuspension of contaminants from bottom sediments, contaminant discharge through groundwater, and atmospheric deposition are all contributing to a maintenance of contaminant concentrations in the Great Lakes food web at levels that threaten the health of fish, wildlife, and humans. Because of the natural processes of bioaccumulation and biomagnification, contaminant levels in predators at or near the top of the food web are of particular concern. In some places, these fish, birds, and mammals exhibit severe problems.

Within the human population, health risks are elevated for those living in areas with polluted air and contaminated groundwater. Even more important, there may be subtle effects on human health that have gone largely undetected and that stem from contaminants in the food web. Certain identifiable subgroups of the population appear to be at elevated risk of exposure. These include human embryos, infants, and children whose parents have bioaccumulated substantial quantities of toxic chemicals that exist in fish and waterfowl. The health effects in the offspring may include altered cognitive, motor, and behavioral development. Preliminary studies suggest that these subtle effects may be far more significant among at-risk populations than cancer and gross physical defects. The need for "more data" is urgent.

Discussion of pollution tends to overshadow vast physical changes that have occurred in the basin. Only a third of the original wetland area now exists. Little old-growth forest is left in developed areas. Transportation corridors have reduced the continuity of wilderness areas. All of this has drastically altered wildlife habitat, reducing natural productivity and the diversity of species.

The pressures on the Great Lakes ecosystem from humans' physical restructuring of the environment continue. Destruction of wetlands and vital habitat probably occurs at a slower rate than it did in years past, but protecting the important areas that are left remains an uphill battle.

## THE COSTS OF SEVERE ENVIRONMENTAL DEGRADATION

Forty-two Areas of Concern (areas where conditions are particularly degraded) have been identified by the International Joint Commission's Great Lakes Water Quality Board since 1973. These include major municipal and industrial centers on rivers, harbors, and connecting channels. Although many of the sites continue to exhibit problems of bacterial pollution, eutrophication, and habitat loss, the dominant concern at all but one today is toxic substance contamination.

In 1985, the eight Great Lakes states and the province of Ontario committed themselves to developing Remedial Action Plans (RAPs) for each Area of Concern, aimed at restoring beneficial uses and encouraging the reestablishment of environmental health and integrity. Preliminary cost estimates are now available for 8 of the 42 RAPS. Based on these early estimates, it is apparent that tens of billions of dollars from both private and public sources will be required for implementation.

As high as these early estimates seem, they reflect only part of the legacy from past action left to the current generation. Neither the plans nor the estimates address conditions throughout the basin, nor do they fully account for the difficult technical issues of:

- contaminated bottom sediments;
- cleanup or containment of contaminants at all the hazardous and solid waste management and industrial and municipal facilities in the basin (including protection and cleanup of groundwater sources);
- further reductions of contaminant emissions and discharges to achieve zero discharge of persistent toxic contaminants; and
- rehabilitation of critical fish and wildlife habitat such as wetlands.

Nor do the cost estimates adequately cover:

- the replacement and maintenance of municipal water and sewage handling and treatment infrastructure that will be required to meet

rising environmental standards, to prevent sewer overflows, to replace aging facilities, and to provide for population growth;
- rehabilitation and maintenance of degraded areas currently not included on the list of 42 Areas of Concern; and
- accidental spills, discharges, and other catastrophes, whether natural or induced by humans.

A comprehensive estimate including all of the above costs is not available. Nevertheless, it is obvious that these costs are enormous. To restore environmental integrity to the Great Lakes basin and maintain the ecosystem in a healthy state will require substantially more than the tens of billions of dollars already identified as necessary to meet immediate problems in the Areas of Concern.

These large costs should be seen in perspective. Not all of the problems can be dealt with overnight, in a year or two, or even in 10 years. The costs will be spread over a long period. The gross annual product of the Great Lakes region exceeds U.S.$1 trillion. Nevertheless, the costs of remedying past wrongs will likely become a much larger factor in the regional economy than they are today, particularly if no investments are made now to prevent the creation of new legacies.

That is the crisis ahead. Already the resources needed to reestablish environmental integrity in the Great Lakes basin may exceed the price that one generation is willing to bear. But a commitment must be made to ensure that the legacy of environmental costs to be left to the future is less than what has been left by the past.

The RAP process offers some insight into how this might be achieved. It is a community-based approach to designing the best possible solution to the particular problems facing each site. It operates on a scale that can foster understanding of the true nature of the issues and the linkage between economic and environmental well-being. Because of the large eventual costs of implementing RAPs and the inevitable trade-offs that must be made, full participation of the community is essential if creative, effective, and equitable solutions are to be found. Though the RAP process has only just begun, and government support has been uneven, a remarkable start has been made. The process represents a revolutionary new approach to environmental decision making for both the United States and Canada. Complex technical and social issues are being dealt with collectively at a grass-roots level. The way is being prepared for the kind of resource commitment that will be required in the future.

## SEVEN PRINCIPLES FOR ACTION

In recent decades, the United States and Canada have made serious and costly attempts to slow the rate of environmental deterioration in the Great Lakes basin. They have spent, collectively, more than U.S.$10 billion building and improving municipal sewage treatment plants in response to the alarm bells that began ringing some decades ago, and have thus avoided turning the Great Lakes into a vast pool of human waste. Major programs have been set in motion to remove and dispose of hazardous wastes. Billions of dollars are still needed to support the RAP process described above.

The overwhelming conclusion of *Great Lakes, Great Legacy?*, however, is that neither country is spending enough, or doing enough, to check the insidious long-term decline of the Great Lakes ecosystem.

On the remedial front, it is painfully clear that only the easiest problems have been tackled and the cheapest remedies, such as curbing the dumping of sewage and toxic chemicals straight into the system, applied. Most of the more difficult challenges lie ahead—such tasks as controlling airborne toxic substances, protecting and restoring groundwater quality, dealing with the problems of toxic metals and pervasive, persistent organic chemicals.

Moreover, the relentless onslaughts of increased population, expanded economic activity, and the resulting higher levels of resource consumption place ever greater strains on the region's natural resource systems and threaten to overwhelm progress in reducing per capita waste and consumption. The dangers of adding new legacies of environmental decay and ecosystem destruction on top of ones that society has yet to remedy are significant.

To resolve the environmental problems of the past and prevent the advent of new crises in the future will require enormous resolve not only on the part of governments but by private citizens and corporations. Seven major principles should guide decision making.*

1. **The environment and the economy must be put on an equal footing, to be weighed and measured together as the basis for development decisions.**

---

*These are presented in different form in chapter 10 of this report. More detailed recommendations for federal, state, and local officials in the United States are presented in *The Conservation Foundation Letter*, 1989, no. 5, available from The Conservation Foundation.

The environment must be a fundamental concern in the mainstream of policy making, not tacked onto the end of the process. Today, the evaluation of economic well-being is divorced from the evaluation of environmental quality, and the former almost always outweighs the latter. The public is now saying that the environment and the economy can be mutually supporting. But, for this to happen, the two must be fully integrated in decision making.

Government programs often pay subsidies to aid economic development—draining wetlands, for example. Such subsidies may promote environmental damage that other government programs attempt to correct. The real long-term costs, including the environmental costs, of all the subsidies, tax breaks, and incentives that promote development should be accounted for at the outset, before projects are approved. Water supply systems, sewage treatment, waste management, and energy supply should be priced to reflect environmental costs and benefits. If such steps are not taken, it is likely that the Great Lakes environment will deteriorate further as the 21st century approaches. But the application of policies to ensure that public services are priced to include all costs would not only reduce environmental damage, it would relieve a great deal of economic pressure placed on financially strapped local governments.

## 2. The operating perspective of governments, industry, and the public must be extended to include the entire ecosystem: water, land, air, and all living organisms.

The oversimplified focus on single aspects of the ecosystem, often at the expense of the ecosystem as a whole, must be expanded to include the broad ecosystem. Pollution control programs that simply shift the risks from air to land to water must be replaced by programs that recognize these cross-media connections. A total ecosystem approach must highlight the importance of other objectives for achieving environmental quality: cutting per capita energy, water use, and generation of waste; recycling; reducing auto emissions and toxic pesticide use; and increasing tree cover and wildlife habitat.

As part of this expanded perspective, a special effort will be required to develop systems of monitoring necessary for establishing the indicators of chemical, physical, and biological sustainability needed to go hand in hand with well-developed measures of economic activity. The implications to the health of the ecosystem of physical disruption, contaminant movement, nutrient cycling, and energy flows are all at

xl
     GREATE LAKES, GREAT LEGACY?

primitive stages of understanding and require attention. It is only through such a broad systemic approach that a comprehensive assessment of the overall economic/environmental health and sustainability of the region will be possible.

3. **Canada and the United States must develop an Ecosystem Charter for the Great Lakes Region to supplement the Great Lakes Water Quality Agreement with a much broader-based arrangement. This charter should recognize the intimate relationships among environmental health, human well-being, and economic activity. A good beginning to this process would be the early adoption of a bilateral accord on transboundary air pollution and the adjustment of the terms of reference of the IJC to go beyond the current focus on water quality.**

The ecosystem charter should set demanding goals for reductions in chemical, physical, and biological stresses on the environment. One such goal would be zero discharge of all contaminants. Another goal would be commitment to a policy of no net losses of wetlands in future development and restoration, where possible, of devastated areas. A third would be to protect natural shorelines from development and to protect special areas of natural beauty, wildlife habitat, or ecological significance. Other goals would include the restoration of bald eagle communities throughout the basin and the restoration of a naturally sustaining fishery. Finally, this charter should recognize the rights and needs of future generations.

4. **Commitments made over the past 15 years must be fulfilled. Governments must set goals, put in place a clear tracking system to monitor progress, and follow through on implementation.**

The goal of zero discharge of persistent toxic substances was set in the U.S. Clean Water Act of 1972 and confirmed for the Great Lakes basin in the Water Quality Agreement of 1978. It is time for these aging commitments to be met, time for governments to follow through on the RAPs with more money and fewer words, time for real muscle to be put behind lakewide toxic management plans, watershed management plans, and shorezone management commitments. Time, in short, for the U.S. and Canadian governments to begin to enforce their laws effectively.

The International Joint Commission has made substantial progress in developing a cooperative program for the two nations. Yet government support—as distinguished from government rhetoric—often has been fainthearted at best, derisive at worst. The U.S. and Canadian governments have tended to marginalize the IJC and not to take advantage of its strength as a cooperative, problem-solving mechanism. In addition, the IJC itself has tended to bow easily to this marginalization and has not pursued its mandate with anything like the vigor and persistence it requires. Much more international cooperation could be facilitated if both sides redoubled their commitment to the IJC.

**5. Governments must act now to increase monitoring and research to promote the understanding of human and ecosystem health conditions in the Great Lakes basin.**

One major conclusion of this project is that, on both sides of the border, monitoring and surveillance to provide critical feedback on environmental quality are grossly inadequate.

A call for more monitoring and research is not an argument to delay action until more is known—clear signals that the ecosystem is unhealthy provide reasonable cause for concern about human health. Rather, it is an argument for supporting long-overdue studies of the links between environmental and human health and ensuring that the findings of these studies are brought to the public's attention.

The human health focus must be expanded beyond concern for such obvious diseases as cancer to subtle, chronic conditions and intergenerational effects. Major tasks include research on human groups at heightened risk of exposure to chemicals, studies of the mechanisms by which toxic substances affect humans and wildlife, enhanced monitoring of wildlife populations, and improved warnings about Great Lakes fish and wildlife to further discourage their consumption by females planning to have children.

**6. In allocating resources available for environmental protection, priority generally should go to prevention first and restoration second.**

The legacy from the past includes an environmental bill for tens of billions of dollars; that legacy has also made clear that it is far cheaper to prevent devastation than to correct it.

The billions society plans to spend on restoration indicate the high value placed on environmental health. But, in the face of demands for large expenditures, priorities will have to be set. Everything cannot be done now or quickly. It is clearly cheaper to prevent the dumping of contaminants in the first place than to attempt to clean them up once they are widespread in the environment. It is cheaper to protect the remaining wetlands and natural shorelines than to pay the high costs of restoring them once lost.

Of course, restoration plans must be pursued vigorously. But it would be folly to spend billions on restoration while neglecting to spend millions on prevention.

**7. A broadly based process of decision making, involving as many people and interest groups as possible, must be utilized and encouraged as a vital part of the ecosystem process.**

It is essential to get the best technical solutions, to promote the most equitable trade-offs in the wrenching processes that lie ahead, and to ensure needed public support for the allocation of the massive resources that will be required. The cooperative approach that is the basis of the IJC, the RAPs (with the involvement of those who have a stake in them), and the lakewide toxic management plans all provide a sound basis to get this process off the ground.

## RECONNECTING: A VISION OF THE FUTURE

To tackle the legacy of the past and the challenges of the 21st century— to restore the health of the Great Lakes ecosystem and to gird it to meet future ecological stresses—will require far-reaching efforts. If the battle is to be won, Canadians and Americans must join together to anticipate rather than react to emerging environmental conditions.

The last time there was a truly historical battle of the Great Lakes, on September 10, 1813, Captain Oliver Hazard Perry—quite rudely, Canadians have always thought—destroyed an entire flotilla of British vessels on Put-In Bay, near Amherstburg, Ontario. The next battle of the Great Lakes will be less dramatic but more momentous, slower, and vastly more costly, but at least this time the United States and Canada are on the same side. The complications of environmental stresses never before encountered—such as global warming due to increased build-up of greenhouse gases in the environment—could greatly complicate strategic efforts to address already known problems.

Both nations—politicians, business leaders, nongovernmental or-ganizations, and others—must work together to develop a vision of a high quality of life in the Great Lakes region. All of these interests must decide where they want to go if they are to begin to get there and, to that end, must build the vision of a life-style that recognizes the intimate relationship between human well-being, a healthy environment, and a prosperous economy. The stakes are much too high to continue dealing with the Great Lakes by waiting for a series of crisis-forced reactions.

Today, actions must work with and adapt to natural processes rather than recklessly try to manipulate and control those processes. If the history of the Great Lakes region teaches anything, it is that nature cannot be bludgeoned into submission. Policies must promote development that is compatible with nature. This will mean, for example, adapting shoreline-use policies to the reality of the natural fluctuations of lake levels and ending subsidies and other incentives to build homes now where water will rule tomorrow. It will also mean deemphasizing fish ranching, an artificially supported sport fishery, in favor of the longer-term goal of restoring the natural sustainability of the lakes to the point where native fish species can thrive and be consumed by humans and wildlife alike.

In the final analysis, it is not institutions that are lacking in the efforts to rescue the Great Lakes basin from environmental degradation. Public and private institutions that already exist can and must be harnessed to a new political will. Above all, institutions and political leaders and the public must develop the foresight to cease looking primarily at the present at the expense of the future. It is then, and only then, that humans will be reconnected with the web that is life and will know that their legacy is an enhanced world for their children.

> Whatever befalls the earth, befalls the sons of the earth. Man did not weave the web of life; he is merely a strand in it. Whatever he does to the web, he does to himself.
>
> —Chief Seattle

# Chapter 1

# An Ecosystem Approach to Great Lakes Policy

Viewed from space, the Great Lakes are an enormous stretch of water extending over 1,000 miles (1,600 km) along the boundary between the United States and Canada. The lakes, described as "sweetwater seas" by French and other European explorers,[1] have been a vital avenue of national and international shipping; sources of drinking water for millions; essential resources for industrial processes and electrical power generation; valuable fisheries serving generations of subsistence, commercial, and sport fishermen; and important recreational and aesthetic resources. From a biological standpoint, they represent a rich and productive assemblage of plants and animals.

The five Great Lakes form part of a still-larger Great Lakes basin, or watershed, including all the surrounding land areas in which the rivers and streams flow into the Great Lakes or their connecting channels (figure 1.1). The Great Lakes occupy almost one-third of the total area of their basin; the over 80,000 other lakes in the basin cover an area about the size of Lake Erie. Few other drainage basins in North America have such a large ratio of water area to land area; no other basin consists of such a continuous chain of large lakes.

Since the early 19th century, the Great Lakes have been a major factor in human settlement and development. The creation of the industrial heartland of North America depended on the access to resources provided by easy water transport, both before and since the coming of the railroad, despite the single major barrier of Niagara Falls. Now, more than 35 million people live within the Great Lakes basin, over 27 million Americans and nearly 8 million Canadians.[2]

1

**Figure 1.1**
**The Great Lakes Basin**

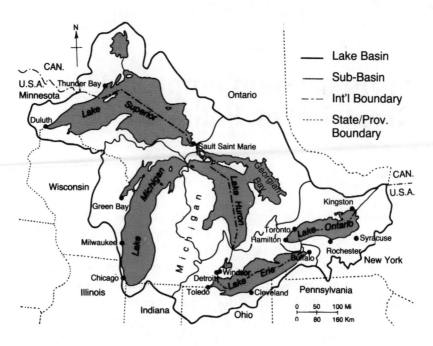

Source: Environment Canada.

## HUMAN IMPACT

Economic growth in the basin often has been explosive, bringing about immense and frequently irreversible environmental changes. For example, during the second half of the 19th century, forest stands in the basin were cleared. Fisheries were devastated by overfishing and loss of habitat. Typhoid, cholera, and other water-related diseases became major sources of death in lakeside towns and cities.

Notable environmental crises continued in the 20th century. Repeated episodes of waterborne diseases early in the century prompted creation of water treatment systems. In mid-century, what remained of the Great Lakes fishery was devastated by the exotic sea lamprey.[3]

By the mid-1960s, Lake Erie was characterized widely as dead or dying, overloaded by wastes from human activities that were only slightly less damaging in the other lakes. The spectacle of a burning river in 1969 symbolized the degradation, when oil and debris in Cleveland's Cuyahoga River caught fire. Commercial fisheries in Lake Erie and Lake St. Clair were closed because of high mercury content in fish tissues. Eggshell thinning and adult mortality in bird populations indicated that DDT (dichloro-diphenyl-trichloro-ethane) and other pesticides were having unexpected and severe effects on wildlife.

Changes over time in the area's wetlands illustrate other human impacts on the basin. As spawning grounds and breeding sites, wetlands are crucial to the biological diversity and productivity of both land and water areas in the basin. Wetlands once extended over almost a third of the present state of Michigan and over more than half of southwest Ontario.[4] Today, throughout the basin, wetlands are but a small fraction of their former size, having been drained for agricultural, industrial, and residential use. Drainage activities continue to the present day.

## THE 1972 GREAT LAKES WATER QUALITY AGREEMENT

In 1972, the United States and Canada signed a Great Lakes Water Quality Agreement. The 1972 agreement addressed the urgent problem exemplified by Lake Erie: excess nutrients (mainly nitrogen and phosphorus) entering the lake as a result of land-based human activities. The nutrients encouraged massive growth of algae and similar microscopic plants in the lake. As this plant growth died and decayed, much of the available dissolved oxygen was consumed in the decay process, and therefore was not available to fish and other organisms. In effect, the lake was being choked to death.

The main strategy used to reduce the nutrient inflow was improved systems of municipal sewage treatment. Since 1972, about U.S.$10 billion has been spent on these systems, and the effect on water quality has been rapid and readily apparent.[5]

The 1972 agreement set in motion a process of intensive research, analysis, and debate. Between 1972 and 1978, major studies were conducted on all the lakes and on the multitude of land-based human activities that likely had an impact on water quality. The stage was set for signing a much more comprehensive accord—the 1978 Great Lakes Water Quality Agreement.

## THE 1978 GREAT LAKES WATER QUALITY AGREEMENT

Through the 1978 agreement, Canada and the United States undertook "to restore and maintain the chemical, physical, and biological integrity of the waters of the Great Lakes Basin Ecosystem."[6]

As defined in the 1978 agreement, and as slightly revised in 1987,

"Great Lakes Basin Ecosystem" means the interacting components of air, land, water and living organisms, including humans, within the drainage basin of the St. Lawrence River at or upstream from the point at which this river becomes the international boundary between Canada and the United States.[7]

What is remarkable about this definition is that it includes everything— air, land, water, plants and animals, humanity, and all the results of human activities.

The agreement takes an "ecosystem approach" to the problems of the Great Lakes' waters. It recognizes, in effect, that to solve many of the Great Lakes' problems requires programs that address the linkages among them. Programs must focus on the physical, chemical, and biological relationships among air, land, and water.

From a management perspective, the ecosystem approach has two major implications. First, the flow of contaminants should be tracked through the Great Lakes to help identify major sources, major effects, and key points at which release of the substances can be prevented. Second, standards and monitoring systems must take account of the movement of pollutants and the risks to humans and other organisms resulting from multiple exposures to pollutants in air, water, and food.

Amendments to the agreement signed in 1987 reflect advances in knowledge since 1978 and underscore the broad perspective of an ecosystem approach: they address airborne toxic substances, groundwater, sediments, and nonpoint sources (for example, urban and agricultural runoff), all of which can contaminate the waters of the lakes.[8]

The 1978 agreement adopts, as a *philosophy*, "zero discharge" of persistent toxic substances (those that remain in the ecosystem for a long time)[9]; as a *policy*, discharges of persistent toxic substances should be "virtually eliminated." For nonpersistent substances, the policy is prohibition of discharges in toxic amounts.[10] Toxic substances are justifiably a priority issue for the agreement, providing a valuable thread through which the complexity of the basin ecosystem can be unraveled and understood. The emphasis on toxic substances also serves as a reminder that, huge though the Great Lakes basin is, it is not a closed system. Toxic substances and other hazards enter or leave the basin via the air and also move downstream into the lower watershed of the St. Lawrence River and ultimately into the Gulf of St. Lawrence.*

## OTHER STRESSES ON THE ECOSYSTEM

The 1978 agreement aims to "restore and maintain the chemical, physical, and biological integrity of the waters of the Great Lakes Basin Ecosystem." But protecting the integrity of the waters requires much more than management of toxic substances. For example, the fisheries of the lakes cannot flourish if habitat for spawning is lost. Introduction of exotic species into the lakes may alter the lakes' food web, and such changes may have an impact on water quality. Administratively, the ecosystem approach implies that full protection of the aquatic ecosystem of the Great Lakes requires close coordination of pollution control policies, habitat protection, and fisheries management.

It is also important to recognize the many stresses on the ecosystem that are independent of water quality concerns. Air pollution has an impact on water quality but, more important, it directly affects the health of people who inhale it. Habitat must be protected not only for the benefit of the Great Lakes' fishery but also for the protection of other living things, particularly rare and endangered species. The many different stresses affecting the ecosystem and requiring attention are summarized in figure 1.2.

The diversity of the many stresses suggests yet another implication of the ecosystem approach: Ecosystem management is the responsibility of more than simply the traditional pollution control and resource protection agencies. The ecosystem approach implies that more agencies and actions must be brought into the search for an improved ecosystem. Decision makers in energy, transportation, agriculture, and other policy areas must raise their sights, reorienting their institutions to pay closer attention and give greater weight to the environmental consequences of their policies.

---

*The Great Lakes basin is the upper watershed of the St. Lawrence River. The Great Lakes Water Quality Agreement does not cover the lower watershed, even though toxic substances do not respect this division.

## Figure 1.2
## Types of Stress Affecting Ecosystem Health

| Stress | Examples |
|---|---|
| Natural processes | Weather-related (e.g., wind, storms, rain, flooding, droughts, freeze-thaw cycles) |
| | Fires destroying forest, grassland, or marsh areas |
| | Disease outbreaks in key species |
| | Natural population cycles in fauna |
| Addition (loading) of substances, heat, radionuclides, etc. | Sand, soil, and other sediment carried and then deposited by streams |
| | Phosphorus, nitrogen, and other nutrients that fertilize plants and lake plankton |
| | Insecticides and contaminants |
| | Carbon dioxide and other gases emitted to atmosphere |
| | Waste heat discharged to air or water bodies |
| Physical restructuring | River and stream damming, diking, or dredging, siltation or other modification of habitat |
| | Shoreline protection (groins, seawalls, etc.) |
| | Forest clearance |
| | Wetland drainage, excavation, and development |
| Removal of renewable and nonrenewable resources | Water withdrawals (from surface or wells), diversions, and consumptive use |
| | Commercial forestry |
| | Fishing (subsistence, commercial, or recreational), hunting, and trapping |
| | Extraction of minerals |
| Introduction of nonnative organisms | Stocking lakes with exotic fish species |
| | Unintended invasion of new aquatic species through canal construction, escape from aquaria, transport on ships' hulls, in ballast water, etc. |

Source: Adapted from Regier (1988).

## THE INSTITUTIONAL ECOSYSTEM

Ecosystems tend to be described in natural terms, but one of the hallmarks of the ecosystem approach as it has developed in the Great Lakes basin is its emphasis on the full range of human institutions—political and economic—that have an impact on the basin. This "institutional ecosystem" seems as complex and diverse as the natural ecosystem. The Great Lakes Water Quality Agreements of 1972 and 1978 were but two of a series of bilateral mechanisms established by Canada and the United States during the 20th century to deal with environment-related issues. Agreements have also been reached on fisheries, migratory wildlife, and other issues. The eight states in the Great Lakes basin and the province of Ontario are parties to yet additional regional and binational arrangements (see box and figure 1.3).

Nongovernmental organizations have been major influences within this institutional ecosystem. Particularly noteworthy have been citizen groups that repeatedly press environmental issues. These groups have helped translate broad public concern for ecosystem health into demands for governmental response.

The economic institutions of the Great Lakes—particularly industries engaged in fish and timber harvesting, mineral mining, manufacturing, and generation of power—have been major shapers of the Great Lakes ecosystem. But the economic forces influencing the Great Lakes ecosystem include more than simply the readily identifiable industries that frequently are the target of public outrage. Those forces also include the multitudes of decisions made by individual consumers, from automobile purchases to gardening practices to energy use.

If the health of the Great Lakes basin is to be restored and maintained, the many elements that comprise the institutional ecosystem will need to work together to achieve this common purpose. The dimensions of this challenge cannot be understated. Canadian ways of doing things differ from those of the United States. Issues of vital importance in Duluth or Thunder Bay may seem of minor importance in Cleveland or Toronto. Habitat rehabilitation may conflict with agricultural objectives or lake-shipping requirements. Individuals may be reluctant to make the lifestyle changes necessary to reduce stresses on the ecosystem. These difficulties notwithstanding, progress thus far indicates that a common view and concerted action to benefit the Great Lakes ecosystem are possible. But, as this report will demonstrate, much more remains to be done.

## Figure 1.3
## Selected Regional Institutions in the Great Lakes Basin

| Institution | Purpose | Members |
|---|---|---|
| International Joint Commission | Provide framework for binational cooperation on air and water pollution issues and the regulation of water flows and levels | 3 appointees from each goverment |
| Great Lakes Fishery Commission | Coordinate maintenance of fisheries | 4 from each side, named by Privy Council and President |
| Council of Great Lakes Governors | Provide a forum on mutual interests, especially economic development and resource protection | Governors, with premiers as associate members |
| Great Lakes Commission | Promote development, use, and conservation of water resources | Gubernatorial appointees and nonvoting representatives from federal and provincial governments |
| Great Lakes / St. Lawrence Maritime Forum | Promote trade and commerce | Includes government and nongovernment organizations |
| International Association of Great Lakes Ports | Promote Great Lakes shipping | 4 U.S., 5 Canadian port authorities |
| Niagara River Toxics Committee | Investigate toxic chemical problems | 2 each EPA, N.Y., Ontario, and Environment Canada |
| Upper Great Lakes Connecting Channels Study Committee | Assess toxics in rivers and Lake St. Clair | Fisheries and environment agencies, with IJC observer |
| Canada-U.S. Programme Review Committee | Advise governments on protection of migratory birds | 3 each from federal government |
| 4 International Boards of Control | Assist IJC decision on levels and flows | Equal members from each side named by IJC commissioners |
| Joint Response Team for Great Lakes | Clean up of oil and hazardous materials spills | Canada and U.S. Coast Guards & other agencies |

Source: Regier (1986); Donahue (1987).

## Canada, the United States, and the International Joint Commission

Formal Canadian-U.S. cooperation on environmental matters affecting the Great Lakes basin began with the signing of the Boundary Waters Treaty in 1909. Article IV of the treaty contained the provision that "boundary waters and waters flowing across the boundary shall not be polluted on either side to the injury of health or property on the other."[1] The treaty also established a unique body, the International Joint Commission (IJC), composed of three persons nominated by the Canadian government and three nominated by the U.S. government. The IJC serves as a vehicle for resolving disputes over the boundary waters shared by the United States and Canada. It has authority to arbitrate specific disputes referred to it, and it judges applications for uses of boundary waters on either side of the international boundary that would affect flows on the other. It also conducts investigations (commonly called "references") of issues referred by the United States and Canada. These functions are exercised throughout the length of the international boundary from Atlantic to Pacific, not only along the Great Lakes.

In 1912 and 1945, in accordance with the provisions of Article IV, the two governments requested investigations of water pollution in the Great Lakes (excluding Lake Michigan, which is not included in the Boundary Water Treaty provisions). The IJC's reports (in 1918 and 1954) may have encouraged national action within each country, but they did not lead to joint action.

In 1964, the two governments requested the IJC to investigate the pollution problems in Lakes Erie and Ontario. The IJC's report in 1970 led directly to the 1972 Great Lakes Water Quality Agreement, which provided for reductions in discharges of phospho-

rus to Lakes Erie and Ontario. The agreement requested the IJC to extend its inquiries to lakes Huron and Superior and to take the lead in investigating the character of nonpoint-source pollution. Under IJC auspices, the International Reference Group on Great Lakes Pollution from Land Use Activities (usually known as PLUARG) prepared a total of 121 reports that, with related research, provided the basis for the ecosystem approach adopted in the 1978 Water Quality Agreement. (The 1978 agreement also includes Lake Michigan, which, because it is wholly within the United States, is not a "boundary water.")

As a legal matter, principal responsibility for implementation of the 1978 agreement, like its predecessor, rests with the two national governments. As a practical matter, responsibility is shared by the two national governments with state, provincial, and metropolitan governments. The IJC has a continuing role to evaluate and report on needs and action relevant to the provisions of the agreement. Since 1981, the commission has issued biennial reports on progress.

Two principal subsidiary bodies have been created to assist the IJC in this task (see figure 1.4). The Great Lakes Water Quality Board acts as the commission's principal advisor; it is composed of senior officials from the government departments directly involved in implementing the agreement. The Great Lakes Science Advisory Board is composed primarily of university and other nongovernmental experts, who advise the IJC on research needs and similar issues. In addition to the IJC offices in Ottawa and Washington, D.C., a Great Lakes Regional Office was established in Windsor, Ontario, for assisting in implementing the provisions of the 1972 and 1978 agreements.

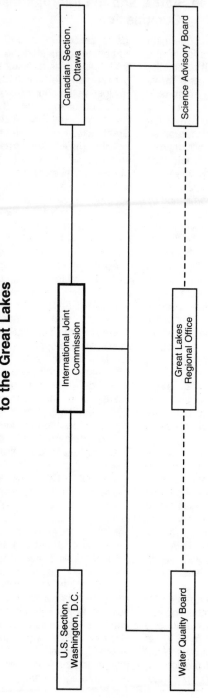

**Figure 1.4**
**Overview of the International Joint Commission Administrative Structure Relating to the Great Lakes**

Canadian Section, Ottawa

Science Advisory Board

International Joint Commission

Great Lakes Regional Office

U.S. Section, Washington, D.C.

Water Quality Board

- - - - Administrative and technical support

Source: National Research Council of the United States; Royal Society of Canada.

## THE FUTURE OF THE ECOSYSTEM APPROACH

To understand an ecosystem requires a knowledge of the main elements of the total system, how these elements work individually, and how they interact with one another. The Great Lakes basin ecosystem is composed of recognizable subsystems, is modified by naturally occurring processes and change, and is vulnerable to stresses of human origin. Although these stresses have caused significant deterioration over the years, the indications are that the basin ecosystem can be restored and maintained if the stresses are reduced and the ecosystem's characteristics and relationships are respected.

It is fair to say that, when Canada and the United States committed themselves in 1978 to protecting the Great Lakes ecosystem, neither the two governments nor the sizable Great Lakes scientific community knew what the commitment would involve. More than 10 years later, they are still finding out. In many respects, it has been a frustrating period: New discoveries often seem to have served only to extend the tangle of environmental relationships, making action more difficult and solutions seemingly ever more complex, difficult, time-consuming, and perhaps ultimately impossible.

Many of the easiest problems have been addressed. What remains for the future is likely to be much more difficult. For example, in 1972, improving the health of Lake Erie seemed largely a matter of reducing inflows of phosphorus from readily identifiable sources. Many of these sources have been controlled, but nutrients from more diffuse agricultural sources also need to be reduced if additional progress is to occur. More generally, it is apparent that future efforts to enhance the health of the Great Lakes ecosystem will require attention to a very wide range of smaller sources that are harder to control, and to problems for which technological solutions have not yet been developed.

The next 10 years will largely determine whether the 1978 commitment to "restore and maintain" ecosystem health in the Great Lakes basin will be fulfilled. Even if the necessary actions are taken and the resources are made available, the vision must then be sustained well into the next century before the task of restoration is completed. Meanwhile, the definition of what constitutes ecosystem health in the basin may be altered by the prospect of significant changes in climate, lake levels, plant growth, and other "greenhouse" effects of global warming in the coming decades.

Future policies for the Great Lakes basin will need to be a mix of rehabilitation and anticipation, between coping with the legacy of deterioration inherited from the past, limiting continuing discharges, and ensuring that undesirable environmental legacies are not created for future generations. Currently, multi-billion-dollar programs to clean up hazardous waste sites address the lurking problems of the past. They represent a hidden "mortgage" bequeathed to this generation by former generations.

Future programs will need to address ongoing pollution, such as continuing discharges to air and water. These, too, will cost billions of dollars. At present, many of these programs have an "end-of-the-pipe," "after-the-fact" quality: They try to solve existing problems rather than to anticipate and prevent them. Moreover, many current programs for pollution control simply shift risks from air to land to water rather than reducing them, reflecting the separate programs for air and water adopted many years ago.

For the future, the ecosystem approach to the Great Lakes basin will require a much greater emphasis on anticipatory programs. These anticipatory programs need to encompass and reduce the broad range of stresses on the Great Lakes ecosystem. More efficient use of energy, less chemically dependent agriculture, and changes in manufacturing processes to reduce dependence on toxic substances—and limit their production—are among the measures that will be necessary. Restrictions on development on vulnerable shorelines, measures to prevent transportation and manufacturing accidents, and controls on ballast water discharges from ships to prevent introduction of exotic species will also be necessary. Reducing stresses on the ecosystem requires such preventive measures.

For those discharges that cannot be prevented, governmental programs will need to take account of the full range of human exposures from air, land, and water and will need to avoid an environmental shell game in which control measures simply shift risks from medium to medium rather than reduce the risks.

The ecosystem approach is as much a philosophical concept as it is a management system. As such, it requires humanity to see itself as part of the ecosystem rather than the dominator of the natural world. The approach embodies principles that affect society's values, lifestyles, and obligations to future generations. As summarized by a group of U.S. and Canadian scientists:

> Two principles should guide conservation of intergenerational equity: the first is conservation of quality, defined as leaving the Great Lakes basin ecosystem

in no worse condition than it was received from previous generations; the second is to conserve options, defined as conserving the diversity of the natural resource base of the Great Lakes.[11]

At present, it is not clear that these principles will be generally accepted or successfully applied in the basin or that the necessary resources and public commitment will be provided and sustained. A start has been made, however, and what is already quite evident is that the ecosystem approach—in both philosophical and management terms—is the only one that appears appropriate for the task.

## REPORT'S OBJECTIVES

*Great Lakes, Great Legacy?* assesses recent trends in ecosystem health, drawing on previous research and data compiled for this report. But the overriding purpose is more than simply to present data in a handy reference. It is to examine how human activities have wrought changes in the Great Lakes ecosystem and suggest how human activities, both within and beyond the basin, must be changed to assure its protection.

The report's approach is broad, beginning with consideration of the difficulties inherent in valuing and measuring the health of the Great Lakes ecosystem.

The central section of the report reviews in greater detail the many human stresses on the Great Lakes ecosystem and some of their measurable impacts. It focuses not only on the water quality of the Great Lakes themselves but also on the water quality of the 80,000 smaller lakes in the basin. It examines not only those airborne toxic contaminants that have an impact on water quality of the Great Lakes but also those air pollutants that are a threat to humans breathing them. It also reviews noncontaminant issues that complement toxic substances on the Great Lakes ecosystem agenda. The central section concludes with an assessment of available evidence on the health of the fish, wildlife, and humans residing in the Great Lakes basin.

The closing section reviews governmental efforts to address pressing ecosystem concerns in the Great Lakes, with principal emphasis on the 1978 Water Quality Agreement, and identifies priority issues deserving further action.

# Chapter 2

# Defining and Measuring Ecosystem Health

[W]e must judge pollution in context. What we call pollution is the perturbation by man of a series of physical and chemical factors and cycles, with consequent effects on living and non-living systems. The scale and nature of this perturbation need to be measured so that we know more clearly what we are doing to ourselves and to the world, and can relate the action we take realistically to the scale of the problem and to the risks.

—M. W. Holdgate, *A Perspective of Environmental Pollution*, 1979.

The goal of the 1978 Great Lakes Water Quality Agreement is to "restore and maintain the chemical, physical, and biological integrity of the waters of the Great Lakes Basin Ecosystem."[1] The agreement, however, does not define "integrity." The ecosystem conditions of pre-European settlement cannot be re-created, if only because 35 million more human beings now live in the basin than did 200 years ago; a new meaning must therefore be found for "integrity." More broadly, it is necessary to define a "healthy ecosystem" in a fashion that addresses not only the waters of the Great Lakes ecosystem but the other components as well.

For much of the last 100 years, public environmental concern has focused on two main objectives: protecting public health and conserving natural resources. From the effects of water-related diseases at the turn of the century, to Love Canal and toxic chemicals more recently, the main priority shaping public opinion and action has been potential health effects from a polluted environment. At the same time, there has been a growing desire to conserve as much as possible of the natural environment: habitat, species diversity, and landscape.

15

The definition of a healthy Great Lakes ecosystem, and the actions necessary to achieve it, ultimately will reflect both objective scientific judgments and subjective public desires. For example, should wetland areas be extended to provide more wildlife habitat? The answer to this question, while it may be informed by scientific advice, ultimately will be provided in the political process.

Despite the uncertainty associated with the definition of a "healthy ecosystem," the concept of ecosystem health helps to unite concern for human health with concern for the health of other parts of the ecosystem; many of the environmental factors relevant to human health are significant also for other parts of the ecosystem. This continuity is especially well illustrated by the phenomena of bioaccumulation and biomagnification within the Great Lakes food web, and it has implications for setting standards, for monitoring, and for research.

## FOOD WEBS, BIOMAGNIFICATION, AND BIOACCUMULATION

Like other ecosystems, the Great Lakes basin ecosystem represents "a community of animals, plants, and bacteria and its interrelated physical and chemical environment."[2] Three biological phenomena—food webs, biomagnification, and bioaccumulation—are of vital significance in defining the health of the ecosystem.

The notion of a food web is a basic description of the organization of life in an ecosystem. On land, plants use energy (in the form of sunlight), basic chemical nutrients, carbon dioxide, and water to create carbohydrates, fats, and protein. This energy is transmitted to the animals that feed on the plants, and the energy may subsequently be transmitted to one or more levels of carnivores, including humans. In lakes and other water bodies, the web begins with the light-dependent diatoms (phytoplankton*) and other forms of vegetation that use phosphorus and other nutrients. Zooplankton feed on such vegetation, fish

---

*Plankton is the collective name for the floating microscopic plants and animals that live in both fresh and salt water. The plants—phytoplankton—in the Great Lakes are mainly algae. The animals—zooplankton—are comprised of protozoans (single-celled organisms), rotifers, copepods, and cladocerans such as the water flea. The zooplankton graze on the phytoplankton and are themselves a major food source for fish.

eat the zooplankton, and predators, including other fish species and birds, consume these fish (figure 2.1).

Organisms at higher levels in the web depend for their food supply on the stability of the web at all lower levels. If something goes wrong lower down, the effect at higher levels can be catastrophic. In several of the Great Lakes prior to the 1970s, for example, increasing phosphorus and other nutrient loadings led to massive growth of algae at the bottom of the web.* The biochemical oxygen demand (BOD) created by bacteria as they decomposed the excessive amounts of algae threatened the survival of other elements in the web that also required oxygen.

During the lifetime of an organism in this food web, some substances that the organism consumes or absorbs are retained in the tissue of the organism—a process known as bioaccumulation. The amount that bioaccumulates in an individual organism depends on many factors, including the concentration of the substance in the prey or food, the amount consumed, and the duration of the organism's life.

Since the organism that is bioaccumulating these substances is normally itself the food supply for the next higher level in the food web, the bioaccumulated substances are conveyed to this higher level. Organisms at the higher level consume large quantities of the lower organisms. As this process is repeated up through the food web, persistent substances become increasingly concentrated, or biomagnified.

Many toxic substances bioaccumulate and biomagnify through the food web, including chlorinated hydrocarbons such as DDT, dieldrin, dioxins, polychlorinated biphenyls (PCBs), and heavy metals such as mercury. In the case of DDT, for example, even though the concentration in a zooplankter—a water flea—is only 1/100 parts per million, the flesh of a fish-eating bird in the same lake system may contain 630 times that concentration (figure 2.2).[3]

The same is true of PCBs. One small zooplankter in the Great Lakes can filter enough water in its short life to collect 400 times the concentration of PCBs in the water. The PCB concentration in the water

---

*"Eutrophic" is the term describing such a nutrient-rich, productive lake. The natural productivity is often visible in the form of algae. When this condition results from nutrients of human origin, it is sometimes labeled "cultural eutrophication," to distinguish it from naturally eutrophic conditions. Less productive lakes are labeled "mesotrophic," and the least productive lakes—like Lake Superior—are labeled "oligotrophic."

**Figure 2.1**
**Simplified Great Lakes Food Web**

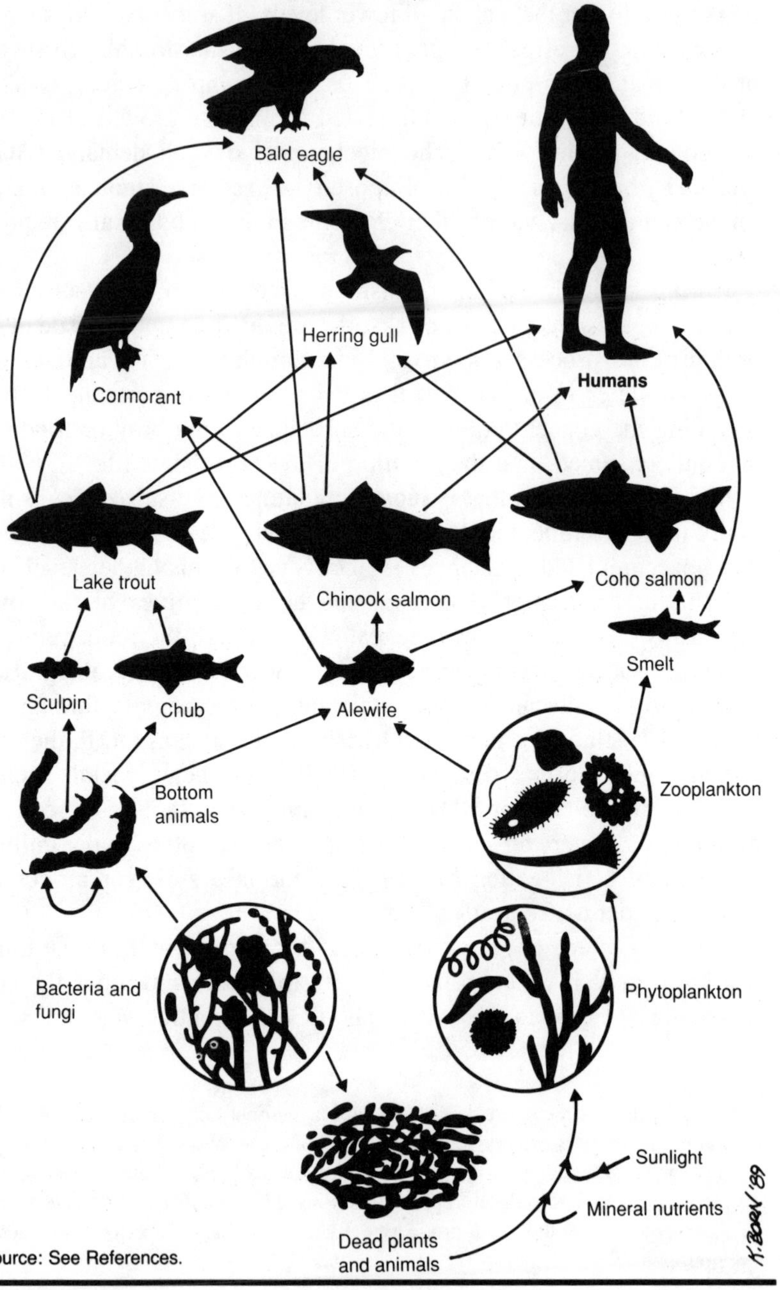


Source: See References.

## Figure 2.2
## Lake Ontario Food Web Biomagnification

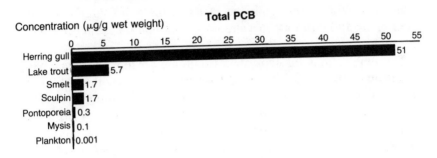

**Total PCB**

Concentration (μg/g wet weight)

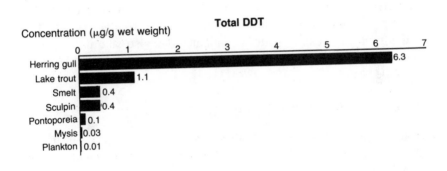

**Total DDT**

Concentration (μg/g wet weight)

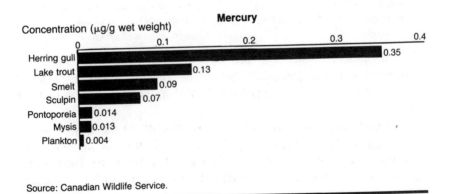

**Mercury**

Concentration (μg/g wet weight)

Source: Canadian Wildlife Service.

may, in fact, be below the threshold of measurement, yet by the time this water flea has been consumed by a mysid, which is swallowed by an alewife, that in turn feeds a lake trout, and the trout has been consumed by a herring gull, the PCBs in the gull's eggs may have been biomagnified to a concentration 25 million times higher than in the water.[4]

The implications for ecosystem health are obvious. Not merely do organisms at higher levels in the food web depend on the stability of the food sources at lower levels, they are also tied through the food web to the quality of the physical and chemical environment: to the condition of the soil, water, and air. What may be a negligible concentration of a toxic substance in the air can become much more significant as it is transferred from the atmosphere to lake waters and as it is biomagnified up the food web. The link to human health is also clear. Humans live longer on average than any other mammal species, so they bioaccumulate substances over a longer period. Depending on their eating patterns, humans may also take in toxic substances that have been accumulated and magnified at many levels in the food web.

## TOXIC SUBSTANCES IN THE GREAT LAKES

The definition of a toxic substance is as much legal as scientific. As defined in the 1978 Great Lakes Water Quality Agreement, a toxic substance is

> a substance which can cause death, disease, behavioural abnormalities, cancer, genetic mutations, physiological or reproductive malfunctions or physical deformities in any organism or its offspring, or which can become poisonous after concentration in the food chain [web] or in combination with other substances.[5]

This definition considers a substance as toxic if the effects occur in any organism, not just in humans. The agreement defines a toxic substance as persistent if it has a half-life* in water greater than eight weeks.[6]

Compilation of a master list of all chemicals in the waters of the Great Lakes basin began in 1975. By 1978, the list included 391 chemicals, and the inventory reached 1,018 in 1983. By 1987, however, a more rigorous review had reduced the total to 362 positively

---

*"Half-life" refers to the time required for half the amount of a substance introduced into a system to be eliminated by natural processes.

identified substances. These have been divided by the Great Lakes Water Quality Board into two groups, a "primary track" that at present includes 11 "critical pollutants" and a "comprehensive track" containing the remaining identified substances[7] (figure 2.3). The critical pollutants in the primary track

> are capable of producing adverse, often irreversible effects in a wide range of mammalian and aquatic species. Because of their ability to bioconcentrate and to bioaccumulate up the food chain [web], the recognized threat to human health and the aquatic ecosystem is significantly enhanced. The concern is further exacerbated because, despite regulatory controls and reductions in ecosystem concentrations for many, all 11 persist at unacceptable levels. These 11 pollutants are representative of a variety of sources, pathways, and uses, and several are members of larger chemical families. Therefore, any action taken for one could be expected to concurrently control or apply to other substances with similar properties. Thus, such action should have a significant impact on the broader toxic substances issue.[8]

Most attention has focused on the 11 critical pollutants' major sources, trends in concentration levels, and additional control strategies. This emphasis on the critical pollutants has been supplemented by efforts to review, systematically, existing information on the comprehensive track pollutants, including their toxicity and potential hazard in the Great Lakes ecosystem.[9]

## ENVIRONMENTAL STANDARDS

Governments routinely use standards to define environmental objectives. Standards frequently identify the concentrations of contaminants allowed in discharges and deemed acceptable in air and water. Standards often incorporate biological measures, such as the concentrations of contaminants in selected organisms; the number and variety of organisms present in certain waters; or the ability of certain organisms to survive in certain discharges.

Standards also are written to require or ban certain actions, in regard to both contaminants and other stresses on the ecosystem. For example, regulations for managing hazardous waste frequently dictate equipment that must be used and procedures to be followed, setback requirements ban unwise development along shorelines, public access to nesting areas of endangered species is restricted to avoid interference with reproduction, and fishing is banned when fish stocks are low.

The 1978 Water Quality Agreement established standards (called

Figure 2.3
Toxic Chemicals of Concern in the Great Lakes Basin:
11 Critical Pollutants Identified by the
IJC's Water Quality Board

| Chemical | Production and Release | Source |
|---|---|---|
| 2,3,7,8-TCDD (dioxin) & 2,3,7,8-TCDF (furan) | Unintentional | Contaminant in herbicides used in agriculture, range and forest management. Also produced as a by-product of combustion of fossil fuels and waste incineration, and through production of pentachlorophenol (PCP), and pulp and paper production processes. 2,3,7,8-TCDD is the most toxic of 75 congeners (forms) of dioxin, and 2,3,7,8-TCDF is the most toxic of 135 congeners of furan. |
| Benzo[a]pyrene (b[a]p) | Unintentional | Product of incomplete combustion of fossil fuels and wood, including forest fires, grills (charcoal broiling), auto exhaust, and waste incineration. One of a large family of polyaromatic hydrocarbons (PAHs). |
| DDT* & its breakdown products (including DDE) | Intentional | Insecticide; used heavily for mosquito control in tropical areas. |
| Dieldrin* | Intentional | Insecticide used extensively at one time, especially on fruit. |
| Hexachlorobenzene (HCB) | Unintentional | By-product of combustion of fuels and waste incineration, and of manufacturing processes using chlorine. Found as a contaminant in chlorinated pesticides. |

| | | |
|---|---|---|
| Alkylated lead | Intentional | Used as a fuel additive and in solder, pipes, and paint. |
| | Unintentional | Released through combustion of fuel, waste, and cigarettes, and from pipes, cans, and paint chips. |
| Mirex† | Intentional | Fire retardant; pesticide used to control fire ants. Breaks down to more toxic form, photomirex, in presence of sunlight. Present sources are residuals from manufacturing sites, spills, and land disposal. |
| Mercury | Intentional | Used in metallurgy. |
| | Unintentional | By-product of chlor-alkali, paint, and electrical equipment manufacturing processes. Also occurs naturally in soils and sediments. Releases into the aquatic environment may be accelerated by sulfate deposition (i.e., acid rain). |
| Polychlorinated biphenyls‡ (PCBs) | Intentional | Insulating fluids used in electrical capacitors and transformers and in the production of hydraulic fluids, lubricants, and inks. Was previously used as a vehicle for pesticide dispersal. PCBs comprise a family of 209 congeners of varying toxicity. |
| | Unintentional | Primarily released to the environment through leakage, spills, and waste storage and disposal. |
| Toxaphene* | Intentional | Insecticide used on cotton. Substitute for DDT. |

*Use restricted in the United States and Canada.

†Banned for use in the United States and Canada.

‡Manufacture and new uses prohibited in the United States and Canada.

Source: The Conservation Foundation.

''objectives'') for some of the primary track, as well as other, pollutants. These standards generally specify acceptable concentrations of contaminants in water or fish. They are intended to protect aquatic life, birds and animals that consume fish, and human consumers of Great Lakes' fish and water. The agreement also establishes procedures for setting additional objectives.

Disputes have arisen over the compatibility of various jurisdictions' standards with the objectives of the 1978 Great Lakes Water Quality Agreement. For example, environmental groups in Wisconsin have challenged the U.S. Environmental Protection Agency's (EPA's) approval of that state's water quality standards, arguing that they are inconsistent with the philosophy of zero discharge and the policy of virtual elimination of persistent toxic substances (see box). The environmental groups, noting the special problems of

---

### Is Zero Discharge Possible?

"Zero discharge" has been adopted in the 1978 Water Quality Agreement as the "philosophy" for achieving the standards for the persistent toxic substances, together with a "policy" to "virtually eliminate" such discharges. A ban on production or restriction on use of a contaminant reflects such a philosophy. For example, with rare exceptions, the use of DDT and dieldrin has been banned in the United States and Canada for many years. Production of PCBs has been banned, and their use is being phased out.

Bans on production and use may be feasible for intentionally produced products, but for those products that are produced unintentionally, achieving zero discharge will be much harder. For example, one of the critical pollutants, benzo[a]pyrene, is emitted when fossil fuels are burned and waste is incinerated. Another, hexachlorobenzene, also is a by-product of combustion and of manufacturing processes using chlorine. Zero discharge of these contaminants is impossible, unless all burning is banned.

Even after bans are put in effect, continued cycling of contaminants in the ecosystem may lead to their persistence at unacceptably high levels. Manufacture of mirex in the Great Lakes basin ceased many years ago. Nevertheless, Lake Ontario's sediments remain heavily contaminated with mirex, and anglers are still cautioned against eating mirex-contaminated fish from Lake Ontario.[1] Even nationwide bans in the United States and Canada may be insufficiently protective. Concentrations of DDT and its breakdown products dropped in the Great Lakes after use of DDT was banned, but fresh DDT still is being found in the lakes. Researchers believe that the DDT is being transported through the atmosphere from Central and South America.

Zero discharge will remain a difficult philosophy to implement, but it provides a powerful symbolic impetus for systematic review and elimination of existing sources of persistent toxic substances.

persistence and bioaccumulation in the Great Lakes, contend that EPA should act more decisively to ensure that standards set by the Great Lakes states meet the goals of the 1978 Water Quality Agreement.[10] The environmentalists' protests are a reminder that the many jurisdictions in the Great Lakes basin must adopt standards acknowledging the biological phenomena in the Great Lakes that magnify risks to living organisms.

The many different stresses on the Great Lakes ecosystem have encouraged a search for better indicators of environmental health. An effort is under way to identify measures that can reflect not only the contaminant stresses on the ecosystem but other stresses as well. As described by a committee of the International Joint Commission's (IJC's) Science Advisory Board, ecosystem objectives provide

> integrative measures for evaluating the state of well-being of different parts of the Great Lakes system. These objectives are intended to provide an overall degree of protection for the lakes by ensuring that multiple stresses do not compound the effects of single stresses and reach a critical stage without being investigated.[11]

An early product of this effort has been a new ecosystem indicator for Lake Superior, incorporated into the 1987 amendments to the 1978 Water Quality Agreement.[12] It is defined in terms of two organisms: a fish (lake trout) at the top of the food web, and a species of benthic organism (*Pontoporeia hoyi*)* at the bottom. The standard includes measures of each organism's abundance and adds that the lake should be comprised of stable, self-producing stocks of lake trout that are free from contaminants at concentrations that adversely affect the trout themselves or the quality of harvested trout. Both organisms require clear, cold water, clean sediments, and undisturbed habitat; in addition, trout require limits on harvesting to assure sustainable populations. If these standards are met in Lake Superior, this would mean that at least three stresses—chemicals, harvesting, and habitat destruction—have been satisfactorily limited.

The search for integrative indicators has extended also to mesotrophic waters (for example, the Bay of Quinte in Lake Ontario, and parts of Georgian Bay in Lake Huron). The Ecosystem Objectives

---

*P. hoyi* is a bottom-dwelling organism that occasionally migrates vertically in the water column at night. It feeds primarily on bacteria in the deposits on the lake bottom.[13]

Committee* of the IJC Science Advisory Board has suggested the walleye as a key community element at the top of the food web, and the mayfly, lower down, as indicators of a healthy mesotrophic system.[14]

Consistent with the importance attached to top predators in the food web, attention has begun to focus on using mammals (for example, otter and mink), birds (for example, terns and eagles), and reptiles (for example, turtles) as integrative indicators. As described more fully in chapter 6, the Ecosystem Objectives Committee has proposed the bald eagle as an indicator of the health of the overall Great Lakes ecosystem, suggesting measures for numbers of eagle sites, eagle productivity, and levels of contamination of eagles and their eggs.

For the future, the search for integrative measures in the aquatic ecosystem needs to be complemented by a search for indicators of the health of terrestrial ecosystems.

## MONITORING

Monitoring is a fundamental requirement for identifying sources of existing problems and newly emerging problems, determining whether standards are being met and whether the ecosystem is healthy. The crucial role of monitoring is reflected in the efforts by the United States and Canada to establish a Great Lakes International Surveillance Plan under the auspices of the 1978 Great Lakes Water Quality Agreement.[15] The IJC commented in 1989 that "necessary elements of the plan have not been implemented, resulting in data gaps and incompatibility of data between the jurisdictions."[16] As appreciation of the many stresses on the Great Lakes ecosystem grows, the demands for monitoring increase and gaps in the monitoring network become more apparent. For example, as recently as 1987, none of the organic pollutants among the 11 primary track pollutants was routinely included in air-monitoring networks.[17]

Advances in monitoring technology have made more complicated

---

*Under the revisions to the 1978 Water Quality Agreement adopted in 1987, the primary responsibility for developing ecosystem objectives is with the parties (Canada and the United States) rather than with the IJC. The Ecosystem Objectives Committee has therefore been dissolved. Many of the objectives developed and recommended by the IJC in the past remain to be considered and adopted by the parties; it remains to be seen how effective the new arrangement will be.

the job of reaching agreement on what constitutes a healthy ecosystem. For example, in the late 1950s, a concentration of 50 parts per million was regarded as the practical equivalent of "zero" in measurements. Thirty years later, contaminants can be detected at 1 part per trillion.[18] Potential risks now surface that previously might have been invisible. This makes more difficult the task of establishing ecosystem priorities, especially in the eyes of a public that has difficulty distinguishing among different levels of risk.

## IMPORTANCE OF BIOMONITORING

The adoption of an ecosystem approach in the Great Lakes basin has emphasized how little is really known about the character and magnitude of the major exchange processes that take place among air, land, and water, and throughout the food web. One form of monitoring that needs to grow even more in the years ahead is biomonitoring: the use of fish and wildlife as ecosystem indicators.

Animals that depend on aquatic food sources and that remain in the Great Lakes basin (preferably in a small part of it) throughout their lives are proving to be excellent monitors of materials that biomagnify in food webs. These animals concentrate toxic substances from the fish they eat and, consequently, are extremely sensitive measures of the contaminants present in the territory they occupy.

Herring gulls demonstrate the utility of biomonitoring. Unlike birds of prey, herring gulls still exist in large numbers and nest in large colonies, simplifying the task of obtaining multiple samples. The herring gulls are year-round residents in the basin, so they reflect conditions within the basin. The monitoring procedure (both for collection and analysis) became easier when it was found that there is a predictable ratio between the organochlorine content of an adult female and that of the eggs she lays. Eggs now are collected each spring, at a number of sites around the Great Lakes, and analyzed for a variety of toxic substances.

This program has demonstrated the benefits of biomonitoring. For example, the first clue that photomirex (the toxic form of mirex) had entered the Great Lakes ecosystem came from herring gull evidence.[19] Also, the herring gull program revealed that the most toxic form of dioxin (2,3,7,8-TCDD) was released as a chemical by-product of the manufacture of pentachlorophenol (PCP), a wood preservative, and retrospective analysis of eggs indicated that levels of TCDD began declining after production of PCP ceased in the region.[20]

The herring gull monitoring program, initiated and carried out by the Canadian Wildlife Service, has had its share of difficulties. First, it was threatened with complete elimination by Environment Canada; only a public outcry saved it. But though it was saved, its operations were pared. Second, the location of monitoring sites depends on the distribution of herring gull colonies, and these are absent in southern Lake Michigan and along the south shore of Lake Ontario.

The herring gull serves as an excellent indicator of the presence of pollutants. But it is less sensitive to these pollutants than other species are—so it shows fewer visible effects from them.* Future monitoring of additional species (such as the double-crested cormorant)† could record health effects as well as contaminant levels in the birds and would provide improved understanding of the association between contaminants and adverse health effects. Cormorant monitoring would complement results from the herring gull program and possibly fill in geographical gaps.

Monitoring, especiallly biomonitoring, includes the preservation of monitored material, such as gull eggs. Advances in analysis techniques or the emergence of previously unrecognized problems may enable these preserved specimens to yield valuable data in the future. Creation of "banks" of biological tissue and sediments was envisioned in the 1978 Water Quality Agreement,[21] and the IJC subsequently recommended that these banks become an integral part of the Great Lakes International Surveillance Plan.[22] Up to the present, however, funding and sponsorship have been lacking, and specimen banking in the Great Lakes basin remains uncoordinated and extremely limited.[23]

Existing biomonitoring activities such as fish tissue programs have provided a wealth of information on the condition of the Great Lakes ecosystem. For example, figure 2.4 displays trends in PCB concentrations in fish and wildlife of Lakes Huron and Superior. The data show drops

---

*Herring gulls still can be used, however, to demonstrate more subtle effects of contaminants. Future herring gull-monitoring programs ought to be broadened to include analysis of gull organs, for assessment of effects known or suspected to occur as a result of exposure to contaminants.

†In a number of locations on the Great Lakes, the offspring of cormorants are exhibiting visible developmental problems.

## Figure 2.4
## PCB Concentrations in Lake Superior and Lake Huron Biota, 1974–1983

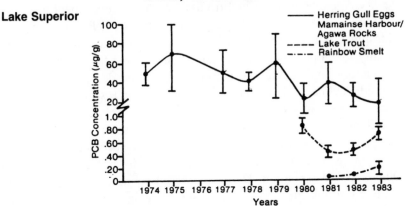

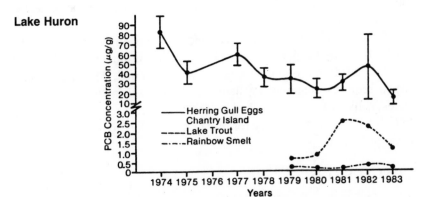

Reprinted with permission from Marlene S. Evans, ed., *Toxic Contaminants and Ecosystem Health: A Great Lakes Focus* (New York: John Wiley & Sons, 1988), p. 495.

in levels in herring gull eggs since the early 1970s. But the uptrend in concentrations in Lake Superior lake trout and rainbow smelt in the early 1980s suggests an influx of PCBs from unknown sources.

As described more fully in chapter 6, scattered research studies have provided disturbing information about the health of many individual species. This information has contributed to the development of remedial steps to restore the health of the lakes. There is little doubt that more biomonitoring is needed. As additional species are monitored more routinely and systematically, a richer picture will emerge of the health of the Great Lakes ecosystem.

## RESEARCH

The 1972 Water Quality Agreement's targeting of phosphorus for control, and the adoption of the ecosystem approach in the 1978 Water Quality Agreement, benefited from a substantial investment made by Canada and the United States in scientific research. But now there is widespread concern that the scientific expertise that made it possible initially to adopt the ecosystem approach may not be available for its satisfactory implementation. During the past decade, there has been a marked decline both in budget allocations for research and in the numbers of scientists being trained in relevant disciplines. For example, in inflation-adjusted dollars, there has been a sharp drop in funding for the U.S. Sea Grant College Program, a major source of support for training new scientists.[24] With both the federal governments in Ottawa and Washington, D.C., concerned about federal deficits, the funding outlook for Great Lakes research remains cloudy. Somehow the modest amounts devoted to Great Lakes research must be protected and enhanced.

The need for increased research funding has been recognized by the Council of Great Lakes Governors, which has promoted development of a U.S.$100 million Great Lakes Protection Fund. The endowment, which requires enabling legislation to be passed in the Great Lakes states, is likely to be established in 1990 and to generate U.S.$7 million to U.S.$10 million annually for research and other activities to combat toxic pollution.[25]

## CONCLUSIONS

A satisfactory definition of "ecosystem health" in the Great Lakes basin remains to be found. Pieces of the definition exist in the form of various standards, but much work still must be done in the pursuit of more robust standards. In a system as complex as that of the Great Lakes basin, it is not surprising that defining health is proving to be such a great challenge.

In defining and working toward ecosystem health, policy makers must determine risk, make choices, and implement policies. Sensible choices and effective policies depend on knowing what is actually happening; this requires a solid commitment to monitoring and research. But the need for additional research must not result in "paralysis by analysis," governmental reluctance to take remedial or preventive action on the grounds that more research is needed.

# Chapter 3

# Legacies and Challenges: Land

In physical terms, the Great Lakes basin (chapter 1, figure 1.1) is defined as including the Great Lakes themselves and the surrounding areas in which the streams and rivers drain to the lakes or to the connecting channels.* When compared to the major rivers of North America, these streams are all relatively short: No part of the basin is more than 200 miles (320 kilometers) from one of the Great Lakes, and, in several places (especially the Illinois shore of Lake Michigan and along the southeastern shore of Lake Erie), the area draining to the basin is only a few miles wide.

The basin is therefore a convenient unit that is easily defined by surface drainage patterns. Nonetheless, it is an ecosystem that is open to many external influences. Weather systems, and the pollutants and other substances they transport, make no distinction between the western suburbs of Chicago, which drain to the Mississippi River, and the North Shore suburbs, which drain to Lake Michigan. Political decisions made in Springfield or Harrisburg may have effects on the basin and its ecosystem that are out of all proportion to the tiny areas of Illinois and Pennsylvania that lie within the basin. The Great Lakes basin is not self-contained; the ''white space'' beyond its edges on the map does not exist on the earth.

---

*The 1978 Water Quality Agreement defines the basin as including that section of the St. Lawrence River that forms the international boundary between the United States and Canada, downstream from Lake Ontario, and the land areas draining to this section.

Within the basin itself, northern and southern zones are a major
contrast. The dividing line runs generally between 44°N and 45°N,
westward from the St. Lawrence to the southern tip of Georgian Bay,
across northern Michigan, and through Green Bay. The contrast in
most places can be recognized easily through differences in land use
and human settlement and results primarily from the interaction of
physical factors: geology, glacial history, and climate. To the north
of the line, the dominant land use is forest; south of the line is specialized and intensive agriculture (figure 3.1).

The basin is also divided into distinct northern and southern zones
by the distribution of the population. The Lake Superior and Lake
Huron basins are sparsely populated. The drainage basins of Lakes
Michigan (especially the southern portion), Ontario (particularly on

## Figure 3.1
## Land Use in the Great Lakes Basin

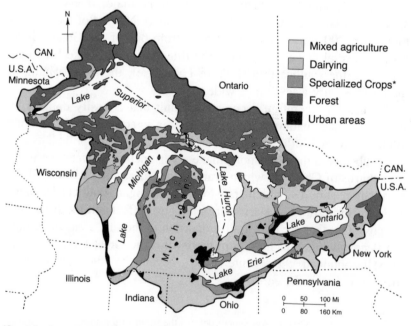

*Specialized crops include fruit and tobacco.

Source: Environment Canada; U.S. Environmental Protection Agency.

the Canadian side), and Erie (mostly in the United States) are, on average, much more densely populated (figure 3.2).

This north-south contrast is also expressed in the incidence and character of environmental problems. Of 42 Areas of Concern as classified by the Great Lakes Water Quality Board, for example, only 10 are located in the northern forest zone (figure 3.3). In the southern zone, the issues that must be faced tend to be more complex and extensive than in the north. In addition to the problems generated by population concentration and industrial activity, the intensive agricultural development in the southern zone has resulted in the movement of fertilizer and pesticide residues into the streams and ponds that drain the land, which means that ultimately the residues are transported to the Great Lakes.

In its first report to the Canadian and U.S. governments on progress in implementing the 1978 Water Quality Agreement, the International Joint Commission (IJC) observed that

a number of pollutants are entering the waters of the Great Lakes System from nonpoint sources. . . . PLUARG* identified croplands as the major source of

## Figure 3.2
## Population Density for Each of the Great Lakes

| Lake | Drainage area in square miles | Population | Population per square mile of drainage area (per square kilometer) |
|------|------|------|------|
| Superior | 49,300 | 663,465 | 13.5   (5.2) |
| Huron | 51,700 | 2,461,115 | 47.6   (18.4) |
| Michigan | 45,600 | 12,051,200 | 264.3 (102.1) |
| Erie | 30,140 | 12,532,770 | 415.8 (160.5) |
| Ontario | 24,720 | 7,375,280 | 298.6 (115.3) |

Source: U.S. Bureau of the Census; Environment Canada; Statistics Canada.

---

*PLUARG was the acronym of the IJC's International Reference Group on Great Lakes Pollution from Land Use Activities. Between 1973 and 1978 PLUARG produced 121 reports based on intensive data gathering and analysis.

**Figure 3.3**
**Areas of Concern in the Great Lakes Basin**

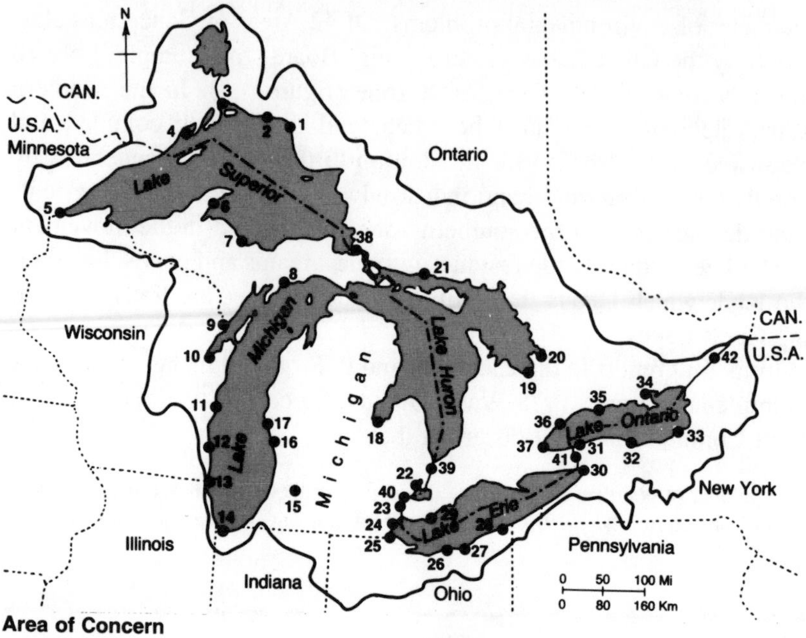

**Area of Concern**

**Lake Superior**
1 Peninsula Harbour
2 Jackfish Bay
3 Nipigon Bay
4 Thunder Bay
5 St. Louis River / Bay
6 Torch Lake
7 Deer Lake / Carp Creek / Carp River

**Lake Michigan**
8 Manistique River
9 Menominee River
10 Fox River / Southern Green Bay
11 Sheboygan Harbor
12 Milwaukee Estuary
13 Waukegan Harbor
14 Grand Calumet / Indiana Harbor
15 Kalamazoo River
16 Muskegon Lake
17 White Lake

**Lake Huron**
18 Saginaw River / Bay
19 Collingwood Harbour
20 Penetang Bay to Sturgeon Bay
21 Spanish River

**Lake Erie**
22 Clinton River
23 Rouge River
24 River Raisin
25 Maumee River
26 Black River
27 Cuyahoga River
28 Ashtabula River
29 Wheatley Harbour

**Lake Ontario**
30 Buffalo River
31 Eighteen Mile Creek
32 Rochester Embayment
33 Oswego River
34 Bay of Quinte
35 Port Hope
36 Toronto Waterfront
37 Hamilton Harbour

**Connecting Channels**
38 St. Marys River
39 St. Clair River
40 Detroit River
41 Niagara River
42 St. Lawrence River

Source: International Joint Commission.

nonpoint* inputs of phosphorus, especially those areas characterized by high-density row crops and fine-grained soils, e.g., north[western] Ohio, south-western Ontario and southern Wisconsin. . . . PLUARG also indicated that a large proportion of the nonpoint phosphorus input to Lakes Erie and Ontario was from large urban areas in these basins, and that organic compounds were entering the lakes from both urban and agricultural areas.[1]

In the northern forested zone, similar nonpoint pollution also occurs, from forest herbicides and insecticides, but the impact on waterbodies and aquatic organisms is less intense. Throughout the basin, land areas are recipients ("sinks") as well as sources of nonpoint pollution.

## EARLY RESOURCE DEVELOPMENT

Despite the immense natural resources of the Great Lakes basin, both political and logistical barriers delayed large-scale settlement and population growth until well into the 19th century. French explorers had found the way through the lower lakes to the fur country in the 16th century, but access from Montreal to the great fur entrepôt at Michilimackinac (northern Michigan) was much easier via the Ottawa River and Georgian Bay, especially because the Iroquois blocked expansion up the St. Lawrence and along the Mohawk Valley until late in the 18th century.

At that time, the opening of the Great Lakes basin became an issue in the American Revolution. The Quebec Act of 1774 had extended the province of Quebec to include Indian territory south of the Great Lakes between the Mississippi and the Ohio rivers.[2] By thus limiting westward expansion of the American colonies beyond the Alleghenies, this became one of the "Intolerable Acts" provoking revolution.

The Revolutionary War and its aftermath eliminated the political barriers to settlement. The Treaty of Paris (1783) and Jay's Treaty (1794) defined the international boundary through the Great Lakes basin.[3] The Northwest Ordinance of 1787 established the basis for settlement and government in what would become the states of Ohio, Indiana, Illinois, Michigan, and Wisconsin.[4] Meanwhile, about 7,500 of the "United Empire Loyalists" who left the former American colonies during or after the Revolution migrated to the area that would later become Ontario.[5]

---

*Nonpoint pollution sources (for example, areas of cropland and forest) are distinguished from point sources such as industrial discharges and sewage treatment plants.

Even though the broad political questions were settled, and were not substantially altered by the War of 1812, significant immigration and settlement in the Great Lakes basin still had to await transport improvements, particularly canals. The Lachine Canal, opened in 1825, was the first stage in bypassing the St. Lawrence River rapids between Montreal and Lake Ontario; by mid-century, Ontario's population had reached 950,000 and had already overtaken that of Quebec.[6] The year 1825 also saw the opening of the Erie Canal, a 364-mile (586-kilometer) link between the Hudson River at Albany and Lake Erie through upper New York State (figure 3.4).

> The effect was explosive. The cost per mile of moving a ton of freight to the Atlantic dropped by 90 percent. People filled the westbound boats. Eastbound, they hauled grain and timber. The price of wheat at Great Lakes ports jumped from 20 cents to a dollar a bushel. The [Erie] canal carried so much business that tolls paid off the entire cost within nine years.[7]

Once backwaters, the Great Lakes now became the focus of settlement and commerce. Canals and, later, railroads were built to Great Lakes ports, especially on the U.S. side of the border. One problem, however, was that as small river-mouth villages such as Cleveland and Chicago expanded into major ports, they lacked natural harbor facilities.

> In those places, harbors were created by dredging the rivers and extending breakwaters out into the lakes. As shipping has expanded, similar work has been done at all Great Lakes ports. Many of these harbor structures have strong local effects on currents in the lakes, often creating erosion or abnormally high deposits on nearby shorelines. Dredging spoils dumped in the lakes cut down on breeding habitat for fish such as lake trout that favor gravel bottoms for laying their eggs.[8]

The erosion, silting, and sedimentation initiated by navigational improvements were increased by agriculture. Though soil erosion is less severe in the Great Lakes basin than in much of the rest of the United States and the Canadian prairies, the process remains a significant means by which pesticides, nutrients, and sediments are transferred to waterbodies. What was a valuable resource on the land leads to siltation of river mouths, wetlands, and other spawning habitat. Where the Maumee River once flowed clear through the Black Swamp, it now carries 2.0 million tons (1.8 million tonnes) of silt a year into Lake Erie.[9] Agriculture continues to be an important activity in the basin and an important factor in the ecosystem.

**Figure 3.4**
**Development of Major Canals and Railroads**
**in the Great Lakes Basin, 1825–1870**

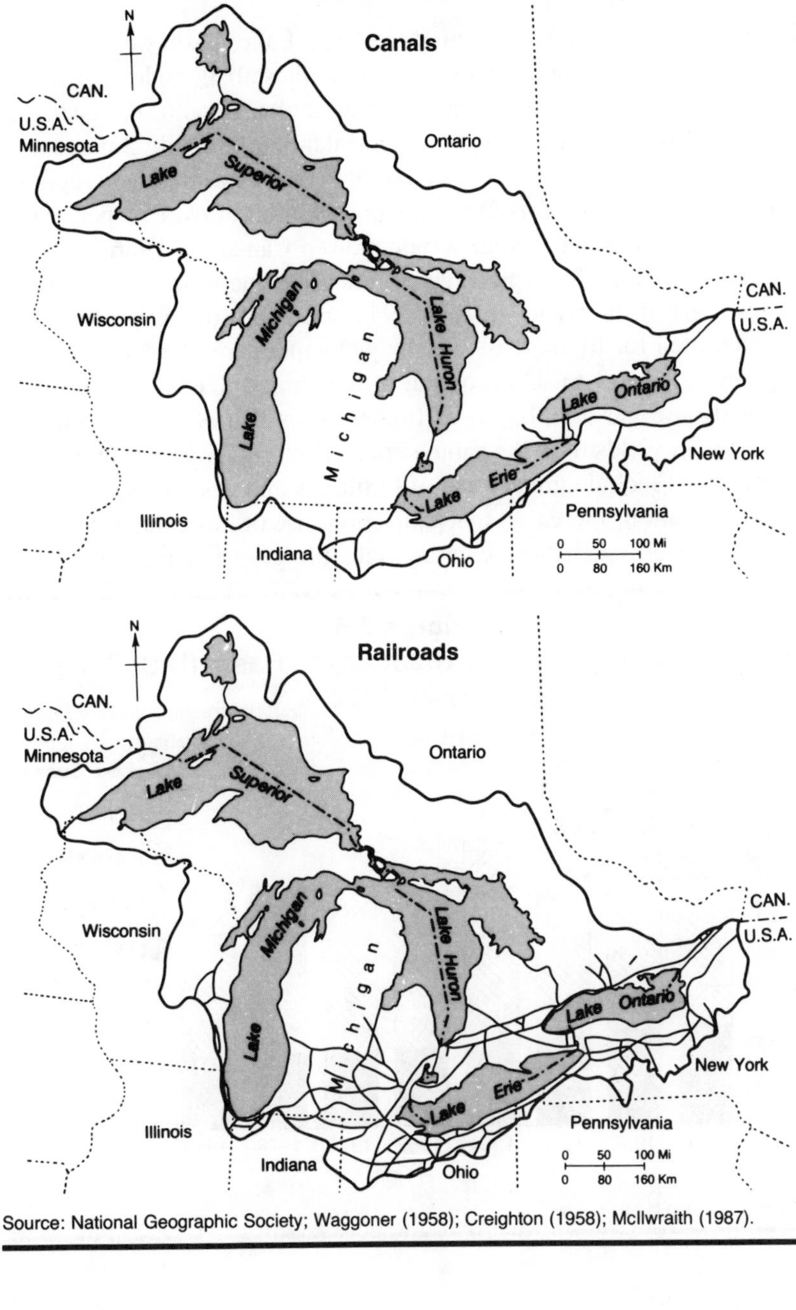

Source: National Geographic Society; Waggoner (1958); Creighton (1958); McIlwraith (1987).

## CURRENT RESOURCE USES

### Agricultural Activities

In terms of land use, 31 percent of the Great Lakes basin was classified
as farmland in the early 1980s, although this statistic hides the strong
contrast between the forested north and agricultural south. For instance,
the Lake Erie basin was 69 percent farmland, while only 3 percent of
the Lake Superior basin was agricultural.[10] One measure of the region's
agricultural importance is Ontario's contribution of over 25 percent of
the value of total agricultural production in Canada in 1986.[11]

Although agricultural acreage declined by one-third in the United
States' part of the basin between 1949 and 1982, this was more than
compensated for by increases in the yields per acre of principal crops
(figures 3.5 and 3.6). Corn output in the United States, for example,
doubled on a per-acre basis, and other crops had at least 50 percent
increases in yields over the same period. Factors that have contributed
to this trend include greater use of fertilizers and pesticides, increased
use of irrigation, increased mechanization, use of more intensive cropping practices (such as increased field tillage), and improved seed

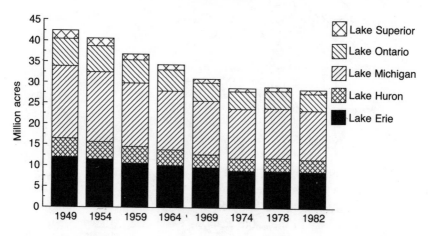

### Figure 3.5
### Total Farmland in the Great Lakes Basin (U.S. Side), 1949–1982

Source: U.S. Bureau of the Census.

**Figure 3.6**
**Yields per Acre for Selected Crops in the Great Lakes Basin (U.S. Side), 1949–1982**

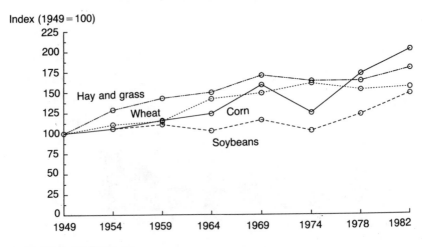

Source: U.S. Bureau of the Census.

varieties.[12] These increased yields, in combination with changes in crop preferences, enabled farmers to increase greatly the total output of corn and soybeans in the Great Lakes region (figures 3.7 and 3.8).

Growth in the use of chemical pesticides and fertilizers has had profound impacts on environmental quality. The principal types of pesticides are herbicides, insecticides, and fungicides. By 1982, herbicides accounted for four-fifths of all pesticides used in the United States.[13] In the United States, 85 percent of herbicides and 70 percent of insecticides are applied primarily to four major crops—corn, cotton, soybeans, and wheat—all of which, except cotton, are major crops in the Great Lakes region.[14] In Ontario, corn, tobacco, and soybeans occupy 35 percent of the agricultural area but account for 84 percent of the pesticides used.[15] Mid-1980s estimates for 21 commonly used pesticides indicated that at least 16,900 tons (15,300 tonnes) of pesticides were being applied annually in the U.S. portion of the Great Lakes basin; 1983 estimates of total pesticide use in the Great Lakes portion of Ontario added another 9,300 tons (8,400 tonnes) to this amount, primarily in the Lake Erie/St. Clair basin (figure 3.9).[16]

From an ecosystem standpoint, pesticides are significant because, by definition, they are toxic substances. Because most of the quantity

## Figure 3.7
## Corn Production in the Great Lakes Basin (U.S. Side), 1949–1982

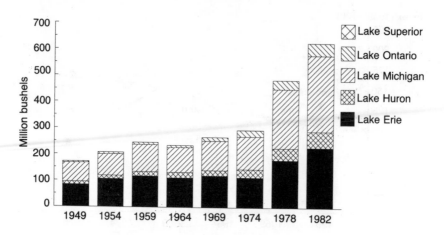

Source: U.S. Bureau of the Census.

## Figure 3.8
## Soybean Production in the Great Lakes Basin (U.S. Side), 1949–1982

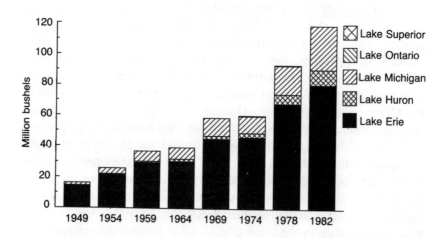

Source: U.S. Bureau of the Census.

## Figure 3.9
## Pesticide Use in the Great Lakes Basin, mid-1980s

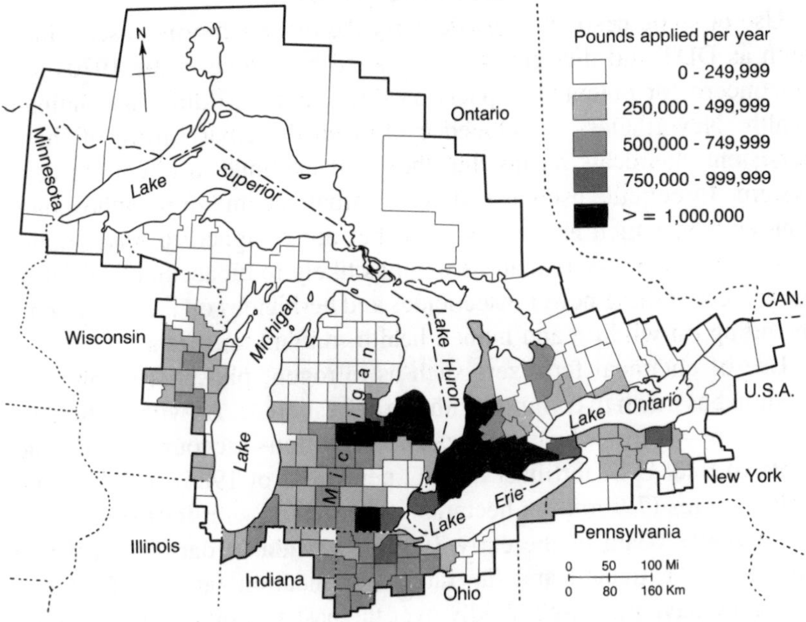

Source: Gianessi (1988); McGee (1984).

that is applied does not reach its target, pesticides have impacts both on the farm and off. When applied, only 4 percent to 20 percent of a pesticide is likely to be taken up by plants, and less than 0.1 percent probably reaches the pests that are the target of the application.[17] What happens to agricultural chemicals after the initial discharge to the environment is not well understood; environmental pathways depend on such characteristics as: how soluble the substance is in water, how readily it adheres to soil particles, how long it persists in the environment, how readily it volatilizes to the atmosphere, in what form it is applied (for example, spray or powder), and when and how much rain falls following application.[18]

As much as half of the pesticides may enter the atmosphere, and exchanges between different media—soil, air, surface water, or groundwater—may continue for a long period, with one medium becoming "a 'source' of residuals to another medium."[19] For instance, it is now known that DDT and its breakdown products, including DDE, have half-lives of 57.5 years, although it was previously thought that DDT would break down much more quickly.[20]

Use of some pesticides, particularly the organochlorine insecticides such as DDT and dieldrin, was restricted beginning in the 1970s out of concern for potential impacts on birds, other wildlife, and human health. Nevertheless, continued cycling in the environment of these persistent chemicals means that they will continue to affect the ecosystem. Insecticide use has shifted to carbamate and organophosphate compounds, which are highly toxic but are designed to break down quickly in the ecosystem and are not as likely to bioaccumulate.[21] But the effects of these newer insecticides and herbicides on the ecosystem, including on wildlife and human health, remain uncertain.

Use of chemical fertilizers such as nitrogen, phosphorus, and potassium has much in common with use of pesticides. As with pesticides, four crops—corn, wheat, soybeans, and cotton—account for the majority of total U.S. fertilizer use (62 percent as of 1985).[22] Some 19.6 million acres (7.9 million hectares) were treated with fertilizers in the Great Lakes basin in the early 1980s.[23] Available data indicate that both the area treated and the rate of application (at least for some nutrients) have increased rapidly over the past several decades. In both the United States and Canada, fertilizers appear to be used most heavily—in terms of area and application rates—in the basins of Lake Erie and Lake St. Clair.[24] Significantly, and perhaps typical of other areas, a 1986 Ontario study found that some farmers applied nearly three times the amount of phosphorus fertilizer recommended by government specialists, with the highest ratios of actual application rates to recommended rates occurring in several counties bordering Lake Erie (figure 3.10).[25]

The increasing use of nitrogenous and phosphoric fertilizers has a direct bearing on efforts to reduce nutrient loadings in the Great Lakes (and other waterbodies in the basin). The PLUARG studies of the mid-1970s suggested that between 35 percent and 80 percent of phosphorus loadings in the lakes were associated with sediment transport, much of which is produced by soil erosion associated with agricultural activities. Of the phosphorus associated with suspended sediments, about 40 percent is in a form that makes it potentially available for use by algae.[26]

While phosphorus loadings throughout much of the Great Lakes

# Figure 3.10
## Fertilizer Use in Ontario, 1980

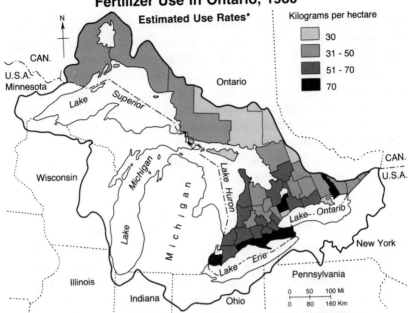

### Estimated Use Rates*

Kilograms per hectare

- 30
- 31 - 50
- 51 - 70
- 70

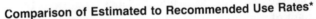

## Comparison of Estimated to Recommended Use Rates*

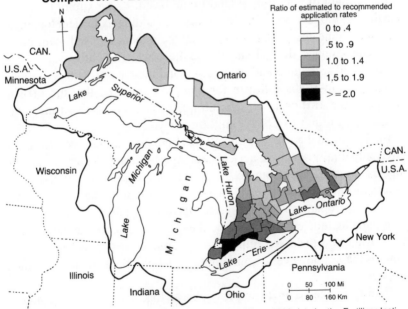

Ratio of estimated to recommended application rates

- 0 to .4
- .5 to .9
- 1.0 to 1.4
- 1.5 to 1.9
- >= 2.0

*"Estimated" refers to the phosphate rate (kg/ha) estimated from 1980 data by the Fertilizer Institute of Ontario. "Recommended" refers to mean annual recommended rates from soil test records (mean value for 1979–80 and 1980–81).

Source: Ontario Institute of Pedology.

have declined, scientists have found that nitrogen loadings to the lakes have risen steadily, at least since the late 1960s and perhaps longer (see chapter 4). The causes and consequences of this trend are not well understood but could be significant if the community structure of Great Lakes phytoplankton shifts as a result of changes in nutrient availability. Although their importance varies by lake, primary sources of nitrogen include atmospheric transport, agricultural fertilizers, and contributions from urban areas.[27]

Soil erosion from agricultural land can have on-farm as well as off-farm impacts; in the Great Lakes basin, the off-farm impacts appear to be more significant. In the United States, the rates of erosion in the agricultural areas of the Great Lakes basin were, as of 1982, largely at or below the "tolerable loss rate" or "T" level (figure 3.11).[28]* There is not universal agreement, however, as to whether the levels established for tolerable loss rates of different soils provide a sufficient basis for maintaining the long-term productivity of soil resources.[29] Regardless, the total volume transported from agricultural lands directly and indirectly to tributaries and the lakes is considerable, because of the amount of agricultural land in the basin, its proximity to water, and the types of soil involved. In addition to adding to nutrient loadings, sediments (and the pesticides that may be attached to sediment particles) can damage the habitat of aquatic organisms, adversely affect water-based recreation and navigation, and increase costs of supplying water. A mid-1980s estimate for Ontario suggested that the off-site (that is, nonfarm) costs of agricultural soil erosion were on the order of C$74.0 million to C$91.2 million per year.[30]

Environmental and economic effects both point to the need for more environmentally sensitive agriculture. Agricultural programs traditionally have emphasized commodity production levels and soil and water conservation. In recent years, programs taking a broader view of agriculture's impact on the ecosystem have been added.† These newer programs include efforts to reduce the off-farm environmental impacts of erosion and to lessen reliance on chemical pesticides. Recent initiatives have, however, been limited in both their scope and their impact.

Efforts in the basin to improve Great Lakes water quality and to

---

*The maximum rate at which soil can be eroded and maintain productivity.

†There also have been some programs over the years aimed at maintaining the viability of smaller family-owned farms.

# Figure 3.11
# Soil Erosion on the U.S. Side of the Great Lakes Basin, 1982*

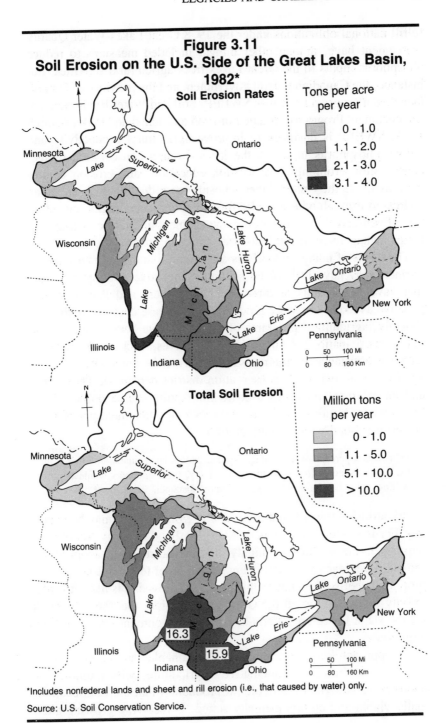

**Soil Erosion Rates**

Tons per acre per year

- 0 - 1.0
- 1.1 - 2.0
- 2.1 - 3.0
- 3.1 - 4.0

**Total Soil Erosion**

Million tons per year

- 0 - 1.0
- 1.1 - 5.0
- 5.1 - 10.0
- >10.0

16.3
15.9

*Includes nonfederal lands and sheet and rill erosion (i.e., that caused by water) only.

Source: U.S. Soil Conservation Service.

fulfill national obligations under the 1978 Great Lakes Water Quality Agreement have, among other things, included measures to reduce phosphorus inputs to the Great Lakes from agricultural activities. For instance, the Canadian federal government and the province of Ontario launched a program known as SWEEP (Soil and Water Environmental Enhancement Program). Initiated in 1985 and scheduled to run through 1993, SWEEP is designed to improve agricultural productivity and reduce phosphorus inputs to the lakes through conservation tillage, conservation cropping, conservation education, and erosion control measures.[31] In the United States, phosphorus-reduction goals are being addressed through educational efforts aimed at encouraging the adoption of conservation tillage, better management of livestock waste, and better management of nutrients used for crop production.[32]

The limits of many such efforts are captured in the verb *encourage*. Farmers may have little or no economic incentive to adopt practices that have no obvious or direct benefit to them and that they may perceive as likely to reduce productivity, increase costs, or both. Historically, agricultural programs of all types have been based on voluntary participation or on positive incentives, such as financial or technical assistance programs, usually provided by university extension agents or soil and water conservation district personnel. The control and enforcement measures used to limit point-source pollution (for example, from industrial discharges or sewage treatment plants) have not been applied widely to agriculture:

> [T]here is a perception that family farming cannot be regulated and that with the current state of [the] agricultural economy, farm operators would be unwilling and unable to shoulder any pollution abatement costs. . . .[33]

But attitudes towards requiring action from farmers may be changing. For instance, in the United States, the Food Security Act of 1985 requires farmers who farm highly erodible farmland to adopt an approved, five-year soil conservation plan in order to receive commodity program benefits.[34] Although this particular provision is likely to apply to only a few farmers in the Great Lakes region, the approach could set the stage for future efforts to reduce environmental impacts from agriculture.

An approach known variously as "sustainable" agriculture, "low-input" agriculture, or "alternative" agriculture, which implies the adoption of patterns of agricultural production that are both economically viable and environmentally sound, is receiving ·growing attention.[35] These patterns will probably entail more intensive managing of farm resources, and switching from a paradigm that maximizes short-term output to one that optimizes long-run returns to the farmer through more efficient use of resources and more environmentally compatible farming methods.[36]

Efforts to avoid the hazards of pesticides by reducing the amounts used are growing in both the United States and Canada. For instance, in Ontario, the provincial government has set a goal of reducing use by 50 percent by the year 2002.[37] In the United States, the Environmental Protection Agency (EPA) recently proposed that the federal pesticide registration law be streamlined so that existing pesticides posing environmental hazards can be removed from use more quickly,[38] and the U.S. Department of Agriculture has initiated a program designed to provide information and support research on low-input sustainable-agriculture farming systems.[39]

Integrated pest management (IPM)—which relies on a mix of biological, cultural, and chemical controls to manage pests—is drawing attention. Farmers may be motivated to use IPM because of its possible cost advantages over traditional chemical use. They may also opt for IPM because of the resistance pests develop to chemicals currently used, environmental hazards caused by heavy pesticide use, potential health risks posed by intensive chemical use, and public pressure for pesticide-free food. In the Great Lakes region, at least five states (Indiana, Ohio, Michigan, Pennsylvania, and New York) and Ontario have small IPM technical assistance and research programs. To date, barriers to more widespread adoption of IPM have included satisfaction with existing control methods, resistance to change, fear of taking financial risks, and perceptions that IPM is complicated to implement and that its effectiveness is unproved.[40]

### Forest Activities: Timber and Paper

From the 1830s, when local demand and waterborne access to markets permitted, the logging industry expanded throughout the Great Lakes basin. For example, 400 million board feet, mainly from white pine in southern Ontario, were sent to the United States through Oswego, New York, between 1864 and 1866.[41]

Although early logging was selective, especially for white pine, subsequent operations were more comprehensive, and "what the loggers didn't get the fires did."[42] Not merely did forest clearance encourage soil erosion, it increased the rate of runoff, causing more flood erosion and warmer temperatures in the runoff water. Conversely, in late summer, streamflow was reduced, and the headwaters of some streams, which under forest would have flowed continuously, dried out seasonally. All of these changes altered significantly the spawning grounds of several important fish species. Logging operations, based usually on floating logs down the principal streams, increased the problem: Dams to control the flow on logging rivers acted as barriers to migrating fish; bark and other tree matter lost during the journey down the stream accumulated on the streambed and eliminated plant and animal life; and the sawmills at the mouths of the logging rivers choked the water with wastes.[43]

For some time, the softwood (coniferous) forests in the Canadian portion of the Great Lakes basin were much less attractive to foresters than the southern hardwoods. This changed after the discovery (around 1840) of wood-based papermaking, which largely replaced the use of cotton and linen rags. The first chemical wood-pulp mill in North America was built in Quebec in 1864. The three main expansions in papermaking in Canada took place at the turn of the 20th century, when exports of raw pulpwood from Canada were prohibited; after the United States removed the tariff on newsprint in 1913; and again in the 1960s.[44]

Papermaking is a chemical process that pollutes soil, water, and air on a major scale. Although many of the processes and waste disposal practices that generated this pollution have been terminated or controlled in recent decades, the problem is far from solved. The latest problem to be recognized is the release of dioxin in pulp and paper effluent. Monitoring studies show that dioxin is released from mills that use chlorine in the kraft process of bleaching pulp and that this dioxin can accumulate in aquatic organisms. In 1988, EPA signaled its intent to tighten controls on discharges of dioxins. In an "interim strategy" for such discharges, EPA indicated it would work with states to update states' water quality standards for dioxin, and would reconsider (and presumably tighten) existing permits governing discharges from paper mills.[45] In Canada, a panel of experts to Ontario's Municipal-Industrial Strategy for Abatement (MISA) program downplayed the importance of paper mills as sources of dioxin, compared to such sources as municipal incinerators, but the panel urged reduction of paper-mill discharges of the entire category of "organochlorines," of which dioxins are a small part.[46]

The legacy of the past is evident in several of the Areas of Concern for which Remedial Action Plans (see chapter 9) are now being prepared in the northern part of the basin. Pulp and paper mills have been major contributors to water quality problems in Jackfish Bay, Peninsula Harbor, Nipigon Bay, and Thunder Bay, all on the northern shore of Lake Superior.[47] Toxic elements in the pulp and paper mill effluents include resins and fatty acids; in addition, the wastes include organic chemicals, metals, and the usual load of bark and other natural wastes.

The release of mercury from chlor-alkali plants associated with paper mills has attracted much attention in recent decades. The toxicity of mercury has been known for a long time,* but it was not until 1967 that it was recognized that mercury released from such industrial plants could be chemically modified and enter the food chain as methyl mercury. The use of mercury has been abandoned in these plants in both the United States and Canada, and mercury loadings of affected lakes, streams, and sediments have declined substantially.[48]

Today, the forests of the Great Lakes region have largely been rejuvenated and are productive components of the ecosystem once again. In the three northern Great Lakes states (Michigan, Wisconsin, and Minnesota), forest products' sales amounted to U.S.$15 billion in 1982 and generated about 150,000 jobs. Forest recreation accounted for about U.S.$2 billion and more than 80,000 jobs.[49] Ontario also has a substantial forest products industry. In 1985, 172,000 people were employed in Ontario's forest products sector, which produced about C$20.2 billion in goods.[50]

As one observer recently described it:

> The Lake States forests truly are enjoying a renaissance. Once cut over, or consumed by disastrous wildfires, the regenerating forests of Michigan, Wisconsin and Minnesota are valued for their timber, recreation opportunities, wildlife, clean water, and scenic qualities. There is a renaissance too in the public's recognition of opportunities to use the forests to diversify the region's economy and enhance its quality of life.[51]

F. Dale Robertson, chief of the U.S. Forest Service, has suggested that, ''the forests in the Lake States have been growing like a savings account with a high interest rate. The timber inventory has increased over 80 percent during the last 30 years. . . . [We] are now in a position to cash in on this investment.''[52] However, not everyone would agree with this optimistic view, and there may be considerable

---

*The phrase ''mad as a hatter'' was a 19th-century recognition of the effect of the use of mercurous nitrate on those employed in felt hatmaking.

disagreement about the way in which the investment should be re-
couped. Nevertheless, within the Great Lakes basin some problems
and some disagreements are more urgent or intractable than others,
and there is much less of a sense of crisis over the forests than for
other ecosystem elements. Accommodation of potentially conflicting uses in the Great Lakes basin probably will be done through
planning for multiple uses—for timber, recreation, aesthetics, energy, and wildlife habitat.

Part of the reason for the sense of optimism—almost compla-
cency—in regard to the "North Woods" of Michigan, Wisconsin,
and Minnesota is a simple comparison with the past. After being
decimated by logging throughout the 19th century and into the 1920s,
the extensive areas of slash suffered widespread wildfires in the
1930s. Consequently, it is only now that mature stands of forest are
evident in the North Woods, almost for the first time within living
memory.[53]

The forests of the late 20th century, however, are not the same
as in the past. Aspen, for example, covers a quarter of the area,
compared to an estimated 1 percent in presettlement times.[54] It has
been suggested that efforts by the U.S. Forest Service to manage
the forests for species diversity (chiefly by providing substantial
species-rich forest-edge habitat) has resulted in a decrease in overall
ecosystem diversity (at least in decreases in the populations of some
sensitive species), because animal and plant species that depend on
large tracts of undisturbed forest have suffered from the more open
pattern prevalent today.[55] This issue has not yet been resolved, in
either scientific or policy terms; it is a measure of the region's forest
rehabilitation, however, that such choices in forest management
policy are now available.

Over the longer term, there is increasing concern about the impact
of climate change, primarily through greenhouse effects. These
changes are anticipated within a single life cycle of a forest stand:

> Slowly, over time, the current species mix of the forests of the Great Lakes
> Basin will change, as the boreal forest moves northwards to be replaced by
> more southerly, temperate species and forest types, constrained only by edaphic
> [soil] factors. A more diverse, hardwood-rich forest community is likely to
> emerge even in the more northerly portions of the basin. It is predicted that the
> decline of the present ecosystems . . . could become evident within 30 to 60
> years.[56]

As the forests come under increasing climatic stress, they may become even more vulnerable to atmospheric deposition* than they are at present.

## INDUSTRIAL DEVELOPMENT

### Growth of the Industrial Heartland

The industrial development of the Great Lakes basin, especially around the lower lakes and the southern part of Lake Michigan, did not begin until the middle of the 19th century. Iron and copper deposits were found in the Upper Peninsula of Michigan in the 1840s, but their large-scale development had to wait until the Sault Canal provided a commercial shipping channel from Lake Superior to the other lakes in 1855, and until the Civil War in the next decade made a major demand for iron. The simultaneous introduction of cheap and large-scale steel making, using the Bessemer converter, reinforced industrial growth. The massive expansion of American railroads fed the lakes' ports with coal and limestone, replacing canal transport, and also provided a demand for iron rails and other iron and steel products.[57]

The legacy of heavy industry is evident today in the bottom sediments in the lakes. The Grand Calumet River and Indiana Harbor Canal on Lake Michigan, for example, contain heavily contaminated sediments and are unable to support healthy aquatic communities. PCBs, heavy metals, and other toxic substances were discharged to the river and canal as a result of direct and indirect industrial discharges, and continue to enter the system via overflows from combined sewers.† Because dredging was halted in Indiana Harbor in 1972, due to restrictions on disposing of contaminated dredged materials in the deep waters of Lake Michigan, contaminated sediments have accrued to a depth of 10 feet (3 meters) in some places. With the drop in lake levels in 1988, some iron-ore freighters have been forced to reduce their loads, and some steel mills are investigating the use of alternative modes of transportation.[58]

The steel industry was not the only cause of environmental degra-

---

*"Atmospheric deposition" refers to the transfer of pollutants from the atmosphere to both land and water surfaces. "Acid rain" is one form of atmospheric deposition. See chapter 5 for additional discussion.

†Where storm sewers are combined with municipal sewage systems, overflows during storms can result in untreated sewage being discharged to waterbodies.

dation. The Precambrian rocks of the Canadian Shield are one of the most accessible storehouses of minerals in the world. Torch Lake, on Michigan's Upper Peninsula, is over 4 square miles in area (1,100 hectares) and has an average depth of 50 feet (15 meters), yet its dimensions have been reduced by a fifth as the result of a century of accumulation of copper-mine tailings and industrial and municipal wastes. Although copper mining and milling ended there 20 years ago, the copper content in the lake water is six to nine times higher than the water quality objective of the IJC.[59] At Sudbury, Ontario, first logging, and then mining and air pollution from nickel-smelting operations, severely devastated local vegetation. These areas have been largely reclaimed.[60]

The beginning of environmental concern in the Great Lakes basin is associated with the problems of human health in U.S. Great Lakes cities that mushroomed as centers of the industrialized economy. Chicago's population in 1830 was about 50; in 1870, nearly 300,000; more than four times that number 20 years later; and 1.7 million by 1900.[61] Chicago was the most spectacular example of growth, but Buffalo, New York, Cleveland, Ohio, and other Great Lakes cities also expanded rapidly.

*Steel mills along Indiana Harbor Canal, East Chicago, Indiana.*
© David Plowden, 1985

Little or no attempt was originally made in these cities to provide basic services such as water purification or sewage treatment, and the inevitable consequence was repeated outbreaks of waterborne diseases. Cholera broke out in the 1890s in Sandusky[62] and in Manitowoc, Wisconsin; typhoid was taken for granted. Whereas in the major European cities at this time the annual death rate from typhoid was around 5 per 100,000 population, in the principal U.S. cities in the Great Lakes basin it was four times higher or more. In Duluth, Minnesota, deaths from typhoid averaged 52 per 100,000 throughout the first decade of the 20th century, and the incidence of the disease was 10 times the death rate. In Sheboygan, Wisconsin, the death rate went over 300 per 100,000.[63] In 1912, the U.S. Public Health Service rightly described the prevalence of typhoid fever as a "national disgrace," because—in principle—its elimination required only a safe water supply.[64] In Canada, the situation was similar. Continual pollution of the water supply by waste outflows caused heavy loss of life in typhoid outbreaks until filtration and chlorination of lake water were introduced in 1912.[65]

Belatedly, these problems were tackled city by city, although more effort was devoted to purifying the water supply than to avoiding its contamination through sewage treatment. As the IJC drily commented in 1951, in regard to the connecting channels between Lake Huron and Lake Erie (St. Clair River-Lake St. Clair-Detroit River):

> Since 1913 a number of sewage treatment plants have been constructed. Notwithstanding the accomplishments of these works, the bacterial load was found in 1946-48 to be approximately three times as great as in 1913. The primary treatment of municipal wastes which has been provided has neither reduced the bacterial load below the 1913 level nor has it even kept pace with the increase resulting from expansion of municipal population and industrial activities.[66]

This experience was characteristic, not merely of municipal water treatment but of the stresses imposed on the natural ecosystem by human activities. Problems accumulated, and legacies were created, much more rapidly than solutions were found and implemented. Frequently, any reductions in stress per person or per unit of production were far outweighed by population growth and by economic growth, especially after World War II.

### Post-World War II Industrial Trends

The Great Lakes basin had by the mid-20th century become the industrial heartland of the United States and, even more so, of Canada.[67]

The Great Lakes region has been particularly strong in the manufacture of durable goods, particularly motor vehicles and related equipment. For instance, as of the mid-1980s, the five-state region of Ohio, Indiana, Illinois, Michigan, and Wisconsin accounted for about 60 percent of all U.S. motor vehicle and equipment production.[68] In Canada, southern Ontario's manufacturing role is similarly noteworthy, especially for motor vehicles.

The recession of the early 1980s hit the U.S. side of the Great Lakes basin hard. The recession accelerated the restructuring of the economy, causing older, less-efficient manufacturing facilities to close and decreasing the relative importance of manufacturing jobs in the regional economy. For example, the five states mentioned above lost 1.1 million jobs in this period: almost three-quarters of the total job loss throughout the United States. About a million of these jobs were in manufacturing industries.[69] The 1980-82 recession affected Canada at least as much as the United States, but the effect in the basin, relative to the rest of the nation, was significantly different. Southern Ontario is not merely the center of Canadian manufacturing, it is also the center of gravity of the Canadian population and the focus of those economic activities that have expanded as manufacturing industry has, in relative terms at least, declined. Whereas the Great Lakes states appeared a "poor relation" in the United States, the recession had less effect in southern Ontario than on regional economies in the rest of Canada.

The proportional share of economic output contributed by manufacturing on the U.S. side of the Great Lakes basin has declined over the past several decades, while services and the related trade and finance, insurance, and real estate industries have steadily increased (figure 3.12). Nonetheless, manufacturing remains important in the region. The outlook for this sector in the United States was healthy in 1989 as a result of facility modernizations and the closure of obsolete facilities, a drop in the value of the U.S. dollar overseas (making U.S. goods more competitive), and growth in demand for the types of goods produced in the Midwest.[70]

The stagnation in the economy felt on the U.S. side of the Great Lakes in the early 1980s can be seen in population trends (figure 3.13). Overall, since 1900 the population of the basin as a whole has grown from around 10 million people to over 35 million, with most of this expansion coming before 1970. Since 1970, most growth has been on the Canadian side of the basin.

Energy-use patterns in the past tended to reflect general economic

## Figure 3.12
## Economic Output in Five Great Lakes States, 1963–1986*

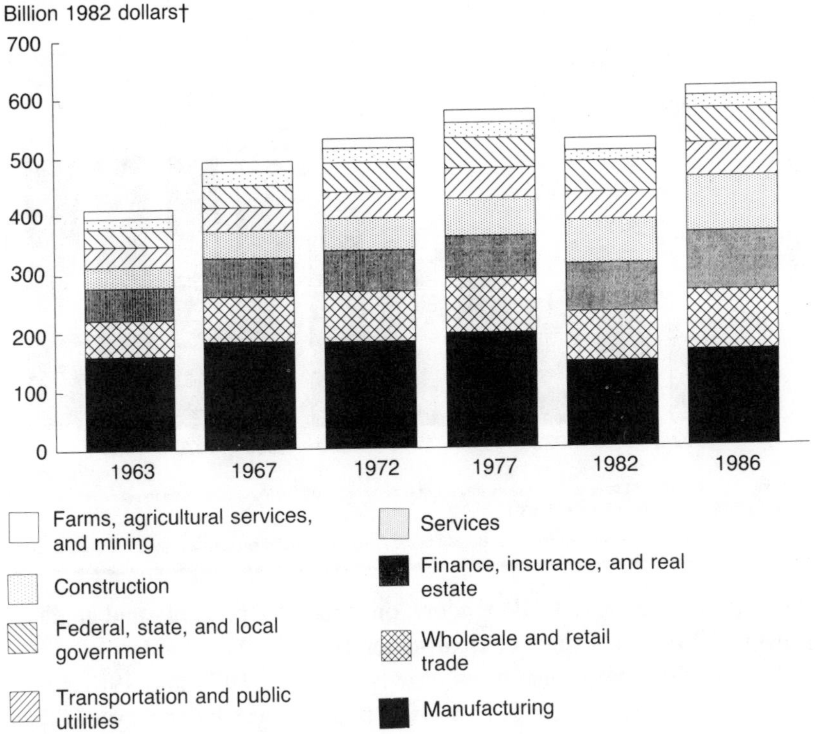
Billion 1982 dollars†
700
600
500
400
300
200
100
0
1963
1967
1972
1977
1982
1986
Farms, agricultural services, and mining
Construction
Federal, state, and local government
Transportation and public utilities
Services
Finance, insurance, and real estate
Wholesale and retail trade
Manufacturing

*As measured by the gross state product.

†Conversions to constant dollars based on the 1982 implicit price deflators for the gross national product.

Source: U.S. Bureau of Economic Analysis.

trends, but since the late 1970s, overall energy consumption in the Great Lakes states has dropped even while economic output has continued to rise. For example, total energy consumption in the eight Great Lakes states in 1986 was 16 percent lower than it had been in 1973, with more than three-quarters of this drop occurring in the industrial sector (figure 3.14).[71] Closure of outdated facilities and more efficient use of energy probably contributed to the drop in manufacturing consumption.

Though overall energy use dropped, total consumption of electricity in the eight states rose 19 percent from 1973 to 1986, with much of this growth in the residential and commercial sectors.[72] As of 1986,

**Figure 3.13**
**Population in the Great Lakes Basin, 1900–1986\***

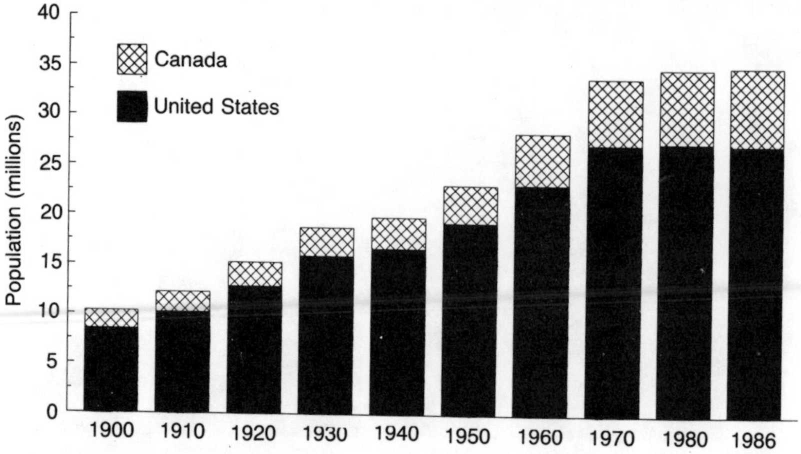

*Estimates for the United States are on the even year of a decade (1900, 1910, etc.); Canadian estimates are for the first year of a decade (1901, 1911, etc.).

Source: Great Lakes Basin Commission; U.S. Bureau of the Census; Environment Canada; Statistics Canada.

the region was heavily dependent on coal (64 percent) and nuclear power (20 percent) for electrical generation.[73]

In Ontario, energy use grew slowly between 1978 and 1987, with a dip in 1981-82 (figure 3.15). Over this period, the energy mix has gradually shifted. The contribution of nuclear energy to total consumption more than doubled, to nearly 20 percent of Ontario's energy supply, while the amount of oil consumed dropped 17 percent to comprise 29 percent of the fuel used.[74]

Not surprisingly, industrial activities over the past century have resulted in a multitude of environmental impacts on the Great Lakes basin, many of which relate to the generation and management of wastes.

## HAZARDOUS WASTES

A short distance from Niagara Falls, one of the great wonders of the world, is a 3,000-foot-long, 60-foot-wide ditch known as Love Canal. Between 1942 and 1953, Love Canal was used as a waste-dumping site by Hooker Chemical Company (now part of Occidental Petroleum Corporation). Hooker placed 21,800 tons (19,818 tonnes) of waste in

## Figure 3.14
## Energy Consumption in the Eight Great Lakes States, by Fuel Type, 1960–1986

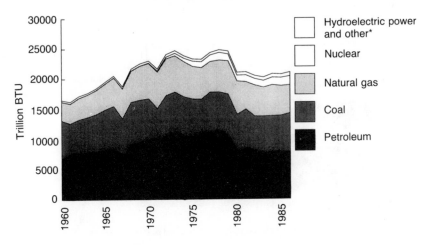

*Includes electricity generated from wood, waste, wind, photovoltaic, solar energy sources.

Source: U.S. Energy Information Administration.

the site, before covering it and selling it to the Niagara Falls Board of Education in 1953 for $1.[75] Over the years, as the neighborhood grew into a suburban area, an elementary school, roads, and homes were built on and adjacent to the waste site area, with some portions remaining as open fields. Though clues surfaced from time to time over the years—strong chemical odors, seeping chemicals, subsidence of parts of the canal (as barrels of chemicals decayed), and rashes and irritated eyes after contact with exposed wastes—most residents had little reason to suspect that a major problem was so close at hand.[76]

Prompted by a 1976 IJC investigation seeking the source of mirex in Lake Ontario fish, the New York State Department of Environmental Conservation began to study the situation.[77] After a series of studies by several agencies (and much ensuing controversy), in August 1978, a dramatic series of events occurred. First, the state health commissioner declared a health emergency and recommended that pregnant women and children under the age of two be evacuated; second, the area was declared a federal disaster area by President Carter; and finally, the governor announced that 239 families would be relocated by the state.[78]

## Figure 3.15
## Energy Consumption in Ontario, by Fuel Type, 1978–1987

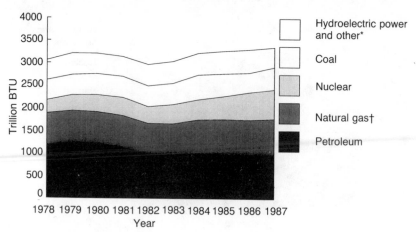

Hydroelectric power and other*

Coal

Nuclear

Natural gas†

Petroleum

*Includes electricity generated from wood, waste, wind, photovoltaic, and solar energy sources.

†Includes natural gas and natural gas liquids.

Source: Ontario Ministry of Energy.

*Technician gathering samples of toxic waste for laboratory analysis.*
Dave Kenyon / Michigan Dept. of Natural Resources

In the decade following, several health studies were conducted (see box), lawsuits were filed for damages and cleanup costs, and many of the houses were demolished. In 1988, a federal district court found Occidental Petroleum Corporation liable for the cost of cleanup, then estimated to be some U.S. $250 million, and the state commissioner of health declared that empty homes in some parts of the Love Canal area could be resettled.[79] However, new information has called into

## Assessing the Health Effects of Love Canal

At the time of the Love Canal incident, most of the answers to the hard questions about human health lay in the future. Were the people living in Love Canal really at risk from cancer and/or reproductive and developmental health effects, or was the fuss over nothing? The future is now here, and soon the questions may be answered.

It is 10 years since the Love Canal story broke. The latency period for many cancers is approximately over. If Love Canal residents were at a risk for cancer, the evidence would be appearing now. Was all the publicity, heartache, and stress really necessary? What is the state of health of the people who used to live there? How many have developed cancer? Of the children born and raised there, how many have children? How healthy are the offspring of the exposed adults? How well have their children fared?

The opportunity for an important epidemiological study on a group (cohort) of people potentially exposed to high concentrations of toxic chemicals is at hand. The New York State Department of Health has reopened the Love Canal files, and the residents from Love Canal are being traced. (Another set of records generated by a group of residents has been sealed in perpetuity by a Supreme Court judge in a claims settlement.) Tracing the 15,000 people today is going to be a monumental task. At the time of the incident, many people were confused and some sought anonymity. Most probably would like to forget the whole affair. Finding a cohort of this nature will not be easy.

People still live on the edges of Love Canal. A line of demarcation between the area of habitability and no-man's-land was drawn arbitrarily down selected streets, between houses, and even along the center of a creek that passes through the community. In 1978 the people within the boundary, if they chose to do so, were given the opportunity to sell their homes to the state and move away. But what about their neighbors directly across the creek, next door, or across the street on the other side of the line? If toxic substances are airborne as well as waterborne (as recent research suggests), might one household be equally as vulnerable as another? Why would people on one side of the creek be better off?

Unfortunately, the Love Canal scenario is being replayed around the world today. People are being exposed to unusual chemicals with little knowledge of their chronic effect. No one would deliberately recreate a Love Canal to study chronic health effects; on the other hand, it would be a mistake not to take the opportunity to follow the Love Canal cohort.

question the validity of the study underlying the commissioner's decision, and the issue remains unresolved.[80]

Down the St. Lawrence River from the Great Lakes basin, an event in the Montreal suburb of St. Basile-le-Grand some years later drew similar attention to a toxic chemical hazard that, like the Love Canal dump, exists in many other places. One summer night in 1988, a warehouse containing 1,500 barrels of oil contaminated with PCBs caught fire, creating a cloud of toxic fumes over an area of at least five square miles and prompting the prolonged evacuation of over 3,300 people. Production of polychlorinated biphenyls has been banned in Canada since 1977, and unessential uses are being phased out. This incident revived concerns in Canada about how to dispose of the 10 million gallons (45.5 million liters) of contaminated liquids currently being stored at some 1,600 sites located throughout the country.[81]

For many people in the Great Lakes region, and indeed throughout the United States, the Love Canal incident epitomized the problems generated by hazardous-waste disposal practices of the past, and the dangers that hazardous wastes can pose. In Canada, the fire at St. Basile-le-Grand prompted unprecedented debate about hazardous waste disposal and became an issue in the 1988 federal election. These, and other hazardous-waste-related incidents since the late 1970s, have led to the strengthening of hazardous-waste management laws in the United States and Canada, as well as to the initiation of remedial cleanup programs. (For discussion of other accident risks, see box.)

Hazardous wastes illustrate very clearly the distinction between dealing with the legacy of the past and avoiding the creation of new legacies. Both U.S. and Canadian legislation recognize that some wastes may be hazardous both to human health and to the health of the ecosystem. Systems and controls have been created to separate such hazardous waste from other types of waste, so that it can be disposed of safely or stored until adequate disposal methods become available. In the past, however, waste was waste was waste, and only the most obvious hazardous items were handled separately. Many former dump sites therefore contain unknown quantities and types of hazardous wastes, mixed haphazardly with other wastes.

In dealing with the legacy of hazardous waste sites, the emphasis necessarily has been on setting priorities, so as to focus on the most serious elements of the legacy, and on remedial action at those sites posing threats to human health and the environment. In the United States, these efforts are best exemplified in the Superfund program;

## Accidents in the Great Lakes Ecosystem

One obvious consequence of continued growth in the scale of human activities in the Great Lakes basin is an increased potential for catastrophic damage, both in the aquatic environment and on land. Transportation accidents are particularly worrisome, such as the 1979 derailment in Mississauga, Ontario (an urban community of 276,000 west of Toronto), of a 106-car train, 1.2 miles (2 kilometers) in length:

Twenty-four cars had derailed. Of these, 22 were tank cars, 11 of which carried propane. Of the others, three contained styrene, four caustic soda, three toluene, one chlorine, and two boxcars contained insulation. Ten propane cars were ruptured and burned, as well as the styrene and toluene cars. One propane car remained intact. The tank car containing 90 tonnes of liquid chlorine began to leak.[1]

Two rapid explosions hurled a tank car half a mile and created a fire that was visible over a radius of 50 miles (80 kilometers). Within a day, the release of toxic gases had forced the evacuation of 240,000 people, and a large proportion of these were not permitted to return for five days, due to continued leakage from the chlorine tank car. The fire burned for more than two days.

One month before the *Exxon Valdez* accident in Alaska's Prince William Sound, the Great Lakes Science Advisory Board expressed unanimous concern

about the growing danger of a spill severely affecting the Great Lakes ecosystem and the drinking water systems of Great Lakes cities. This danger is greatly enhanced by the evidence of substantial substance abuse among transportation workers.[2]

Discharges from accidental spills can dwarf the routine discharges of substances allowed under existing regulatory programs. For example, a report sponsored by the IJC's Science Advisory Board cited two incidents in the St. Clair River pertaining to styrene. In one case, the amount spilled was equivalent to that contained in 1.5 years of a company's routine discharge and, in the other, was equivalent to almost 1,500 years of continuous discharge.

The Science Advisory Board report further noted that a major release of radioactivity from an accident at one of the 14 nuclear generating stations in the basin "would have a calamitous impact that could dwarf all previous incidents" reported at these plants.[3]

---

in addition, each of the Great Lakes states has its own remedial action or Superfund-type program.

By 1989, the National Priority List of the U.S. Superfund program contained 890 sites, of which 116 are within the Great Lakes basin. A further 273 sites have been proposed for inclusion in the program, of which 23 are in the basin.[82] The sites are distributed through 70 of the 181 counties in the basin (figure 3.16). Many of the counties with the highest concentrations of sites border the Great Lakes. The sites included in the Superfund program, however, are only those with the

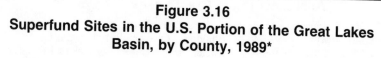

**Figure 3.16**
**Superfund Sites in the U.S. Portion of the Great Lakes Basin, by County, 1989\***

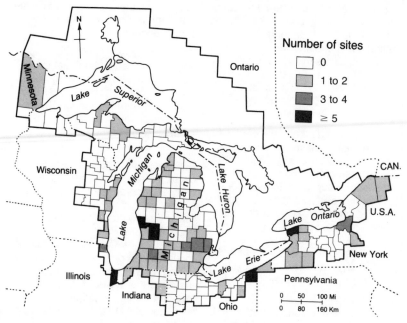

\*Includes both proposed and final sites on the National Priority List as of April/May 1989.
Source: U.S. Environmental Protection Agency.

worst contamination. Sites not qualifying for this program usually become the responsibility of state governments. State agencies often play a role in the federal Superfund-site cleanup process as well. With the enactment of a state Superfund in Pennsylvania in 1988, all of the Great Lakes states now have their own site cleanup programs. Although the amount and sources of funding vary, the objectives and characteristics of these programs are similar. As in the federal program, states generally try to identify problem sites and establish priorities for cleanups. Wisconsin's priority list, for example, contained 173 sites in 1987, of which 65 were in the Great Lakes basin.[83]

The magnitude of the problem is not really known yet, however. EPA's overall inventory of sites in the United States that either cause or have the potential to cause environmental harm contained nearly

3,600 sites in the Great Lakes basin as of 1989. In Ontario, the province has conducted a waste site inventory. The Ministry of the Environment (MOE) has begun to assess systematically those sites from the inventory expected to pose the most serious hazards, and MOE regional offices conduct additional investigations and cleanups of waste sites on an as-needed basis.[84]

Although the idea of initiating a Superfund type of program in Canada has been discussed, to date no such effort has been adopted by either the federal or Ontario government. In mid-1989, however, the Canadian Council of Resource and Environment Ministers (CCREM) proposed that the party responsible for the waste should pay for the cost of cleanup of contaminated sites, and estimated that this would account for about 95 percent of waste sites in Canada. The cost of cleaning up the remaining 5 percent of sites for which responsible parties could not be identified would be shared by federal and provincial governments. In addition, waste sites on publicly owned lands would be cleaned up by the responsible agency. The nationwide cleanup effort is expected to cost C\$250 million initially.[85]

As of 1988, Ontario's MOE had identified 7 sites, of 156 examined, for which further study was needed because of potential hazards to human health or the environment. Another 186 sites were being evaluated to determine whether more detailed investigations would be required.[86] Probably a more realistic indication of the scale of the problem is that there are 3,850 active and inactive waste sites in the province, of which perhaps 80 percent are in the Great Lakes basin. Of those in the basin, 1,748 are thought to have the potential to pose health hazards to humans.[87]

It is difficult to evaluate the effectiveness of these programs, given the enormous size and complexity of the problems that have to be addressed. In the United States, much criticism has been directed at EPA for its management of the Superfund program.[88] Spending on Superfund grew dramatically in the 1980s, but fiscal pressures and management concerns raised by a number of reviewers are bringing these large expenditures under increasing scrutiny.

In addition, the program's Hazard Ranking System, which provides the technical basis for decisions to include an individual site in the program, has been criticized on the grounds that it pays insufficient attention to effects on human health resulting from contamination of the food web. When the U.S. Congress amended the Superfund law in 1986, it required EPA to revise the ranking system to include impacts on the food web.[89] EPA has proposed such revisions, which focus to a large extent on the aquatic food chain.[90]

In both Canada and the United States, the implications of the legacy of hazardous wastes inherited (including from the recent past) have led to the adoption of cradle-to-grave systems that track wastes from the point of generation, through the transport stage, until a final disposal site is reached.[91] This concept was extended in Canada in 1988, to include the entire life cycle of development, manufacturing, storage, transportation, use, and disposal, with the passage of the Canadian Environmental Protection Act (CEPA).[92] At present, CEPA provides for controls on nine groups of designated "toxic substances."[93] In February 1989, Environment Canada announced another 44 substances scheduled for assessment and possible designation as "toxic substances."[94] CEPA also will be applied to new substances and to toxic substances entering international trade.[95]

These hazardous-waste tracking systems can provide a better picture of how much and what types of waste are generated and require management, and they provide a system of accountability so that improper disposal can be detected (figure 3.17). A 1988 estimate by the Ontario Waste Management Corporation estimated the generation of "primary subject wastes" (which include liquid industrial and hazardous wastes) at 4.0 million tons (3.6 million tonnes) per year in Ontario alone. Based on this figure, Environment Canada estimates the national total to be in the neighborhood of 6.6 million tons (6.0 million tonnes).[96] Waste management agencies in the eight Great Lakes states estimate that about 58.3 million tons (52.8 million tonnes) were generated in 1985, out of a total of 271 million tons (246 million tonnes) nationwide.[97] Although this is obviously an area in which good data are desirable, to date most information has been at least confusing, if not inaccurate. For instance, one analyst reported that:

> Surveys performed for the USEPA have produced generation figures for the eight Great Lakes states ranging from 51.8 million to 105.9 million [metric] tons. The total of the eight states' 1985 reports to the USEPA, by contrast, is only 18.3 million [metric] tons.[98]

Such disparities probably reflect different definitions, conversion factors, and the like, and in any case may be of limited use, because it is the character and strength of the toxicity that often matter more. It also has been suggested that the production of hazardous or toxic wastes may be decreasing even while data show the opposite trend;

## Figure 3.17
## Hazardous Waste Generation in the Great Lakes Region, 1985

| State/Province | Estimated Generation million tons (million metric tons) | Type of Waste Included in Reported Estimates |
|---|---|---|
| Illinois | 2.5 (2.3) | Hazardous waste as defined by RCRA in 40 C.F.R. 261 |
| Indiana | 2.2 (2.0) | Hazardous waste as defined by RCRA in 40 C.F.R. 261 |
| Michigan* | 3.9 (3.5) | In addition to RCRA waste, state generation estimates include three waste groups defined under Michigan Act 64. These categories are (a) waste with EP Toxicity for Copper and Zinc, (b) waste categorized as "severely toxic," and (c) commercial chemicals and process waste specific to industries located in Michigan, such as Dow Chemical. This amount, however, is insignificant when compared to the estimated generation of RCRA waste. |
| Minnesota | 0.4 (0.4) | RCRA-defined hazardous wastes, PCB wastes, used oil if it is not recycled, and other State-listed wastes. |
| New York | 16.0 (14.5) | Hazardous waste as defined by RCRA, plus a small amount of PCB wastes. |
| Ohio | 4.1 (3.7) | Hazardous waste as defined by RCRA in 40 C.F.R. 261. |
| Ontario† | 3.9 (3.6) | Liquid industrial and hazardous wastes as defined in the Ontario Environmental Protection Act, Regulation 309. |
| Pennsylvania | 29.1 (26.4) | Hazardous waste as defined by RCRA in 40 C.F.R. 261. |
| Wisconsin | 0.1 (0.1) | RCRA waste plus a small amount of soil contaminated with chlorinated solvents. |

*Michigan's estimate is for 1986 (preliminary).
†Ontario's estimate is for average annual generation, as of 1987.

Source: See References.

this may occur as reporting systems are extended to more producers and include more items that would not have been regarded as hazardous or toxic until comparatively recently.

Most wastes are treated and disposed of on-site at the point of generation; the balance are shipped to off-site facilities. Significant quantities of waste are transported via trucks, trains, and ships in and out of the Great Lakes basin. Responsibilities for responding to spills and other emergencies are shared by state, provincial, and federal agencies.* The IJC's Science Advisory Board found that data bases on spills and emergency response programs are inadequate, and that programs lack effective coordinating mechanisms.[99]

In creating sustainable development policies for the future, it is becoming clear that a distinction should be drawn between substances that are too hazardous to be permitted in normal use—or sometimes in any use (for example, certain CFCs and PCBs)—and those that can be used subject to effective controls, especially in regard to disposal. One of the most significant consequences of a decade of concern about toxic and hazardous wastes has been the recognition that so many of the items taken for granted in daily life are potentially harmful to the ecosystem or to human health. The task in most cases is to ensure that potential harm does not become actual harm. Reducing the amount of waste produced in the first place is a crucial first step, but providing safe hazardous-waste disposal methods, and ensuring that these are used effectively, is no less important. While some measures are being implemented in the Great Lakes basin to reach these goals, more can, and must, be done.

## SOLID WASTES

In the past, little or no attempt was made to separate hazardous household or industrial waste from nonhazardous wastes, except when the implications for human health were immediate and obvious. This lack of management control is in part responsible for the legacy of contamination emanating from former mixed-waste sites in the Great Lakes basin. In recent years, with the enactment of the Resource Conservation and Recovery Act (RCRA) in the United States in 1976 and Ontario's 1985 amendments to its Environmental Protection Act of 1971, different types of waste have been defined more precisely, and protective

---

*These responsibilities apply to all hazardous materials, products, and wastes.

management and disposal practices have been prescribed for many waste categories.

Municipal solid waste (a small proportion of total waste generated)[100] represents a significant management challenge, especially to urban governments. The amount and environmental hazard of waste generated, and proposals for changes in methods for handling it, have made municipal solid waste a high-profile environmental issue.

In statistical terms, each of the 35 million residents of the Great Lakes basin generates approximately 4.5 pounds (2 kilograms) of municipal waste per day; enough, collectively, to bury 484 football fields in a layer 10 stories high each year.[101]* These wastes, disposed of by households, industries, commerce, and government, cause problems because of their sheer volume, and create environmental risks as well. At present, in both the United States and Canada, most of this waste is deposited in landfills, with relatively small proportions being incinerated or recycled.

The environmental impacts of wastes depend on their nature and the methods selected for their treatment. Tracking their impact can be complicated. For example, if paper printed with an ink that contains lead is put in a landfill, the lead may leach downwards into the groundwater. If the paper is burned in an incinerator, the lead may either be emitted to the air or retained in the ash, which will later be transferred to landfill. If the paper is recycled, the "deinking" process may transfer the lead to sludge, wastewater, or to the new product. Lead in sludge may subsequently be released when the sludge is incinerated, spread on land, or composted.[102]

Limits on the capacity of existing disposal sites are reaching crisis proportions in many areas, especially in big cities such as Chicago, which expects to exceed its landfill capacity within five years.[103] In 1989, only Wisconsin among the Great Lakes states had more than 10 years of landfill capacity remaining; Ohio and Pennsylvania had less than 5 years.[104] Although some facilities are closing as they reach capacity, others (for example, in Wisconsin and New York) are being forced to close because they do not meet current environmental standards.[105]

Disposal costs are also increasing rapidly. As with any scarce commodity, as landfill space has dwindled, the price of using that space

---

*Only 373 fields under Canadian football rules, however.

has risen. Localities with low tipping fees* have found that imports from other jurisdictions threaten to overwhelm local capacity. In the hope of preserving landfill space for local use, municipalities are raising tipping fees substantially. Metropolitan Toronto, for instance, opened a landfill in 1983 that was expected to last for at least 20 years. It is now expected to close by the mid-1990s because of volume from other areas that has been higher than anticipated. As a result Metro Toronto has increased its rates for private haulers from C$18 to C$50 per metric ton.[106] Akron, Ohio, has recently doubled its tipping fees for haulers from outside the area, from U.S.$15 to U.S.$30 per ton.[107] In addition to these higher fees, transportation to sites that are farther away is adding to disposal costs for those communities that must export their wastes.

Increasingly stringent environmental standards are also causing costs to rise. For example, new regulations proposed by EPA in 1988 include restrictions on locating facilities on floodplains, fault zones, and similar sites; procedures for excluding hazardous wastes; requirements for groundwater monitoring; corrective action if groundwater standards are exceeded; performance standards for closure and post closure care; and demonstration of financial responsibility by owners for such care and for cleanups.[108] Many state and provincial regulations have become increasingly stringent; Ontario, for example, requires groundwater monitoring, "where there is a possibility of water pollution resulting from the operation of a landfilling site."[109] Taking such factors into account, one 1988 estimate put the cost of developing a new state-of-the-art landfill at over $400,000 per acre.[110]

Finally, the siting of new facilities, whether they are landfills, incinerators, transfer stations, or even recycling centers, has become extremely difficult in many places. Public opposition, based on concern for human health effects, environmental impacts, and property values, has slowed the development of new solid waste facilities. In the past, even in the vicinity of major metropolitan areas, as one landfill site reached capacity, another was acquired and opened up. This has become increasingly impractical, on grounds of cost, availability of nearby sites, and local opposition.

What has been striking about the approach taken for municipal solid

---

*Tipping fees are the fees paid when a load of waste is delivered to a landfill or incinerator. Other solid-waste management costs include transportation, labor, equipment costs, and administrative expenses.

waste management until recently is that it has run almost completely counter to the solid-waste management profession's theoretical hierarchy of preferred methods for waste disposal.[111] First, whenever possible, the amount and toxicity of products, packaging, and other items entering the municipal waste stream should be reduced before they become wastes, so as to conserve natural resources, eliminate contaminants, and reduce waste disposal costs. Second, whenever possible, materials should be reused or recycled rather than discarded, in order to capture valuable materials in the waste stream. Third, wastes that cannot be recycled or reused should be incinerated, in order to recover the energy in the materials and to reduce the volume of the material. Last, any remaining nonrecyclable, noncombustible wastes should be landfilled with proper environmental controls.[112]

Paradoxically, however, waste management decisions have tended to reverse this logical hierarchy. Traditionally, as much waste as possible has been sent to landfills, with incineration as the alternative. Recycling and waste reduction were not serious options until comparatively recently. Recycling was often rejected because it was regarded as intrusive for householders and uneconomic as a means of waste management. Recycling and source reduction involved the creation of physical and commercial systems with which waste managers were unfamiliar; they were also subject to the vagaries of variables perceived by state and local officials to be uncontrollable. For instance, in the early 1970s recycling efforts suffered in some areas because of fluctuations in the commodities markets on which scrap materials collected through recycling efforts were sold. Source-reduction initiatives often failed because solid waste managers—especially at the local level—were unable to influence substantially the many product and package design decisions in the private sector that shape the composition of the municipal waste stream.

This situation is changing significantly in response to the constraints facing solid waste management. Michigan, for example, intends to shift from disposing 85 percent of the solid waste stream in landfills to a situation in 2005 in which landfills account for only 10 percent to 20 percent of the waste stream (excluding incinerator ash) (figure 3.18).[113] Most attention in the Great Lakes region is focusing on the development of waste reduction and recycling programs, composting programs, and waste-to-energy incineration facilities, although many areas are also actively trying to site new landfills and upgrade old ones.

2

**Figure 3.18**
**Solid Waste Management Strategies in Michigan**

| Management method | Early 1980s | Goal for 2005 |
|---|---|---|
| Reduce | — | 8–12% |
| Reuse | — | 4– 6% |
| Compost | — | 8–12% |
| Recycle | 7% | 20–30% |
| Incinerate with energy recovery | 8% | 35–40% |
| Landfill | 85% | 10–20% |

Source: Michigan Department of Natural Resources.

The need for alternatives to landfills is widely acknowledged, but the development of waste-to-energy facilities has been controversial. Originally incineration was welcomed as a large-scale technology that could significantly reduce the volume of waste to be disposed of, with only minimal changes needed in existing waste collection practices. It also had the additional benefit of generating energy that could be used or sold. Recently, however, incineration has faced growing opposition, based primarily on uncertainty about the environmental and health effects of air emissions and disposal of fly and bottom ash, and the high (and often overbudget) costs of facility development. Many proposals for new incinerators have been abandoned, delayed, or modified.[114]

The fight over a Detroit waste-to-energy incinerator, which will burn 2,400 tons of processed solid waste daily, exemplifies the controversy. Since the facility is less than three miles from Windsor, Ontario, and emissions could drift into Canada, the government of Ontario, together with several environmental groups, sued the Greater Detroit Resource Recovery Authority to force the installation of better pollution control equipment than was originally planned. The Detroit agency has resisted the improved controls, on grounds of cost. Litigation was still in progress in mid-1989, with the incinerator scheduled to open in July 1989. In March 1989, the controversy was fueled further by state tests of ash from test burns of the incinerator. Levels of cadmium and lead detected in the ash may require it to be managed as a hazardous waste.[115] The issue has also now been referred to the

IJC through revival of a 1975 reference* on international air pollution in the Detroit and Windsor areas.[116]

One of the most encouraging trends is the development of recycling programs throughout the Great Lakes region. Many state, provincial, regional, and local governments have made recycling a major component of their solid-waste management strategies. For example, New York State passed legislation in 1988 requiring separation of recyclables in all communities by September 1992.[117] Ohio's State Solid Waste Management Advisory Council adopted a plan in 1989 that calls for a 25 percent reduction of landfilled wastes by 1994 and a ban on landfilling yard wastes as of 1993.[118] Ontario's "blue-box" program (named for the containers for recyclable material distributed to each household and collected at curbside) is a component of a plan to divert 25 percent of the municipal waste stream by 1992, and 50 percent by 2000. More than 1.5 million households participated in the program by 1989, and it is anticipated that this figure will rise to 3 million by 1995.[119]

As with strategies for disposal, administrative arrangements for solid waste management may need radical rethinking if the problem is to be tackled effectively. Disputes among neighboring jurisdictions are increasing, with the Detroit incinerator the most obvious example at present. The old nursery principle that those who create a mess should also clean it up was for a long time a reasonable basis for regarding waste disposal as a function to be exercised at the local level. It is still a principle strongly held by those who understandably object to their rural municipality becoming a disposal site for wastes from a metropolitan area. In many parts of the Great Lakes basin, however, it is difficult to see how local responsibility can be sustained, except in regard to the cost of disposal. The necessary space and other requirements for disposal no longer exist in many of the political units where the waste is generated.

State and provincial governments were able in the past to limit their role to overall regulation of disposal systems. Increasingly, however, they are being forced to intervene between hostile jurisdictions, impose solutions that local governments are unwilling or unable to adopt for themselves, and develop overall strategies for waste reduction and

---

*A reference is a request to the IJC by Canada and the United States for an investigation and report concerning an issue of mutual concern.

disposal. In the United States, solid-waste management issues have also become regional and, indeed, national. Some of the questions for which multistate or federal initiatives may be necessary include interstate transport of solid waste, development of markets for recyclable materials (such as newspaper and plastic), and formation of source reduction strategies.[120]

## PARKS AND PROTECTED AREAS

The legacy of human activity in the Great Lakes basin is not only one of modification and defilement, but also one of appreciation and delight in the natural environment. A great variety of protected areas have been created in the Great Lakes basin, covering thousands of acres. Some of these areas are quite large, while others are extremely small. The size, purpose, and degree of policy control exerted differ enormously from one area to another too. Thus, it is difficult to compare recreational parks with areas protected for their wilderness value, or tiny sites that have been protected to ensure the survival of a rare animal or plant species with a place containing unique historical or architectural features. One recent study captured the diversity of protective mechanisms in Ontario with this listing of types:

> national parks; national wildlife areas; Canadian heritage rivers; migratory bird sanctuaries; provincial parks; wilderness areas; provincial wildlife management areas; crown game preserves; fish sanctuaries; the parks of the St. Clair, Niagara, and St. Lawrence Parks Commissions; environmentally sensitive areas (ESAs) that have been incorporated into an official plan; conservation areas which protect sites identified as ecologically significant; and properties owned by conservation groups.[121]

The list of U.S. types of protected areas is at least as complex.

Historically, areas have been protected for two principal reasons that may often conflict:

- preservation of resources (natural, scenic, wildlife, cultural, historical), and
- use of resources (recreational, timber, tourism, hunting, fishing).

Over time, the elements included within these categories, and their relative importance, have changed. For example, the first category has been extended to include protection of plant and animal habitat and biological diversity.

The underlying tensions between preservation and use have been

*Boats on Black River with steel mill on opposite bank, Lorain, Ohio.*
© David Plowden, 1985

evident since at least the beginning of the 20th century. In recent years, however, pressures and tensions have both intensified and diversified. Greater demand for recreation and leisure activities has caused such problems as overcrowding of camping and other facilities, elimination of wildlife because of habitat loss, soil compaction or erosion on trails, inadequate septic systems, increased air pollution, and wildlife kills caused by automobile traffic. New activities such as hang gliding, snowmobiling, use of all-terrain vehicles, and cross-country skiing add to management conflicts. Other pressures, such as atmospheric deposition and other forms of toxic pollution, may stem from sources far beyond the boundaries of the protected areas.

The Great Lakes themselves are especially important both for recreation and for wildlife habitat. Some of the coastal parks in the basin are in great demand. Boating is extremely popular—Michigan, with 746,979 registered boats in 1987 (7.5 percent of the U.S. total), had more registered boat owners than any other state in the nation.[122] Sport fishing, too, is enormously popular throughout the region (see chapter 6).

Although the shoreline and near-shore zone are often of critical importance, protected areas can be found throughout the basin. Over the last 20 years, for example, 83,000 acres (36,000 hectares) have been purchased by Ontario as part of an overall plan to protect the Niagara Escarpment throughout its 450 miles (725 kilometers) from the Niagara River to the tip of the Bruce Peninsula.[123] State, provincial, federal, and private funds are also being allocated to protecting natural areas such as those in the Carolinian forest zone of southwest Ontario.[124]*

---

*The need for a basinwide protection plan is discussed in chapter 6.

# Chapter 4

# Legacies and Challenges: Water

Water is the most obvious and distinctive feature of the Great Lakes basin ecosystem. Within the several stages of a complex hydrological cycle (figure 4.1), water can be found in its three phases—liquid, vapor, and solid. It moves in rivers, lakes, and seas at the earth's surface. Above the surface, it moves in the atmosphere, and below, it moves as groundwater. It evaporates from ground or lake surfaces and is transpired by plants. Water vapor condenses as cloud droplets and falls as snow or rain.

As water moves through the hydrological cycle, it carries other substances, including nutrients and contaminants, in solution or suspension. These percolate downward through soils to groundwater or are brought to the surface from below by groundwater flow or pumping. Many substances evaporate (often referred to as "volatilization") to the atmosphere and travel over long distances before falling out as wet (or dry) deposition. Water also scours streambeds, erodes valleys, and attacks shorelines. Eroded material is transported by water in solution or suspension and later is deposited as deltas or as sediments in rivers, lakes, or seas. Finally, water is essential for all plant and animal life in the ecosystem. It is both a physiological necessity and the medium in which aquatic plants and animals exist.

Concern for water quality within the Great Lakes basin, within the context of the 1978 Great Lakes Water Quality Agreement, has historically emphasized the quality of the five Great Lakes themselves. But equally deserving of attention are the basin's groundwater resources, the sediments that can serve as sources of contaminants cycling through the system or

## Figure 4.1
## Great Lakes System Hydrological Cycle

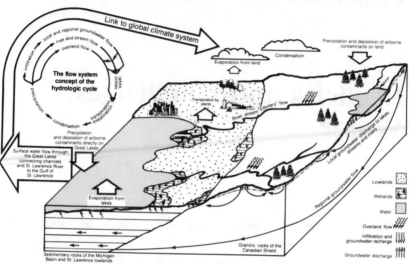

Source: Institute for Research on Public Policy.

as sinks where these settle and are buried, and the surface waters of inland rivers, streams, and lakes other than the five Great Lakes. This chapter takes a broad view of water issues in the Great Lakes basin, encompassing both these aspects of water quality and the companion issue of managing water quantity in the Great Lakes.

## GROUNDWATER

Groundwater is important from two perspectives—as a direct source of water for consumption and as a mechanism for transporting contaminants. In the Great Lakes basin, about 7.5 million residents depend on groundwater for their drinking water.[1] Meanwhile, contamination of groundwater continues, from abandoned solid- and hazardous-waste management dumps, operating industrial facilities, agriculture chemicals, and many other human activities. Recent indications from the Niagara River area suggest that contaminants transported in groundwater from hazardous waste sites and from under operating industrial facilities may be at least as significant as all point sources of contaminants combined.

Despite the growing realization of the important role of groundwater, it remains largely a "missing link" in understanding the ecosystem. Out of sight and usually out of mind, groundwater has only recently attracted the attention it deserves. Little is known about the ground-water system of the Great Lakes basin. However, groundwater does behave in accordance with some basic, easily understood principles.

Water from rain and snowmelt percolates through the soil, initially through an unsaturated zone and then into a saturated zone.* The water table marks the top of the saturated zone. In the Great Lakes basin, groundwater within the saturated zone usually moves from highland recharge zones to lowland discharge zones. It follows various path-ways, discharging eventually into surface water systems such as streams, marshes, ponds, or lakes. Alternatively it may enter surface soils, to be evaporated or transpired through vegetation.

Depending on climatic, topographical, and geological conditions, the pathway from infiltration to exit may be tens of meters or many kilometers. The flow is usually so slow that even in shallow, "local" flow systems, the travel time may be measured in years or decades. If the flow enters a deeper "regional" system, thousands of years may pass before the water emerges. Older groundwater usually acquires a marked chemical content from natural sources and as a result is often "hard."

Discharging groundwater is often a key factor in sustaining wetlands, streams, lakes, and vegetation systems through dry periods. Human over-use of groundwater can therefore adversely affect streams, rivers, and wetlands that depend on it for a significant portion of their flow.

The overall direct contribution of groundwater to the total volume of water in the five Great Lakes and their connecting channels has not been firmly established. Preliminary work on Lake Ontario concluded that this contribution was negligible.[2] Studies on Lake Michigan indicate that groundwater discharge through the lake bottom sediments may be as much as 18 percent of the contribution of tributary flow to the lake.[3]

Such estimates of direct groundwater flow to the main lakes do not take account of the groundwater contribution to upland lakes, streams, and rivers that subsequently feed the Great Lakes. American research-ers have estimated that over half the streamflow entering the Great Lakes basin from the United States may be from groundwater inflow.[4] In contrast, the average contribution of groundwater to streamflow on

---

*A saturated zone is one in which all pore spaces within porous earth materials are filled with water.

the Canadian side of the basin has been estimated as less than 20 percent, because of different geological conditions.[5]

Factors such as rock or soil composition and the degree of rock fracturing produce different zones in the subsurface for storage or transport of groundwater. Zones through which substantial amounts of groundwater move relatively easily are termed *aquifers*; they are tapped for water supplies. In contrast, *aquitards* may not store large quantities and do not transmit water easily; they may play a critical role in waste management. For example, site selection for Ontario's new toxic-waste disposal facility included a key requirement for a subsurface geology of silts and clays (an aquitard) that would naturally limit contaminant migration from both accidental spills and regular waste management activities.

## Groundwater Use and Abuse

Initial interest in groundwater stemmed from its use as a drinking water source. In Michigan, for example, approximately half the residents, about 4.6 million people, depend on groundwater as their sole source of drinking water. Over 18,000 new wells are installed each year in the state. About 530 million gallons (2 billion liters) of groundwater per day are withdrawn: 41 percent is used for public water supplies, 30 percent for domestic uses in rural areas, 14 percent for irrigation, 12 percent by industry from its own wells, and 3 percent for livestock.[6]

Wells intersect and "interrupt" the natural groundwater system. If the amount extracted is more than the natural system can replenish, the effect is that of mining, and the water table (reflected in well-water levels) can be seriously lowered. This is dramatically illustrated in the Chicago-Milwaukee area. In the late 1800s, when wells were first drilled, water flowed naturally under pressure so great that it would, if allowed, rise 130 feet (40 meters) above ground level in an open standpipe. Continuous pumping since then has caused water levels in the Chicago area to drop, on average, 800 feet (244 meters). One quarter of the fall has occurred since 1971.[7] Water levels in some Chicago area wells are now 100 to 150 feet (30 to 46 meters) below sea level,[8] and the growing cone of influence extends well beyond the boundaries of the Great Lakes hydrologic basin, causing groundwater to flow northwest from Indiana, west from Lake Michigan, and south from Wisconsin.[9]

Similar groundwater mining has been a concern, although not as extreme, in the Lake Winnebago area and in Green Bay, Wisconsin.[10] It appears to be an emerging problem in some growing rural residential areas in southern Ontario,[11] although, in general, it is much less of a problem on the Canadian side of the basin than on the U.S.

Groundwater quality is of concern because of groundwater's direct use for a variety of purposes including drinking water and because of its influence on surface water. Major natural dissolved constituents include sodium, calcium, magnesium, bicarbonate, sulfate, chloride, and silica. Many other constituents may be present, including iron, strontium, potassium, carbonate, nitrate, and fluoride. These not only give distinctive "flavor" to local water supplies; they can also be of concern for human health, especially on a long-term basis. In Wisconsin, for example, several high-capacity deep wells (most of them within the Great Lakes basin) have radium concentrations exceeding recommended standards. Further, radon gas, present in host rocks and subsequently dissolved in groundwater, can be released into the air in domestic showers and can accumulate in dwellings.[12]

Investigations of groundwater in the Niagara Peninsula (Ontario) have turned up benzene, toluene, and xylenes (collectively known as BTXs) that are "very probably" derived naturally from petroleum-bearing sedimentary host rocks.[13] These BTXs are chemically equivalent to some of the contaminants that leak into the groundwater from hazardous waste sites; they may ultimately need to be included in estimates of contaminant discharge to the Niagara River.

It is, however, contamination of groundwater from human sources that is of greatest concern. These sources can be grouped into three broad categories:[14]

- waste disposal;
- diffuse or nonpoint sources, such as the use of chemicals in agriculture and forestry; and
- accidental discharges, including spills and leaks.

Three broad types of contaminants may enter the groundwater from such sources:

- simple inorganic substances, such as nitrates from septic tanks, feedlot wastes, fertilizers, and salt from highways;
- heavy metals, usually from industrial sources such as plating works; and

- complex synthetic organic compounds, derived principally from industrial and manufacturing processes and the use of pesticides.

The synthetic organic compounds cause the greatest concern, especially a subgroup known as dense nonaqueous phase liquids (DNAPLs). These have been produced in large volume by the chemical industry since the 1940s for such diverse purposes as dry cleaning, wood preservation, and automobile production and repair. Contamination by these heavy organic liquids, such as carbon tetrachloride or trichloroethylene, is usually much more difficult to deal with than, say, petroleum leaks. Small volumes of DNAPLs can contaminate large volumes of groundwater: Because of their density, migration is slow and not governed by the same principles as typical groundwater flow; furthermore, the locations of most spills or leakages that took place prior to the last 10 or 20 years are not known. Finally, cleanup of much of this contamination is not feasible with existing technology.[15]

Injection of liquid waste into deep wells has long been a common method of waste disposal that may directly affect the groundwater flow system. On the U.S. side of the St. Clair River, for example, 63 injection wells are in current operation, 2 are temporarily abandoned, and 7 have been permanently plugged and abandoned.[16] In Lambton County on the Canadian side, about 35 deep wells were used to dispose of industrial wastes during the period from 1958 to 1972 and are still used for the disposal of waste brines.[17] Several studies have been carried out to determine whether the injected materials have affected aquifers or surface waters. This does not appear to have happened, although upward movement of waste may have occurred locally during injection and may have come from poorly sealed disposal wells and from abandoned oil and gas exploration wells.[18] Additional research is needed to establish whether contaminated groundwater is moving across the international boundary in deep formations.

What is more common is the transport of toxic or hazardous wastes through groundwater at shallow depths, to contaminate well water or discharge into streams, rivers, or lakes. This possibility accounts for the designation of so many licensed disposal sites in Ontario as class A: potentially hazardous to human health.

In Michigan, over 3,000 sites have been inventoried that have a potential for causing groundwater contamination and may require discharge or storage permits. There are 1,778 identified sites where toxic and hazardous substances have been released to the environment in quantities that are, or may become, injurious to public health or the environment. As of January 1988, 69 of these sites were also on the federal Superfund list; 35 Michigan municipal well systems were known to have been affected by toxic contaminants, and over 950 private residential wells had become polluted.[19]

As recently as 1984, when the Niagara River Toxics Committee (NRTC) issued its final report,[20] it was found impossible, because of lack of data, to make any quantitative estimate of the transport of contaminants by groundwater to the Niagara River from hazardous waste sites. Only in 1988 was a preliminary estimate attempted.[21] Over 215 hazardous waste disposal sites were identified by the NRTC in New York's Erie and Niagara counties. Of these sites, 164 were within three miles of the river and 61 had a significant potential to pollute the river. Another 8 had some potential for off-site migration or were hydraulically linked to Lake Erie or the Niagara River. Five sites on the Canadian side of the river had a similar potential (figure 4.2).

No attempt has yet been made to estimate toxic transport from the Canadian sites. Preliminary assessment of transport from the U.S. sites to the Niagara River, however, suggests the following:

- Estimates of total potential contaminant loadings range from about 117 pounds (53 kilograms) per day to 4,566 pounds (2,071 kilograms) per day.
- The "best estimate" of total potential was 694 pounds (315 kilograms) per day.
- Using "best professional judgment," the estimate of current total actual loadings of the river from the waste sites through the groundwater was 70 percent of the total potential or about 478 pounds (217 kilograms) per day.
- Of this actual loading, 394 pounds (178 kilograms) per day was estimated to consist of organic compounds.

These estimates are highly tentative, particularly for individual chemicals, and much more research and monitoring are needed.* Nevertheless, their implications are profound. Figure 4.3 suggests that the current contribution of contaminants via groundwater may be roughly

---

*Concern for groundwater contamination in the Niagara Peninsula led the U.S. Environmental Protection Agency to fund a $1.7 million, five-year study by the U.S. Geological Survey of regional hydrology, scheduled for completion in 1991.

# Figure 4.2
## Waste Sites in the Niagara River Area*

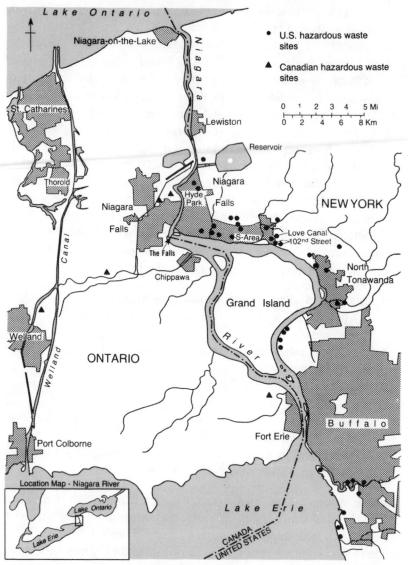

*Sites include those identified by the Niagara River Toxics Committee for the Canadian side and hazardous waste sites included in a study of potential sources of contamination by the U.S. Geological Survey and U.S. Environmental Protection Agency.

Source: *Canadian Geographic*; U.S. Geological Survey and U.S. Environmental Protection Agency.

## Figure 4.3
## Comparison of Current Point and Nonpoint Loadings to the Niagara River

| Loading | Kilograms per day | Pounds per day |
|---|---|---|
| U.S. point source total (1986) | 245 | 540 |
| Canadian point source total (1987) | 62 | 136 |
| U.S. nonpoint (groundwater) source total (1987) | | |
| —Best estimate | 315 | 694 |
| —Low estimate | 53 | 117 |
| —High estimate | 2,071 | 4,566 |

Source: Ontario Ministry of the Environment; New York Department of Environmental Conservation; Gradient Corporation; GeoTrans Inc.

equal to the contribution from all point sources combined (using the "best estimate" of groundwater sources).

If this is so, then "cleaning up the Niagara River"—and Lake Ontario—becomes substantially more difficult. To achieve zero discharge from point sources takes effective action, time, and money but otherwise is relatively straightforward. However, the four major Superfund sites in the area (Love Canal, 102nd Street, S-Area, and Hyde Park) alone contain approximately 334,000 tons (304,000 tonnes) of chemical waste. They are situated in complex hydrogeological situations, all are hydraulically connected to the Niagara River, and all are characterized by off-site migration of chemicals.[22] Only Love Canal has been isolated thus far, with constant pumping and monitored ring wells to prevent further migration of contaminants. In the case of Hyde Park, approximately 40 tons (36 tonnes) of PCBs alone are estimated to be already in the bedrock outside the waste dump proper; alternative calculations put the amount as high as 83 tons (75 tonnes).[23] Only about 40 percent of the nonaqueous phase chemicals have been identified,[24] and cleanup of much of this contamination is not feasible with existing technology.[25]

In the Niagara River area, in addition to contaminant movement through groundwater from hazardous waste sites, the flow of contaminated groundwater from beneath operating industrial facilities may also be significant. For example, a 1984 study of conditions below the Hooker Chemical Niagara plant found highly elevated levels of contaminants, at least some of which were seeping into sewers that flow into the Niagara River. Levels as high as 740 milligrams per liter of organic halogens (organic compounds of chloride, fluoride, benzene, and toluene) were found in the groundwater of the upper bedrock.[26]

Despite the general lack of knowledge of groundwater conditions, the evidence that is available underscores the importance of the annex on contaminated groundwater added to the Great Lakes Water Quality Agreement in 1987. This requires Canada and the United States to:

> Identify existing and potential sources of contaminated groundwater affecting the Great Lakes; [and to] Map hydrogeological conditions in the vicinity of existing and potential sources of contaminated groundwater.

With considerable optimism, the annex also requires that the two countries:

> Control the sources of contamination of groundwater and the contaminated groundwater itself, when the problem has been identified.[27]

To date, only limited action has been taken by government and industry to restrict discharges of contaminants into the groundwater system. As time passes, the long-term consequences of inaction become more profound.

## SURFACE WATER QUALITY

In many ways, surface water is the unifying element in the Great Lakes basin ecosystem. The pattern of surface water drainage defines the basin. The Great Lakes and their connecting channels are the dominant feature of the geography, and vegetation, wildlife, and the human population are intimately connected to the quantity and quality of surface waters. Although much remains to be discovered, and monitoring systems must be improved, scientific knowledge of surface waters is much better than knowledge of the atmospheric linkages to the ecosystem and is incomparably better than the understanding of groundwater behavior.

Surface water quality concerns are of two kinds: (*a*) conventional pollutants or water chemistry changes involving bacteria, nutrients (for example, phosphates and nitrates), and other substances such as chloride and silica; and (*b*) toxic contaminants, including organic compounds, metals, and radioactive elements.*

Although considerable generalization about the quality of surface waters is possible, local situations may depart significantly from the norm, especially on lake shorelines or in specific sections of inland streams, rivers, and lakes. Around the Great Lakes, and in the connecting channels, the most severely degraded areas are included among the 42 Areas of Concern defined by the International Joint Commission's (IJC's) Great Lakes Water Quality Board (chapter 3, figure 3.3).

The following section considers water quality in the basin from a geographical perspective, starting at the top of the system (inland streams, rivers, and lakes) and descending through the Great Lakes and their connecting channels to the St. Lawrence River.

## Inland Streams, Rivers, and Lakes

Over 80,000 inland lakes lie within the drainage basin. The number is imprecise, since jurisdictions use different definitions of the minimum lake size included in their inventories. However, the lakes cover an area of roughly 11,000 square miles (28,000 square kilometers), an area larger than that of Lake Erie. An estimated 466,000 miles (750,000 kilometers) of upland rivers and streams lie in the basin. About 67 percent of the inland lakes, and a comparable proportion of the rivers and streams, are in Ontario; Michigan accounts for 13 percent, while an additional 8 percent are found in Minnesota.

A partial assessment of the quality of these inland bodies of water has been compiled for the United States, pursuant to requirements of the federal Clean Water Act. These assessments generally indicate whether waterbodies can fulfill designated uses (for example, swimming and fishing). Because streams may be highly degraded from a healthy natural condition, yet may still meet designated uses (for example, for industry), this rating system has only limited value as an indicator of ecosystem health.

No equivalent overall assessment is carried out in Ontario. The Ministry of the Environment is sensitive to problem areas and indi-

---

*The implications of contamination for the health of fish, wildlife, and humans are explored in chapters 6 and 7.

vidual conservation authorities* are aware of local degradation, but the information is scattered. New monitoring, required as part of the Municipal/Industrial Strategy for Abatement (MISA),† should lead to a vastly improved understanding of chemical loadings to the environment, but there is no overall assessment of the physical, chemical, and biological state of the environment.

In Ontario, the dominant concern is acidification of the thousands of inland lakes, streams, and ponds that lie in the Canadian Shield rocks, north of about 45° N. Here, substantial amounts of acid deposition are received with little to counteract increased acidity in the receiving waters. Further south, the underlying sedimentary rocks commonly include limestone, which offers a neutralizing capacity to counteract the effects of acid deposition.

The acidity of hinterland lakes in the northern part of the basin appears to be a key factor in elevated and unacceptable levels of mercury in fish. The mercury may be natural or deposited from the atmosphere; the increased acidity enhances its availability to fish.[28]

In the agriculturally rich area of southwestern Ontario, severe degradation of inland rivers and lakes has occurred as a result of municipal waste and agricultural practices (chemicals and suspended solids). Examples include the Thames River and the Grand River.

Only 33 percent of inland lakes are on the U.S. side of the basin, but the higher population density and level of industrial activity south of the international boundary have resulted in a significantly higher degree of degradation. Within the basin, only Minnesota lakes appear to be in largely good condition. Ninety-two percent of Minnesota lakes are reported as supporting designated uses; in this region, the designations require waters to satisfy stringent criteria for fishing and swimming. (Minnesota has, however, issued advisories warning against consumption of mercury-tainted fish from some of its lakes.[29])

---

*There are 38 such authorities, which operate under the jurisdiction of the Ontario Ministry of Natural Resources, although they do not cover the whole of the Ontario portion of the basin.

†The MISA program, launched in 1986, is Ontario's effort to regulate systematically municipal discharges and eight categories of major industrial discharges. MISA significantly strengthens Ontario's water pollution control efforts by providing for mandatory reporting of routine discharges and by imposing more stringent discharge standards. In its emphasis on mandatory reporting and industry-by-industry standard setting, MISA resembles programs carried out under the Clean Water Act in the United States.

The situation is different in the other states. In Michigan, 296 of 297 watersheds are affected by nonpoint source pollution.[30] Fully 70 percent of inland lakes either do not or only partially support designated uses or are threatened. In Wisconsin, 40 percent of the state's streams are degraded or threatened by nonpoint sources, and 80 percent of inland lakes suffer from eutrophication.[31]* In Ohio, 94 percent of inland lakes either do not support or only partially support designated uses or are threatened.[32] Nonpoint sources causing eutrophication are the dominant problem in Ohio.[33] Throughout the Great Lakes states, many stream segments and lakes are degraded by toxic contaminants from point sources.[34] Comparison of recent state assessments of inland water quality with earlier analyses suggests some noteworthy improvements in conditions; yet bacterial problems, excessive nutrients, and elevated levels of toxic contaminants remain significant problems in many of the inland areas.

Inland waters that drain to the Great Lakes can contribute significant amounts of contaminants to the lakes. The extent of this contribution is not well known. The IJC's Water Quality Board has noted major shortcomings in monitoring of tributaries for phosphorus and has reported that many tributary monitoring programs do not provide data on contaminants.[35]

## The Great Lakes and Their Connecting Channels

The five Great Lakes share some notable characteristics that influence the quality of their waters. First, their large surface areas make them vulnerable to direct pollution from the air ("atmospheric deposition"). However, air-water interactions can also help to cleanse the lakes of some contaminants, as if the lakes were exhaling. Second, the relatively small proportion of land within the drainage basin leads to quick delivery, through tributary flow, of any contaminants introduced in upland areas. Third, the low volume of flow-through (less than 1 percent of the volume of the Great Lakes leaves through the St. Lawrence River each year), coupled with the high retention times of several of the lakes (figure 4.4), means that contaminants can be retained in the system for many years.

Despite these common characteristics, each of the Great Lakes and

*See chapter 2 for discussion of the trophic status of lakes.

## Figure 4.4
## Physical Characteristics of the Great Lakes

| Lake | Area of Lake | Area of Drainage Basin | Average Depth | Volume | Retention Time |
|---|---|---|---|---|---|
| Superior | 31,700 sq. mi. 82,100 sq. km. | 49,300 sq. mi. 127,700 sq. km. | 483 ft. 147 m. | 2,900 cu. mi. 12,100 cu. km. | 191 yr. |
| Michigan | 22,300 sq. mi. 57,800 sq. km. | 45,600 sq. mi. 118,000 sq. km. | 279 ft. 85 m. | 1,180 cu. mi. 4,920 cu. km. | 99 yr. |
| Huron | 23,000 sq. mi. 59,600 sq. km. | 51,700 sq. mi. 134,000 sq. km. | 195 ft. 59 m. | 850 cu. mi. 3,540 cu. km. | 22 yr. |
| Erie | 9,910 sq. mi. 25,700 sq. km. | 30,140 sq. mi. 78,000 sq. km. | 62 ft. 19 m. | 116 cu. mi. 484 cu. km. | 2.6 yr. |
| Ontario | 7,340 sq. mi. 18,960 sq. km. | 24,720 sq. mi. 64,030 sq. km. | 283 ft. 86 m. | 393 cu. mi. 1,640 cu. km. | 6 yr. |

### Depth Profile of the Great Lakes

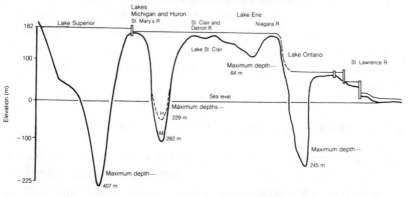

Source: Environment Canada and U.S. Environmental Protection Agency (1987); Great Lakes Tomorrow.

their connecting channels is unique. Biological, chemical, and physical characteristics vary greatly, as do patterns of human activity.

### Lake Superior

Lake Superior is the second-largest freshwater body in the world, both by area and by volume. It contains half the water in the Great Lakes system. Practically the whole of the drainage basin, as well as the lake itself, is located on ancient rocks of the Canadian Shield. Its drainage area is 95 percent forest-covered; there is little agricultural activity (chapter 3, figure 3.1) and a low population density.

## Figure 4.5
## Total Phosphorus Concentrations in the Great Lakes*

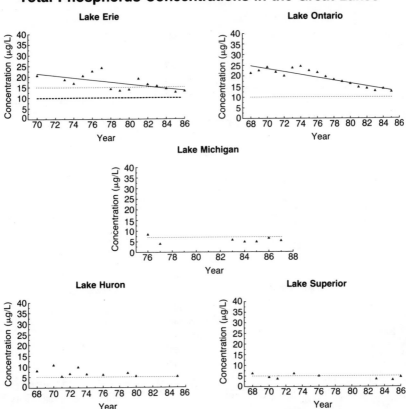

*Dotted lines represent the acceptable in-lake concentration of total phosphorus for western Lake Erie (15 g/l), Lake Huron (5 g/l) Lake Michigan (7 g/l), Lake Ontario (10 g/l), and Lake Superior (5 g/l). The acceptable phosphorus level for central and eastern Lake Erie is 10 g/l (dashed line).

Note: Regression lines indicate a significant change (p = 0.05) over time using the two-tailed T-test.

Source: Great Lakes Water Quality Board.

Not surprisingly, therefore, Lake Superior is the least degraded of the lakes. For example, phosphorus levels are the lowest in the system, targets for discharges from municipal sources are being met, and ambient levels have not changed significantly since the mid-1960s.[36] (See figure 4.5 for recent trends in phosphorus concentrations in the lakes and figure 4.6 for trends in loadings of phosphorus.)

There has been, however, a steady growth in nitrates. Nitrate concentration in Lake Superior tripled (from 75 parts per billion to 236

## Figure 4.6
# Estimated Total Phosphorus Loadings in the Great Lakes

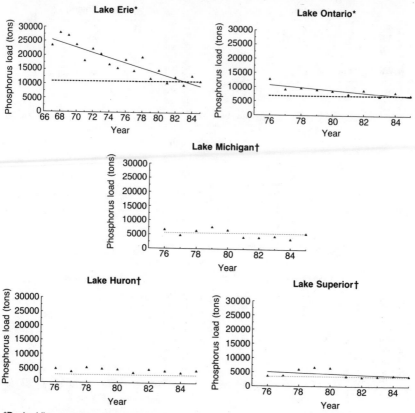

*Dashed lines represent the phosphorus loadings required for Lake Erie (11,000 t/yr.) and Lake Ontario (7,000 t/yr.) to meet the goals set in the Phosphorus Load Reduction Supplement to annex 3 of the 1978 Great Lakes Water Quality Agreement.

†Dotted lines represent loadings that would result if all municipal plants over one million gallons per day limit their phosphorus discharges to 1 mg/l. To achieve this goal, the load targets for Lake Huron, Lake Michigan, and Lake Superior would be 2,800, 5,600, and 3,400 tons per year, respectively.

Note: Regression lines indicate a significant change (p = 0.05) over time using the two-tailed T-test.

Source: Great Lakes Water Quality Board.

parts per billion) between 1906 and 1959 and rose another 24 percent (to 311 parts per billion) between 1959 and 1976.[37] Nitrate levels have also been rising in the other lakes. Although loadings from nonpoint sources such as agriculture may well contribute to increased nitrate levels in Lakes Erie and Ontario, and although earlier increases to

Lake Superior may have been due partly to municipal point source discharges, the continuing increase in Lake Superior probably comes from atmospheric sources.[38] (See figure 4.7 for recent trends in concentrations of nitrate and nitrite in the lakes.)

The role of the atmosphere in Lake Superior's nitrate loadings extends to contaminants as well. In the mid-1970s, chlorinated organic residues, with no possible local source, were found in fish in an isolated lake in the middle of Isle Royale.[39] Lake Superior is particularly sus-

**Figure 4.7**
## Nitrite and Nitrate Concentrations in the Great Lakes

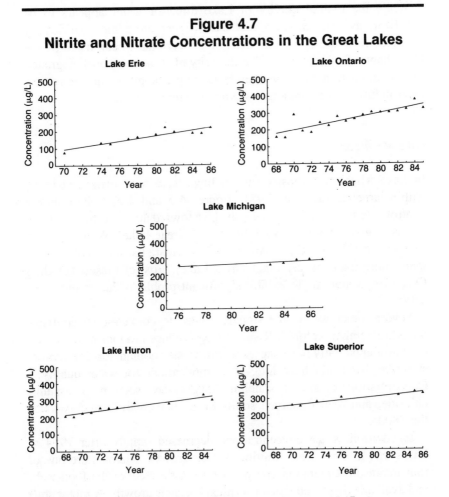

Note: Regression lines indicate a significant change (p = 0.05) over time using the two-tailed T-test.

Source: Great Lakes Water Quality Board.

ceptible to atmospheric contaminant inputs because of its large surface area and surface-to-basin-area ratio, its long chemical and water residence times, the dominance of precipitation over streamflow in the water supply to the lake, and regional meteorological patterns that transport airborne pollutants from urban/industrial centers.[40] Recent estimates suggest that over 90 percent of some contaminants entering Lake Superior do so from the atmosphere, although the total quantities of these contaminants entering the lake from all sources are generally less than those reaching the other lakes.[41]

While the overall quality of Lake Superior water appears to be excellent, as with all the Great Lakes there are some significantly degraded local areas. Seven Areas of Concern have been listed by the IJC (chapter 3, figure 3.3). The majority of these have been degraded by a combination of discharges from pulp and paper mill activities, local industry, and municipal sewage treatment plants.[42]

*Lake Michigan*

In Lake Michigan, phosphorus loadings have been estimated to be within target levels since 1981 (figures 4.5 and 4.6).[43] Phosphorus controls are successfully moving the lake toward the oligotrophic status set as a goal in annex 3 of the 1978 Great Lakes Water Quality Agreement.[44] However, 10 Areas of Concern are listed for Lake Michigan (more than for any other Great Lake). Five of these, including Green Bay, continue to exhibit significant problems due to eutrophication.[45]

Several other worrisome signals related to conventional contaminants are being monitored. Rising nitrogen concentrations in the southern basin apparently have caused a shift in the zooplankton community structure that could have long-term implications for water quality.[46] Concentrations of sulfate, calcium, magnesium, sodium, potassium, chloride, and total dissolved solids have all increased steadily since the 1800s.[47]

In addition, silica concentrations decreased rapidly after 1954 to levels that in 1969 were limiting diatom growth. Diatoms are one of four major phytoplankton groups that lie at the base of the food web, and available dissolved silica is critical for their growth. A major shift in silica dynamics appears to have occurred.[48] Recently, concentrations of dissolved reactive silica seem to have remained stable or increased slightly.[49] A crash of the diatom population would eventually be felt throughout the food web.

In terms of toxic contaminants, Lake Michigan probably is the second most degraded of the Great Lakes, after Lake Ontario. Lake Michigan fish contain the highest levels of DDT and PCBs in any of the Great Lakes. Levels of DDT, PCBs, and dieldrin consistently are higher in fish taken from the southern end of the lake.[50] However, concentrations throughout the lake of most contaminants in fish (for example, mercury and PCBs) are declining.[51]

Concentrations of individual metals in open water remain low for Lake Michigan. However, the total impact of metals in Lake Michigan may be significant. In an attempt to address the potential toxicity of metal mixtures, the Aquatic Ecosystem Objectives Committee of the IJC's Science Advisory Board developed the "toxic unit sum concept."[52] This concept states that the sum of the ratios of each metal concentration to its respective objective concentration should not exceed 1.0.* When the sum is greater than 1.0, it is expected that subtle adverse effects on biota will occur. The aggregate toxic sums based on median total metal concentrations of 11 metals for each of the Great Lakes are listed in figure 4.8.

### Lake Huron

Water quality in Lake Huron has deteriorated only slightly from conditions that existed in the early 1800s. The significant changes are

**Figure 4.8**
**Toxic Sums for the Great Lakes Based on**
**Median Total Metal Concentrations**

| Lake | Toxicity unit sum |
|------|-------------------|
| Lake Michigan | 4.16 |
| Lake Erie | 3.91 |
| Lake Ontario | 1.96 |
| Lake Huron | 0.81 |
| Lake Superior | 0.49 |

Source: Great Lakes Water Quality Board.

*The "objective concentration" refers to the goals established for each substance in the Water Quality Agreement or proposed by the IJC.

confined to areas adjacent to centers of human activity such as Saginaw Bay and the various harbors and estuaries around the lake.[53]

Early work that compared conditions between 1906/07 and 1956 found little change in concentrations of calcium and of sodium plus potassium but a doubling, during the same period, of chloride and sulfate.[54] More recent data covering the period 1968 to 1985 indicated relatively constant chloride levels, close to the 1956 levels and well below levels of concern.[55]

In contrast to Lake Michigan, soluble silica showed a significant increase between 1971 and 1980.[56] The cause of this increase appears to be as mysterious as that of the decline in Lake Michigan.

The long-term increase in nitrate plus nitrite is continuing (figure 4.7). For Lake Huron, the annual rate of increase is less than that of Lake Ontario and the central basin of Lake Erie, but greater than that for Lake Superior and the southern basin of Lake Michigan.[57] In addition to atmospheric inputs, nonpoint source loading (mainly agricultural runoff) is significant in the southern part of the lake and in parts of Georgian Bay.

Phosphorus levels indicated no statistically significant change between 1971 and 1985 (figures 4.5 and 4.6). Georgian Bay levels are generally lower than those found in Lake Huron proper. The highest concentrations occur in Saginaw Bay. Estimated annual phosphorus loadings for Lake Huron, between 1976 and 1985, were above, but within 15 percent of, the target for loadings established in the Water Quality Agreement.[58] All four Areas of Concern listed for Lake Huron are characterized by elevated phosphorus levels.[59]

In general, the trophic status of the open waters of Lake Huron has remained unchanged from the oligotrophic/meso-oligotrophic conditions reported in 1971.[60]

Few reliable historical data exist for assessing trace metals in Lake Huron waters. Of 14 metals reported in 1980, only 2 (cobalt and vanadium) were identified as increasing in concentration.[61]

## Lake Erie

Lake Erie has a larger surface area than Lake Ontario, but it is the smallest lake in volume. It is the southernmost, warmest, and most biologically productive; it is also the only lake that frequently is completely ice-covered under winter climatic conditions. Lake Erie divides naturally into three major basins: western, central, and eastern. The western basin is the shallowest, probably has the most important fish spawning and nursery grounds, and is used extensively for recreation.[62] Its natural characteristics and its proximity to Detroit and Toledo make it the basin most vulnerable to change.

The aquatic ecosystem of Lake Erie has altered dramatically and visibly over the past 150 years, and especially in recent decades. By the 1960s, degradation had become extreme. Massive algal blooms were occurring, and several near-shore areas were devoid of visible higher aquatic life. Twenty years later, the lake itself has visibly and invisibly improved in quality. Rapidly developing urban waterfronts appear to reflect this change. As elsewhere, however, new and more complex problems have been identified as a result of initiatives originally sparked by the eutrophication issue.

The reduction of phosphorus loadings to Lake Erie and subsequent ecosystem recovery is an encouraging success story. Annual loadings by municipalities and industry were reduced from a high of 30,800 tons (28,000 tonnes) per year in 1968 to 12,298 tons (11,180 tonnes) per year in 1985, only slightly above the long-term target (figure 4.6).[63] Open-lake concentrations of total phosphorus have responded accordingly (figure 4.5).

The improvements in Lake Erie largely reflect conditions along the north shore of the western basin and the surface waters of the central basin. Oxygen depletion in the deep waters of Lake Erie's central basin continues to be a problem;[64] the sediments in the basin are estimated to have released 2,200 tons (2,000 tonnes) of phosphorus in 1985.[65]

Although phosphorus levels are the most common indicators of water quality conditions in Lake Erie, other chemicals are also important. For example, the salt industry uses salt deposits beneath the western part of the basin. Discharges of waste brine caused chloride levels in Lake Erie to rise from about 8 parts per million in 1920 to about 25 parts per million in the early 1960s. By 1985, levels had returned to those found in the late 1930s, with much of the improvement attributable to elimination of waste brine pollution.[66]

As elsewhere in the lakes, nitrogen loadings and resultant ambient levels are increasing steadily. Apparently these are influenced heavily by use of nitrogen fertilizers. For example, research on the Maumee River demonstrated a very close relationship between the increased use of nitrogen fertilizers in the watershed between 1900 and 1975 and rising concentrations of nitrates.[67] Atmospheric loading of nitrogen nutrients to the lake is estimated to represent about 13 percent of the total nitrogen load per year. A large part of this probably represents agricultural fertilizer previously lost to the atmosphere.[68]

Lake Erie appears to be almost as contaminated with heavy metals as is Lake Michigan (figure 4.8). In the late 1970s, the Detroit River was found to contribute 66 percent, 32 percent, and 67 percent of the cadmium, lead, and zinc loads, respectively, while all sewage and atmospheric sources combined contributed 26 percent, 49 percent, and 22 percent, respectively. Over 40 percent of the metal loading is retained in the lake, and, in the case of lead, 65 percent is lost to the basin sediments. It is evident that the most important source of contamination to the lake remains the Detroit River, which has been identified as the principal target for reducing loadings to the open lake.[69]

Lake Erie receives a substantial burden of organic contaminants, although 1986 surveys found that only PCBs exceeded the Water Quality Agreement objectives. The excessive levels occurred in the western regions of the lake, coinciding with inputs from the Detroit River.[70] Compounding the problem is the legacy of PCB accumulation in the lake bottom sediments, which can act as a contaminant source long into the future.

Despite the relatively heavy loadings of toxic metal and organic contaminants to Lake Erie, contaminant levels in fish flesh rank close to Lakes Huron and Superior and are well below those of Lakes Michigan and Ontario.[71] It has been suggested that this may be explained by the continuing near-eutrophic conditions in the western basin of Lake Erie. Large amounts of organic material continue to be produced at the bottom of the food web, causing a mass-per-unit volume of associated contaminants that is lower than it would be if smaller quantities were produced.[72] The relatively low contaminant concentration at the bottom of the food web continues as a ripple effect through the entire food web. In addition, particulate matter tends to settle out relatively quickly in the shallow waters of Lake Erie and carries with it many contaminants that are adsorbed onto the particles.

In addition to the Detroit and Niagara rivers at each end of Lake Erie, the IJC's Water Quality Board has listed eight Areas of Concern around the lake (chapter 3, figure 3.3). Almost all these areas are characterized by a broad range of problems, including conventional pollutants, heavy metals, toxic organics, contaminated sediments, eutrophication, and severe degradation of fish and wildlife habitat.

*Lake Ontario*

Lake Ontario is the last in the Great Lakes chain and was the first to be influenced by European settlement. It is the smallest (by surface area) but has an average depth slightly greater than Lake Michigan and much greater than Lakes Erie or Huron. As shown in figure 4.9, there are three major depositional basins in the main part of the lake, with a fourth near Kingston and the outlet to the St. Lawrence.

Within the lake, about 90 percent of the inflowing water from the Niagara River circulates in a period of a few months, with currents moving in a generally counterclockwise motion.[73] The result is a relatively short mixing time that ensures the distribution of any introduced contaminant throughout the lake in one to two years.[74] It has been suggested that the evaporation of some contaminants to the atmosphere might significantly assist the self-cleansing of Lake Ontario within a few years, if all sources of contaminants were eliminated.[75]

Increases in Lake Ontario of total dissolved solids, calcium, chlo-

## Figure 4.9
## Great Lakes Depositional Basins

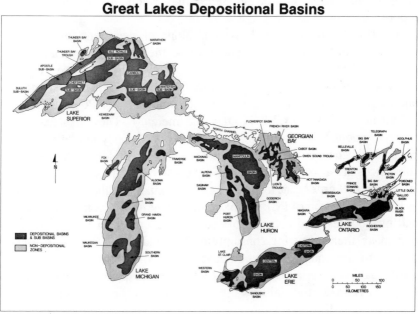

Source: Eisenreich et al. (1983).

um, potassium, and sulfate probably began around 1910 and continued through 1965.[76] These increases were the most dramatic in all the Great Lakes. However, in the mid-1970s, trends changed markedly and assessments during the period 1977 to 1983 showed decreasing levels for almost all major ions.[77]

Total phosphorus in the surface waters of Lake Ontario peaked in 1973 (figures 4.5 and 4.6). All measured forms of phosphorus have declined since that time, and current estimates indicate that the total loading of phosphorus is close to the target value.[78]

Like the other Great Lakes, Lake Ontario has experienced a trend of increased concentrations of nitrate plus nitrite that has continued from early in the century to the present (figure 4.7). In Lake Ontario, a shift in algal species composition has resulted, but the long-term implications remain unclear. As in Lake Erie, in contrast to the upper Great Lakes, direct agricultural runoff rather than atmospheric deposition is the probable cause.[79]

Trace metal concentrations in open Lake Ontario waters are generally below IJC objectives. However, toxic sums in the lake, which vary from a low of 1.61 in central waters to a high of 2.31 in nearshore areas at the western end of the lake,[80] may potentially affect aquatic biota.

In terms of diversity and concentrations of persistent toxic substances, Lake Ontario is recognized to be the most contaminated of the Great Lakes.[81] The edible portions of fish tissue in the larger specimens of some Lake Ontario sportfish—most frequently salmon and trout—exceed Canadian and/or U.S. standards for PCBs, mirex, chlordane, dioxin, 2,3,7,8-TCDD, and mercury. They also exceed more stringent U.S. Environmental Protection Agency guidelines for hexachlorobenzene, DDT and metabolites, and dieldrin. The latter substances are also found in the ambient water column at levels above standards and criteria designed to protect human health.

Bioaccumulation of PCBs, dioxin, chlordane, mirex, dieldrin, DDT and metabolites, and octachlorostyrene has occurred in fish to levels that make them unfit for consumption by wildlife. PCBs, iron, and aluminum are found in the ambient water column at levels above standards and criteria designed for protection of aquatic life. Deformities and reproductive failures attributed to toxic contaminants have been found in fish-eating birds.

This said, data on concentrations of contaminants in fish and wildlife indicate substantial improvements since the 1960s. For the most part, this improvement reflects the controls placed on the manufacture and use of certain chemicals such as PCBs, DDT, mercury, and mirex. However, inputs of some contaminants may be increasing (for example, dioxins and furans),[82] and since the early 1980s no apparent trend has been evident for some substances (for example, mirex), suggesting continuing inputs or recycling within the lake ecosystem. (Figure 4.10 displays the distribution of mirex in Lake Ontario's sediments in 1977.) Enhanced sampling and analytical technology has led to the detection of previously unmonitored substances.[83] There is now an overall sense that the concentrations of problem toxic substances in Lake Ontario may be stabilizing at unacceptably high levels.[84]

If Lake Erie was pivotal in the development of action on eutrophication, Lake Ontario and the Niagara River are similarly central to the present concern over toxic contamination. Monitoring systems, lake-atmosphere exchanges, groundwater discharge, release by lake bottom sediments, and the quality of the inflow from the rest of the Great Lakes basin are all of major importance in Lake Ontario. Understanding their interactions and cumulative effects is crucial in solving problems of toxic contaminants throughout the Great Lakes basin.

## Figure 4.10
## Mirex Distribution in Lake Ontario Sediments, 1977

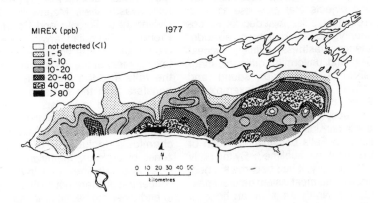

MIREX (ppb)                              1977

☐ not detected (<1)
▨ 1-5
▨ 5-10
▨ 10-20
▨ 20-40
▨ 40-80
■ >80

0  10  20  30  40  50
kilometres

From "Sources, Fate, and Controls of Toxic Contaminants," by R.L. Thomas, J.E. Gannon, J.H. Harting, D.J. Williams, and D.M. Whittle, in *Toxic Contamination in Large Lakes, Volume III*, edited by Norbert W. Schmidtke. Copyright 1988, Lewis Publishers, Inc., Chelsea, MI. Used with permission.

*The Connecting Channels*

The connecting channels are the conduits linking the Great Lakes. In general, water moves through the connecting channels quickly and in large volume, contaminants are diluted and quickly conveyed further down the system, and the rivers tend to scour their beds rather than deposit sediments along them. Direct atmospheric loading is insignificant compared to direct point and nonpoint sources and tributary flow.

Conventionally, five connecting channels are recognized in the Great Lakes. Three, the St. Clair River, Lake St. Clair, and the Detroit River, link Lake Huron and Lake Erie. The St. Marys River drains Lake Superior into Lake Huron, and the Niagara River, in two distinct sections separated by Niagara Falls, drains Lake Erie into Lake Ontario (see box on Niagara Falls).

The contrasts among the individual channels are at least as significant

---

## Niagara Falls—From Sublimity to Toxicity

In the late 18th century, the word *sublime* came to be used to describe the combination of "overwhelming awe, the contradictory reaction of terror yet attraction" evoked by natural landscapes and spectacles such as Niagara Falls.[1] Edmund Burke attempted to define the qualities of natural objects that give rise to such feelings; his list[2] included terror, obscurity, power, darkness, solitude, silence, vastness, infinity, succession and uniformity, difficulty, magnificence, light, color, sound, and "bitters and stenches" (examples of these last are presumably hot springs and active volcanic areas). As Elizabeth McKinsey has recently shown, Niagara Falls became the "icon of the American sublime."[3] By the early 19th century, it had become the best known and most visited natural spectacle in North America, an honor it still retains.

The 20th century meaning of *sublime* is not quite the same as that of Edmund Burke. Nor are contemporary perceptions of Niagara Falls. In the mid-1980s, two centuries after the falls were first called "sublime," rather different qualities were being discovered and documented. The Niagara River Toxics Committee was investigating the loadings of toxic substances to the Niagara River via groundwater contaminated by nearby toxic waste sites. Meanwhile, the University of Toronto and Pollution Probe (a Canadian environmental organization) were investigating the toxic content of the mists rising from the falls and the implications for transfers from the mists to the atmosphere and to tourists. The University of Toronto and Pollution Probe found that the mists contained toxic chemicals, including PCBs, benzene, chloroform, methylene chloride, and toluene. The levels of concentration were not high enough to endanger the health of those who inhaled the mists, but Pollution Probe suggested that contaminants might subsequently fall out from the atmosphere and enter the food web.[4]

as their common features. However, by their nature, they have all become foci for crossing points, settlement, and industrial activity. In several respects, for example, the St. Marys River has affinities with the much more intensely developed St. Clair area. In both settings, power generation, shipping traffic, and discharges of nutrients and toxic substances from industrial and municipal point sources, as well as urban nonpoint discharges and combined sewer overflows, have contributed to degradation of receiving water, fish, habitat, sediment, and benthos quality. With both rivers, the deterioration has been greater on their Canadian sides, and, in both cases, steady improvements in water quality have been recorded during the last two decades.

Both the Detroit River and the Niagara River have been the focus of intensive concern and research on water quality deterioration, with problems being concentrated overwhelmingly on the U.S. side of these rivers. However, all the connecting channels, reinforced by their trans-boundary position, have been and continue to be areas with particular significance for water quality.[85] All, except Lake St. Clair, have been designated Areas of Concern, and 3 other Areas of Concern (the Clinton, Rouge, and Buffalo rivers) are adjacent or tributary to connecting channels (chapter 3, figure 3.3).[86]

## The St. Lawrence River and Links to the Great Lakes

Of the 537-mile (864 kilometer) length of the St. Lawrence River, the international section extends 114 miles (184 kilometers) from the outlet of Lake Ontario to Cornwall, Ontario, and St. Regis Akwesasne, New York. The remainder is under Canadian jurisdiction.

In terms of flow, the contribution from the Great Lakes ranges from 100 percent at the outlet of Lake Ontario to 95 percent at Cornwall/St. Regis Akwesasne and 61 percent at Sept Iles, Quebec.[87] Because of the relatively rapid movement of water through the system, the St. Lawrence River will respond and recover quickly if contaminant sources can be eliminated.

Three distinct life zones can be identified along the St. Lawrence: the freshwater, brackish, and saltwater zones.[88] The freshwater zone extends from the outlet of Lake Ontario to Cap Tourmente, Quebec, below Ile D'Orleans; the brackish zone from there to Baie St. Paul on the north shore and Sainte-Anne-de-la-Pocatiere on the south shore; beyond is saltwater. The St. Lawrence system includes 214 square miles (554 square kilometers) of wetlands, 80 percent of which are located in the freshwater zone.

The Great Lakes, particularly Lake Ontario, have been implicated as the major source of mirex, PCBs, DDT and its derivatives, and volatile hydrocarbons to sediments, water, benthos, and fish in the St. Lawrence River, particularly the upper reaches. Further, water entering the St. Lawrence has elevated levels of dissolved metals. However, 7 of the 11 priority toxic contaminants identified in Lake Ontario also have been associated with local industrial sources along the river; cleanup of the St. Lawrence will require action at local sources, as well as in the Great Lakes.

Tributaries to the river are key, not only in terms of flow, but also biologically. The brackish zone, the tributary/main river interface where fresh- and saltwater meet, is particularly rich in life. For example, the interface between the waters of the Saguenay and St. Lawrence is the preferred habitat of beluga whales.*

Riverine lakes (Lacs Saint-François, Saint-Louis, Saint-Pierre), tributary dam reservoirs, and the estuary act as sinks much as the Great Lakes do. In these depositional areas, the integrated effect of all upstream sources is felt. Unfortunately, these areas are often highly productive zones of broad species diversity and, as such, are particularly sensitive and vulnerable.

For the St. Lawrence, it is reasonable to extrapolate the experience of the Great Lakes and suggest that fish, wildlife, and humans that are dependent on the aquatic system for food are at elevated risk. Nevertheless, the level of understanding of the contaminant issue on the St. Lawrence is inferior to that of the Great Lakes.

## Contaminated Lake, River, and Stream Bottom Sediments

Bottom sediments in the Great Lakes basin range in quality from completely uncontaminated to classification as hazardous waste. Contaminants can reach sediments via surface water or through groundwater. Once contaminated, sediments can become a long-term source of contaminants to surface water and, therefore, to the aquatic ecosystem.[89]

Overall concentrations of contaminants in Lake Superior bottom sediments generally are lower than in the other Great Lakes. Lake Huron's levels are above those of Lake Superior but generally below

---

*See chapter 6 for discussion of beluga whales.

those of the lower lakes. Conditions in Lake Ontario are probably the most degraded, although high levels of some contaminants are found at specific locations in Lakes Michigan and Erie, the connecting channels, and many of the tributary lakes, rivers, and streams. For example, Lake Michigan has some of the sediments most highly contaminated with PCBs; in Waukegan Harbor, concentrations as high as 500,000 parts per million (a 50 percent concentration) have been found in the sediment.[90] Local areas throughout the system, including 41 of the 42 Areas of Concern, have problems with contaminated sediments.

In the Great Lakes themselves, bottom sediments that were recently deposited are significantly less contaminated by both toxic metals and organics than are those deposited earlier. However, accumulated loadings and internal lake processes that serve to slowly distribute sediments to the broad depositional basins (figure 4.9) combine to create a long-term source of contaminants to the surface water system.

For example, in Lake Ontario, although the contaminant plume emanating from the Niagara River is no longer so strongly evident in the most recent (top) layer of bottom sediments, PCB concentrations in the sediments of the lake's three main depositional basins show little change from the early 1970s to the mid-1980s.[91] In waters of the western basin of Lake Erie, no improvement in PCB levels has been recorded. This could indicate a continuing source via the Detroit River, but the lack of improvement may also be due to release of accumulated PCBs in existing sediments.[92]

Degraded conditions are also found in the bottom sediments of the connecting channels, even though the areas of accumulation are relatively small. Concern exists not only about contaminants for which dredging guidelines exist but also about other contaminants such as hexachlorobenzene (HCB), polyaromatic hydrocarbons (PAHs), phenols, DDT and the metabolites, phthalate esters, and volatile organics. Oil and grease are a particularly severe problem.[93]

Burial of contaminated sediments by ongoing sedimentation may be important to the long-term recovery of the lakes. Burial may result in a certain amount of natural "sealing" of lake bottoms. However, this depends on rates of sedimentation, which are high in Lake Erie but very low in Lakes Michigan and Superior.

Resuspension and re-solution of contaminants occur as a result of several processes, including storms, dredging, and boating. When dredging is required to maintain navigation channels or for other purposes, the resuspension of contaminants in the water column that may take place can become a serious problem. During the period 1975 to 1979, 62 percent of dredging activity occurred in Lake Erie (including Lake St. Clair), 15 percent in Lake Michigan, and less than 10 percent in each of the other three lakes. The volume of dredged material removed in the U.S. portion of the basin during these five years was more than 10 times the amount removed in Canada.[94]

Contaminated sediments have been assigned hazardous waste status and are listed on the Superfund priority list at three U.S. sites, all of which are Areas of Concern on Lake Michigan (Waukegan Harbor, Grand Calumet River/Indiana Harbor Canal, and Sheboygan).[95]


## Conclusions—Water and Sediment Quality

Trends and conditions in water quality and sediments in the Great Lakes basin offer a mixed picture of program successes, unacceptably high levels of continued contamination, and uncertainty about conditions. Reductions in phosphorus loadings and levels are the most obvious sign of program success. Reduced levels of particular toxic substances in sediments and organisms reflect the success of restrictions or bans on chemical use and production, although levels of such contaminants as mirex, PCBs, and dieldrin remain unacceptably high in many places.

Controlling phosphorus loadings to the Great Lakes from major point sources and products was relatively easy. Phosphorus removal could be readily accomplished at municipal sewage treatment plants, and laws requiring reductions in phosphorus were passed quickly in most (but not all) jurisdictions. Characterizing and addressing problems of contamination by toxic substances are proving more difficult. Both under IJC auspices and pursuant to other organizational arrangements made by Great Lakes jurisdictions, several significant planning activities have been launched as a prelude to remedial and preventive action.

These include the Niagara River Toxics Committee (1981-84),[96] the Niagara River Toxics Management Plan (ongoing), the Upper Great Lakes Connecting Channels Study (1984-89),[97] and the development of the Lake Ontario Toxics Management Plan.[98] All of these initiatives are consistent with annex 2 of the 1978 Water Quality Agreement, as amended in 1987, which commits Canada and the United States to develop Lakewide Management Plans for open lake waters, "to reduce loadings of Critical Pollutants in order to restore beneficial uses."[99] These Lakewide Management Plans are the open-water counterparts of the Remedial Action Plans being developed for near-shore Areas of Concern.

Programs to address groundwater concerns are just getting under way. In commenting on the first progress reports submitted by the United States and Canada on implementation of the groundwater annex to the Great Lakes Water Quality Agreement, the Great Lakes Water Quality Board noted in 1989 that there had not yet been any movement toward bilateral coordination of groundwater programs, nor had a standard approach to sampling and analysis of contaminants been agreed on.[100]

Contaminated sediments remain the area where the greatest technological innovation will be required to address existing problems. The Water Quality Board, in its 1989 report, noted that no technologies have been used within the Great Lakes basin "to remediate large volumes of contaminated sediments *in situ*."[101] The board observed that the only options currently available are to dredge contaminated sediments or to leave them in place, but disposal of the dredged material remains a major problem. Sediments constitute "the major reservoir of pollutants in the Great Lakes system,"[102] and they are likely to remain so for many years. Canada and the United States must mount an ambitious effort to develop appropriate technologies for cleansing contaminated sediments, to minimize the period that the Great Lakes ecosystem is contaminated with this legacy of the past.

## WATER QUANTITY ISSUES

Great Lakes water quantity issues have drawn almost as much attention as water quality issues during the past 25 years. The lakes hold an almost inconceivable volume of water—5,439 cubic miles (22,684 cubic kilometers).[103] This is approximately 20 percent of the world's fresh surface water.[104] Spread evenly, the lakes would flood an area the size of North America to a depth of three feet.[105]

Water quantity issues can be divided into three categories:

- problems caused by substantial year-to-year changes in lake levels;
- the opportunities, real or imagined, for structural and similar means of maintaining near-constant levels; and
- prospects for major diversions, involving transfers to and from the Great Lakes, primarily to meet water demands outside the basin.

### Influences on Lake Levels

Levels of the Great Lakes vary on a very short-term basis due to storms. On a seasonal basis and on a longer-term year-to-year basis, lake level alterations are due to changes in the balance between precipitation, inflow, and runoff, on one hand, and evaporation and drainage, on the other.

The short-term variations can be dramatic and can cause substantial amounts of damage along vulnerable shoreline areas. An extreme example, commonly cited, is the December 2, 1985, storm that caused the water level of Lake Erie to rise 7 feet (2.1 meters) at Buffalo at the eastern end of the lake, while dropping levels 8 feet (2.4 meters) at Toledo on the western end (figure 4.11).

Seasonal variations lead to changes of about 12 to 18 inches (30 to

**Figure 4.11**
**Effect of Storm on Lake Levels in Lake Erie,**
**December 1985**

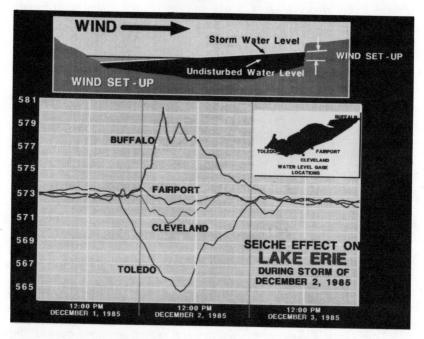

Source: U.S. Army Corps of Engineers.

46 centimeters), with lows usually occurring in January or February, and highs from June to September.[106]

During the 1980s, four of the five Great Lakes (all but Ontario) reached record high levels.* Previous record highs had been recorded in the 1950s and 1970s, and record lows in the 1920s, 1930s, and 1960s[107] (figure 4.12). The difference between record low and record high levels is nearly 7 feet (2.1 meters).[108] It is not surprising that record high lake levels were reached in 1986; for 13 of the 16 years beginning in 1970, precipitation was above the long-term average.[109] (In a recent wet year—1979—the net gain to Lake Erie was 48 inches [1.2 meters], compared to the addition of 12 to 14 inches [0.3 to 0.4 meters] during the dry 1960s.)[110]†

By July 1989, as a result of a period of reduced precipitation, the lakes had dropped substantially, returning to average long-term levels or to levels just above them; for example, Lake St. Clair dropped nearly 2 feet (0.61 meters) and Lakes Michigan and Huron dropped 2.5 feet (0.76 meters) from the record levels of 1986.[111]

The United States and Canada have constructed a series of works in the Great Lakes basin that divert water to and from it and that facilitate navigation and generation of hydroelectric power. For example, there are controls on the exits from Lakes Superior and Ontario. Some control can also be provided by varying the Ogoki-Long Lac diversions to Lake Superior, the Chicago diversion from Lake Michigan, and the flow through the Welland Canal between Lakes Erie and Ontario. The existence of these works perpetuates the belief held by many individuals (particularly the wishful thinking of those whose shoreline property is subject to damage from high water) that humans can substantially control lake levels. In fact, human influences on lake levels are miniscule compared to natural ones. For example, it was recently estimated that human structures change the level of Lake Superior by 4.5 inches (11 centimeters) and of other lakes by even smaller amounts.[112] Through the years, additional construction plans have been suggested, one of which would change the level of Lake Erie by as much as 13 inches (33 centimeters).[113] But, in all

---

*These records are based on data collected since 1900.

†The net gain is the change resulting from the addition of water by precipitation and runoff and the removal of water by evaporation. Global warming will alter precipitation and evaporation in the basin. It is estimated that this climate change will produce a sharp decline in lake levels. See figure 4.13 and additional discussion in chapter 5.

## Figure 4.12
## Fluctuations in Annual Mean Water Levels in the Great Lakes, 1900–1988

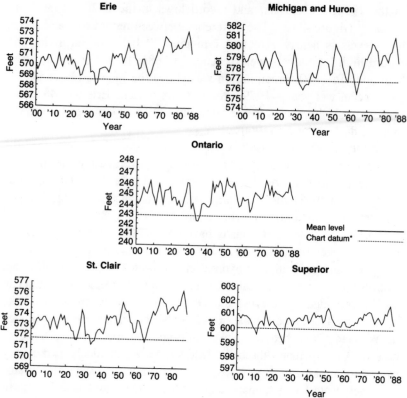

*The reference level for surface level measurements, or chart datum, is the plane upon which navigation chart depths and federal navigation improvement depths are based. Changes in lake level are measured in feet.

Source: National Oceanic and Atmospheric Administration; Great Lakes Environmental Research Laboratory; U.S. Army Corps of Engineers, Detroit District.

cases, either economic costs have been estimated to exceed economic benefits or it has been concluded that undesirable environmental impacts would result.[114] In mid-1989, an IJC study group concluded that "systemic measures aimed at affecting system-wide water level fluctuations are probably futile."[115]

Diversion of lake waters has been an issue not only because of high levels that cause problems in the basin but also because the lakes are eyed enviously by water-short regions elsewhere. Since 1959, at least

## Figure 4.13
## Potential Impacts of Global Climate Change
## on Great Lakes Water Levels*

| Lake | AES | Estimated lowering in centimeters GLERL | GLI |
|------|-----|------------------|-----|
| Superior | 21 | 39-43 | 29-80 |
| Michigan/Huron | 59 | 86-252 | 58-96 |
| St. Clair | 48 | 73-200 | 45-79 |
| Erie | 44 | 63-165 | 40-71 |
| Ontario | † | † | † |

*Reductions in Great Lakes water levels projected to occur as a result of a doubling of atmospheric $CO_2$ levels.

†In all cases, the large decreases in water supply projected for Lake Ontario resulted in reductions in water levels beyond the model capabilities (and beyond the limits of current regulation of Lake Ontario).

Source: Environment Canada, Atmospheric Environment Service; U.S. Great Lakes Environmental Research Laboratory; Great Lakes Institute.

five separate proposals have been made or studies conducted concerning major diversions into and/or from the lakes.[116] For example, the Grand Canal concept would divert water from the Hudson Bay drainage basin to the Great Lakes for distribution to arid regions of the United States and Canada. James Bay, south of Hudson Bay, would be sealed off from Hudson Bay by a dike. The saline water in James Bay would eventually be replaced through natural runoff by freshwater. This would be pumped and transported to the Great Lakes through a series of canals and then be channeled and pumped to arid regions. The plan's estimated cost would be C$79 billion to C$100 billion.[117] Major diversion proposals of this magnitude have not been endorsed by Great Lakes jurisdictions. The 1985 Great Lakes Charter (see chapter 9), signed by the eight Great Lakes states and the provinces of Quebec and Ontario, declares regional opposition to diversions of water from the Great Lakes that would have adverse impacts on lake levels, in-basin uses, and the Great Lakes ecosystem.[118]

The levels of the Great Lakes are a concern for a broad range of interests. The quantity of water in the lakes and accompanying changes in lake levels have major implications for the ability of shippers to use Great Lakes ports and for utilities to generate hydroelectric power. Changes in lake levels also influence demands for dredging, and its associated impact on water quality, and have other impacts on the ecosystem.

Human interventions to manage lake levels have been the focus of repeated IJC studies requested by the United States and Canada. In 1964, during a period of low water levels, the two nations asked the commission to examine measures to reduce extremes in water levels. Reporting in 1976, the commission indicated that only limited regulation of actual water levels was advisable. The commission addressed lake levels again in 1985 in a report on consumption and diversions, stemming from a reference given it in 1977. The investigation acknowledged the complexity of the consumption and diversion issue and again argued against further management of lake levels.[119]

In 1986, during the record high water levels, Canada and the United States once again asked the IJC to investigate "methods of alleviating the adverse consequences of fluctuating water levels in the Great Lakes-St. Lawrence River Basin."[120] In mid-1989, the IJC's Levels Reference Project Management Team released the initial results of its work. As noted above, the study group argued that specific measures to affect systemwide water level fluctuations are futile. It acknowledged the complexity of lake level issues, noting that "the issue of water levels is not a single, simple problem, but a cluster of problems, each identifiable but interrelated and interdependent in ways which have to be made very clear."[121] In moving forward to the second phase of its work, the work group will emphasize developing a set of binational principles as guides for decision making and further definition of an overall strategy and general plan for action.[122]

## Shoreline Management

In the mid-1980s, as the waters of four of the Great Lakes rose to record high levels, coastal areas became a focus of great attention. Many shoreline residents clamored for some type of government action to protect them from the rising waters (by managing lake levels or building protective structures) or to compensate them for damages. Elected officials were under great pressure to "Do Something!"

Since systematic human measures to change lake levels do not have a major impact, it is far wiser to manage shorelines to keep human structures from vulnerable areas. In a 1976 report, an IJC study group recommended that nonstructural methods of dealing with fluctuating water levels, such as planned and regulated development along shorelines, should be explored.[123] But regulating use of land along the shores of the lakes has proved difficult.

In the United States in the early 1970s, the federal government enacted

*Damaged house, Lake Michigan shoreline, Manistee County, Michigan.*
Great Lakes Commssion

the Coastal Zone Management Act. This legislation provided federal assistance to state governments to develop and implement coastal management plans that would reconcile the many conflicting uses of coastal areas.* This program was purely voluntary; states were free to participate or not as they saw fit. Four of the eight Great Lakes states—New York, Wisconsin, Michigan, and Pennsylvania—adopted approved plans. These four together represent a vast majority of the U.S. Great Lakes shoreline. The failure of other states to adopt plans illustrates the controversial character of shoreline management. For example, proposed coastal legislation in Illinois in the 1970s failed to pass because of public opposition to provisions for setbacks in erosion-hazard areas and for increased public access to the lakeshore in private residential areas. Ohio ceased its involvement because of private landowners' and industrial and commercial

---

*These plans were to address the considerable competition for the shoreline among different human user groups. Especially in urban areas and scenic rural areas, landowners and local governments see shorelines as ripe for residential development. Recreational enthusiasts see them as providing bathing beaches and access points for boating. Often, there is conflict between development for private purposes and allowing continued public access. Furthermore, some shoreline areas, such as wetlands, should not be developed at all.

developers' concerns over proposed erosion-hazard setback requirements.[124] However, in late 1988, building on the work of a citizen initiative, the Ohio Coastal Resource Management Task Force, Ohio adopted
legislation authorizing development of a state coastal zone management
plan.[125]

Advocates of greater shoreline protection in the United States have
also urged that the federal Coastal Barrier Resources Act (CBRA) be
extended to the Great Lakes. This law, protecting undeveloped barrier
islands along the Gulf and Atlantic coasts of the United States, dis-
qualifies developers of these lands from participation in the federally
subsidized flood insurance program and prohibits federal spending for
activities that encourage development.[126] In late 1988, Congress amended
the CBRA, requiring the Department of the Interior to recommend
undeveloped coastal barriers along the shore areas of the Great Lakes
appropriate for inclusion in the national coastal barriers system.[127] The
Interior Department made these recommendations in early 1989, but
as of August 1989 they had not been adopted by Congress.

Coastal protection also has been of great concern in Ontario. However, as in some U.S. states, appropriate action to manage shoreline
uses has been slow in coming. One Canadian researcher concluded in
1987:

> Despite repeated calls for more aggressive municipal control of development
> on flood- and erosion-prone shorelines, progress has been painfully slow in
> Ontario.... It appears easier to attack natural processes than modify human
> behavior.[128]

In 1986, the Ontario Shoreline Management Review Committee recommended that the provincial Ministries of Natural Resources and of
Municipal Affairs develop a shoreline management plan for Ontario,
to be implemented by conservation authorities within the province.
The committee recommended that conservation authorities apply regulations controlling construction of dwellings and other structures in
hazard areas. At the time, only 5 of 27 authorities along the Great
Lakes had such regulations in place.[129]

In both Canada and the United States, the public evidently has been
slow to accept limits on development along shorelines. If the ecosystem
approach is to be implemented in the Great Lakes basin, however,
adapting to nature, rather than managing it, must be given greater
priority.

# Chapter 5

# Legacies and Challenges: Air and Climate

When concern over air quality developed in the United States and Canada several decades ago, the problem appeared to consist essentially of excessive local concentrations of common pollutants such as sulfur dioxide, particulates (that is, dust and other solid particles), carbon monoxide, and ozone.* At unhealthful concentrations, these pollutants can irritate or damage human respiratory systems or damage vital organs.

Nowadays, air quality is recognized increasingly as a much more complex problem or group of problems. Urban air represents a soup containing many substances that pose serious risks to human health and to the environment. But the air quality problem is one that involves not merely the local consequences of emissions but their long-distance effects as well. Moreover, it also involves the exchange of pollutants between the air and other media.

One of the most significant results of the adoption of the ecosystem approach in the 1978 Great Lakes Water Quality Agreement has been a growing recognition of the significance of atmospheric factors in the Great Lakes basin ecosystem. As the International Joint Commission (IJC) observed in 1986,

many more toxic chemicals and low ambient concentrations of chemical mix-

---

*Ozone in the lowest layers of the atmosphere can impair breathing and produce other harmful health effects. Ozone in the upper layers of the atmosphere, presently threatened by chlorofluorocarbons, protects humans from harmful ultraviolet radiation.

tures threaten the health of the ecosystem to an extent and in ways that were not realized in 1978, and many are not adequately addressed by existing monitoring and control programs.[1]

The need for additional monitoring was addressed by the United States and Canada in amendments to the 1978 Water Quality Agreement adopted in 1987. These amendments provide for the establishment of an Integrated Atmospheric Deposition Network. It will, however, take another decade or more for this network to adequately describe toxic deposition throughout the Great Lakes basin.

These problems of inadequate data are compounded by the absence of meaningful boundaries. Even though the Great Lakes basin is not a closed system, its land and water areas can be clearly defined. No such boundaries, real or arbitrary, can be defined for the region's atmosphere. The notion of an "airshed," analogous to a drainage basin or watershed, is meaningless, as was vividly demonstrated by the hemispheric transport of radionuclides after the Chernobyl meltdown or of particulate matter after the Mount St. Helens eruption.

It is more realistic to think in terms of an "atmospheric region of influence" for the Great Lakes (figure 5.1).[2] This is the area most recently traversed by air masses affecting the Great Lakes basin. These air masses may contain pollutants released into the atmosphere several days earlier and hundreds or thousands of miles away. The basin itself remains the focus of interest, but the sources of, and solutions for, Great Lakes basin problems may be as much outside the basin as in it.

The latitude of the Great Lakes basin, between 40°N and 50°N, is of key importance. Throughout the year, the basin lies within the zone of west-to-east air movement around the Northern Hemisphere. Inflow of air that has a recent origin east of the basin is fairly infrequent; from west, south, and north, however, the basin is open to heat, cold, and moisture and to pollutants that may have been transported hundreds or thousands of miles from their source. The same basic westerly circulation leads to transport of these same elements out of the basin eastward, northward, or southward.

As part of the hydrological cycle (see chapter 4), water is deposited as rain or snow and then evaporates to the atmosphere from the land and surface water of the basin. The familiar precipitation/evaporation exchanges between the atmosphere and land and water surfaces are mirrored by similar exchanges of other substances, including toxic pollutants. These are not merely deposited by the atmosphere but are

## Figure 5.1
## Atmospheric Region of Influence for the Great Lakes Basin*

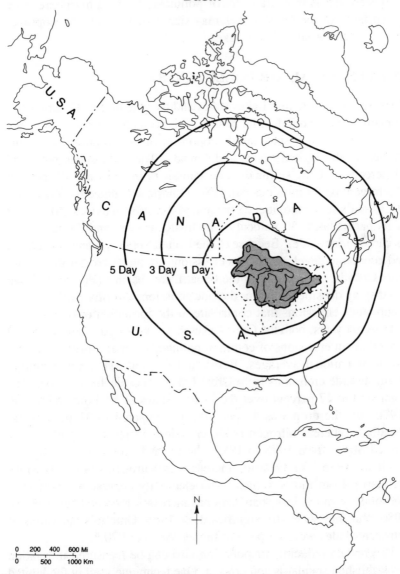

5 Day   3 Day  1 Day

N

0   200   400   600 Mi
0         500      1000 Km

*Lines indicate the median location of airborne contaminants originating 1, 3, and 5 days before their arrival in the Great Lakes hydrological basin.

Source: International Air Quality Advisory Board.

also transferred to the atmosphere from point and nonpoint sources. Residues from agricultural fertilizers and pesticides evaporate (volatilize) from croplands and other vegetation. Recently, researchers have suggested that similar transfers of pollutants to the atmosphere from the surfaces of the Great Lakes may significantly assist the improvement of water quality in the lakes.

## CONVENTIONAL AIR POLLUTANTS

Because the eight Great Lakes states and the province of Ontario have so many urban and industrial centers, it is scarcely surprising that they are the source of a substantial proportion of the common pollutants emitted in the United States and Canada. The eight states produced 41 percent of U.S. sulfur dioxide emissions in 1985 and 28 percent of nitrogen oxide emissions.[3] In 1980, Ontario accounted for 38 percent of Canada's sulfur dioxide, 28 percent of its nitrogen oxides, 20 percent of its particulates, 30 percent of its hydrocarbons, and 29 percent of its carbon monoxide.[4] Because of the United States' greater population and economic development, its emissions are much greater than those from Canada, particularly in the Great Lakes basin.[5] (Figures 5.2 and 5.3 display densities of sulfur dioxide emissions and of volatile organic compounds emissions that contribute to the formation of ozone.)

In recent years, both the Great Lakes states and Ontario have achieved reductions in emissions of common pollutants that are, in many cases, ahead of national averages. Between 1975 and 1985, for example, sulfur dioxide emissions from Great Lakes states declined 21 percent, compared to 17 percent over the United States as a whole; in Ontario (1970-80), the drop was 45 percent, as compared to 31 percent nationally.[6] Whereas nitrogen oxide emissions increased slightly in the United States from 1975 to 1985, the Great Lakes states managed a small decrease.[7] In Ontario, increases in nitrogen oxide emissions (primarily from motor vehicles and electricity generation) were proportionately much less than national increases recorded for 1970 to 1980. But they were still significant. In 1984, Ontario's emissions of nitrogen oxides were 29 percent higher than in 1970.[8]

Progress in reducing air pollution also can be measured in relation to established standards and criteria. One technique used in the United States is to identify the counties in which national ambient-air quality standards have not been achieved. Between 1978 and 1989, there was a considerable drop in the totals (that is, more counties achieved the

**Figure 5.2**
**Density of Sulfur Dioxide Emissions from Human Sources in the Continental United States and Canada**

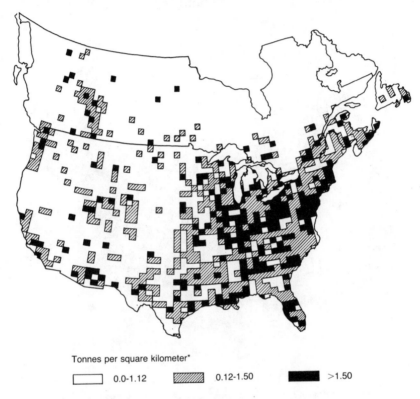

Tonnes per square kilometer*

☐ 0.0-1.12     ▨ 0.12-1.50     ■ >1.50

*1.0 metric tons per square kilometer equals 2.9 tons per square mile. Grid size is 80 x 80 kilometers.

Source: National Acid Precipitation Assessment Program.

standards), both nationally and in the Great Lakes basin (see figure 5.4).[9]

Changes in monitored concentrations of pollutants can result from shifts in industrial activity or in weather. For example, increases in temperature and sunlight can promote formation of ozone. Likewise, counties identified as violating standards may also change if the standards are changed. The improvement shown for ozone between 1978 and 1989 reflects at least three factors: relaxation of the ozone standard

## Figure 5.3
## Density of Volatile Organic Compound Emissions from Human Sources in the Continental United States and Canada

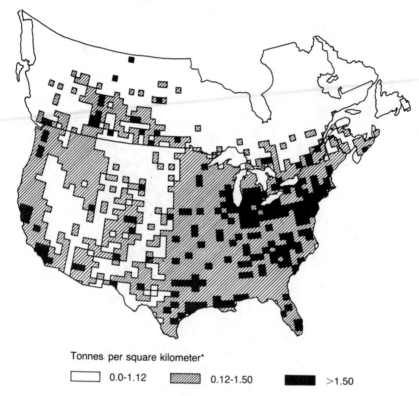

Tonnes per square kilometer*

☐ 0.0-1.12     ▨ 0.12-1.50     ■ >1.50

*1.0 metric tons per square kilometer equals 2.9 tons per square mile. Grid size is 80 x 80 kilometers.

Source: National Acid Precipitation Assessment Program.

in the United States, changes in measurement techniques, and some reduction in actual emissions.

Ozone remains the most serious national air pollution problem in the United States, in terms of the number of individuals subject to unhealthful levels of pollution. The hot summer of 1988 increased substantially the number of counties, in the Great Lakes basin and throughout the United States, that failed to achieve the national air

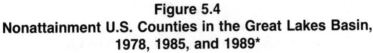

**Figure 5.4**
**Nonattainment U.S. Counties in the Great Lakes Basin,**
**1978, 1985, and 1989***

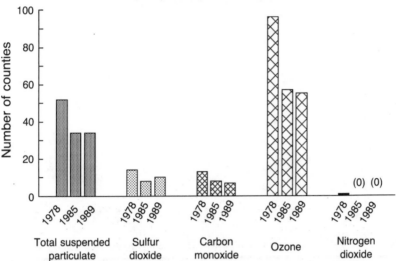

*"Nonattainment" means that a county did not meet the standards as of the latest data available and that a State Implementation Plan had not yet been approved by EPA. Changes in attainment status can reflect actual changes in emissions, changes in standards, or changes in measurement techniques. Designations for 1989 are based on air quality measurements through 1987.

Source: U.S. Environmental Protection Agency.

quality standard for ozone. Ozone pollution in many locations was worse in 1988 than in any other year of the 1980s (figure 5.5). The designations in figure 5.4, based on data through 1987, do not reflect the increases in ozone levels in 1988.

The substantial, though uneven, progress shown in the Great Lakes states toward lowering measured levels of air pollution is mirrored in Ontario. Between 1977 and 1986, improvements were reported in monitored levels of sulfur dioxide, carbon monoxide, nitrogen dioxide, nitric oxide, and total suspended particulates. There was less evidence of a downward trend in the soiling index (a measure of smaller particulates that may pose a greater health risk than larger particulates) and in hydrocarbons.[10]

Yet another perspective on progress is provided by the changing frequency with which air pollution advisories are issued in Ontario. These advisories have been based on measurements of sulfur dioxide and the

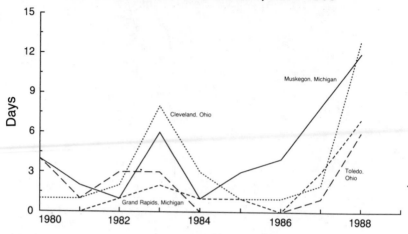

**Figure 5.5**
**Number of Days Exceeding Ozone Standards for 4 U.S. Great Lakes Cities, 1980-1988**

Source: Michigan Department of Natural Resources; Ohio Environmental Protection Agency.

soiling index but do not take ozone into account. Advisories have been issued most frequently for Hamilton—on 23 occasions in both 1971 and 1979 but only 12, 8, and 5 times in 1982, 1984, and 1986, respectively. No advisories were issued for any other Ontario city in 1986.[11]

Ozone remains a problem in Ontario. Whereas both urban and rural violations of Canada's air quality objective for ozone seemed to decline somewhat between 1979 and 1986, they had a dramatic upswing in 1987 and 1988 (figure 5.6).[12] Ozone is not only a local problem in urban areas; it is a regional one having international implications. The flow of ozone from the United States contributes an estimated 50 to 60 percent of background ozone concentrations in southern Ontario, making improvement in Ontario dependent on reductions across the border.[13] Long-distance transport of ozone also may be significant for agriculture throughout the southern part of the basin. Rural ozone monitors in Ontario, for example, have recorded amounts above the level likely to cause significant yield losses in such sensitive crops as soybeans and white beans.[14]

The Ontario air quality criterion for ozone is violated many hours per year more in Ontario than the U.S. air quality standard for ozone is violated in the United States.[15] Ontario's air quality is not necessarily worse than that of the United States: the Ontario air quality criterion

## Figure 5.6
## Ozone Trends in Southwestern / South Central Ontario, 1979-1988

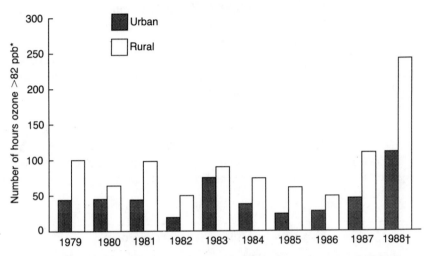

*82 parts per billion is the Canadian ambient air quality objective for one-hour concentrations of ozone.

†Estimated.

Source: Environment Canada.

is tougher than its U.S. counterpart. Air quality in the United States would look much worse if judged against Canadian standards. For example, using data from U.S. sites, the International Air Quality Advisory Board, which reports to the International Joint Commission (IJC), showed that during summer months ozone levels registered at these sites would exceed a Canadian national ozone objective (almost identical to the Ontario criterion) 12 to 15 times more frequently than they exceed the looser U.S. standard.[16] Whether judged against U.S. or Canadian standards or guidelines, ozone levels in the U.S. are higher than ozone levels in Canada.[17]

## THE CHALLENGE OF THE TOXIC SOUP

The number of pollutants in the air is much larger than the list of common pollutants on which pollution control efforts have concentrated thus far. Some of the many volatile organic compounds that contribute to ozone formation may also represent a more direct risk to human health. These include, for example, benzene, chloroform, carbon tetrachloride, and vinyl chloride; metals such as cadmium, chromium, arsenic, and asbestos may also pose risks.

An illustration of the variety of substances in this "toxic soup" is provided by a recent inventory of air pollution emissions in a heavily polluted area of southeast Chicago (see box, "Southeast Chicago's Toxic Soup."). Detailed inventories of this sort are exceptional. In general, few data are available on either emissions of toxic pollutants or their concentrations in the atmosphere. (However, in 1989, significantly more data on emissions became available in the United States [see box, "Enhanced Information on Chemical Discharges..."].)

The lack of specific data about atmospheric toxic pollutants was demonstrated most forcibly when the U.S. Environmental Protection Agency's (EPA's) Great Lakes National Program Office reported in

---

### Southeast Chicago's Toxic Soup

Southeast Chicago has "perhaps the most serious combination of concentrated industrial activity with high population density" in the midwestern United States.[1] A combined federal-state-local inventory was designed to estimate emissions of 51 substances, 32 of which are potentially cancer-causing.[2] The survey, using a variety of calculation techniques, estimated emissions for 43 of the 51 substances. For 15 substances, annual emissions were estimated to be 1.1 tons (1 tonne) per year or less; for 11 other substances annual emissions were 110 tons (100 tonnes) per year or more. (See figure 5.7 for estimated emissions in 1984 of eight selected pollutants.)

Some substances are emitted primarily by motor vehicles, others primarily from point sources (for example, industrial facilities), and still others from consumer-oriented sources such as refueling of autos, wood burning in fireplaces and wood stoves, and dry cleaning. Most benzene emissions come from point sources, with coking operations at steel mills constituting a majority of the point source emissions.[3] About 71 percent of the benzene emissions from mobile sources come from vehicles traveling arterial (nonfreeway) roads.[4] Consumer sources produce most of the emissions of methylene chloride. Aerosol cans and paint stripping produce about 75 percent of the methylene chloride emissions from such sources.[5] Of the perchloroethylene emissions, about 67 percent come from dry cleaning operations, and another 32 percent from degreasing operations.[6] Ethylene is emitted primarily by automobiles.[7] Two sewage treatment plants in southeast Chicago produce about 27 percent of the area's acetone emissions and 16 percent of its styrene emissions, but produce insignificant percentages of other substances.[8]

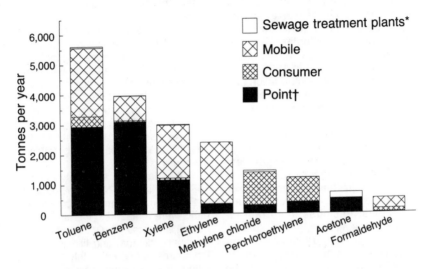

**Figure 5.7**
**Estimated Emissions of 8 Toxic Air Pollutants**
**in the Southeast Chicago Area, 1984**

*Includes waste facilities and sewage treatment plants.

†Includes steel mills and other industrial sources.

Source: U.S. Environmental Protection Agency.

1987 that none of the organic pollutants on the IJC's Primary Track (those of greatest significance for water quality) is routinely monitored in the atmosphere.[18] (Figure 2.3 in chapter 2 lists the Primary Track pollutants.) In a similar vein, consultants reporting to an IJC workshop on atmospheric deposition indicated that, except for lead, what data are available on emissions of these pollutants in the Great Lakes basin are either questionable or unacceptable.[19] This dearth of information about a major factor affecting ecosystem health is reflected in the new annex on Airborne Toxic Substances added to the Water Quality Agreement in 1987, requiring creation of an integrated network to monitor atmospheric deposition.[20]

Emissions to the air from pollution control activities themselves have attracted growing attention in recent years. This is partly because of increasing knowledge. It also demonstrates a recognition that past programs of pollution control were often developed without much regard to possible impacts on other media.

## Enhanced Information on Chemical Discharges to Air, Land, and Water Required by U.S. Superfund Legislation[1]

Information on discharges of toxic pollutants to air (as well as to land and water) is sparse, as noted throughout this chapter. However, amendments to the U.S. Superfund legislation, enacted in 1986, promise to provide more information than previously has been available on discharges from major industrial sources. The amendments, known as the Emergency Planning and Community Right-to-Know Act of 1986, require the U.S. Environmental Protection Agency (EPA) to establish an inventory of routine toxic chemical emissions from certain facilities. Facilities in certain industrial categories, using specific chemicals in large amounts, are required to submit information to EPA on maximum amounts of the chemicals on-site and on how much enters the air, land, and water annually.

Initial reports were released by EPA in April 1989. In releasing the data, and describing their meaning for human health, EPA cautioned that the estimates of annual emissions represent only the first step. Releases do not equal exposure, and the annual estimates say nothing about rates of release, concentrations in specific locations, or extent of public exposure.

EPA's data indicate that during 1987 an estimated 2.7 billion pounds (1.23 billion kilograms) of contaminants were released to the air by reporting industries. The states of Ohio, Michigan, Indiana, and Illinois were the source of approximately 18 percent of the toxic emissions to the air reported to EPA.

Several forms of pollution control may themselves be potential sources of air pollution, though the evidence on this possibility is limited. One EPA study of the municipal sewage treatment plant in Philadelphia, Pennsylvania, found that the plant was a major contributor of organic chemicals to the city's air; subsequent studies of another 30 plants suggested, however, that the Philadelphia situation appears to be exceptional.[21] Few analyses of sewage treatment emissions have been done in the Great Lakes basin, but the detailed study of toxic emissions in southeast Chicago concluded that the two plants in the area accounted for only a very small fraction of the total pollution risk.[22]

Elevated mercury concentrations in St. Louis Bay, near Duluth, Minnesota, demonstrate how pollution problems can be shifted around in pollution control activities. The sludge from Duluth's wastewater treatment plant is disposed of by incineration. The incinerator is fueled by municipal solid waste, which contains mercury from paints, batteries, and other sources. Water from the plant is used to cool the gases escaping from the incinerator and then is returned to the plant.

This recycling of water increases the mercury concentration of the sludge. Some of the mercury released in combustion escapes to the atmosphere. Elevated concentrations of mercury in the bay have been found when the incinerator has been operating.

Plants that incinerate municipal solid waste have proved extremely controversial in recent years (see chapter 3). They can emit a wide range of air pollutants, including acid gases (hydrochloric acid and sulfur dioxide), metals (lead, zinc, and cadmium), and organic compounds such as dioxins and furans.[23] Technologies to control emissions from incinerated municipal waste have advanced considerably in recent years. From its National Incinerator Testing and Evaluation Program, Environment Canada has concluded that these technologies can reduce emissions significantly.[24] Much depends, however, on how the plants are operated. If operators are not well-trained, supervision is inadequate, or equipment is not well maintained, emissions can reach unacceptable levels. The technology to burn waste has become more sophisticated and it requires sophisticated management to assure its proper operation. Local objections to new incineration facilities may generate questions that are not answerable with available data. In the absence of convincing data, communities may feel understandably that the potential for significant air pollution exists.

If data are sparse on such well-defined facilities as sewage plants and incinerators, they are even worse on atmospheric emissions from hazardous and other waste dumps. Both Michigan and Wisconsin have found undesirable emissions from hazardous-waste sites and municipal landfills; it seems probable that if such investigations were conducted more widely, the problem might be seen to be a general one.[25]

## LONG-RANGE TRANSPORT AND DEPOSITION OF POLLUTANTS

The Great Lakes are particularly vulnerable to contaminants showered on them from the atmosphere. They have large surface areas on which pollutants can be deposited, and they are near to and downwind of such major pollution sources as cities, chemical complexes, coal-fired power plants, and agricultural lands. Several of the major toxic chemicals deposited from the atmosphere are known to biomagnify in the fish and birds of the lakes, posing risks to these organisms and to the humans that consume them (see chapters 6 and 7).

In principle, the complex movements of pollutants through different parts of the environment can be described through a mass-balance model.* In practice, however, the data requirements needed to make reasonable estimates of the many processes involved are large, and sufficient data for these calculations usually are not available. Uncertainties are substantial even with the best available data on atmospheric and nonatmospheric inputs to the Great Lakes, such as those for PCBs (figure 5.8).[26] These uncertainties aside, it is clear that the atmosphere contributes a sizable proportion of PCBs to the Great Lakes, especially the upper lakes.

DDT and toxaphene, two of the 11 Primary Track critical pollutants, clearly demonstrate the significance of long-range transport of pollution to the Great Lakes basin.[27] Toxaphene was used in the United States from the late 1940s until 1982. Its use in the Great Lakes basin, however, was minimal, since its principal use was to control insects on cotton crops in the southern states. Nevertheless, high levels of toxaphene were found in Great Lakes fish in the late 1970s, as well as in fish sampled in the Atlantic and Pacific oceans. Equally striking is the continuing deposition of DDT in the Great Lakes basin, despite restrictions on its use in the United States and Canada since 1972. It appears that much of the DDT currently being deposited in the basin is atmospherically transported from Central and South America.

Acid deposition (for example, acid rain) has perhaps the highest

### Figure 5.8
### PCB Inputs to the Great Lakes and Fractions Attributed to Atmospheric Pathways

| | Total Inputs kg per year | Atmospheric Direct | Indirect* |
|---|---|---|---|
| Lake Superior | 606 | 90 | 0 |
| Lake Michigan | 685 | 58 | 0 |
| Lake Huron | 636 | 63 | 15 |
| Lake Erie | 2520 | 7 | 6 |
| Lake Ontario | 2540 | 6 | 1 |

*Indirect inputs are airborne pollutants deposited on an upstream lake that subsequently flow into another lake downstream.

Source: International Joint Commission.

*In a mass-balance model, the amount of a contaminant entering the system, minus the amount retained or transformed, equals the amount leaving the system.

profile of the long-range transport problems.* It has been a major issue in Canadian-U.S. relations for more than a decade, because much of the acid rain falling in Canada is attributed to sources in the United States, and the United States has failed to adopt a national program to address it.

Damages to aquatic ecosystems—fish deaths and changes in food webs—are perhaps the best-documented adverse effects of acid deposition.[28] In eastern Canada, Canadian scientists estimate that about 14,000 lakes have been acidified, and many thousands more are vulnerable.[29] In regional studies of acidic lakes, U.S. researchers have found that the Upper Peninsula of Michigan, where 9 percent of the lakes have acidities of less than pH 5.0, is third, behind the Adirondacks and Florida in number of acidic lakes.[30]† In north-central Wisconsin, 41 percent of the lakes are especially acid-sensitive; that is, they have very limited ability to neutralize the acids added to them.[31]

Deposition of nitrogen oxides from the atmosphere may also contribute to rising levels of nitrogen in the Great Lakes. The IJC's Water Quality Board has expressed concern about rising levels of nitrates and nitrites in the lakes.[32] These levels have risen steadily for at least 20 years. They remain far below regulatory levels established for drinking water, however, and hence are not regarded as a threat to human health.[33]

Acid deposition is also thought by many to contribute to forest decline in eastern Canada and the eastern United States, although it has proved difficult to distinguish acid's impact from those of other air pollutants and natural stresses.[34] Concern over acid deposition is not limited to its effects on natural systems; the pollutants that contribute to its formation can adversely affect human health.[35]

The acid deposition problem serves as a reminder of the increasing scope and scale of pollution problems. During the 1960s, large percentages of emissions of sulfur dioxide came from tall stacks.[36] During the 1970s, very tall stacks (such as the "superstack" at Sudbury, Ontario) were sometimes used to reduce the local impact of emissions,

*Acid deposition is the deposit to the surface of the earth of acidic or acidifying materials from the atmosphere in wet or dry form.

†Readings on the pH scale, from 0-14, are measures of acidity and alkalinity. 7.0 is neutral; lemon juice has a pH of about 2.0. The scale is logarithmic so that, for example, a change from 6.0 to 5.0 represents a tenfold increase in acidity. Few fish species can survive in water with pH less than 5.0.

but these merely thrust the emissions higher in the atmosphere, transferring the damage to more distant locations.[37]

Regional ozone and acid deposition problems, the long-range transport of contaminants that bioaccumulate in the Great Lakes food web,
and growing appreciation for the complex character of urban air pollution all serve as a reminder that adopting an ecosystem approach to
the Great Lakes will not be easy. Some solutions must be found within
the Great Lakes basin, but clearing the air will require substantial
action far beyond it.

## THE PROSPECT OF CHANGING CLIMATE IN THE GREAT LAKES BASIN

Clearly, the attempt to adopt an ecosystem approach in the Great Lakes
basin has been handicapped immeasurably by inadequate data. That
is not surprising: Only when an ecosystem approach was adopted in
1978 did it become evident how much needed to be discovered about
the relationships among so many different ecosystem components.
Progress toward a healthy and sustainable ecosystem and economy in
the Great Lakes basin will take time—several decades at least. The
progress that has been made in the two decades since environmental
concern for the Great Lakes became acute makes such a time perspective less discouraging than it might be otherwise.

However, a major and largely unexpected complication has been
added to the task: the prospect of significant change in the climate of
the Great Lakes basin even as the attempt is being made to restore
ecosystem health. Increasingly, it seems as though restoration of ecosystem health will need to be defined in terms of climate conditions
that are unlike those of today and that indeed have no precedent in the
period of human history.

By now, few people are totally unaware of current scientific concern
for the "greenhouse effect," caused by increases in atmospheric concentrations of carbon dioxide and other "greenhouse gases."* The
implications, especially in the next 40 to 60 years, were examined at
an international conference that took place in 1988 in Toronto. Par-

---

*Combustion of fossil fuels is a major source of greenhouse gases. The Great Lakes
states produce 29 percent of the carbon emitted from all fossil fuel burning in the
United States. Reducing fossil fuel burning would also lower emissions of trace
metals.[38]

ticipants at the conference concluded that among the changes to be anticipated by a continuation of present trends is a rise in the mean surface temperature of the Earth of 2.5°F to 8°F (1.5°C to 4.5°C) before the middle of the 21st century. Further:

> Marked regional variations in the amount of warming are expected. For example at high latitudes the warming may be twice the global average. Also, the warming would be accompanied by changes in the amount and distribution of rainfall and in atmospheric and ocean circulation patterns.[39]

The uncertainty associated with such estimates is considerable. In particular, longitudinal (east-west) changes are less easy to estimate than are latitudinal changes. Defining the probable effects within a specific area such as the Great Lakes basin is therefore highly speculative.

However, if the changes are anywhere near the magnitude foreseen by some,[40] it is evident that the effect on the Great Lakes basin ecosystem will be profound (figure 5.9). For example, the forest species

## Figure 5.9
## Potential Effects of Global Climate Change on the Great Lakes Region*

| Variable | Effect |
|---|---|
| Temperature | Average annual temperature up by 4-5 degrees C. Winter warmer by 5-6 degrees C and summer warmer by 3-4 degrees C. |
| Precipitation | Up |
| Evaporation and evapotranspiration | Up enough to overshadow precipitation increases. |
| Runoff | Down |
| Snowpack | Reduced by 50 to 100 percent |
| Snow season | Shortened by 2 to 4 weeks |
| Ice cover | Reduced, perhaps gone |
| Soil moisture | Reduced |
| Supply of water | Reduced by 15 to 30 percent |
| Great Lakes water levels | Reduced |

*General conditions to be expected in the Great Lakes region from a doubling of carbon dioxide in the earth's atmosphere

Source: Institute for Research on Public Policy.

now growing over a large proportion of the basin may, within the lifetime of a single stand, be incompatible with the climate of the future—a change that would have immense economic and ecological implications. Some crops such as corn and soybeans may become uneconomic because of drought conditions, while horticulture may become more feasible.[41] Winter skiing may disappear from the southern part of the basin, at least as a commercially viable activity.

Among the most obvious effects are those to be expected from changes in the character of the Great Lakes themselves. These changes include the prospects of a longer shipping season, as ice forms later and breaks up earlier. But the substantial lowering of lake levels that is expected might make it more difficult to enter certain ports without increased dredging (chapter 4, figure 4.13). Lower levels would also have profound implications for shoreline use and protection, wetlands, and practically every other aspect of the Great Lakes ecosystem and economy. A recent study of Lake Erie, for example, suggests that over half the marinas that currently exist would be inoperable if the lake declined to the levels anticipated.[42]

There is too little space in this volume to examine the implications of climate change in the Great Lakes basin in substantial detail. More research is needed before the consequences of the greenhouse effect for the basin can be evaluated with any confidence. When that research is conducted (and much of the necessary research and data collection is already being initiated), it may be both possible and necessary to adjust the objectives and management strategies of the ecosystem approach to the conditions probable within a few decades. Since the greenhouse effect is a global phenomenon, similar adjustments and forward-looking strategies will be needed worldwide. Because an ecosystem approach to the problems of the present has been adopted, the Great Lakes basin is already in a better position to cope with future changes than is much of the rest of the world.

# Chapter 6

# Fish, Wildlife, and Habitat

Our fate is connected with the animals.
—Rachel Carson, *Silent Spring*, 1962

[T]oxic chemicals ... may ... exert adverse biological effects at dilute concentrations and bioaccumulate in aquatic organisms in the food chain to toxic proportions.... Organisms exhibiting these effects are potentially useful as an early warning system to alert to potential threats to humans and biota.
—International Joint Commission (IJC),
*Second Biennial Report*, 1984

Crashes in fishery stocks, gross defects and population declines in birds, and the death of ranch mink and their offspring when fed Lake Michigan coho salmon were early signals about 30 years ago of major problems in the health of the Great Lakes ecosystem. The problems reported stemmed from overharvesting, habitat disruption, and toxic chemicals. Today, fish and wildlife populations continue to be endangered in areas of high contamination. Even if chemical stresses are reduced, fish and wildlife populations cannot thrive if suitable habitat is unavailable. Experience also shows that, if harvesting practices are not controlled carefully, populations of targeted species will crash.

## ORGANISMS AT THE BASE OF THE
## GREAT LAKES FOOD WEB

Scientific and popular interest in the organisms of the Great Lakes basin has generally been concentrated on the animals, birds, and fish close to the top of the food web. However, as noted in chapter 2,

131

these organisms depend for their well-being on the stability of the food web at lower levels. Healthy conditions at the base of the food web are crucial to the survival of organisms higher up.

Far less is known about the microscopic organisms at the base of the food web—phytoplankton and zooplankton—than about the higher organisms, particularly with respect to the effects of toxic contamination. The state of knowledge about phytoplankton was summarized in a recent report:

> Phytoplankton, as a collective group, generally are sensitive to toxicants. Because of their rapid physiological response and short generation time, it is possible to detect deleterious effects of toxicants in relatively short periods of time.... [However,] the ability to predict the effects of a toxicant on natural phytoplankton communities is confounded by a variety of physical and biological factors that make data interpretation difficult.[1]

The same is true of the zooplankton: "Very little information exists on the effects of toxic substances on the community structure of Great Lakes zooplankton."[2] Additionally, it is known that benthic (bottom-dwelling organisms) communities evolve in response to toxic contamination from diversity to predominence by less desirable organisms.[3]

The lower levels in the food web are also sensitive to levels of nutrients. Excess nutrients in Lake Erie and other lakes caused massive production of algae; consumption of oxygen during the bacterial decomposition of these algae reduced the dissolved oxygen in the water, depriving other organisms of the oxygen they needed to survive. In another instance, the amount of dissolved silica in Lake Michigan declined after 1954 to levels that, by 1969, appeared to have limited diatom growth. As noted in chapter 4, a crash of the diatom population would eventually be reflected throughout the food web. Throughout the Great Lakes, levels of nitrate plus nitrite have increased in recent years; at present there is insufficient knowledge to determine whether this is likely to have beneficial or harmful impact at lower levels of the food web.[4]

## ORGANISMS AT THE TOP OF THE GREAT LAKES FOOD WEB

Generalizations about the health of animals at the top of the food web are based mainly on individual studies of specific species or populations and on data from programs that regularly monitor selected fish species and herring gulls. If the results of these individual studies and data bases are reviewed and compared, some disturbing trends and convergences become apparent. Figure 6.1, for example, summarizes reports in the scientific literature on the state of wildlife populations, focusing on identifiable health effects.

In many instances, where troubled populations have been observed around the Great Lakes, relatively high concentrations of at least one contaminant have been found in individual animals (in at least nine species) and in the eggs of egg-laying species.[5] Animals, such as bald eagles and mink, that live near the shoreline where pollution is greatest have been found to accumulate more toxic substances than do members of the same species living inland. The inland populations of eagles also show fewer signs of trouble.[6] (See box, "The Bald Eagle")

Despite the *association* between health effects and concentrations of contaminants, it is very difficult to prove that individual contaminants have *caused* specific effects in wildlife populations (see box, "Toxic Substances and Health Effects in Wildlife"). Efforts to prove cause-and-effect relationships through controlled laboratory experiments have only limited application to the natural ecosystem, because of uncertainties about exposure, consumption habits, and other characteristics of animals in wild conditions. Despite unexpected and significant population declines among many Great Lakes species, the only specific chemicals to which a cause-and-effect relationship in wildlife has so far been assigned unequivocally are DDT and the product to which it decays, DDE; these have been shown to cause eggshell thinning (and therefore reproductive failure) in bird species.[7]

The problem of linking cause with effect, even in relatively straightforward situations, was illustrated by a 1983 study that showed "clear impairment of the reproductive capacity of Forster's terns on Green Bay."[8] Poor hatchability, lower body weight, increased ratio of liver weight to body weight, edema, low numbers of hatchlings maturing to the point where they were able to fly, poor nest success, and parental abandonment were all noted in the Green Bay colony. Predation also contributed to poor nesting success. Some of these characteristics had been described in earlier literature as known effects of dioxins and PCBs in species of birds.

As part of the study, eggs were exchanged between the "dirty" Green Bay colony and a "clean" inland colony, and eggs from both colonies were also placed in artificial incubators. The results suggested that both intrinsic factors (embryotoxicity and chick mortality) and extrinsic factors (such as lack of parental care) contributed

## Figure 6.1
## Population, Organism, and Tissue Effects Found in Great Lakes Animals

| Species | Population Decline | Reproduct. Effects | Eggshell Thinning | "Wasting" | Gross Defects | Tumors | Target Organ | Immune Suppress. | Behavioral Changes | Generational Effects |
|---|---|---|---|---|---|---|---|---|---|---|
| Bald eagle | x | x | x | x | | | x | | | x |
| Beluga whale | x | x | n/a | | | x | x | x | | |
| Black-crowned night heron | x | | | | x | | x | | | |
| Caspian tern | x | x | | x | x | | | | x | |
| Chinook/coho salmon | n/a | x | n/a | x | x | x | x | | x | x |
| Common tern | x | | | x | | | x | | x | |
| Double-crested cormorant | x | x | | | x | | x | x | x | |
| Forster's tern | x | x | x | x | x | | x | | x | x |
| Herring gull | x | x | x | x | x | | x | x | x | x |
| Lake trout | x | x | n/a | x | x | | x | | x | x |
| Mink | x | x | n/a | x | | | x | | x | x |
| Osprey | x | x | x | | | | | | | |
| Otter | x | | n/a | | | | | | | |
| Ring-billed gull | x | | x | x | | | x | x | | |
| Snapping turtle | x | x | | x | x | | x | | | x |

x = Observed effects that have been reported in the literature. Cells not marked do not necessarily mean there is no effect; only that no citation was found.

n/a = Not applicable.

Source: The Conservation Foundation.

## The Bald Eagle

The bald eagle has been in North America for a million years. It is an opportunistic carnivore, scavenging for carrion, stealing food from other birds, and preying on other live animals. Since the last of these activities requires the most energy, it is the least preferred. During a typical 24-hour day in winter, the bald eagle will roost for 68 percent of the time, loaf for 30 percent, fly 1 percent, and feed for the remaining 1 percent. Despite all this adaptation to energy conservation, the bird still requires about 450 to 500 calories per day, from a protein-rich diet that is high in fats.[1]

Of the million years of its existence, the last 100 may have been the most precarious for the bald eagle. At the turn of the century, bounties were being paid for the "unwanted and dirty predator"; its habitat was also being reduced, especially on the U.S. side of the Great Lakes basin, by forest clearance and other human activity. But early in the 20th century, the bald eagle became the object of increased protection and seemed to be recovering well until the 1940s. Then came a rapid population decline in the continental United States and in some areas of Canada.

Following the banning and restric-tion of DDT and dieldrin, most of the troubled populations across North America made remarkable recoveries. Unfortunately, this was not so in the Great Lakes. In 1986, there were reported to be only 25 nests on the Lake Superior shoreline, 4 on Lake Michigan, 4 on Lake Huron, and 12 at the western end of Lake Erie. There were no nests on Lake Ontario. A small population of six pairs remained on the north shore of Lake Erie through the 1970s and early 1980s.[2] Nesting success along the shores has been relatively poor when compared with inland populations.[3]

The bald eagle's preference for fish and birds (herring gulls in some instances in the Great Lakes) and other aquatic food sources has made it particularly vulnerable to chemicals that biomagnify in the system. The bald eagle is an excellent indicator of toxic contamination because it sits at the top of the food web.[4]

Because of the eagle's position and sensitivity, the Ecosystem Objectives Subcommittee of the Great Lakes Science Advisory Board recommended in 1989 that "the bald eagle ... be used as an ecosystem objective to define the virtual elimination of persistent toxic substances

to the lack of nesting success in the Green Bay colony as compared to the clean colony. There were also significantly higher concentrations of PCBs and dioxins in the Green Bay eggs, but it was noted that other compounds "should not be discounted as causative factors in the reproductive impairment of nesting Forster's terns on Green Bay."[9] The indications of toxic effects were clear, but cause and effect could not be established indisputably. The weight of evidence suggests that the basic causes of the problems of the Forster's terns were PCBs and dioxins, but other causes have not been completely ruled out.[10]

from the Great Lakes Basin Ecosystem."[5] As recommended, the objective would specify how many pairs of eagles live around the lakes, how productive they are, and what should be the maximum concentrations of toxic substances in eagle eggs and brains.

*America's national symbol has had difficulty reproducing along the shores of the Great Lakes.*

Dave Kenyon/Michigan Dept. of Natural Resources

## Reproduction Problems and Population Decline

Researchers have found that animal species at the top of the Great Lakes food web have shown occasional and, in some cases, long-term reproductive problems and/or population declines since the 1950s. Among these are the bald eagle,[11] black-crowned night heron,[12] Caspian tern,[13] common tern,[14] double-crested cormorant,[15] Forster's tern,[16] herring gull,[17] osprey,[18] and ring-billed gull;[19] the Beluga whale,[20] mink, and otter;[21] the lake trout;[22] and the snapping turtle.[23] All of

## Toxic Substances and Health Effects in Wildlife: The Challenge of Linking Cause and Effect

How do environmental scientists prove that a chemical caused an observed effect in wild populations of organisms? This issue is not new to human health specialists or epidemiologists, who have developed criteria to test their ideas and evidence for a variety of diseases, but the concept of applying the criteria to fish and wildlife diseases is new.

At a 1989 meeting hosted by the International Joint Commission, researchers discussed the criteria and applied them to evidence linking chemicals found in the Great Lakes to effects found in fish, wildlife, and human populations. The first criterion is *time order*: Can it be shown that the effect occurred only after exposure to the suspected chemical and not beforehand? The second is *strength of association*, related to how often the effect is seen in the populations exposed to the suspected chemical in comparison with the frequency in an unexposed population. The third criterion, *specificity*, addresses the fact that some chemicals cause very specific effects and that some effects are caused only by specific chemicals. The fourth, *consistency on replication*, considers whether the effect still occurs when populations are exposed in different

places and at different times and whether other related species are also affected when they are exposed. The fifth criterion, *coherence*, considers whether the supposed causal linkage makes biological sense, whether it fits with existing biological facts and theory, and whether there is a plausible biological mechanism for the observed effect. If the evidence linking a relationship between an observed effect and a suspected chemical holds up for these five criteria, there is a strong inference that the chemical caused the effect. However, a strong inference does not mean that the link has been proved.

The workshop presentations demonstrated the value of the five criteria as a valid way to discuss case histories in wild populations as well as in humans. Presentations at the workshop also showed that, for many of the case studies, vital pieces of information do not exist. The studies together imply, however, that the presence of persistent toxic substances in the Great Lakes has caused significant effects on the reproduction and survival of populations of fish and wildlife. The findings reported at the workshop are a warning for humans, as discussed more fully in chapter 7.[1]

these animals derive their sustenance from animals in the Great Lakes food web, especially fish.

## Metabolic Changes

Ten species, including mammals, birds, reptiles, and fish, showed changes in fat metabolism and disposition of body fat. In extreme circumstances, a condition called ''wasting'' was reported: The animals appeared lethargic, lost their appetites and weight, and eventually died. In some cases, emaciated and dead birds exhibited low body fat and high concentrations of organochlorines.[24]

## Birth Deformities

Species of mammals, reptiles, birds, and fishes in the Great Lakes basin have also shown birth defects significantly more prevalent than in control populations less exposed to toxic contaminants.[25] The most publicized of these are found in chicks in colonies of double-crested cormorants; born with crossed bills, they are unable to feed themselves after leaving the nest. In four island colonies in Green Bay, between 1983 and 1987, bill defects in young birds were 42 times greater than in colonies outside the Great Lakes basin.[26] Other birth defects encountered in both double-crested cormorants and other bird species include club feet, shortened appendages, missing eyes, no brains, major organs outside the body, and abnormal accumulations of fluid in tissue (edema/ascites).[27]

*Double-crested cormorant embryos from two northern Green Bay colonies. Birds are suffering from defects such as ascites (abdominal or subcutaneous edema), gastroschisis (stomach outside body), unmetabolized yolk sac, crossed bills, and hemorrhaging.*

U.S. Fish and Wildlife Service

## Hormonal Changes

Samples of herring gulls from Lake Ontario collected in 1975 and 1976 showed cellular and anatomical changes in embryos and newly hatched chicks that caused feminization of male chicks and overdevelopment of female reproductive organs. Elevated concentrations of DDE and other residues were found in eggs from the same population.[28]*

## Tumors

Tumors have been observed in whales in the estuary of the St. Lawrence River (see box).[30] In addition, unusual numbers of facial tumors, both benign and malignant, have been reported in various Great Lakes fish species such as the brown bullhead, a bottom-feeding catfish.[31] Extensive epidemiological, pathological, and histological† research also clearly demonstrates that this and other fish species develop liver tumors in the presence of known carcinogens and carcinogen-containing sediments.[32] However, direct cause-and-effect relationships have not been established, and other pollutants have not been ruled out. The reported occurrences of cancer and precancerous tumors are only in fish and whales, in contrast to the occurrence of other health effects distributed more widely among species.

## "Generational" Effects

In six species—the bald eagle, Caspian and Forster's terns, herring gull, lake trout, and snapping turtle—the scientific literature implies that some stress on parents (for example, exposure to chemical contaminants) affects the well-being of an embryo or newborn.[33] These effects include those problems mentioned above: metabolic, hormonal, and target-organ‡ changes that are manifested by "wasting," abnormal ontogeny (development), and immune suppression (lowering of an organism's ability to withstand disease).

---

*Western gull eggs, when injected with ambient concentrations of DDT and its estrogen-like isomers in a laboratory, became feminized.[29] In this laboratory study, males developed ovarian tissue and oviducts.

†Histological research deals with organisms' tissues.

‡Target-organ damage can occur in such organs as the thyroid, liver, kidney, or brain. Thyroid problems have been noted in herring gulls.[34] A liver condition called porphyria, aggravated by the presence of organochlorine chemicals, has been found in herring gulls in contaminated areas in the lakes.[35]

## Troubled Beluga Whale Population in the St. Lawrence Estuary

Toxic contaminants in the beluga whale population found in the St. Lawrence estuary demonstrate how far the Great Lakes food web can stretch. The belugas, found in the St. Lawrence estuary, at the confluence of the St. Lawrence with the Saguenay River, are perhaps "the most polluted mammal(s) on earth."[1] Among the 25 toxic chemicals so far discovered in these whales are 8 of the 11 critical pollutants designated by the IJC's Great Lakes Water Quality Board (see chapter 2, figure 2.3). Of particular significance is the presence of mirex and its decay product, photomirex. So far as is known, no mirex was ever produced along the St. Lawrence River or the St. Lawrence estuary. It was, however, produced by a plant near Niagara, New York, and used and accidentally spilled at a plant on the Oswego River, both in the Great Lakes basin. Present sources for mirex have been traced to these locations.

Only in 1988 was the apparent link between these sources and the whales found, in the form of Atlantic eels migrating from the Great Lakes to the Atlantic Ocean. It appears that the eels accumulate the mirex in or near Lake Ontario; from the amount of mirex found in the whales, it is estimated that each whale consumes 194 pounds (88 kilograms) of eels annually, more than 600 miles (960 kilometers) from the presumed origin of the chemical.[2]

Concentrations of organic chemicals have been found in the whales' fat at levels higher than those of other animal species exhibiting reproductive losses.[3] Both tumors and target-organ damage have been found, as well as probable suppression of immune responses. This population of whales, once hunted, has been reduced to approximately 10 percent of its estimated size of a century ago, despite protective measures undertaken since 1950. A simulation model constructed by scientists suggests that above average mortality of young adults may be contributing to the population decline.[4] Habitat destruction may also be a factor.

## Behavioral Changes

Health effects in wildlife may be behavioral as well as physiological. For example, it is increasingly suggested that apparent "indifference" to incubating eggs by parent gulls, nocturnal abandonment of incubation by terns (making owl predation easy), and behavioral problems in lake trout fry (for example, swimming upside down) may be attributed to toxic chemicals.[36] Female/female pairing of herring gulls was reported in northeastern Lake Michigan in 1978.[37]* However,

---

*Western gulls, on Santa Barbara Island off the coast of California, were observed with the same condition. Up to 14 percent of the nests of gulls in this colony exhibited double clutching, attended by two females.[38]

most studies of wildlife behavior have not been combined with analyses of chemical contamination.

## LINKING WILDLIFE EFFECTS WITH LABORATORY STUDIES

The challenge remains to demonstrate *causal relationships* between chemicals and health effects. Evidence from animal studies in laboratories is especially noteworthy. *Associations* between wasting (body weight loss, loss of weight gain), immune suppression (thymus gland atrophy), birth defects (cleft palate), and exposure to certain PCB congeners* and 2,3,7,8-TCDD (dioxin) have been demonstrated in laboratory animals.[39]

Reproductive and developmental effects have been reported for all of the IJC's critical pollutants except toxaphene.[40] All have been found to be immunotoxic in animal or animal tissue studies.[41] All, except benzo[a]pyrene, are neurotoxic in animals.[42] Several chemicals have been found to cause birth defects and physical deformities, immunotoxic and neurotoxic effects in the offspring of exposed animals, and decreased birth weights and suppressed weight gain in the offspring.[43]

Many of the same anomalies have been reported in a number of Great Lakes wildlife species (see figure 6.1). Not all chemicals have been tested for these effects. With recent improvements in technology, scientists are gaining an improved appreciation of the mechanisms of action by which chemicals affect organisms, particularly at the cellular level, although much more needs to be learned (see box, "Chemical Action"). Even lacking full understanding of cause and effect, the many associations found thus far between concentrations of chemicals and harm to wildlife provide compelling justification for controlling the chemicals and reducing exposures.

## HABITAT DESTRUCTION, HUMAN DISTURBANCE, AND EXPLOITATION

Physical restructuring of much of the Great Lakes has placed considerable stress on wildlife populations. Such restructuring includes forest removal, draining of wetlands, damming of streams, widespread in-

---

*PCBs are found in 209 configurations (congeners), some of which are more toxic than others.

## Chemical Action at the Cellular and Subcellular Level

Breakthroughs in understanding what residues of toxic chemicals in wildlife and animal tissue mean in terms of health have been made by researchers in laboratories working at the cellular and subcellular level. Researchers are rapidly accumulating information that provides a picture of the mechanism of action of these chemicals. For instance, it is now evident that several PCB, dioxin, and furan congeners have similar effects at the cellular level.[1] Separating their effects in wildlife may be impossible, however, because they are generally found together in most samples.

The difficulty of establishing causal relationships between toxic substances and an adverse health effect is also exacerbated by the multitude of the mechanisms of action of so many of the toxic substances. Individual substances have more than one effect and more than one target site of effect. In other words, their effects can be very general. For example:

- DDE, dieldrin, lindane, mirex, PCBs, and toxaphene block communication between cells. Normal metabolism and development of a cell may be disrupted because movement of nutrients, electrolytes, and hormones in and out of the cell is blocked by the presence of the contaminants.[2]

- 2,3,7,8-TCDD, furans, benzo[a]pyrene, chlordane, DDE, dieldrin, HCB (hexachlorobenzene), b-HCH (an isomer of lindane), mirex, PCBs, and toxaphene induce enzyme activity. In most instances, this activity transforms these substances to a more soluble form, thereby enhancing their excretion from the body (2,3,7,8-TCDD is an exception). During induction, normal products of the endocrine hormone system can be released in this manner as well. This activity may disrupt the role of steroid hormones in the endocrine system, affecting growth and sexual maturation, although the extent of this impact is not fully known.[3]

- Except for benzo[a]pyrene, the literature suggests that all of the critical pollutants are capable of upsetting the normal endocrine balance in laboratory animals. The structures of DDT/DDE are quite similar to an estrogen hormone. In addition, DDE induces enzymes that break down male hormones. Dioxin is known to be both a pro-estrogen and antiestrogen. As enzyme inducers, a number of chemicals of concern enhance the breakdown of steroid hormones.[4]

troduction of monoculture agriculture, urbanization, and industrialization (see box, ''Wetlands Drainage''). Energy intensive recreational use of basin resources, such as boating, waterskiing, snowmobiling, and use of all-terrain vehicles, can be particularly stressful on wildlife populations during nesting periods or during the winter (when animals may be having difficulty satisfying their energy needs).

Because there have been no systematic censuses of historic popu-

## Wetlands Drainage and Protection

The biological productivity of wetland areas is enormous, and they play a vital role in the life cycle of many of the most significant fish and wildlife species in the Great Lakes basin. For example, the marshes, estuaries, lagoons, and channels that make up the wetlands of the St. Clair River delta "are among the most productive areas in the Great Lakes."[1] These areas provide spawning habitat for more than a dozen fish species, as well as resting places for huge numbers of ducks using the Atlantic and Mississippi flyways, and constitute exceptional habitat for many species of land-based wildlife.[2]

Economic growth along the shores of the Great Lakes, especially in the southern zone, has caused profound changes in the character of the shoreline. In effect, a shoreline has often been created by human action, replacing wetlands that existed before the period of European settlement. These wetlands often formed part of much larger wetland areas in the basin (figure 6.2). It has been estimated, for example, that almost one-third of the land area of Michigan was once wetland.[3] Wetlands covered 60 percent of southwest Ontario (Essex, Kent, and Lambton counties).[4] At the western end of Lake Erie, a wetland shore between the Maumee River and Sandusky Bay extended as the Black Swamp for 1,500 square miles (3,885 square kilometers) southwestward across the Indiana state line. By the early 1900s, the swamp had been almost entirely drained for agriculture(figure 6.3).[5] In both the United States and Canada, wetland drainage was traditionally regarded as development and improvement.

Over the last 20 years or more, however, in both countries, there has been growing awareness of the crucial ecological role of wetlands and a growing consensus that remaining wetlands should be protected and, if possible, extended. In principle, this goal should be achievable, if only because most of the wetlands suitable for development were drained long ago. Some areas drained for agricultural use have indeed already been abandoned and could revert to a more natural state.[6] In practice, however, subsidy and other programs promoting agricultural wetland conversion still continue in Ontario.[7] Some forms of development (for example, shopping malls) also find wetland conversion economically attractive, even without government subsidies.

The attention being given to wetlands protection by governments and conservation groups in the United States and Canada indicates a growing recognition of the role that wetlands play in the ecosystem.[8] The changing attitudes appear to be bringing about a reconsideration of policies and programs that have long encouraged wetland drainage, particularly for agricultural use.

lations of wildlife in the basin, there is no way to estimate the extent of damage to wildlife caused by habitat destruction. However, more information is available concerning the impact of harvesting, especially of fish, as discussed in the fishery section below.

Distant habitat destruction can be as threatening to Great Lakes wildlife as local changes. For example, the wood duck was almost

## Figure 6.2
## Wetland Losses in the Great Lakes Region*

| Location / Area | Wetland Assessment |
|---|---|
| Southwestern Ontario | 80% loss since presettlement |
| Southern Ontario | 61% loss since presettlement |
| Lake St. Clair wetlands | 85% loss since presettlement |
| Minnesota | 76% loss since 1953 |
| Wisconsin | 50% loss since presettlement |
| Illinois | 90% loss since presettlement |
| Indiana | 86% loss in areas studied |
|  | 71% loss in northern Indiana |
| Michigan | 71% loss since presettlement |
| Ohio | loss of almost the entire 1,500 sq. mi. Black Swamp |
| Pennsylvania | no overall assessment found |
| New York | no overall assessment found |

*Estimates are state- or province-wide unless otherwise noted.

Source: Weller (1988).

## Figure 6.3
## Presettlement Extent of the Black Swamp in Northwestern Ohio

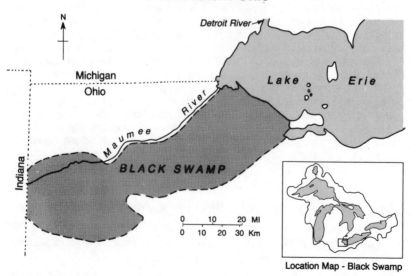

Source: Forsyth (1960).

extirpated in the early 1900s as the result of overharvesting. In the aftermath of the signing in 1918 by Canada and the United States of a treaty to protect migratory birds, the wood duck made a remarkable comeback.[44] It was protected until 1941, when hunting was again permitted. The wood duck depends on calm water, beaver ponds, wooded cover, and cavities for nesting, but, equally important, it needs swamps for overwintering. As with many migrating species, protection of this species depends upon preservation of critical habitat in areas thousands of miles distant. Increased channelization of swamps in the American South, where the wood duck overwinters, is threatening its existence.

## The Piping Plover and Lynx

The impact of habitat destruction and human disturbance is illustrated by two species of Great Lakes animals, the piping plover and the lynx, which have dramatically different habitat needs.

Of the some 2,000 breeding pairs of piping plovers in the United States and Canada, fewer than 20 pairs spend the summer in the Great Lakes region.[45] Although this species of plover was once able to breed on the shores of all of the Great Lakes states, it now breeds successfully only in six counties in northern Michigan.[46] The piping plover occupies a very fragile, dynamic, and limited habitat; the species usually makes its nests on barren sand or gravel beaches adjacent to dunes.[47] In many areas, this type of habitat is subject to significant stresses, caused by beach stabilization efforts, water level fluctuations, and recreational use.[48] Because of its responsiveness to habitat alteration and human disturbance, the piping plover serves as a sensitive indicator of stress on a very ephemeral segment of the ecosystem.

The U.S. Fish and Wildlife Service (FWS) has prepared a recovery plan for the piping plover, pursuant to the federal Endangered Species Act. Unlike all other piping plover populations that are listed as threatened, piping plover populations on the Great Lakes are listed as endangered. The plan aims to foster the recovery of the piping plover population so that 150 pairs will breed in the Great Lakes region, including 100 in Michigan, 15 in Wisconsin and Minnesota, and 35 elsewhere.[49] After extensive information gathering, land acquisition and management options will be reviewed, and action taken based on priorities: (a) to prevent extinction, (b) to maintain current population levels, and (c) to provide full recovery of the species. Habitat acqui-

*Piping plover photographed near Grand Marais, Michigan, along shoreline of Lake Superior.*

Dave Kenyon/Michigan Dept. of Natural Resources

sition, restricting human disturbance, and protecting winter habitat are a few steps to be taken.[50]

Lynx are distributed widely throughout Canada. Populations generally follow 10-year cycles of highs and lows. In years of high population, lynx are found occasionally in the upper Great Lakes states. The species lives in climax boreal* forests having a dense understory; a lynx can range as much as 18 miles per day. Its prime food source is the snowshoe hare. The lynx population declined severely around the turn of the century because of overhunting, but by the 1960s the lynx had reappeared in much of its former range. However, within recent years the peaks of the population cycles have decreased considerably. It is speculated that increased trapping along the southern

---

*A climax boreal forest is a northern forest in the final stage of ecological succession.

edge of the lynx's range, human interference, and habitat destruction are the cause of the dips in peak population. There is concern that excess trapping during low points in the cycle may reduce the chance of maintaining an adequate breeding stock.[51]

## Protection Strategies for Wildlife Species

In 1987, the IJC's Science Advisory Board launched a project to review and evaluate practical means for identifying and protecting important "natural heritage areas." The project may lead to development of Heritage Area Security Plans, natural area counterparts to the Remedial Action Plans being developed for the 42 degraded Areas of Concern around the lakes. This project, together with a related project funded by a private Canadian foundation, has assembled information on known protected and unprotected areas along the coastal zone of the Great Lakes. The project's long-range goal is:

> to create a system of protected areas along the Lakes that would collectively protect sufficient examples of the full range of diversity to be found there, as well as areas of critical importance for fish and wildlife. Priorities for developing this system would then go to securing sites that filled important "gaps."[52]

This project demonstrates how the ecosystem approach embodied in the Water Quality Agreement encourages cooperative action beyond the achievement of traditional water quality objectives. It also suggests how a broad basinwide perspective can be useful in setting priorities. For example, a report from a project workshop noted that:

> Blanchard's Cricket Frog[s] (Acris crepitans blanchardi), known historically from about six sites in southern Ontario, now occur at only two sites on Pelee Island. Thus, they are rare and endangered in Canada. However, they are alive and well throughout much of the rest of their range in the Great Lakes basin, so expensive efforts to save them on the island would be a dubious venture.[53]

In a related effort, the Nature Conservancy of Canada and the Nature Conservancy of the United States have begun establishing a Canadian National Conservation Data Center, fashioned after the natural heritage programs established by The Nature Conservancy in the 50 states. Work begun in Ontario should benefit the protection efforts in the Great Lakes basin. This cross-boundary cooperation by the two private organizations, which rarely had coordinated their efforts in the past, provides yet another example of the importance of private transboundary efforts for ecosystem protection in the Great Lakes.[54]

## FISH IN THE GREAT LAKES

The history, present state, and future of the Great Lakes fishery are matters on which there are strong divergences of opinion and on which opinions and emotions are easily aroused and strongly held. Much of this can be traced to the character of the fishery as a common property resource—a resource that has considerable economic significance but is shared among many users instead of being owned or rented as is farmland. As Garrett Hardin pointed out 20 years ago, the tragedy of such common property resources is that economically rational behavior by individuals may ultimately lead to destruction of the resource.[55]

Since fish are an economic resource, a potential conflict exists between maximizing economic returns from it and restoring and maintaining ecosystem health. At the extreme, there is no conflict: if a lake has become too polluted to support fish life, then the ecosystem is not healthy and the fishery resource does not exist. But to assume that "what is good for the fishery resource is good for the ecosystem" is an oversimplification. On land, agriculture usually attempts to maximize the value of the resource, but such efforts can often have severe repercussions on the wider environment. More broadly, agriculture almost always involves the replacement of the natural ecosystem by a manipulated or artificial ecosystem. The same is increasingly true of fisheries, especially in enclosed areas such as the Great Lakes.

From the perspective of current environmental quality and future policy options, three principal sets of factors can be seen to interact with one another, though the effects of these factors both in the past and at present are extremely diverse. These main factors are: (*a*) differences in natural characteristics from one lake to another (and even from one part of the same lake to another); (*b*) the respective roles of commercial, sport, and subsistence fisheries; and (*c*) factors directly contributing to the decline or rehabilitation of individual species and fish stocks.

### Natural Characteristics

Although comparisons are frequently made between the relatively healthy conditions in the upper lakes (especially Superior and Huron) and the problems of the recent past in the lower lakes, significant natural differences between the lakes as fish habitats have always existed. Lake Erie, shallower and in a warmer latitude than Lake Superior, does not offer ideal habitat for oligotrophic (cold water) species such

## Figure 6.4
## Selected Fish Species in the Great Lakes

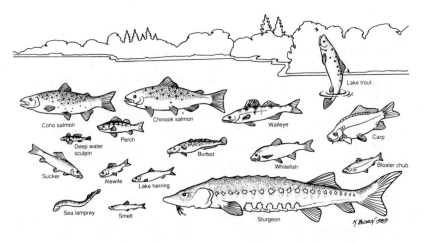

Source: Grzimek (1974); Kuchenberg and Legault (1978); Scott and Crossman (1973).

as whitefish and lake trout. (Figure 6.4 displays several of the different species in the lakes.) The latter have in the past sustained robust populations in the deeper parts of Lake Erie, but they are near the southern limits of their range and were therefore more vulnerable to stresses such as overfishing, loss of spawning grounds, competition from other species (including exotics), and climate change.

The comparative warmth of Lake Erie has been suggested as a reason why the sea lamprey did not thrive there and had comparatively little destructive effect after its appearance there in 1921.* In contrast, it thrived in the colder waters of the upper lakes and devastated their fisheries.[56]

There are also obvious differences between Lake Ontario and the other lakes. Lake Ontario is easily reached by fish moving upstream from the St. Lawrence River, but Niagara Falls is a formidable barrier to their movement further upstream to the other lakes (although exotic species have managed to move further upstream via canals and boats). Lake Ontario is quite deep (especially as compared to Lake Erie), and

---

*It has also been suggested that the lamprey did not thrive in Lake Erie for lack of satisfactory spawning areas.

it was the home (until the late 19th century) of an indigenous land-locked population of Atlantic salmon. Much debate has been devoted to the question of whether the sea lamprey was indigenous to the lake or arrived via early canals. It was certainly present in the lake by 1850.[57]

## Commercial, Sport, and Subsistence Fisheries

Fishing in the Great Lakes can be separated into three types: commercial fisheries, sport fishing, and native nations fisheries.* Subsistence fishing by native people predates large-scale settlement of the Great Lakes basin. In the last two centuries, commercial fisheries dominated until recently. There are virtually no long-term statistics on either subsistence or sport fishing.[59]

A dramatically enlarged sport fishery has been created since the 1960s. In New York State, for example, the economic benefits related to this form of recreation rose from nearly zero in 1968 to an estimated U.S.$100 million per year in 1985.[60] For all five of the Great Lakes in 1985, it was estimated that sport fishermen spent about $2 billion for angling.[61]

The transformation was caused by the decision in the 1960s to introduce fast-growing Pacific salmonids (especially the Coho salmon) into the Great Lakes on an experimental basis. At that time the early battles to control sea lampreys appeared to be having an effect. Lamprey control would, it was anticipated, ultimately benefit the native lake trout, but it was expected that lake trout would take a considerable time to reestablish themselves in large numbers. Meanwhile, it was expected that introduction of Pacific salmonids would be a powerful influence in controlling the excess numbers and biomass represented by another exotic species, the alewife. Alewives had proliferated as the population of the lake trout that preyed on them diminished (see box, "Sport versus Commerce").

The landed value of commercial fishing in the Great Lakes in 1985—about $41 million—is much smaller than the $2 billion estimated to have been spent that year by sport anglers.[62] The large differences in economic returns between sport fishing on one hand and commercial fishing on the other have encouraged Great Lakes jurisdictions to adopt

---

*There are 350,000 native people and 7,000,000 acres of federally recognized native lands within the Great Lakes-St. Lawrence River basin.[58]

*Sport fishermen displaying chinook salmon caught in Lake Huron.*

*Dave Kenyon/Michigan Dept. of Natural Resources*

policies that restrict commercial fishing in favor of angling. It is, however, not yet clear that the two activities necessarily compete severely with each other, and some jurisdictions (for example, Wisconsin and Canada) have acted to ensure the continuation of their commercial fisheries.[63]

The tension between sport and commercial fisheries increases when the rights of native people are added to the equation. For many native

## Sport versus Commerce: The Alewife in Lake Michigan[1]

The conflicts that exist between sport and commercial fishing interests may in some cases be more perceived than real, but this does not reduce their present significance. The alewife provides a good example. This small exotic followed the lamprey into the upper lakes, and because the lamprey and other factors reduced the number of predators, it rapidly became a nuisance, except in the cold waters of Lake Superior. First reported in Lake Michigan in 1949, by the 1960s it represented over 80 percent of the number of fish in the lake and half the total biomass. Such instability climaxed in spring 1967, when starvation combined with cold weather caused hundreds of millions of alewife carcasses to wash up on Lake Michigan's beaches.

The sardine-like alewife has no direct value as a sport fish, but it can be harvested commercially for use in fishmeal, fertilizer, and pet food. By 1958, the Lake Michigan commercial catch amounted to more than 500 tons (445 tonnes). This had little effect on total numbers, and, after the 1967 die off, the stocking of Lake Michigan with exotic coho and chinook salmon was, in part, an attempt to control alewife numbers.

Twenty years later, the situation has reversed itself. Now it is the continued viability of the alewife that is the focus of attention. There was a sharp decline in numbers in the early 1980s, although it is not clear whether this was due entirely to salmonid predation or whether predation was reinforced by the effects of a series of cold winters (see figure 6.5).[2] Meanwhile, alewives have come to represent over 70 percent of the diet of Lake Michigan salmon and trout, and commercial fishing for alewife is seen by sport fishing interests as competitive and threatening. As one fishery economist observed:

> Given the low commercial value of alewives, if we're trading salmon for cat food, there would be a case for reducing the alewife harvest— if an alewife shortage actually exists.[3]

Only a few decades ago the alewife was an indicator of ecosystem instability and deterioration. Now, both commercial and sport fishing depend heavily on this exotic species. Moreover, the size of the alewife population influences water quality in Lake Michigan.[4] The central role of the alewife demonstrates yet again the difficulty of developing appropriate management policies designed to restore and maintain the health of the Great Lakes ecosystem.

nations, fishing was a main or subsidiary source of food prior to 19th-century European immigration into the Great Lakes basin, and the rights to such indigenous food resources were generally retained in the treaties signed by native groups with both the Canadian and U.S. governments. This 19th-century view, which saw native fishing as essentially limited to subsistence, is being superseded by more recent policies that encourage native nations to reduce their dependence on government assistance by developing the resources available to them. From this perspective, the Great Lakes fisheries represent a resource

## Figure 6.5
## Alewife Catch in Lake Michigan, 1957–1987*

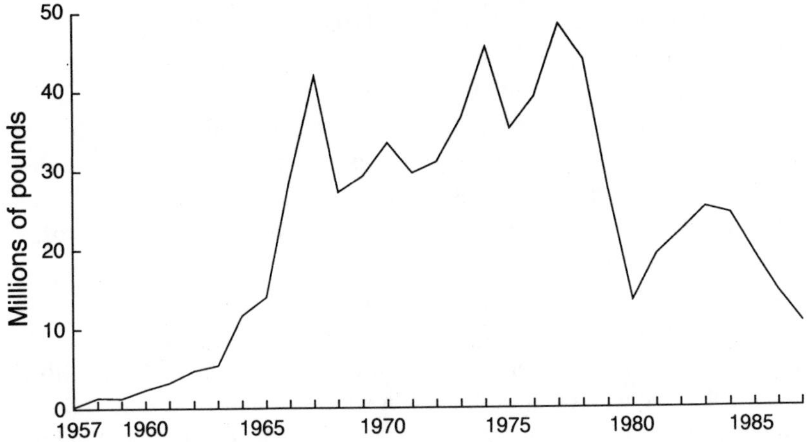

*Includes commercial harvest only.

Source: Great Lakes Fishery Commission; National Oceanic and Atmospheric Administration; Ontario Ministry of Natural Resources.

that can be developed by native nations for both commerce and recreation income, as well as for direct consumption within the group.

In recent years in both Canada and the United States, there has been considerable conflict over native fishing, sometimes with strong racial overtones.* The more extreme sport fishing interests resent the exercise of historic treaty rights, including techniques (such as spearfishing) that are not open to anglers. From the viewpoint of native peoples, their present take of both fish and other wildlife (for example, deer and waterfowl) represents a tiny fraction of the numbers harvested by others.[64]

### Ecosystem Deterioration: Environmental Damage, Overfishing, Exotics, and Toxics

"A century of change, a decade of recovery" is one recent summary of the fish resources of the Great Lakes:

---

*In the United States, the main battles have focused on the Chippewa of northern Wisconsin. In Ontario, efforts were made in the early 1980s to develop a provincewide agreement on native fishing rights, but these were beset with controversy.

virtually every major change in the fish resources of the Great Lakes during the past century was directly or indirectly caused by humans, masking any subtle effects that might have been the result of ecological succession.[65]

When Europeans reached the Great Lakes in the 17th century, about half the biomass of the lakes is estimated to have consisted of fish weighing more than 10 pounds (4.5 kilograms). Since true commercial fishing did not develop until the 19th century (and offshore fishing until the middle of that century)—it is understandable that a belief developed in the interim that the resource was inexhaustible.[66]

Even before overfishing exposed the fallacy of this belief, deforestation, fires, pollution of spawning areas by sawmills, damming of tributaries, and the conversion of coastal wetlands to agriculture or urban-industrial uses all shifted the ecological balance against the fisheries. Forest clearance, for example, increased silt and sediment flow, raised tributary water temperatures in summer, and increased the seasonal variation in stream flow. The consequent low flows in winter meant greater freezing of the stream bed and destruction of fish eggs.

Regular surveys of the United States commercial fish catch began in 1879, mainly because it had already become evident that the resource was in decline. The natural response was to increase the fishing effort, and the U.S. commercial catch reached a peak of 59,500 tons (54,091 tonnes) in 1899. Although some species, notably the sturgeon, were certainly overfished almost to extinction, the overall decline in the commercial catch was probably due to a combination of causes: not just overfishing but also destruction of habitat (especially for spawning) and possibly the indirect effect of these changes on the food web on which other fish species depended.

Similar interactions of habitat deterioration and overfishing continued during the early decades of the 20th century, including the collapse of the lake herring in Lake Erie in the mid-1920s. By that time, the sea lamprey had invaded the lake, but it was not a significant factor in the collapse.

Elsewhere, however, it was a different matter. By the end of the 1930s, the lamprey was established in all the upper lakes:

> With no natural predators in the lakes to control it, the parasite wreaked havoc among the Great Lakes fish populations, particularly lake trout and whitefish. The annual commercial catch of lake trout from Lakes Michigan and Huron dropped from a total of more than 5,500 tons [5,000 tonnes] in the early 1940s to less than 100 tons [91 tonnes] just 15 years later....
> The burbot and whitefish populations in the upper Great Lakes were similarly

devastated, and then the lampreys attacked the lakes' walleyes and suckers. Perhaps aided by overfishing, the lamprey wiped out many of the large cisco species in the three upper Great Lakes.... Hundreds of commercial fishing operations also became extinct.[67]

Destruction of the fisheries in the upper lakes by the sea lamprey from the 1930s on also achieved something that all the other stresses imposed on the fishery during the previous half century had not led to: it produced the first effective intergovernmental cooperation on Great Lakes fisheries management, both within and between the United States and Canada. This was formalized in the 1955 convention that created the Great Lakes Fishery Commission (GLFC) (see box, "Great Lakes Fishery Commission").

The commission devotes most of its work to implementing a program to eradicate or limit the sea lamprey in the Great Lakes. The adoption in the late 1950s of TFM and Bayer 73* as lampricides during the several years of the larval stage dramatically reduced the size of the lamprey problem. Lamprey numbers are only a tenth of what they once were. However, eradication may not be feasible, and lampricides now form part of an integrated program that must be continued indefinitely. Ironically, some of the measures to improve fisheries habitat—removing of dams, reducing sedimentation, and improving water quality—benefit the lamprey as well as the fish on which it preys.

The lamprey problem may get worse in the future. The commission acknowledged in 1986 that a population of lamprey in the St. Marys River (the outlet of Lake Superior) could not be controlled using existing techniques, and that control efforts would have to be increased to protect the fishery in Lake Huron.[68] Even worse, the commission's budget is inadequate. If funds provided by the United States and Canada are not increased, the commission expects to reduce applications of lampricides in Lakes Michigan, Huron, and Ontario by 40 percent. Experts project that, as a result of this diminished effort, sea lamprey in Lake Ontario could double in 10 years, with fishable stocks of lake trout and salmon decreasing by 50 percent.[69] It is reasonable to assume that the fisheries of Lakes Michigan and Huron would also suffer.†

---

*TFM: 3-trifluoromethyl-4-nitrophenol; Bayer 73: 2',5-dichloro-4'-nitrosalicyanilide.

†Since the economic rewards to the region from lamprey control are so substantial, the states and Ontario may want to fill the funding gap themselves.

## The Great Lakes Fishery Commission[1]

The Great Lakes Fishery Commission was created by the Convention on Great Lakes Fisheries, signed by the United States and Canada. The convention was spurred by the lamprey problem in the lakes. By 1955, when the convention took effect, lake trout production in Lakes Huron and Michigan was 99 percent lower than the average commercial catch during the 1930s.

The commission was given responsibility to coordinate fishery research and management, to advise governments on measures to improve the fisheries, and to develop measures and implement programs to control sea lamprey. The commission is comprised of eight commissioners, four appointed by Canada and four by the United States. It conducts its sea lamprey control and research through the U.S. Fish and Wildlife Service and Fisheries and Oceans Canada. Sixty-nine percent of the commission's budget is provided by the United States, based on the value of the whitefish and lake trout fishery prior to the lamprey invasion.

Although most of its budget is devoted to lamprey control, the commission also serves as the secretariat for a sizable committee structure involving representatives of fishery management and research agencies and the academic world. Technical committees deal with habitat, the sea lamprey, and control of fish diseases. A Council of Lake Committees and individual lake committees, comprised of senior staff members from fishery management agencies, develop and coordinate studies and policies on a voluntary basis.

Under the commission's auspices, the fishery management community developed in 1980 a Joint Strategic Plan for Management of Great Lakes Fisheries, whose principal goal is

to secure fish communities, based on foundations of stable self-sustaining stocks, supplemented by judicious plantings of hatchery-reared fish, and to provide from these communities an optimum contribution of fish, fishing opportunities, and associated benefits to meet needs identified by society for wholesome food, recreation, employment and income, and a healthy human environment.

The lake committees have since been working to translate this broad goal into more specific goals for each lake, although each jurisdiction's fishery managers are free to follow their own policies if they wish.

The commission, with justifiable pride, notes that "from a condition which can only be described as devastated, development of the fisheries has been spectacular." It acknowledges that much of this success has been "bioengineered" through control of the lamprey, stocking of native species and exotics, and other measures. It recognizes further that the development and maintenance "of balanced fish communities supported by natural reproduction is not yet attainable."

The final phase in the deterioration of the fisheries began with the recognition that toxic chemicals were biomagnifying in the food web and were bioaccumulating in many of the predators at levels unsafe for human consumption. This affected both the commercial fishery and the nascent sport fishery; it affected indigenous species and also the exotic salmonids that were being introduced to restock the lakes as lamprey control became effective. PCBs and mercury were soon added to the list of contaminants, and the now ubiquitous "fish advisories" warning against consumption of different species were introduced (see chapter 7).

Figures 6.6 and 6.7 display the waxing and waning of the fortunes of the commercial fisheries during the past century in two of the Great Lakes—Superior and Erie. Similar figures can be drawn for other lakes. The statistics for Lake Superior demonstrate the workings of a "fishing up" process, in which commercial fishermen shift their emphasis from fish with high value to those with lower value, because of declining catches of higher value fish.[70] In the 1880s, practically the entire commercial catch consisted of lake trout and whitefish. The proportion of these species declined to less than 10 percent in the mid-1960s; although there has been a significant recovery, the total catch is much less than it was a century ago.

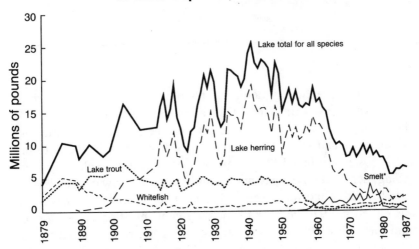

**Figure 6.6**
**Commercial Catch of Selected Fish Species
in Lake Superior, 1879–1987**

*Canadian officials began to list harvest figures for smelt only after 1952

Source: Great Lakes Fishery Commission; National Oceanic and Atmospheric Administration; Ontario Ministry of Natural Resources.

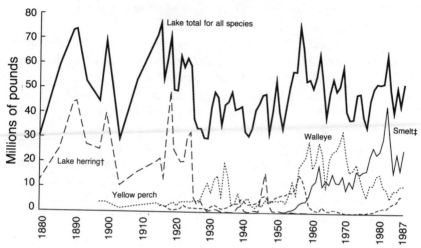

**Figure 6.7**
**Commercial Catch of Selected Fish Species**
**in Lake Erie, 1879–1987***

*Commercial catch total for Lake Erie began to be reported in a consistent historical fashion only after 1913

†Since 1961, the reported commercial catch of lake herring has been under 10,000 pounds annually

‡Canadian officials began to list harvest figures for smelt only after 1952

Source: Great Lakes Fishery Commission; National Oceanic and Atmospheric Administration; Ontario Ministry of Natural Resources.

Figure 6.7 graphically demonstrates the crash of the lake herring population in Lake Erie in the 1920s, a crash attributed to overfishing.[71] The walleye catch in Lake Erie, like the herring, has experienced striking rises and falls. The sharp decline from the mid-1950s to the late-1960s is attributed to a combination of factors, including overfishing, degradation of spawning areas by siltation, low oxygen levels, and changes in the food web.[72] The commercial fishery for walleye was closed in 1970 because of mercury contamination. This moratorium was followed by development of a cooperative interjurisdictional strategy for rebuilding the resource and limiting harvests. The walleye catch has rebounded since the 1970s. As one observer has noted, "Recovery of the walleye population has been phenomenal—beyond anyone's expectations."[73]

## FISHERIES MANAGEMENT AND ECOSYSTEM OBJECTIVES: CONVERGENCES AND DIVERGENCES

After such a sorry tale, extending over more than a century, it is understandable that many involved in the Great Lakes fisheries take pleasure and pride in the trends during the past "decade of recovery." Nevertheless, it is clear that, over the next decade or so, improving ecosystem health and expanding opportunities may emphasize policy dilemmas that did not have to be faced when the overriding imperative was to arrest the deterioration. One dilemma that has already been mentioned is the conflict between commercial, sport, and native interests in the fisheries. Another is the conflict between limiting nutrients to protect water quality, and providing a bountiful fishery. As stated baldly in a publication of the Sport Fishing Institute:

> Abatement of nutrients by "shutting off the faucet" while stocking millions of recreational fish could result in no food for these fish and have a negative impact on a multimillion dollar economic infrastructure around Lake Ontario and the other Great Lakes.[74]

Questions also have been raised about the relative importance to be given to stocking of exotic salmonids, as compared to achieving the longer-term objective of achieving a self-sustaining fishery based on native species. Maintaining the exotic salmonid fishery can be regarded as a short-term goal that produces an economic return from the lakes until the longer term objective of restoring self-sustaining lake trout stocks is achieved. But the two goals may come in conflict.

A self-sustaining, contaminant-free population of lake trout has been established under the Water Quality Agreement as an indicator of a healthy ecosystem in Lake Superior. The Ecosystem Objectives Subcommittee of the IJC's Science Advisory Board, in its final report, considered whether the lake trout should be used as an indicator of ecosystem health for both Lakes Michigan and Huron.[75] Critics of the use of the lake trout for this purpose point out that lake trout are not reproducing extensively in either lake and that the exotic salmonids have become the predominant predators. Some of the critics have suggested instead using the exotic salmonids as ecosystem indicators.

The subcommittee argued that it would be inappropriate to use the exotic salmonids as indicators of ecosystem health. Not enough is known about them on a long-term basis, they have shorter life spans than the trout (so they do not bioaccumulate toxic substances for as long a period), and they are more restricted than the trout in their behavior and in their habitat requirements. In fact, the subcommittee stated, "the presence of large numbers of exotic species, whether through deliberate introduction or merely serendipity, should in itself be regarded as one of the symptoms of ecosystem malaise."

The subcommittee recommended future use of the lake trout as an indicator of ecosystem health for Lake Huron, but it acknowledged that using the trout for such a purpose in Lake Michigan might not be possible because of the emphasis in Lake Michigan on stocking exotic salmonids:

> Current management goals for Lake Michigan may preclude the possibility of achieving a healthy ecosystem based on lake trout alone because of present fishery management policies which encourage [exotic] salmonid production. Currently, the best we can hope for on Lake Michigan is a state of health based on a mixture of lake trout and exotic salmonids, with the implicit understanding that these types of semi-indigenous mixed fish assemblages are less predictable, more subject to emergent surprises and may even, on occasion, mask ecosystem insufficiencies.

In their recent efforts to refine their goals under the Joint Strategic Plan for Great Lakes Fisheries, the fishery managers for many of the lakes (but not Lake Michigan) are giving higher priority to the longer-term goal of restoring self-sustaining stocks of native fish such as lake trout.[76] One incentive for this changing priority is the expense of maintaining fish hatcheries and the vulnerability of hatchery-reared stock to epidemics of disease. As the Ontario Ministry of Natural Resources has noted with respect to Lake Ontario:

> Brown trout, rainbow trout, and the pacific salmons ... have often required expensive, high-risk hatchery support to provide sufficient numbers for a sport fishery. Native, naturally reproducing fish species, on the other hand, are very predictable, cost-effective, and have little risk of failure.[77]

Because of the emphasis during the past decade on stocking exotic salmonids, and the benefits these have produced for anglers, the Great Lakes have, in a sense, become a "fish ranch" at the upper levels of their food web. Although fishery managers now attach greater importance to self-sustaining native species, there probably will continue to be conflicts between this objective and serving the angling community. For example, in Lake Michigan, stocking of salmon has slowed since 1984 to avoid overtaxing the forage base.[78] Lower salmon runs are prompting pressures to increase the allowable catch of lake trout.[79] Recent data indicate a forage shortage in Lake Superior. As a result, lake trout are growing more slowly than expected, raising the question of whether fishery managers should cut back stocking of the rainbow trout and salmon that compete with the lake trout.[80]

Stocking policies have an influence not only on the mix of top predators in the lakes, but also on lower levels of the food web and, indirectly, on measures of water quality. This interconnection of fisheries management and water quality management has been explored in IJC-sponsored workshops focusing on Lake Michigan and Lake Ontario. At issue in these workshops has been the interaction of "top-down" (fisheries management) and "bottom-up" (phosphorus reduction) strategies in improving water quality. The initial workshop, for Lake Michigan, concluded that bottom-up control reduced phosphorus levels during the winter in that lake, which then lowered the amount of spring phytoplankton and chlorophyll. In addition, salmonid predation reduced the number of alewives, which feed on zooplankton. Large zooplankton (*Daphnia pulicaria*) therefore increased in number. In turn, the zooplankton's grazing on phytoplankton increased, with the net result that the clarity of Lake Michigan's water during the summer improved. (Water clarity is one measure of water quality.) (Figure 6.8 describes the mechanisms of bottom-up and top-down strategies.)[81]

The Lake Ontario workshop, convened in 1987, concluded that bottom-up control had significantly reduced phosphorus concentrations in Lake Ontario, producing some minor changes in the composition of the phytoplankton community. At the time of the workshop, effects of predation by salmonids were only beginning to become apparent, and some workshop participants urged continued monitoring of the lake's response.

The participants at the Lake Ontario workshop noted a fundamental question for management agencies: "Are the phosphorus management and fishery management strategies compatible?" They observed that these two management strategies "may in the long run promote ecosystem instability if they are not carefully coordinated." The answer to the question of how much stocking and phosphorus control is too much "depends on the relative priorities of management goals, i.e., maximizing fish production, maximizing economic returns, maximizing water clarity, and restoring native species."[82]

Historically, the fisheries management community within the Great Lakes basin, operating under the umbrella of the Great Lakes Fishery Commission, has worked largely separately from the pollution control community operating under the umbrella of the International Joint

## Figure 6.8
## "Top-Down" and "Bottom-Up" Management Mechanisms in Lake Michigan

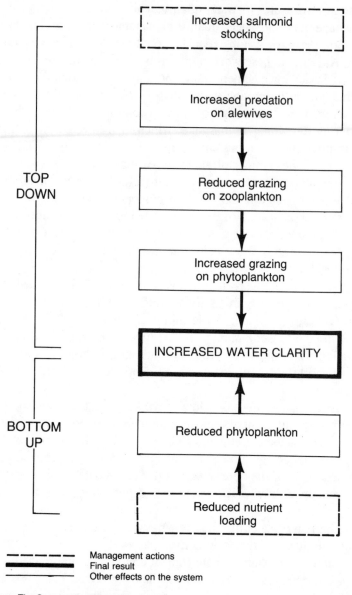

Source: The Conservation Foundation.

Commission. Members of the fishery management community have had an interest in the ecosystem approach to managing the lakes, and there have been considerable informal contacts among members of the two communities. Nevertheless, only within the past several years have the formal contacts begun to grow. The questions raised at the Lake Ontario workshop on the food web make clear that it is now more urgent than ever that the two communities—and the two commissions—expand both their formal and informal ties.

# Chapter 7

# Human Health

Humans are positioned at the top of both the terrestrial and aquatic food webs. As such, they risk being exposed to the persistent toxic substances that build up in food resources. Indeed, consumption of top wildlife predators may be the most significant way in which humans are exposed to environmental contaminants. It should not be surprising, then, that those animals that are at or near the top of the natural food web are sentinels or indicators of hazards that may also affect humans.

Media attention to the health of animals in the Great Lakes basin has generated growing concern by citizens for their own well-being. People are asking such questions as: Is water from the Great Lakes, or from wells in the basin, safe to drink? Are the fish, birds, and other wildlife in the basin safe to eat? Are the physical and behavioral problems of wildlife populations likely to occur in nearby human communities? Should I be concerned about the effects of toxic substances in the Great Lakes basin on my health? (See figure 7.1 describing the routes of human exposures to toxic substances.)

These are straightforward, reasonable questions. Unfortunately, they are very difficult to answer with equal directness and simplicity, for several reasons:

- *Lack of understanding of biochemical processes.* Associations between the presence of a toxic substance and a particular illness or other health impairment in wildlife may suggest a relationship, but absolute proof that a particular substance caused an effect in wildlife may be difficult to find. As noted in chapter 6, for only

165

## Figure 7.1
## Simplified Model of Persistent Toxic Substances in Aquatic Ecosystems

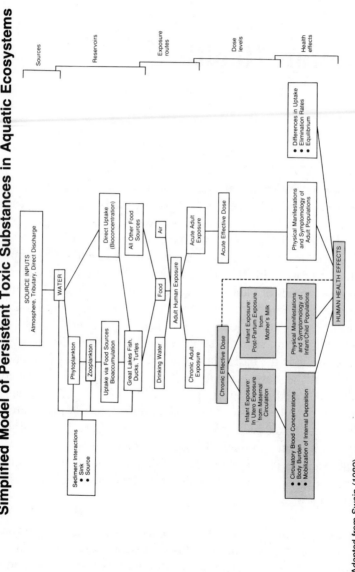

Source: Adapted from Swain (1982).

one chemical—DDT—has a clear cause-effect relationship been established with a health effect in wildlife; in this case, eggshell thinning in a number of bird species.[1]

- *Time lags and multiple exposures.* Cause-effect relationships are particularly difficult to establish when there are long time lags between exposure to contaminants and development of health problems. A health effect may result from exposure to a toxic substance years earlier or from the cumulative effect of many years' exposure. Furthermore, because humans are normally exposed to multiple contaminants simultaneously, and this exposure involves several different pathways (for example, ingestion of food and water, and inhalation), the difficulty of linking individual substances to effects on health is compounded. Also, several toxic substances may have the same effects, making it hard to distinguish the effects of exposure to one substance from the effects of another.

- *Lack of data.* Although many studies of health effects have focused on cancer and on effects observable in the short term, such as acute poisoning, less research has focused on noncancerous effects and the effects of longer-term exposures to low levels of substances. To detect some effects, large-scale surveys may be needed. These, however, are likely to be expensive and time-consuming, and the information required may be difficult to obtain or be regarded as an invasion of privacy.

For many of the problems likely to be caused by toxic chemicals, there are more reliable data for effects on wildlife than for effects on humans. Since most animals have shorter lives than humans, generational effects* can be easier to trace. It is also easier to obtain samples from wildlife (for example, by gathering herring gull eggs) or to perform postmortem studies on animals (necropsies) to investigate the extent of toxic contamination.

---

*The term *generational effect* as used in this report is a condition observed in an offspring as the result of parental exposure. The exposure is passed on to the offspring via transfer of a substance from the mother; the offspring may exhibit effects not visible in the parents. These developmental problems appear to be *congenital* rather than *genetic*; that is, they are the result of direct exposure to the toxic substances by the germinal cells (the sperm and the egg) and the fetus *in utero*. The effects are therefore not hereditary. Many chemicals of concern have been found in the reproductive organs of both men and women: the testicles,[2] ovarian follicle,[3] and placenta.[4] Toxic substances are also passed to human offspring via breast milk (see text below).

- *Difficulty of moving from general to specific statements of risk.*
  Individuals concerned about environmental risks frequently want
  to know, "Is the air, water, or food safe for me and my family?"
  The answer may depend very heavily on what people eat and
  how much, where they live and work, their lifestyles, and their
  individual sensitivities.

## THE EVIDENCE FROM WILDLIFE

If organisms in aquatic food webs can act as an "early warning system"
for humans, what do these and other wildlife sentinels indicate? Important clues—lines of evidence—include*:

- Similar physiological and health anomalies have been found across
  a wide range of species in the Great Lakes ecosystem (see chapter
  6, figure 6.1). These anomalies frequently are associated with
  toxic substances. It therefore is prudent to search for indications
  of similar health effects in exposed human populations, especially
  since the same toxic chemicals found in wildlife tissue are also
  found in human tissue.[5]
- Relatively few symptoms of adverse health effects have been
  encountered in adult specimens of wildlife. Most of the problems
  are encountered in the offspring.
- Even though complete causal evidence may be lacking (such as
  the exact mechanism of action that causes changes at the cellular
  level), some of the health effects observed in wildlife have been
  reproduced in laboratory animals. These include wasting, birth
  defects, immune suppression (lowering of an organism's ability
  to withstand disease), and target organ damage.[6]†
- Cancerous tumors that appear to be linked to toxic contamination
  have been found in whales[7] and fish,[8] but (as figure 6.1 indicates)
  cancer is far from the most significant or frequent health or physiological anomaly in wildlife.
- The evidence from animal studies is insufficient to state whether
  toxic chemicals block one another (antagonism) or multiply one

*See chapter 6 for a more complete review of this evidence.
†Target-organ damage could occur in such organs as the thyroid, liver, kidney, or
brain.

anothers' effects (synergism).* Researchers have demonstrated both antagonism and synergism in laboratory animals with mixtures of dioxins and PCBs.[9] It is reasonable to assume that exposure to multiple toxic substances probably is additive in many situations, based on limited animal studies.

These indications are valuable, but they must be viewed with caution. It is well known that effects of toxic substances vary significantly from one organism to another, between sexes, and between species. Nevertheless, the potential significance of the evidence from wildlife remains considerable. In particular, the relatively long period between birth and childbearing in humans means that humans can accumulate substantial amounts of toxic substances that they can transfer to their offspring.

## EVIDENCE FROM PUBLIC HEALTH DATA ON EFFECTS IN LARGE HUMAN POPULATIONS

Both Canada and the United States routinely collect data on causes of death (mortality) and certain illnesses and diseases (morbidity). These normally are available on a national, provincial/state, or county basis. The quality of the morbidity and mortality data is inconsistent across the continent, making comparisons among areas difficult.

### Cancer Incidence

Data on the incidence of cancer around the Great Lakes are limited. Several states have no registries to record cancer incidence. Other registries were initiated only recently. The data that are available indicate considerable variations in the incidence of different forms of cancer in counties around the Great Lakes. An analysis of the New York State cancer registry found the incidence of respiratory cancer relatively high throughout the Niagara Falls area, but there was no evidence of higher liver cancer, lymphoma, or leukemia among those living near Love Canal than in the rest of upstate New York.[10]†

---

*Antagonism means 3 plus 3 is less than 6; synergism means 3 plus 3 is greater than 6. Additivity means 3 plus 3 equals 6.

†See box, "Love Canal," in chapter 3.

## Cancer Mortality

U.S. statistics on cancer mortality through 1980 do not indicate that Great Lakes counties, as a whole, suffer from substantially higher cancer mortality rates than nonbasin counties.[11] In response to concern over toxic substances leaking into the Niagara River, Health and Welfare Canada analyzed mortality data on a countywide basis in the Canadian portion of the Great Lakes basin.[12] The study showed (a) statistically significant variations among and within individual Great Lakes counties and (b) no consistency in cancer mortality or types of cancer mortality between municipalities in Niagara County.

## Reproductive Outcomes

Data collected regularly on birth defects are also inconclusive. For example, reports of cleft palate and cleft lip in the first week after birth indicated that the incidence in Canadian counties along the Lake Erie shoreline was generally average or below average in the period 1973-81, compared to the rest of Ontario (figure 7.2).[13] Another study, involving data from 1970 to 1973, for five Ontario municipalities in the Niagara region, found that birth outcomes were similar to those elsewhere in the province. Although the Lake Ontario shoreline showed a higher incidence of cleft palate, this condition also extended northward—moving away from the lakes. Incidence varied from year to year, and in almost all instances the number of cases was low. The pattern again was unpredictable and was more related to urban and industrial development (population density) than to proximity to the lakes.[14]

It is not surprising that these general mortality and morbidity data indicate nothing unusual around the Great Lakes. Public health officials do not routinely gather information on the subtle developmental effects that may be of greatest concern.

## EVIDENCE OF HUMAN EXPOSURE FROM TISSUE ANALYSIS

Exposure to toxic substances is not unique to the Great Lakes, as a number of tissue-monitoring programs have confirmed. Human contamination is a global problem because of the persistence of "tissue-loving" chemicals released in the last 50 years. Because chemicals are so ubiquitous, separating exposed individuals from unexposed has

## Figure 7.2
## Incidence of Cleft Palates in Ontario, 1973–1981

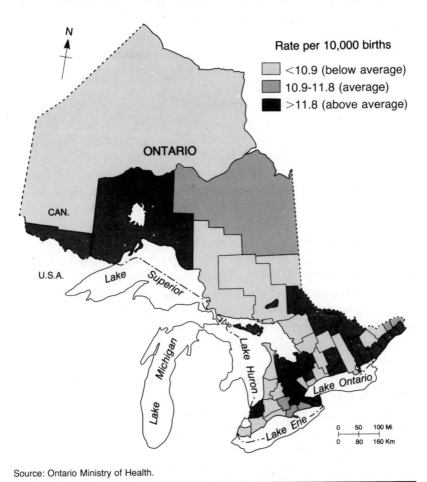

Rate per 10,000 births

☐ <10.9 (below average)
▨ 10.9-11.8 (average)
■ >11.8 (above average)

Source: Ontario Ministry of Health.

become a major epidemiological challenge. Wide-ranging monitoring programs have revealed that almost everyone in Canada and the United States is exposed to a number of toxic chemicals that are found in wildlife tissue.

For example, 2,3,7,8-TCDD (dioxin) is generally found in all human adipose tissue sampled in developed countries (including the United States and Canada).[15] Hexachlorobenzene (HCB) was found in 98 percent of the human adipose tissue sampled throughout the United

States over a 10-year period;[16] DDE, in 99.1 percent of the samples in a U.S. study;[17] and beta-HCH (a contaminant released with the pesticide lindane) in 100 percent of the samples taken in a survey of six Canadian municipalities along the Great Lakes[18] and in breast milk nationwide in Canada.[19] Nothing in the Great Lakes region consistently signals higher human contamination than anywhere else; for some contaminants, the concentration levels are lower than in other areas of both Canada and the United States.[20]

There are no long-term human-tissue-monitoring programs in the Great Lakes basin that can provide measures of changes in human exposure to toxic chemicals. Because of the limitations of the monitoring (for example, differences in protocols for sampling and analysis; variations in mathematical and statistical approach) that has been done, it cannot be said with confidence that the concentrations of these chemicals in human tissue of persons in the basin have changed in the past decade or are significantly different from those in human groups outside the basin. In the case of beta-HCH and HCB, there are indications that these may be increasing in adipose tissue.[21] Certainly, the frequency of detection has increased, but this may be more due to advances in techniques of measurement than to increased exposure.

What is most troubling, because it so clearly demonstrates the persistence of toxic substances in the food web, is the fact that concentrations of organochlorine pesticides and PCBs in breast milk in 1982 were not noticeably different in either Canada or the United States from those found 20 years earlier.[22] Photomirex, the degradation product of mirex, is found almost universally throughout Canada (even in northern indigenous populations),[23] where there have been no reported uses or production. Concentrations of dioxins and furans were similar throughout Canada and comparable to levels found in the United States and Sweden.[24] Because the technology to measure dioxins and furans in tissue is quite new, there are no long-term data to assess whether these are decreasing or increasing in the tissues of the general population. It would not be surprising if some unusual concentrations were to be found as research and monitoring are extended.

## EVIDENCE FROM STUDIES OF INDIVIDUALS

A series of reports has been published on an ongoing study undertaken in response to concern over the effects of eating Lake Michigan fish on reproductive outcomes.[25] This study is searching in humans for subtle developmental effects that may signal exposure to some of the same toxic chemicals found in wildlife. These reports have focused on the health of individuals potentially at risk—fish-eating mothers and their infants.

The 1981 study screened 8,472 women to determine their history of fish consumption and examined 242 infants of women who were accustomed to eating fish from Lake Michigan on a regular basis. Seventy-one controls were selected from among nonfish eaters. Information was collected on mothers' consumption of Lake Michigan fish during their lifetimes, during their pregnancies, and during lactation. The fish-eating mothers' consumption was equivalent to about two or three lake trout, coho, or chinook salmon dinners per month. Data show that length of gestational period, birth weight, skull circumference, and cognitive, motor, and behavioral development of the infants were adversely affected by the mothers' lifetime consumption of Lake Michigan fish. In each case, the differences were slight, but statistically different from the controls.*

Among the results of this study, the rate of consumption of contaminated fish species per year from Lake Michigan was associated with PCB concentrations in the mothers' breast milk and sera.[27] In turn, there was an association between the mothers' serum PCB concentrations and the infants' cord serum PCB concentrations.[28] The latter finding is consistent with other studies outside the basin investigating the transfer of maternal PCBs to the fetus and infant.[29]

When the infants were retested at age seven months, the researchers found that the total amount of fish consumed by the mother in all years prior to conception, as well as the amount of PCBs (measured as Aroclor 1260) in the umbilical cord serum, was associated with infants' decreased visual recognition memory (a measure of neurological development).[30] Furthermore, the health effects found in the Lake Michigan fish-eater study were confined to offspring. No health effects of fish eating were reported in the mothers.

The 242 mothers who consumed Lake Michigan fish ate approxi-

---

*Infant weight was 160 to 190 grams (0.35 to 0.42 pounds) lighter than controls. Skull circumference was 0.6 to 0.7 centimeters (0.23 to 0.27 inches) smaller. Gestation period was 4.9 days less. Compared with weight and gestation period, head circumference was disproportionately small.[26]

mately 14.74 ± 12.76 pounds (6.7 ± 5.8 kilograms) per year.* The average U.S. citizen consumes approximately 15.7 pounds (7.2 kilograms) of commercial fish per year.[31]† The mothers ate fish for an average of 15.9 ± 9.1 years preceding childbirth. During pregnancy, their consumption dropped to 9.02 ± 9.68 pounds (4.1 ± 4.4 kilograms) annually.

Follow-up tests of the infants at age four have been undertaken, but the results have not yet been published. At present, another study of pregnant women is being completed in Green Bay, Wisconsin. It is essential that more studies of this nature be conducted to test the conclusions of the first.

## EXPOSURE PATHWAYS

Measurements of actual exposure to toxic substances generally are difficult to obtain; only estimates are available. Such estimates sometimes are generated by modeling. For example, a model has been developed in Canada of the probable relative importance of exposure to dioxin via different routes, and similar models are being developed for lead, PCBs, and other contaminants.[32]

### Ingestion of Food

Present evidence indicates that the main route of exposure for toxic substances in the Great Lakes is through ingestion of food (see, for example, the results shown in figure 7.3 of a Toronto study based on purchase of food grown within the Great Lakes region). Substances found in the Great Lakes ecosystem, that bioaccumulate in fish tissue, include dioxins, chlordane, DDT/DDE, furans, HCB, lead, lindane, mercury, mirex, octachlorostyrene (OCS), PCBs, toxaphene, and tributyltin. Most of these are included in the International Joint Commission (IJC) Water Quality Board's primary track of critical pollutants (see chapter 2, figure 2.3). Of these, relatively elevated concentrations in human tissue of chlordane,[33] DDT/DDE,[34] HCB,[35] lindane,[36] mercury,[37] mirex,[38] and PCB[39] have been associated with those who regularly eat fish (figure 7.4).

---

*The first figure in the text represents the average consumption, followed by the standard deviation.

†This figure is based on total commercial catch of 3.9 billion pounds (1.5 billion kilograms) and total imports of 3.2 billion pounds (1.2 billion kilograms) in 1987.

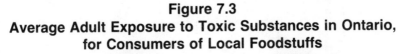

# Figure 7.3
## Average Adult Exposure to Toxic Substances in Ontario, for Consumers of Local Foodstuffs

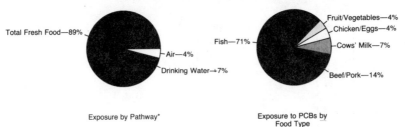

Total Fresh Food—89%

Air—4%

Drinking Water—7%

Fish—71%

Fruit/Vegetables—4%

Chicken/Eggs—4%

Cows' Milk—7%

Beef/Pork—14%

Exposure by Pathway*

Exposure to PCBs by Food Type

*Estimates based on consumption of fresh food grown in southern Ontario and purchased in local food stores. Includes exposure to aldrin, dieldrin, DDT, g-HCH (lindane), a,b-HCH, HCB, and PCB.

Source: K. Davies, Department of Public Health, City of Toronto.

PCBs are transferred to the infant through breast milk; milk fat is indeed a significant pathway through which PCBs[40] and dioxins[41] are excreted by the mother. In the Lake Michigan fish-eater studies, only the more highly chlorinated PCBs (Aroclor 1260) were found in measurable concentrations consistently, as compared with the lesser chlorinated PCBs (Aroclor 1016).[42] (The highly chlorinated PCBs appear to be more toxic and persistent than the lesser chlorinated ones.) During early nursing, an infant may consume almost six times the recommended consumption guideline for PCBs for an adult weighing 154 pounds (70 kilograms), and after seven months the infant may still be exposed to twice the acceptable adult dose.[43] Additionally, it is recognized that breast milk contains only the toxic congeners* of dioxin, which are passed on to the infant.[44]

The Wisconsin Department of Health sampled blood from selected sport fishermen statewide in 1984 for PCB and DDE. Human PCB levels surge within hours following a meal of contaminated fish and take about a week to decline.[45] As fish consumption increases, both PCB and DDE serum levels increase also. In the survey, anglers with

---

*As noted in chapter 2, figure 2.3, dioxins are found in 75 different forms (congeners), some of which are more toxic than others. 2,3,7,8-TCDD is the most toxic form of dioxin.

## Figure 7.4
## Toxic Chemicals Found in Fish and Human Tissues

| Toxic chemicals associated with generic effects | Concentrates in fish | Associated with fish eaters* | Found in human† Follicle | Testicle | Placenta | Breast milk | Human carcinogen‡ |
|---|---|---|---|---|---|---|---|
| 2,3,7,8-TCDD (a,c) | + | | | | | | O |
| B[a,b]P (a) | + | | | | | + | E |
| Chlordane (a,c) | + | + | + | + | | | O |
| DDE/DDT (a,b,c) | + | + | + | + | + | + | O |
| Dieldrin (a,b,c) | + | + | + | | + | + | O |
| HCB (a,c) | + | + | + | + | + | + | E |
| Lead (alkyl) (c) | + | + | | + | + | + | O |
| Lindane (a,b,c) | + | + | + | + | + | + | O |
| Mercury (c) | + | + | + | + | | + | O |
| Mirex (a,b) | + | + | | + | + | + | O |
| PCB (a,b,c) | + | + | + | + | + | + | E |
| Toxaphene (a,b,c) | + | | | | | + | O |

a = enzyme inducer
b = gap junction intercellular communication blocker
c = disrupts endocrine control
E = equivocal
O = no evidence
+ = positive
Blanks = no citation found
(Effects are explained in chapter 6.)

*Toxics associated with one or more generic effect that concentrate in fish tissue and for which human residues show an association with those who eat fish.
†Toxics that have been reported in ovarian follicles, testicles, placentae, and breast milk.
‡Conservation Foundation characterization of evidence of human carcenogenicity, based on human epidemiological studies.

Source: The Conservation Foundation.

the highest PCB concentrations ate 50 percent more fish than those who were less contaminated. The anglers also ate three times more fish than the national average (sport and commercial fish combined). There was a positive relationship between DDE concentrations and the amount of sport fish consumed. Figure 7.5 compares PCB serum levels in Iowa farmers who did not eat fish, Michigan farmers, Michigan farmers who painted their silos with PCB, and fish eaters (see box). It also compares serum PCB values of Michigan residents who ate fewer than 6 pounds of fish per year with those who ate more than 23 pounds of fish per year.

The importance of fish as an exposure route for PCBs has been summarized by one researcher as follows:

> In terms of exposure potential, it is possible to breathe the air in the rural Lake Michigan basin and drink its water for a lifetime before achieving the same effective exposure that one would receive from eating a single one pound fish meal of Lake Michigan lake trout.[46]

## Ingestion of Drinking Water

The ingestion of municipally treated drinking water from the Great Lakes is considered to be a minor exposure pathway for pollutants when compared with food.* The same general statement cannot be made for groundwater, partly because of lack of information and also because of known localized instances of groundwater contamination.[48] Although drinking water may not carry detectable concentrations of toxic chemicals, the cumulative effect of long-term, low-dose exposure to drinking water and other pathways cannot be ignored; it is important to reduce concentrations in all exposure pathways.

## Inhalation and Other Pathways

Inhalation is, in most instances, a minor pathway of exposure for toxic substances when compared to ingestion of food. However, it can be significant for certain volatile organic compounds (such as tetrachlo-

---

*A recent U.S. Environmental Protection Agency regulation requires all municipal drinking water systems which do not meet established limits on coliform concentration and turbidity to install charcoal filtration systems. Filtration removes the largest part of the organic chemical contaminants and trace metals.[47]

## Figure 7.5
## Human Exposure to PCBs

### Median PCB Sera Levels in Humans

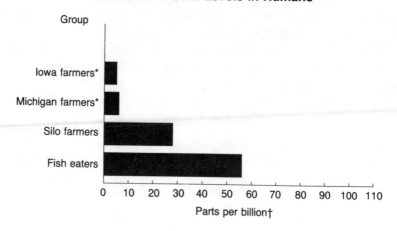

### Median Serum PCB Values
### Among Michigan Communities in 1973

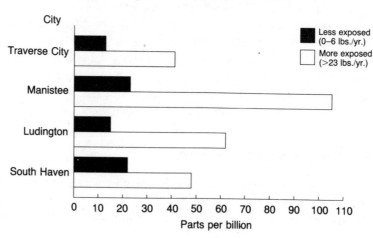

*Source of exposure unknown.

†1 pound = .45 kilograms, and 1 part per billion = 1 microgram/kilogram.

Source: Adapted from Humphrey (1983).

## Fish Advisories

To discourage consumption of tainted fish that may pose a risk to human health, the province of Ontario and state governments in the United States issue advisories to those fishing their waters, indicating which fish are safe to eat and which are not. The advisories differ in format among the various jurisdictions, although efforts have been made to develop a standard format, especially in the United States. The advisories may also differ in their conclusions about which fish are safe to eat and which are unsafe, because of different methodologies and standards used to determine risk. Risk to health has often focused on cancer, although other effects are also taken into account, as in the case of mercury. The annual bulletins are advisory only; individual fishermen and others may choose to ignore the warnings.

The Ontario government's 303-page *Guide to Eating Ontario Sport Fish* is the most comprehensive and detailed of the fish advisories available around the Great Lakes.[1] It lists, for the Great Lakes and a large number of other lakes and streams in the basin, the types of fish that should not be consumed at all or whose consumption should be limited, with special limitations for children under 15 and women of childbearing age. The guidebook also lists the contaminants of concern and their health effects and provides information on trends in contamination.

There has been considerable discussion among concerned officials and members of the public about the adequacy of fish advisories. Great Lakes states generally base their advisories for sport fish on regulatory limits for commercial fish established by the U.S. Food and Drug Administration (FDA). These limits are based on national averages for consumption. FDA itself acknowledges that the

*Sign warning anglers not to eat fish.*
Marcella S. Martin

national limits may not fully protect the health of those around the Great Lakes and elsewhere who consume larger amounts of fish than the average American.[2] Moreover, most FDA limits were established in the early 1970s and therefore fail to reflect more recent scientific findings and new scientific technologies. A recent review of the FDA limits for DDT and dieldrin, published by National Wildlife Federation (NWF) scientists, has suggested that sport fish with concentrations of DDT or dieldrin one-fifth and one-third of the existing FDA levels should be covered by consumption advisories, because of cancer risks believed to exist at these lower levels of contamination.[3]

Greater recognition of the possible effects on offspring from the mother's total lifetime consumption of fish should be considered. Based on the weight of the evidence from Great Lakes wildlife research and laboratory animal and tissue studies, females who intend to bear children should not eat contaminated fish until they pass child-bearing age.

Recent research on PCBs provides an additional reason to reevaluate the adequacy of fish advisories. Advisories discouraging fish consumption because of PCB contamination have been based on measurements of total PCBs in sampled fish.* It now appears that some PCB congeners are more toxic than others and that the most toxic PCB congeners tend to bioaccumulate the most,[4] so advisories should be based on congener-specific analysis. Moreover, scientists have developed a method—called dioxin enzyme induction equivalency testing—by which the toxicity of multiple pollutants can be assessed relative to the most toxic form of dioxin.[5] Fish advisories might be made more stringent if they incorporated these and similar recent findings.

---

*PCBs are measured against standards for commercial products such as Aroclor 1260 or Aroclor 1248, which contain different ratios of the 209 PCB congeners.

roethylene commonly used for dry cleaning).* Volatile organic compounds (VOCs) may volatilize from domestic water as it leaves the tap, raising concentration levels in indoor air. ''Showerhead'' exposure involves both inhalation and dermal (through the skin) sorption; dermal sorption can be a major route of exposure for VOCs in some instances.

Little is known about the risk from a number of other pathways, except that the possibility of exposure exists. These pathways include body contact with lake water (for example, in swimming); dermal sorption from other bathing; exposure at the air-water interface (for

---

*The U.S. Environmental Protection Agency (EPA) estimates that the amount of lead in children's blood varies considerably, depending on the levels of airborne lead to which they are exposed. For example, lead levels in the air that are above the lower third of the EPA ambient-air quality criterion for lead can cause an exposed child's blood-lead level to be double that of the level resulting from exposure to normal background levels of lead in food, water, and dust.[49] With certain other substances—for example, the conventional air pollutants like carbon monoxide and sulfur dioxide—inhalation *is* the primary pathway of exposure. These are not among the persistent toxic substances that are the major concern of this chapter.

example, just above lake surfaces[50]), where it is estimated that PCBs concentrate; and body contact with lake sediments and suspended organic material.

### General Exposure

Toxic substances produced or released during combustion and similar processes result in widespread contamination. These substances include benzo[a]pyrene, dioxins, furans, octachlorostyrene, hexachlorobenzene, cadmium, lead, and mercury. Available evidence suggests that exposure to several of these (for example, cadmium,[51] lead,[52] octachlorostyrene,[53] and PCBs[54]) varies according to proximity to urban or industrialized areas, whether they are in the Great Lakes basin or not. Several studies have shown that levels of PCBs do not appear to be higher in people living near PCB waste sites or spills.[55] However, mirex, produced in a relatively small geographical area near Lake Ontario, does appear to be more highly concentrated in tissues of people living along the Lake Ontario shoreline.[56]

## POTENTIAL HEALTH EFFECTS FROM PRINCIPAL TOXIC SUBSTANCES FOUND IN THE GREAT LAKES

Although human tissue undoubtedly contains an array of toxic substances, little is known about the effects of such residues on human health. There may be no measurable health effect at all associated with toxic substances at the levels generally found in human tissues. The clinical effects of residues on human health, either singly or in association with one another, are generally not yet understood. As noted previously, more is known at present about the effects of toxic substances in animals (mainly through controlled laboratory experiments) than about the effects of toxic substances in humans. However, nine of the IJC's critical pollutants have been associated with adverse effects in the human nervous system.[57]

These chemicals appear to pose more of a risk as influences on human development than as carcinogens. But the effects of exposure during development often are subtle; they may not be readily evident at birth and in early childhood unless they are the focus of carefully designed studies. For example, the neurological deficits seen in the infants in the Lake Michigan fish-eating study, or those found in groups of children exposed to lead, are quite subtle and would not be recognized in a random sample of children unless special testing procedures were used.[58] Public health authorities are currently searching for new techniques to measure exposure. Because of the generic nature of the chemicals at the cellular level (see box, chapter 6), a combination of effects (a syndrome) may eventually be described as constituting a symptom of a toxic induced disease.[59]

Much of the available information about reproductive and developmental effects in humans is being assembled as the result of studies of accidental poisonings and industrial exposure in different parts of the world (involving, for example, cadmium, dioxin, PCBs, HCB, and methylmercury).[60] Almost nothing is known about the cumulative effects in humans of low doses acquired from the general environment. The study of fish-eating mothers cited earlier is the type of study needed to gather greater knowledge about developmental effects from long-term, low-dose exposure.

## SUMMARY AND IMPLICATIONS

A suite of chemicals has been introduced into the Great Lakes environment. They are persistent and bioaccumulate and are biomagnified through the food web. Neither the chemicals themselves nor the quantities in which they are released into the environment are unique to the Great Lakes basin. However, the characteristics of bioaccumulation and biomagnification in combination with a relatively contained aquatic system* do lead to relatively high concentrations of these chemicals in fish and wildlife in the Great Lakes.† Following the introduction of these chemicals into the Great Lakes, health anomalies have been found in those wildlife populations holding significantly higher concentrations of chemicals than unaffected populations. The majority of effects are found in the offspring of wildlife; parental exposure seems to be the cause of problems that are more developmental than carcinogenic.

From studies of laboratory animals and animal tissues (see chapter

---

*Chemicals can be retained in the system for long periods; flushing times for most of the lakes are quite long. See chapter 4, figure 4.4.

†Because of the substantial and accessible wildlife populations around the Great Lakes, these problems became apparent to wildlife researchers more readily than they would have in less populated systems. Extensive colonies of nesting birds contributed the numbers and visibility needed to record health effects in wild populations. There is evidence that problems of this nature have occurred in other aquatic systems, such as Puget Sound, Boston Harbor, and the Baltic Sea.[61]

6), it is evident that chemicals affect a variety of body tissues and organs; they may disrupt normal cell function, nutrition, and development. The results include overt birth defects, and subtle changes in the immune system, metabolism, and behavioral and sexual development of offspring.

In terms of human health, conclusions about the effects of exposure to toxic contaminants in the Great Lakes fall within the realm of inference. It appears that the dominant pathway of exposure is through food. The largest doses of a number of contaminants are to fetuses and infants through maternal transfer via the placenta and breast milk during periods of rapid development. The most vulnerable groups are likely to be the offspring of those who regularly consume wildlife predators at the top of the food web (fish, waterfowl, turtles, and other species).

The weight of present evidence suggests that human health probably is affected by exposure to the persistent chemicals found in the ecosystem. Citizens' concerns will not be put to rest until it is clear that the health effects being seen in Great Lakes wildlife are not being manifested in their own offspring. Conclusions about human health effects at present depend far too much on disturbing indications rather than on solid knowledge.

More effort must be directed toward studies of behavioral, developmental, and immune system characteristics as well as of stages of sexual development in growing children. These studies are especially needed in population groups where the parents are likely to carry chemical residues significantly above those in the majority of the population.

A long-term commitment to researching effects and reducing exposures is the only course to take. Funding should be provided for several different types of research activities—especially development of inexpensive, noninvasive technologies for measuring exposure to chemicals, and identification of new techniques for assessing health effects at the early stages of disease and those resulting from exposure to multiple chemicals. Building on this work, sustained funding should be provided for studies that focus on suspected exposed groups, such as fish eaters. These efforts will require substantial cooperation among many government agencies, including those concerned with public health, environmental protection, food safety, and resource management.

In the absence of evidence that human residues of some of the contaminants are declining appreciably, it is apparent that all exposure pathways should be of concern because of the cumulative nature of

*Children fishing along dock near Sarnia Bay on the St. Clair River in Ontario.*
Lambton Industrial Society

these chemicals. The need to reduce exposure to potential health hazards is emphasized in the 1989 report of the Health Committee of the IJC's Science Advisory Board:

> One possibility is to borrow one of the axioms of the public health movement—preventive health care. . . . In environmental terms, this could mean financing programs to reduce or eliminate chemical exposures, as a preventive health measure. Indeed, the explicit concept of the virtual elimination of discharges of persistent toxic chemicals, contained in the Great Lakes Water Quality Agreement, is already giving effect to the concept of preventive health care for the Great Lakes Basin Ecosystem.[62]

How then are the simple questions asked at the beginning of this chapter to be answered?

*Is water from the Great Lakes, or from wells in the basin, safe to drink?* Municipally treated drinking water from the Great Lakes is a minimal exposure pathway for pollutants when compared with the food pathway. Risks appear negligible for the IJC-targeted pollutants and others in municipally treated water. The safety of groundwater varies among locations.

*Are the health problems of wildlife populations likely to be repeated in nearby human communities? Are the fish, birds, and other wildlife in the basin safe to eat?* These questions now appear closely related to each other. On one hand, the wildlife that appear to exhibit health-related problems due to toxic contamination depend on local conditions and local sources of food to an extent that is quite atypical of most human beings, wherever they live in North America. But, on the other hand, it has become clear that human beings, like other predators, can accumulate toxic substances and, especially in the case of persistent chemicals like PCBs, do so over much longer lifetimes than most animals. In addition, human beings apparently are most vulnerable to toxic contamination before and soon after birth. There do, therefore, seem to be grounds for concern about the effects that consumption of fish, waterfowl, and other animals close to the top of the food web may have on the health of individuals in the next generation. Authorities have been wise to warn women of childbearing age and children under 15 years of age not to eat much of the fish, but they may need to make their warnings even more stringent.

*Should I be concerned about the effects of toxic substances in the Great Lakes basin on my health?* For the great majority of the human Great Lakes population, the answer is yes, but no more so than for the rest of the continent. Toxic contaminants are widespread, and little is known about their long-term effects. However, those groups dependent, through need or preference, on fish and other wildlife for a substantial proportion of their food, and those living in areas having polluted air or contaminated groundwater do have greater grounds for concern.

The deterioration of the lakes and, in particular, the status of the wildlife in the basin have caused the residents, scientists, and governments of the Great Lakes basin to focus on the implications for human health to a greater extent than in places where the signals are less obvious. Individual researchers and the institutions of the Great Lakes basin are leaders in environmental health issues, relative to other regions of the world. Most of the messages coming from the Great Lakes "early warning system"—such as the need for health concerns to extend well beyond their present sharp focus on carcinogens and the need to give particular attention to the effects of toxic substances on fetuses and offspring—have universal significance.

# Chapter 8

# State of the Ecosystem: A Summary Synthesis

The Great Lakes basin ecosystem is a vast and complex set of processes and relationships, the main elements of which have been analyzed in the preceding chapters. Given the scope and detail of that analysis, it is easy to lose sight of the overall ecosystem—separating land, water, and other principal elements makes it easy to forget their essential interdependence.

Figure 8.1 highlights the principal conclusions about ecosystem conditions drawn in the preceding chapters. The figure also indicates the time period during which ecosystem health may be restored; for some problems, remedial responses will produce quick results, while for others the payoff will only be seen by future generations. The spatial contexts shown indicate the geographic area within which problems exist and responses are necessary. Some problems are local and can be solved locally; others are broader and require action both within and beyond the basin.

## Figure 8.1

## Indicators of Ecosystem Health in the Great Lakes Basin

### A. Contaminants in the Environment

| Element | Recovery Time | Spatial Context | Status |
|---|---|---|---|
| 1. Air quality | days to months | local to global | Air quality probably has improved over the last two decades because of declines in emissions of various pollutants. Quality still is unsatisfactory in many areas, principally because of high levels of ozone. The problem of airborne toxic pollutants is not yet well defined or addressed. Atmospheric deposition remains a problem for water quality, aquatic organisms, and vegetation. More reductions in emissions are needed. |
| 2. Surface water quality | months to years | basin | Substantial progress on excess nutrient problems has been made in the last two decades, by resolving crisis situations in Lakes Erie and Ontario, although trophic conditions still are not at targeted levels in some areas. Eutrophication and acidification remain serious problems in many inland lakes within the basin. Concentrations of nitrogen compounds have been rising at least over the last two decades in the Great Lakes, and their implications are not yet clear. Nonpoint pollution (urban and rural) remains a serious problem. Cumulative concentrations of metals in three Great Lakes are at elevated levels. Forty-two degraded Areas of Concern require a massive remedial effort. Although concentrations of some pollutants meet ambient water quality standards, concentrations are still high enough to cause serious contamination problems in fish and other wildlife. |

| | | | |
|---|---|---|---|
| 3. Contaminated sediments | decades | basin, river, and lake bottoms | Sediments contaminated with metals and organic compounds are a serious problem in 41 of 42 Areas of Concern. In many locations, sediments remain a continuing source of contaminants and excess nutrients for the food web. Concentrations of many contaminants in recent sediments are significantly less than in older sediments, with some exceptions. |
| 4. Groundwater | decades to centuries | basin | Water sources are contaminated in various locations throughout the region. Degraded conditions stemming from persistent toxic substances will last long into the future. Groundwater can be a major source of contaminants to surface water. Preventive activities are in their infancy, so groundwater quality is degenerating. |

**B. Fish and Wildlife**

| | | | |
|---|---|---|---|
| 5. Body burdens of toxics | years to decades (generational effects) | local to continental | Contaminant levels in many organisms are substantially lower than they were in the early 1970s, but declines appear to have leveled off and present trends are difficult to interpret. For many substances, levels remain above objectives specified in the Water Quality Agreement or other guidelines and standards. Continued high levels for substances whose use has been restricted signals releases of contaminants previously deposited in the ecosystem, continued release from improper storage of remaining stocks, and remaining uses in remote areas. |
| 6. Population status | years to decades | local to continental | Populations of many bird species are recovering. Problems remain for specific species or populations in particular locations. Some key species, such as lake trout, still are unable to establish self-sustaining populations in several lakes. Biota are threatened in acidifying inland lakes. |
| 7. Habitat | days to centuries | basin | The pace of habitat destruction is substantially reduced from earlier eras, but protection of remaining habitat is still a concern. A coordinated basinwide effort is needed. |

| | | | |
|---|---|---|---|
| 8. Fisheries | years to decades | local to basin | A substantial reduction in the lamprey population during the past 20 years and heavy stocking of exotic salmonids and other species has permitted development of a robust sport fishery. The forage base for the fishery may be limited due to controls on phosphorus discharges. The artificially managed "fish ranch" in the lakes may be quite fragile, and the future of the commercial fishery still is uncertain. |
| **C. Terrestrial Conditions** | | | |
| 9. Forests | decades | local to basin | Many forests are maturing after recovering from massive overcutting and fires during the late 19th and early 20th century. The future increasingly is seen in managing public lands to allow for multiple uses of forest resources. Forests are at risk from transported air pollutants, such as ozone and acid deposition, with a prospect of widespread stress in the coming decades from climate change. |
| 10. Wetlands | years to decades | local | Two-thirds of the original wetlands in the basin have been destroyed since the beginning of European settlement. The key role of wetlands in the Great Lakes ecosystem is now recognized. Public policies encouraging wetland destruction must be adjusted to make them consistent with wetland protection goals. |
| 11. Soil erosion | years to decades | local to basin | Available data indicate that erosion generally is below the threshold of concern for short-term, on-site productivity, but there is growing evidence of serious impacts on water quality due to transport of nutrients and pesticides from agricultural areas. |
| 12. Agricultural productivity | years to decades | local to basin | Yields of major crops have risen dramatically through use of fertilizers, pesticides, new varieties of crops, and other changes in farming practice. Economic and environmental doubts about long-term sustainability of chemically dependent agriculture are prompting growing interest in alternative farming practices. |

| 13. Shorelines | days to years | basin | Record high levels of the Great Lakes in the mid-1980s increased demand by riparian landowners for protection. There is continued public reluctance to accept that substantial year-to-year changes in levels are beyond cost-effective human control. Long-term declines are envisaged due to global warming. Greater emphasis is needed on shoreline management to prevent development in vulnerable areas, protect habitat, and allow multiple use. |

## D. Human Conditions

| 14. Human health | days to years | local to global | Available public health data on birth defects and cancer incidence are inadequate as indicators of health effects that may arise from biomagnification and bioaccumulation of toxic substances in the Great Lakes food web. Subgroups at risk may be offspring of those who consume sizable amounts of fish and other predators. A special effort is needed to develop measures for and examine the incidence of subtle developmental problems in groups at risk. Other probable risks to human health occur in areas of contaminated air and groundwater. |
| 15. Economic conditions | months to years | local to global | The Great Lakes basin is the manufacturing heartland of the United States and Canada. The U.S. side was affected strongly by the recession of the early 1980s. A general recovery is underway, speeding the transition from manufacturing dominance towards a more service-oriented economy. Facility modernization has benefited the environment. |

# Chapter 9

# From Agreement to Action: Implementing Programs

> A river or lake system, its waters, the living things they support, the lands
> beside them, the living things the land supports and the ways in which the land
> is used—all these, including human communities, comprise a system, with all
> the complex interrelatedness the word implies.
>
> On the other hand, the political administration, use, management . . . of that
> system form an extraordinary jigsaw puzzle bearing no relationship to the form
> of the system itself. Federal-provincial agreements, watershed management,
> conservation areas, and recognition of the need for ecosystem-based planning
> are all important steps, but clearly there is a long reach still to be travelled.
>
> —Canadian Environmental Advisory Council,
> *Land Use Planning and Sustainable Development in
> Canada*, 1989.

When Canada and the United States adopted an ecosystem approach
to water quality problems in the Great Lakes basin in 1978, they
recognized that policies and actions to restore and maintain the integrity
of the ecosystem need to be as comprehensive and integrated as the
ecosystem itself. The binational 1978 Great Lakes Water Quality
Agreement falls short of being a completely comprehensive approach
because of its focus on water quality. However, because water so
pervades the ecosystem, the actions necessary to implement the agreement represent a major portion of what is required to restore overall
ecosystem health. This chapter examines key elements of the effort to
implement the agreement since 1978. It indicates the institutional
mechanisms and resources required if the effort is to succeed, and it
points to some of the principal elements of national action and bina-

tional cooperation warranted by a truly comprehensive ecosystem approach.

For good reasons, Canada and the United States did not establish a "superagency" to implement the agreement. Instead, the two countries gave the job to existing federal, state, provincial, and local agencies, coordinating their activities primarily with and through the International Joint Commission (IJC). The two national governments assumed the obligations embodied in the agreement, but implementation involves many governmental and nongovernmental initiatives in both countries. These initiatives have had mixed success. The support given in principle to the ecosystem approach has not always been backed up in practice by the human, financial, and other resources needed to achieve the agreement's objectives.

Much of what has been attempted, and a large and expensive part of what remains to be done, consists of pollution control: after-the-fact efforts to clean up polluting discharges or waste dumps and contaminated sediments inherited from the past. At the same time, a start has been made on a "new agenda," anticipatory and preventive in character, to minimize present and future stresses to the Great Lakes ecosystem. Obvious and essential in principle, this new agenda requires major changes in attitudes and actions by energy, agriculture, transportation, industry, and other sectors whose understanding of ecosystem health has not matched their impact on the ecosystem.

## THE ORGANIZATIONAL PROBLEM

To appreciate both the novelty and the continuity represented in the 1978 agreement, one must see it in a broad historical context. As indicated in chapter 1, the agreement did not emerge from a vacuum; the institutional mechanisms for implementing the agreement draw on long-established national and binational institutions.

The basic element in this historical context is the Boundary Waters Treaty of 1909. This treaty provided a framework for subsequent cooperation between the United States and Canada on water (especially but not only in the Great Lakes). It created the IJC, and it included the basic principle that the boundary waters and waters flowing across the boundary "shall not be polluted on either side to the injury of health or property on the other."[1] This framework, and this principle, were used in subsequent decades, but to investigate pollution rather than to prevent it.

The existence of this treaty and of the IJC facilitated the 1972 Great Lakes Water Quality Agreement. In turn, despite its limited immediate objective—reducing nutrient flow to the lower lakes—the 1972 agreement enabled the IJC to create the International Reference Group on Pollution from Land Use Activities (PLUARG). PLUARG's more than 100 reports during the next six years were crucial in putting the ecosystem approach at the core of the 1978 agreement.

By adopting the ecosystem approach as the basis of the 1978 agreement, Canada and the United States committed themselves to an enterprise that was as novel and uncharted as the Boundary Waters Treaty had been 70 years earlier. In 1909 it had been necessary to create a new type of institution, the IJC, to implement the treaty's provisions. One option for carrying out the comprehensive undertaking of 1978 might have been to create a new binational body—a "Great Lakes Basin Water Quality Authority"—with powers over the whole area and in all the diverse fields affecting water quality. Such a body, to be successful, presumably required a substantial degree of authority, independent of other governmental structures, and assured funding. It is understandable that the United States and Canada did not create such a body—it would have involved transferring national sovereignty to "a state within a state."

A binational body of this kind would have encountered great difficulties in achieving a consistent approach throughout the basin, given the substantial differences in political philosophies between the United States and Canada. Legislation and related actions in the United States tend to be very detailed, specifying the kinds of regulations to be issued by the executive branch and deadlines for them. However, enormous amounts of time and energy are consumed in fighting over implementation, and litigation is the norm. This approach contrasts markedly with the situation in Canada, where legislation tends to state the general direction of policy but leaves considerable discretion to ministers and their departments to determine the scale, scope, style, and speed of implementation. There has traditionally been much less opportunity for public review of executive decisions than exists in the United States, and even less opportunity for judicial review.

Some U.S. observers find the discretion and apparent lack of accountability in the Canadian system disconcerting, and the U.S. system appears extremely cumbersome and unnecessarily adversarial to many Canadian observers. It would be very difficult for a single agency to impose a single system on both parts of the basin, and virtually impossible for such an agency to operate simultaneously in the two contrasting styles.

Furthermore, additional constitutional and legislative differences in the two systems of government would make a single agency unworkable in practice. In Canada there are clear areas of federal environmental jurisdiction, but, since both natural resources and municipal affairs are clearly within provincial jurisdiction, provincial governments have primary responsibility for environmental protection and natural resource management. In contrast, in the United States, the federal government has broad authority to address environmental issues and to define the major steps that states and local governments must take to develop and administer environmental programs. This federal intervention has been supported strongly by the courts. Some states have programs more stringent than federal requirements, but many others allow their programs to be shaped largely by federal demands.

More broadly, however, the relationship between provincial governments and the federal government in Canada differs profoundly from federal-state relations in the United States. Canada's small number of provinces, and the consequent influence that the major provinces can have on national affairs, explains the difference, at least in part:

> Federal-provincial conferences in Canada have no parallel in the United States. The president does not sit down with fifty governors to attempt to hammer out agreement on joint policies or programs. The number of states would make it impossible, but equally would the disparity in status and power between the president and the governors with whom he would be dealing.[2]

Another contrast is that the Canadian government does not possess the constitutional power that the U.S. government has to override state authority so that international agreements can be implemented.* Before Canada can agree with the United States on the Great Lakes ecosystem's health, it must first of all agree with Ontario. The Municipal-Industry Strategy for Abatement (MISA) initiative in Ontario is a major element in Canada's implementation of the agreement. However, if the Ontario government were unwilling to adopt or implement such a strategy, the federal government could neither compel it to do so nor

---

*The Great Lakes Water Quality Agreement is not a treaty signed by the president and ratified by the U.S. Senate. But the U.S. federal government can nevertheless require states to accomplish many of its goals through federal legislation, as noted in the text.

intervene with a comprehensive set of actions of its own.* In the United States, by contrast, if a state fails to develop a satisfactory program under the federal Clean Water Act to control municipal and industrial discharges to surface waters, the federal government develops and implements such a program.

In short, although both Canada and the United States share a common purpose in the Great Lakes basin, their political philosophies and systems of government are so different that an attempt to achieve that purpose through a single basinwide agency would not be feasible.[3]

## IMPLEMENTATION WITHIN EXISTING STRUCTURES: COOPERATION AND COORDINATION

The 1978 Great Lakes Water Quality Agreement defines its purpose and general and specific objectives to be achieved: It defines a role for the IJC, it identifies needed programs (for example, controls on point- and nonpoint sources on land, controls on discharges from ships, controls on dredging, and monitoring), and it commits the two national governments to seek necessary cooperation from state and provincial governments.[4]

Some of the difficulties that have been encountered stem from the broad ecosystem approach of the agreement. Even within the two federal environmental agencies (the U.S. Environmental Protection Agency [EPA] and Environment Canada) achieving a unified view of air, land, and water issues in the Great Lakes basin has taken years to accomplish—and is likely to remain an ongoing problem.[5] Securing the understanding and commitment of nonenvironmental agencies (for example, those dealing with energy and transportation) is even more difficult and time-consuming.

These problems become still more complex when multiple levels of government are included. The task has been easier on the Canadian side than in the United States, since the Canadian area defined in the agreement is contained within one province. Ontario officials participated in the negotiation of the agreement and its revision, and formal Canada-Ontario agreements have complemented the international undertakings. Comparable federal-state agreements to implement the

---

*MISA represented a significant strengthening of Ontario's program for controlling water pollution, but it was not launched until 1986—eight years after the 1978 Water Quality Agreement was signed.

agreement are absent on the United States side, although the states bear major responsibility for conducting programs to meet the agreement's goals. Such agreements would enhance state accountability for carrying out the agreement.[6] In both countries, furthermore, many of the daily tasks of environmental management and pollution control are in the hands of a large number of municipal and other local governments.

## THE ROLE OF THE INTERNATIONAL JOINT COMMISSION

Beyond essentially national problems, coordinated binational analysis and action are needed. Here, the IJC has a crucial and visible role, although the nature of that role has been the subject of debate and disagreement since the agreement was reached in 1978. In part, this debate was inevitable, since the agreement created expectations that could not be realized as quickly as was hoped. In part, however, the misunderstandings reflected ambiguity in the language of the agreement, especially over the extent of the IJC's implementation role. The IJC was to assist in implementing the agreement by helping to coordinate joint activities of the parties,* but it was sometimes unclear where the line should be drawn between the parties' responsibility and the IJC's. This uncertainty had implications, both for the parties' unwillingness to take on certain responsibilities and for the IJC's ability to evaluate independently the parties' activities.

Some groups are reluctant to abandon the idea of having a strong IJC manage the Great Lakes ecosystem. For example, in 1989, in response to disappointment over the implementation of the agreement by both Canada and the United States, Greenpeace demanded that

> the two federal governments restructure the IJC and invest in it the sole authority responsible for ecosystem management of the Great Lakes basin.[7]

Nevertheless, the philosophical and structural problems mentioned previously continue to put significant limits on how active the IJC can be in implementing the agreement. In 1984, the IJC reminded the Canadian and U.S. governments:

> It is the task of federal, state and provincial governments to integrate and co-

---

*The governments of the United States and Canada are referred to as "the parties" in the agreement.

ordinate governmental activities, supply scientific expertise and provide technical and financial resources. They are responsible for program implementation.[8]

The 1987 protocol to the agreement clarified the IJC's role, drawing a clearer line between its evaluative responsibilities and the parties' responsibilities for implementation. The IJC interpreted the protocol as follows:

> The principal function of the Commission under the Great Lakes Water Quality Agreement is the provision of advice to governments... The Commission sees as its primary activities therein, the assessment of the state of the Great Lakes, the assessment of the effectiveness of governmental programs to fulfill the Purpose of the agreement and, more specifically, the analysis of reports and plans prepared pursuant to the agreement.[9]

The IJC provides the formal meeting ground for many of the binational governmental and scientific activities involved in implementing the agreement. The IJC's principal advisor in discharging its duties is the Great Lakes Water Quality Board. Since this board has been composed entirely of government officials concerned with water quality problems, questions have been raised about the independence of IJC assessments. The commission asserts that members of both the Great Lakes Water Quality Board and the Science Advisory Board "serve . . . in a personal and professional capacity, not as representatives of their agencies or employers."[10]

The Water Quality Board's reports may be less hard-hitting than those issued by nongovernmental advocacy groups, but they nevertheless have advanced the agenda of ecosystem rehabilitation through such actions as identification of critical pollutants and Areas of Concern. Moreover, both the Water Quality Board and the Science Advisory Board, through their reports, have encouraged a "single vision" of the problems facing the restoration and maintenance of water quality that did not exist before the agreement. The structure of subcommittees and task forces developed by the boards has also extended the "invisible college" of Great Lakes researchers to include administrators and others who play key roles in implementing the agreement.

Relations between the IJC and the parties in regard to the agreement became better defined by the 1987 protocol, but some broader questions remain concerning other functions that the IJC could perform to foster achievement of the agreement's objectives. Article VII of the agreement gives the IJC investigative power (using various means ranging from data collection to public hearings) and the power to publish and report its views to the public as well as to state, provincial, and federal governments. The potential influence that these powers give the commission is considerable, but its use of them during the first decade of the agreement has been extremely limited.

Many different reasons can be advanced to explain the IJC's low profile. These include the clear rejection by both national governments during the 1970s of an expanded and more aggressive role for the IJC,[11] the nature and duration of commissioners' appointments, the small size of the IJC staff, and the ecosystem learning process through which everyone, including the commission, has passed since 1978. It would be difficult to point to specific topics that might have been addressed more effectively if the IJC had "gone public" about them. Even where the IJC has made recommendations, these frequently have not been responded to by the United States and Canada.[12]* Nevertheless, the IJC should continue to test the limits of the parties' tolerance for criticism.

The IJC has the power to report to the public "concerning any problem of water quality in the Great Lakes System,"[13] and its regional office in Windsor is empowered to "provide a public information service for the programs, including public hearings, undertaken by the Commission and its Boards" in connection with the agreement.[14] Neither of these powers has, however, been exercised as fully as it might be. This has been a particular source of frustration to the nongovernmental organizations concerned with Great Lakes issues—organizations with which the IJC might have cooperated more effectively to develop public commitment to the agreement and a "sense of the basin" among the public. These organizations have characterized the IJC's biennial public meetings as

> a frustrating, dissatisfying experience for those few citizen activists who have been able to attend. No serious opportunity has been provided . . . for the residents of the Great Lakes basin to present their assessment of Great Lakes water quality and to participate in policy making.[15]

A public hearing scheduled for the IJC's biennial meeting in October 1989 in Hamilton, Ontario, represents a clear attempt by the com-

---

*The 1987 protocol revising the Water Quality Agreement sought to increase the parties' accountability by requiring them to report on progress in implementing various provisions of the revised agreement (concerning, for example, Remedial Action Plans, Lakewide Management Plans, groundwater, sediments, and airborne pollutants). These reports could be used to respond to IJC recommendations.

mission to address this complaint. Interested groups have been invited to make statements to the IJC regarding implementation of the water quality agreement. Whether this is the beginning of a much more vigorous use by the IJC of its public hearing and reporting powers remains to be seen.

## REMEDIAL ACTION PLANS: ECOSYSTEM HEALTH IN LOCAL CONTEXTS

In a very real way, the Remedial Action Plans (RAPs) for Areas of Concern represent the major test of the ecosystem approach in the Great Lakes basin and also are the means through which that approach will affect large numbers of individuals and institutions. The 1990s will be the crucial period. Areas of Concern originated in the first reports prepared by the Water Quality Board in the early 1970s. From 69 "problem areas" identified in 1974, the number, the criteria for recognition, and the terminology all changed during the next 10 years. In particular, the board decided in 1981 to replace the ad hoc notion of "problem areas" with an ecosystem perspective. "Areas of Concern" would be "based on environmental quality data for all media (sediment, biota, and water)," and the areas would be evaluated according to uniform criteria.[16]

Since 1983, the Water Quality Board has recognized 42 Areas of Concern in the Great Lakes basin (see chapter 3, figure 3.3). Seven of these are along the shoreline of Lake Superior, 10 on Lake Michigan, 4 on Lake Huron, 6 on Lake Erie, 7 on Lake Ontario, and 8 are either connecting channels or are rivers that are tributary to connecting channels.[17] Twelve areas are in Canada, 25 in the United States, and 5 (all of them connecting channels) extend across the international boundary.

The 42 locations vary widely in geographical size, water quality problems, and size of local population. All, however, show biological communities affected by contaminants; all but one are characterized by toxic contamination of sediments and most by toxic substances in the water (figure 9.1). Most major cities on the lakes, from Duluth, Minnesota, to Rochester, New York, are in or close to Areas of Concern, although Chicago, Illinois, is only on the periphery of the Grand Calumet River–Indiana Harbor Canal area. In some cases, there is a single basic problem: for example, discharges from pulp and paper mills on the north shore of Lake Superior; radionuclide and heavy metal residues from radium and uranium refining during the 1930s and

## Figure 9.1
## Summary of Water Quality Problems Identified in Areas of Concern

| Ref. no.* | Area of Concern | Toxics in water | Toxics in sediments | Health advisories on fish | Fish tumors† | Impacted biological community | Elevated bacteria levels | Elevated phosphorus levels | Dissolved oxygen depletion |
|---|---|---|---|---|---|---|---|---|---|
| | **Lake Superior** | | | | | | | | |
| 1 | Peninsula Harbour | Y | Y | Y | ND | Y | N | | N |
| 2 | Jackfish Bay | Y | Y | Y | ND | Y | Y | Y | Y |
| 3 | Nipigon Bay | Y | Y | Y | ND | Y | Y | N | N |
| 4 | Thunder Bay | Y | Y | Y | Y | Y | Y | N | Y |
| 5 | St. Louis River / Bay | Y | Y | Y | ND | Y | N | Y | N |
| 6 | Torch Lake | Y | Y | Y | Y | Y | N | N | N |
| 7 | Deer Lake / Carp Creek / Carp River | N | Y | Y | ND | Y | N | Y | Y |
| | **Lake Michigan** | | | | | | | | |
| 8 | Manistique River | Y | Y | Y | ND | Y | N | N | N |
| 9 | Menominee River | Y | Y | Y | Y | Y | N | N | N |
| 10 | Fox River / Southern Green Bay | Y | Y | Y | Y | Y | Y | Y | Y |
| 11 | Sheboygan Harbor | Y | Y | Y | ND | Y | N | N | N |
| 12 | Milwaukee Estuary | Y | Y | Y | ND | Y | Y | Y | Y |
| 13 | Waukegan Harbor | Y | Y | Y | ND | Y | N | N | N |
| 14 | Grand Calumet / Indiana Harbor | Y | Y | Y | ND | Y | Y | Y | Y |
| 15 | Kalamazoo River | Y | Y | Y | ND | Y | Y | Y | Y |
| 16 | Muskegon Lake | N | Y | N | ND | Y | N | Y | Y |
| 17 | White Lake | Y | Y | Y | ND | Y | N | N | N |
| | **Lake Huron** | | | | | | | | |
| 18 | Saginaw River / Bay | Y | Y | Y | N | Y | Y | Y | Y |
| 19 | Collingwood Harbour | N | Y | Y | ND | Y | Y | Y | N |

| # | Location | 1 | 2 | 3 | 4 | 5 | 6 | 7 | 8 |
|---|---|---|---|---|---|---|---|---|---|
| 20 | Penetang Bay to Sturgeon Bay | N | Y | N | ND | Y | Y | Y | N |
| 21 | Spanish River | Y | Y | Y | ND | Y | Y | Y | N |
| | **Lake Erie** | | | | | | | | |
| 22 | Clinton River | N | N | N | ND | Y | Y | Y | Y |
| 23 | Rouge River | Y | Y | Y | Y | Y | Y | Y | Y |
| 24 | River Raisin | Y | Y | Y | Y | Y | Y | Y | Y |
| 25 | Maumee River | Y | Y | N | ND | Y | Y | Y | Y |
| 26 | Black River | Y | Y | Y | Y | Y | Y | Y | Y |
| 27 | Cuyahoga River | Y | Y | N | ND | Y | Y | Y | Y |
| 28 | Ashtabula River | Y | Y | Y | ND | Y | Y | Y | Y |
| 29 | Wheatley Harbour | N | Y | Y | ND | Y | Y | Y | Y |
| | **Lake Ontario** | | | | | | | | |
| 30 | Buffalo River | Y | Y | Y | Y | Y | Y | Y | Y |
| 31 | Eighteen Mile Creek | Y | Y | Y | ND | Y | N | N | N |
| 32 | Rochester Embayment | Y | Y | Y | ND | Y | Y | Y | N |
| 33 | Oswego River | Y | Y | Y | ND | Y | Y | Y | N |
| 34 | Bay of Quinte | Y | Y | Y | N | Y | Y | Y | Y |
| 35 | Port Hope | Y | Y | Y | Y | Y | N | Y | Y |
| 36 | Toronto Waterfront | Y | Y | Y | Y | Y | Y | Y | N |
| 37 | Hamilton Harbour | Y | Y | Y | Y | Y | Y | Y | Y |
| | **Connecting Channels** | | | | | | | | |
| 38 | St. Marys River | Y | Y | Y | Y | Y | Y | Y | N |
| 39 | St. Clair River | Y | Y | Y | N | Y | Y | Y | N |
| 40 | Detroit River | Y | Y | Y | Y | Y | Y | Y | N |
| 41 | Niagara River | Y | Y | Y | Y | Y | Y | Y | N |
| 42 | St. Lawrence River | Y | Y | Y | ND | Y | Y | Y | N |

Y = yes    N = no    ND = no data

*See figure 3.3 in chapter 3 for map showing location of each Area of Concern.

†In many cases, where fish tumors have been found, further work is warranted to determine the extent of the problem and the causative factor. In other cases, fish tumors have been directly linked to contamination in the sediments.

Source: International Joint Commission.

1940s at Port Hope on Lake Ontario. Where the local population is large, however, the problems are usually diverse, substantial, and of long standing.

The RAPs represent three kinds of tests of the ecosystem approach: scientific, financial, and political. The IJC is responsible for reviewing and commenting on the plans at three stages:

- Stage 1—when a definition of the problem has been completed;
- Stage 2—when remedial and regulatory measures have been selected; and
- Stage 3—when monitoring indicates that impaired beneficial uses have been restored.[18]

In its 1989 report, the Water Quality Board commented on the adequacy of the first eight RAPs submitted to the IJC.[19] More than half of these were found inadequate at stage 1 (problem definition). Despite this, the board reported ''considerable progress'' and expressed its satisfaction with the RAP program as a whole.[20]

The IJC clearly requires a high standard in the preparation and implementation of RAPs, especially in regard to their comprehensiveness. This need places even greater significance on the financial test: Can the necessary financial resources be made available to implement the RAPs effectively?

To a considerable extent, this question is premature. It will be some time before the second stage (selection of remedial and regulatory measures) has been completed for most RAPs, and only then can the costs of the plans be reliably estimated. However, even at the present preliminary stage, it is evident that costs will be substantial, and it has been suggested that in some cases they may be prohibitive. The principal problems in the Rouge River Area of Concern, for example, are caused by 185 combined sewer overflows (CSOs) and by contaminated bottom sediments. As elsewhere, the resolution of the sediment problem is still undefined; one estimate suggests that the capital and finance costs needed to make improvements to Rouge River's existing separate sanitary sewers and to construct CSO control projects will total U.S.$1.8 billion over 20 years. Similar problems are being encountered, and similarly high control costs are envisaged, in the Grand Calumet River/ Indiana Harbor Area of Concern.[21] By one estimator's calculations (see box), the overall costs for all the Areas of Concern ''to reestablish some semblance of ecosystem integrity'' are likely to be counted in

## What Will It Cost to Clean Up Areas of Concern?

At the request of the Institute for Research on Public Policy, Statistics Canada's David Rapport reviewed the initial estimates generated for cleaning up the RAPs and identified some of the major unknowns surrounding them.[1]

As of early 1989, costs had been estimated for 10 Areas of Concern, with the total for the 10 ranging between U.S.$2.8 billion and U.S.$5 billion. The bulk of these costs are for two areas of concern, the Rouge River, where U.S.$1.8 billion may be required to address storm water runoff, and the Grand Calumet River/Indiana Harbor Canal, where costs may total as much as U.S.$1.6 billion for clean-up. There is considerable uncertainty regarding estimated costs, especially the cost of dealing with contaminated sediments, which are a particularly severe problem in Grand Calumet River/Indiana Harbor Canal. The cost of managing contaminated sediments depends on the type of remedial action to be taken (from monitoring to removal) and the type of process used to treat the sediments. For example, treatment of contaminated sediments can cost from U.S.$30 to U.S.$1,800 per cubic yard, depending on the process required.

Leaking landfills and waste sites are another major source of uncertainty. The RAPs do not include clean-up costs for such places. Citing work by Cate Leger of the Northeast-Midwest Institute, Rapport notes that 27 Areas of Concern on the U.S. side have leaking dumps; there are several thousand hazardous waste sites with potential impact on the Great Lakes basin, and some 92 potential sites have been identified in the Grand Calumet River/Indiana Harbor Canal area. Individual sites could cost millions of dollars to clean up, adding to a total of billions of dollars in expense.

Based on these and other considerations, Rapport guesses that a minimum estimate for the cost of cleaning up the areas of concern is U.S.$100 billion to U.S.$500 billion. He adds: "If this proves correct, it is likely a price that cannot or will not be paid." Thus, the damage already done to the health of the Great Lakes ecosystem is not likely to be repairable in total, or perhaps even in large part.[2]

From his guess about the cost of cleaning up the mistakes of the past, Rapport says "the lesson is clear": there must be "a redoubling of efforts aimed at prevention of further degradation."

---

tens of billions of dollars, and a minimum estimate for restoring integrity may be between U.S.$100 billion and U.S.$500 billion.

Fortunately, this estimate may be too high. The cost estimates that are currently available are fragmentary and unreliable. In those areas where problems are straightforward, costs may not be exorbitant. If there are technological breakthroughs (for example, in biotechnology) for addressing contaminated sediments and hazardous waste sites, projected expenses for such problems may drop.

Nevertheless, it is undeniable that the RAPs will be expensive. Funding 42 RAPs simultaneously will be a major burden, especially in key jurisdictions such as Michigan and Ontario. These financial demands will test severely public and political commitment to the Water Quality Agreement.

There is not space in this report to summarize the problems in the 42 areas and the different approaches to their solution that are being developed. Instead, two representative Areas of Concern are discussed briefly: Hamilton Harbour at the western end of Lake Ontario, and Fox River and Southern Green Bay on the Wisconsin shore of Lake Michigan.

## Hamilton Harbour

If the Cuyahoga or Rouge rivers have in the past symbolized water quality deterioration in the U.S. portion of the basin, Hamilton Harbour is the archetypal problem area on the Canadian side.

Hamilton Harbour is an almost-enclosed body of water at the western tip of Lake Ontario (figure 9.2). It is triangular in shape and about 8 square miles (2,150 hectares) in area. It is separated from the open water of Lake Ontario by a narrow sandbar through which the Burlington Ship Canal has been cut to provide navigation access to the harbour. The total area of the Hamilton Harbour drainage basin is 208 square miles (49,400 hectares).

The harbour is well known to many Canadians and Americans, since the Queen Elizabeth Way linking Toronto with Niagara Falls and Buffalo is carried across the sandbar and canal on the Burlington Skyway Bridge. Beneath the bridge, in a rather symbolic location, is the Canada Centre for Inland Waters, a federal government research institute.[22]

When seen from a vehicle on the Queen Elizabeth Way, the dominant impression is of the largest concentration of heavy industry in Canada. The Stelco and Dofasco steel mills are waterside plants that are partly built on reclaimed land. Hamilton is the second largest Canadian port on the Great Lakes, and the sixth largest in Canada. Behind the industrialized waterfront is a metropolitan area, within the Hamilton Harbour watershed, of approximately 500,000 people.

The problems of Hamilton Harbour are therefore those that would be expected of an almost-enclosed body of water that has deteriorated over generations of industrial activity and urban growth. One of the main problems is the amount of ammonia ($NH_3$) discharged by industry and sewage treatment plants. In spring, the levels of ammonia are so high that they are toxic to fish. During the summer, bacteria convert

## Figure 9.2
## Bird's Eye View of Hamilton Harbour

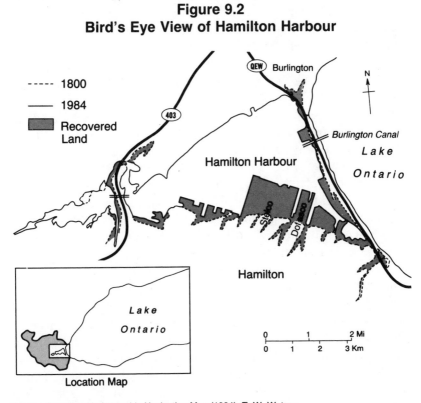

Source: Canadian Hydrographic Navigation Map (1984); T. W. Watson.

much of the ammonia to nitrate. This eliminates the toxicity problem but creates another, since 40 percent of the available oxygen is consumed in this conversion. Low dissolved oxygen levels are a particular problem in the deeper waters (hypolimnion) of the harbour in summer. The only link to Lake Ontario is the ship canal, which has a maximum depth of 31 feet (9.4 meters). This means that in summer the only exchange between the harbour and the lake is of relatively warm water that remains on the surface. The deeper water is consequently deprived of oxygen in summer, so that oligotrophic (cold water) fish species such as whitefish or lake trout must leave the harbour if they are to survive.

In many areas of concern, efforts to rehabilitate the environment are taking place in advance of a formal RAP. Over the last two decades, the Hamilton Harbour RAP team has noted, major improvements have been recorded: several species of birds have returned, the number and diversity of fish species are increasing, and the number and type of worms inhabiting the bottom sediments have improved.[23]

The cost of these achievements has been about C$300 million, spent by industries and all levels of government on pollution abatement programs. For example, industrial loadings of ammonia to the harbour, a key problem, have been reduced from about 24,000 kilograms per day (52,910 pounds per day) in 1967 to about 857 kilograms per day (1,889 pounds per day) in 1987. There has, however, been no comparable reduction in ammonia loadings from municipal sewage treatment plants. Hamilton and Burlington together added over 6,000 kilograms per day (13,228 pounds per day) from 1985 to 1987. In the past, municipal plants merely added to the base load from industry. Now, however, the problem is with these plants, not with industry.

A "stakeholders'" group is defining the goals of the Hamilton Harbour RAP. The group consists of 49 people representing "agencies, organizations, institutions, government departments, industries and private citizen groups who make use of, wish to make use of, or in some manner have jurisdiction over the use of Harbour water."[24] (Public participation programs have so far been established in 32 of the 42 Areas of Concern, but not all employ stakeholder groups.)[25]

The stakeholders' group produced its list of goals for the harbour at the end of 1986. The list is lengthy and varied, but it became apparent that, if three key goals can be achieved, there should be little difficulty in attaining the others. The key issues concern a naturally reproducing fishery for both warm- and cold-water species, enhanced wildlife habitat, and water quality that would permit swimming.

Although the plan has not been completed or approved, substantial action is being taken to achieve the various goals defined by the stakeholders. Moreover, the act of creating the plan may itself contribute to the goals being accepted as feasible and appropriate, rather than impractical and idealistic, as they would probably have seemed two decades ago. To achieve a reduction in ammonia loadings by the sewage treatment plants that would bring total loadings in the harbour within target limits will cost C$9 million; in view of the C$300 million spent already by industry and others, this does not seem an impossible sum.*

---

*Even then, the two treatment plants will still discharge over 3,000 kilograms of ammonia per day (6,614 pounds per day), whereas Stelco and Dofasco are spending C$13 million to cut the 870 kilograms per day (1,918 pounds per day) they discharged in 1987 to 270 kilograms per day (595 pounds per day).

Ammonia is only part of the problem, however. One of the key challenges will be to deal with the discharge of raw sewage into the harbour from municipal sewage treatment plants. This, as in many other communities, occurs when combined sewage and storm water runoff exceeds the capacity of the treatment system during periods of high runoff. The only alternative to an extremely costly reconstruction and separation of sewage and storm drains is to construct tanks in which the overflow can be retained and then recirculated for treatment when flows diminish. The regional municipality has initiated such a containment program, but:

> It is estimated that [C]$60 million may be needed to control CSOs [combined sewer overflows]. At the present rate of commitment of funds, the Regional Municipality will take in the order of 20-40 years to complete the program. If funds were not limiting, the CSOs could probably be controlled within 5 years.[26]

It is this type of reordering of priorities that RAPs must achieve if they are to succeed.

## Fox River/Southern Green Bay

There are no steel mills at the southern end of Green Bay, and the population of the lower Fox River valley is smaller than that of the Hamilton Harbour watershed: about 400,000.[27] Nevertheless, there are striking similarities as well as differences when the two Areas of Concern are compared.

Ecologically, Green Bay is often regarded as a freshwater estuary, with characteristics that contrast both with its tributary rivers and with the open waters of Lake Michigan, from which it is separated by a chain of small islands. The early history of the area, in terms of environmental deterioration, is a familiar one: forest clearance and associated pollution of the rivers and Green Bay, increased runoff from the cleared lands when converted to agriculture, damming of the Fox River for hydropower, and overfishing combining with oxygen depletion caused by paper mill discharges. At present, there are 13 paper mills and 5 major municipal sewage treatment plants along the Fox River.

Although deterioration began in the mid-1800s, it was, as in other Areas of Concern, the post-World War II period that combined an increasing rate and scale of pollution with significant public concern. The yellow perch catch in southern Green Bay fell from 2.4 million pounds (1,089 tonnes) in 1943 to 162,000 pounds (73 tonnes) in 1966. Green Bay's public beach was permanently closed in 1943 due to fecal coliform bacteria, and in the 1950s the city was forced to take its drinking water from Lake Michigan, since the groundwater table was dropping and Green Bay was regarded as too polluted.

The Green Bay RAP is remarkable for its degree of citizen involvement. A Citizens' Advisory Committee and four technical advisory committees advised the Wisconsin Department of Natural Resources in the plan's development. The citizens' committee identified the 10 most pressing problems to be addressed by the plan and a desired state for the lower river and bay by the year 2000 (figure 9.3). The latter took a very broad, ecosystemic view, encompassing good water quality, a balanced edible sport and commercial fishery, balanced shoreline use, productive wildlife and plant communities, and an economical transportation network. The plan established quantitative targets, such as densities of wildlife populations, concentrations of contaminants, and wetland acreage.[28]

One of the major reasons for the technical sophistication of the plan, and the substantial citizen involvement, lies in the foundation about 20 years earlier at the University of Wisconsin of a substantial Sea Grant program. Green Bay became a focus for research that documented both the water quality deterioration's scale and character and the scope for rehabilitation. Prior to development of the RAP, in response to the federal Clean Water Act, water quality and the Green Bay fishery had shown marked improvement. Further improvement via the RAP is being promoted by building on the substantial reserve of expertise developed in the community during the past 20 years. The RAP for this area was among the first to be completed, and the first to be approved at stage 1.[29]

Both Hamilton Harbour and Green Bay demonstrate the potential that RAPs offer for communities to develop a vision of how they would like their future environment to look and measures to achieve it. RAPs provide, at a local level, a vehicle for rehabilitating the existing ecosystem, minimizing future problems, and paving the way for a broadly integrated consideration of both economic and environmental concerns. The challenge to those developing RAPs for other areas is to meet or better the ambitious objectives for community involvement and ecosystem rehabilitation set in Hamilton Harbour and Green Bay and to find the means to pay for the required programs.

In all the Areas of Concern, considerable cooperation will be required to ensure that plans developed in the RAP process do not gather dust. Carrying RAPs to fruition, from the initial planning stages to deployment

# Figure 9.3
# Present State and Desired Future State
# of the Lower Green Bay Ecosystem

## Present State

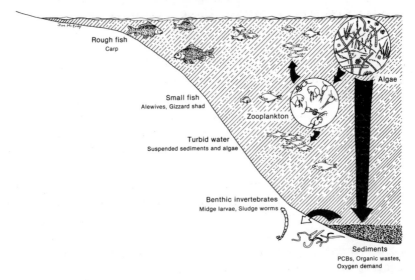

## Desired Future State

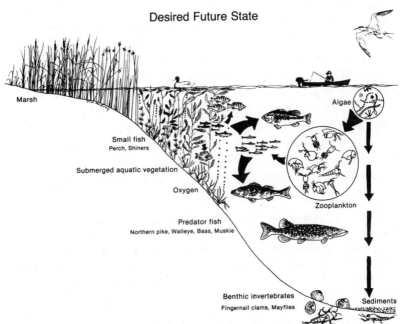

Illustrations courtesy of Jim McEvoy, Wisconsin Department of Natural Resources.

of often expensive remedies, will require a substantial commitment of resources from both the public and private sector and the creation of institutions to assure sustained public and private involvement.

## AGREEMENTS ON WATER QUALITY AND QUANTITY MANAGEMENT AMONG STATES AND PROVINCES IN THE GREAT LAKES BASIN

The 1978 Water Quality Agreement represents a national commitment by the United States and Canada, but it has also facilitated cooperation and coordinated action by the governments of the states and provinces in the Great Lakes basin. As noted earlier in this chapter, the constitutional powers possessed by Ontario and the other Canadian provinces to deal with the environment are substantial. In the United States, the general shift of responsibility from Washington, D.C., to the states during the 1980s has involved the environment as well as many other fields, even though the federal government remains the dominant authority. It is, therefore, not surprising that the Great Lakes states and Ontario have found increasing reason to coordinate their activities through formal agreements. Because of its concern for the St. Lawrence, Quebec is frequently also a participant.

The most notable achievements in recent years are the 1985 Great Lakes Charter and the 1986 Great Lakes Toxic Substances Control Agreement (GLTSCA). Both are voluntary arrangements to share information and to take a unified stance in protection of Great Lakes resources. Both contain the types of bold, forward-looking management principles found in the 1978 Great Lakes Water Quality Agreement. Both were initiated by the Council of Great Lakes Governors, formed in 1983 by six of the eight Great Lakes states (subsequently joined by New York and Pennsylvania), to promote regional economic development and the protection and enhancement of water resources in the basin.[30]*

The charter and the GLTSCA stress the economic and environmental

*Creation of the council was, in part, a response to the void created in 1981 by abolition of the Great Lakes Basin Commission. The Great Lakes Basin Commission was abolished by the Reagan administration, along with other regional water planning commissions. Its major contribution during the 1970s had been the *Great Lakes Basin Framework Study*, a planning document (for the U.S. side only) designed to guide conservation, use, and development of water and land resources in the Great Lakes area through the year 2000. The multivolume report brought together analyses by a wide range of federal agencies, working in cooperation with state and local governments.

importance of the Great Lakes and the need to manage the lakes in an integrated fashion. The charter is a nonbinding, good-faith agreement among the states and provinces; it was motivated in large measure by a desire to resist potential pressures for the transfer of Great Lakes water to more arid regions. The charter asserts that diversions of water resources from the Great Lakes basin will not be allowed if, individually or collectively, such diversions would have significant, adverse impacts on lake levels, in-basin uses, and the Great Lakes ecosystem.[31] The charter commits the parties to develop a common data base on water resource use and a cooperative management program that includes an inventory of surface water and groundwater resources. The charter entitles the signatory governments to prior notice and consultation on major new or increased diversions of basin water by other signatories, if the governments to be notified and consulted have previously adopted legislation for registering and regulating large withdrawals.

The charter has now been signed by all eight Great Lakes states and the provinces of Ontario and Quebec. By the end of 1988, nearly all of the jurisdictions had taken the actions (for example, adopting legislation) entitling them to prior notice and consultation. The data base has been established in another regional organization, the Great Lakes Commission.* The cooperation between the Council of Great Lakes Governors and the commission on this matter is a reminder of the cooperative arrangements frequently struck in the Great Lakes basin among the jurisdictions to help overcome institutional fragmentation.

The GLTSCA, signed in mid-1986 by the eight Great Lakes states, is an extremely ambitious document that commits the signatories to reducing toxic substances in the Great Lakes basin.† It calls for better integration of permitting processes for discharges to different media, development of coordinated groundwater management programs, interstate cooperation in hazardous waste management planning, ex-

---

*The Great Lakes Commission should not be confused with the defunct Great Lakes Basin Commission. The Great Lakes Commission was established in the late 1960s by an interstate compact consented to by the U.S. Congress. The commission is composed of representatives of the eight Great Lakes states appointed by the governors and legislatures of the states. The commission focuses on issues of economic development, resource management, and environmental quality.

†In 1988, Ontario and Quebec signed a memorandum of understanding with the states to implement the agreement in Canada.

change of information on fish contamination, development of common health advisories on fish contamination, and a host of other measures. The signatories have agreed in principle to develop a strategy for greater consistency among jurisdictions in the environmental permits they issue and to develop mechanisms for incorporating the effects of toxic air emissions on Great Lakes water quality into air emission permits.

Implementation of this agreement is, however, in its earliest stages. Information exchange and increased understanding by all parties represent important steps, but much harder steps lie ahead. The key tests of progress in implementing the agreement's provisions will be the firm adoption of more consistent and protective water quality standards, similar commitment to air pollution control programs that provide for enhanced monitoring and regulation of toxic air pollutants, and allocation of resources to create the various monitoring programs called for in the deliberations of various work groups operating pursuant to the agreement.

## PUBLIC INFORMATION AND INVOLVEMENT

The free flow of information and ideas between concerned citizens and government officials is an essential element in the development and implementation of public policy. Complaints about public information and public involvement have been commonplace in environmental controversies, although in recent years, access to information and opportunities for public involvement in programs have improved.

Generally speaking, public access to information—the right to be informed—and structured public participation in government decision making—the right to be heard—have been less readily available in Canada than in the United States. Arguably, this reflects the predominant political culture in both countries. Canadians historically have placed greater trust in their government to act in their best interest, while the United States has provided many opportunities to make sure that individual rights to be informed and heard are protected.

In the United States, under the federal Freedom of Information Act passed in 1966, a well-structured process has governed the release of information. Many state governments also have adopted freedom of information laws. Periodic tempests over secrecy notwithstanding, it is relatively easy to gain access to government-gathered information in the United States. In Canada, the process has been slower. A 1978 handbook on Canadian environmental law complained that in Ontario there was no established public procedure for citizens to obtain information, and, generally, when requests for information are made, "civil servants . . . maintain a rigid policy of releasing as little information as possible."[32]

Provision of environmental information and public participation have improved in Canada since the late 1970s. One observer has characterized the transition as an evolution from statutory silence to enlightened administration to statutory recognition of public participation.[33] A federal Access to Information Act was adopted in the early 1980s, and a similar measure subsequently was adopted by Ontario. More recently, Environment Canada engaged in a broad process of public consultation in developing the new Canadian Environmental Protection Act (CEPA), and the act itself contains provisions for public participation.

Information has also flowed somewhat more freely from Ontario where, for example, the Ministry of Environment has annually published volumes describing the compliance of individual municipal and industrial dischargers with water pollution abatement guidelines. Canada's and Ontario's programs for citizen involvement and information continue to evolve, with citizen groups pressing for further opening of the process.

Citizen participation has also been a major issue in the international context. For example, concerned about the inadequacy of efforts by the IJC, the United States, and Canada to solicit public input on prospective revisions to the Great Lakes Water Quality Agreement, Great Lakes United convened 19 "citizens' hearings" around the lakes in mid-1986 to air citizen concerns about the lakes and recommendations for improvements in implementing the agreement.[34]*

Two developments of particular importance to public information and involvement have been the growth of "basinwide" nongovernmental organizations and the increasing use of "stakeholder groups" in developing environmental policy. It is presumably as difficult for citizens to adjust to an ecosystem approach to environmental rehabitation as it is for governments, and it is also not easy to make this

---

*In 1987, Canada and the United States recognized the growing importance of citizen concern and knowledge in the international arena. Representatives of Great Lakes United, the National Wildlife Federation, and the Sierra Club were granted formal observer status for the two-party negotiations of revisions to the Great Lakes Water Quality Agreement.

adjustment for an area the size of the Great Lakes basin. Although there are literally hundreds of nongovernmental bodies with a direct concern in one or more aspects of the Great Lakes basin ecosystem, the last 10 years or so have seen the emergence of several organizations—for example, the Center for the Great Lakes and Great Lakes United—that are explicitly binational, basinwide, and responsive to the ecosystem approach of the Great Lakes Water Quality Agreement (see box). As one observer has noted, such organizations have rapidly assumed a prominent role in Great Lakes management, not only as a governmental "watchdog" but as a means to assume vital functions (for example, coordination and special studies) once undertaken by public institutions.[35] In a separate category is the International Association for Great Lakes Research, which over a longer period has done much to strengthen the "invisible college" of academic and other researchers on which the ecosystem approach depends for much of its knowledge and understanding.

"Stakeholder groups" have become an important participatory mechanism consisting of both governmental as well as nongovernmental representatives. They seem particularly suited to the multifaceted character of ecosystem issues. For example, the "cradle-to-grave" management approach to chemicals that underlies the 1988 CEPA was the product of a stakeholders' group (the Task Force on the Management of Chemicals), with 12 members representing industry, governments, labor, environmental groups, and consumers.[36] As noted already, stakeholder groups are becoming particularly significant in developing RAPs in Areas of Concern.

## PROVIDING THE RESOURCES

Setting a price tag on the 1978 Great Lakes Water Quality Agreement is difficult because of the multiplicity of objectives, the almost infinite numbers of actions and processes relevant to the agreement, and the countless numbers of entities involved. It is relatively easy to measure spending for discrete federal programs and discrete federal agencies. For example, a review of federal spending in the United States for some Great Lakes programs shows a cut in financial support during the 1980s for programs clearly related to the Great Lakes (see box, "Federal Funding for U.S. Great Lakes Programs").

Assessing state environmental agency spending for Great Lakes programs is less easily accomplished. State accounting systems are quite

## The Rise of Binational NGO Activity

The growing regional consciousness in the Great Lakes—and the importance of private action to encourage and sustain this consciousness—is reflected in the activities of two nongovernmental organizations (NGOs), Great Lakes United (GLU), and the Center for the Great Lakes.

GLU, formed in 1982, consists of more than 180 member organizations and 800 individual members in the eight states and two provinces bordering the Great Lakes and the St. Lawrence River. Its membership includes environmental groups, locals of the United Auto Workers in the United States and auto workers in Canada, sportsmen's organizations, cities, counties, and others. The organization receives its support not only from organizational and individual members but also from private foundations, mostly in the United States, that historically have had an interest in Great Lakes issues. Its major focus has been the critical environmental problems of the Great Lakes basin, including implementation of the Water Quality Agreement and GLTSCA, as well as diversions of water from the basin. GLU has produced citizen agendas for cleaning up several of the Great Lakes, has cosponsored "Great Lakes Week" for legislators and administration officials in Washington, D.C., and publishes a periodic tabloid newspaper on Great Lakes environmental issues. In GLU's own words, it "has provided the catalyst for Great Lakes' citizens to be involved in the decisionmaking process." GLU is governed by a board of directors from both the United States and Canada.

The Center for the Great Lakes, a second binational organization, is a nonprofit research and communication organization formed in 1983. With offices in Chicago and Toronto, and with support from private foundations, corporations, individual donors, and government agencies, the center has focused on promoting sound public policies for environmental protection, resource management, and economic development. The center conducts research, sponsors binational meetings of public officials from the United States and Canada, and has forged good working relationships with the Council of Great Lakes Governors and state officials in the United States. Its research reports have included a guidebook on alternative shoreline management strategies, surveys of waterfront developments, and a feasibility study for the Great Lakes Protection Fund sponsored by the Council of Great Lakes Governors. The center also has published a directory of Great Lakes natural resources organizations and is establishing a Great Lakes information center.

Both of these organizations demonstrate the important role nongovernmental organizations play in generating information, coordinating activities among jurisdictions within the United States and Canada, and fostering ties among private and public organizations spanning the international boundary.

## Federal Funding for U.S. Great Lakes Programs

Federal programs directed specifically at the Great Lakes suffered greatly during the 1980s (figure 9.4). The EPA Large Lakes Research Station was targeted for closure by the Reagan administration, only to be saved by congressional action. But even while being saved by Congress, its budget was cut. EPA's funding for Great Lakes research between 1980 and 1987 declined 60 percent in inflation-adjusted dollars.[1] The budget of EPA's Great Lakes National Program Office, which has principal responsibility within the agency for overseeing implementation of the Water Quality Agreement, decreased 58 percent in inflation-adjusted dollars during the same period. The program office's budget has increased markedly since 1987, reflecting new responsibilities assigned by amendments to the federal Clean Water Act, but its funding still falls far short of funds authorized by Congress.

Between fiscal years 1980 and 1987, funding for the Sea Grant program in the Great Lakes states fell 23 percent; Sea Grant was another program targeted for extinction by the Reagan administration during its early years, only to be saved by Congress at reduced levels of funding.

These funding decisions serve as a reminder that, while the United States has agreed in principle to support an ecosystem approach to Great Lakes management, in practice funding cuts made implementation of that approach much more difficult. In early 1989, a coalition of Great Lakes organizations, including environmental groups, the Great Lakes Commission, and the Council of Great Lakes Governors, called for a marked increase in federal spending on Great Lakes programs. Five federal Great Lakes programs (the EPA Great Lakes National Program Office and Large Lakes Station, the National Oceanic and Atmospheric Administration's Great Lakes Environmental Research Laboratory, the Fish and Wildlife Service's National Fisheries Research Center, and the Great Lakes Fishery Commission) had been appropriated an estimated $27.8 million in FY1989; $25 million was being sought by the new Bush administration for FY1990. Noting a host of important spending needs, including continued lamprey control, research on toxic effects, establishment of a wildlife specimen data bank, and wetlands monitoring, the regional groups stated that an ideal budget for these offices in FY1990 would be $49 million.[2]

complex, and Great Lakes programs are not budgeted separately. For the one state entirely in the basin, Michigan, the budgetary picture for environmental programs during the 1980s was particularly bleak (see box, "Michigan's Environmental Budget").

Budget data for Environment Canada and the Ontario Ministry of the Environment have not been systematically reviewed. Certain Ontario programs, such as MISA and enforcement, are generally recognized to have had substantial budget increases in recent years. But, at the federal level in Canada, there has been a sustained effort to

**Figure 9.4**
**Funding History of Selected Great Lakes Programs,**
**in Constant Dollars, 1980–1989**

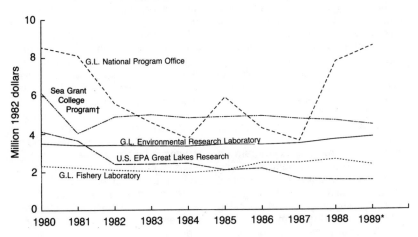

*Estimated.

†For the Great Lakes only.

Source: U.S. Environmental Protection Agency; Northeast-Midwest Institute.

"downsize" the federal civil service, especially after the Progressive Conservatives replaced the Liberals as the party in power in 1984. Environment Canada has been affected by these cuts.

In the United States and Canada, environmental programs will likely command more government attention in the 1990s than in the 1980s, but they will continue to struggle for funding, especially at the federal level. Public concern for environmental issues is mounting in both countries, so the national governments now attach high priority to the environment. But federal governments also are concerned about accumulated budget deficits. Action to reduce these deficits will inevitably threaten the federal allocation to Great Lakes issues in the United States and Canada. Such budget constraints do not bode well for environmental programs. A heavy burden for implementing RAPs and other activities will fall on state, provincial, and local governments. Provision of this funding will represent a major test of political and public commitment to environmental improvement.

## Michigan's Environmental Budget

The gap between state spending and state needs for environmental programs is illustrated most starkly in the state of Michigan. Michigan was especially hard hit during the U.S. economic recession of the early 1980s, and it is still returning to economic health.

The state's Department of Natural Resources (DNR) suffered a 9 percent cut in personnel between FY1980 and FY1989.[1] It lost much of its ability to monitor water quality and, as of early 1987, had only one person to administer a program on soil erosion and sedimentation.[2] The state groundwater-discharge permit program had a 13-year backlog, and the air quality program had a backlog of 5,000 operating permits.[3]

For FY1989, the governor sought $1.1 million as part of a Great Lakes initiative, but the legislature appropriated only $600,000.[4] No state funds were appropriated for RAPs; other sources of funding for them were found.

In November 1988, Michigan's voters passed a bond issue that includes $425 million for cleaning up toxic waste sites, $150 million for solid waste problems, $25 million for Michigan's contribution to the Great Lakes Protection Fund sponsored by the Council of Great Lakes Governors, and $70 million for state parks.[5] However, the bond issue did not address much of the fundamental problem of understaffing that plagues DNR's programs. Higher taxes, user fees, or other funding mechanisms are needed to support personnel increases.

## COMPLIANCE

Standards, regulations, guidelines, and other measures limiting the discharge of pollutants are key administrative tools used to achieve environmental goals. As discussed in chapter 2, the stringency of standards limiting discharges is hotly debated. That question aside, standards become meaningless if they are not complied with.

Jurisdictions in both the United States and Canada routinely gather and publish statistics on compliance. In all jurisdictions, government regulators depend heavily on voluntary action. Nonetheless, a sizable rate of noncompliance does raise questions about the reasons for noncompliance and what is being done about the situation.*

Administrators generally separate compliance by municipal sewage treatment plants from compliance by industrial dischargers. In Ontario, the Ministry of the Environment (MOE) reported that, in 1986, only 61 percent of 385 municipal sewage treatment plants assessed met all

---

*Dischargers comply with requirements for such diverse reasons as a general sense of civic duty, concern for public image, confidence in the fairness and equitable application of a standard, and fear of punishment for violations.

their discharge obligations.[37] Forty-nine percent of the 258 facilities in the province required to meet stringent phosphorus-discharge control requirements failed to do so consistently.

Industrial compliance also leaves much to be desired. In Ontario in 1986, 41 percent of 154 dischargers reporting failed to comply with annual average limits for discharges; this figure rose to 71 percent for compliance with monthly average limits on discharges. Thirty-one percent of the dischargers violated one or more discharge requirements for six months or longer during the year.[38] The 154 dischargers for which compliance data have been gathered represent but a small portion of the many thousands of industrial dischargers in Ontario, since most dischargers have not been required to report to MOE. Most of the others currently discharge to municipal sewage systems, and little is known about these discharges. Under Ontario's new MISA program, an enhanced effort is being made to address them.

The Great Lakes states contain 30 percent of the major municipal facilities in the United States that must comply with final discharge standards.[39] As of late 1987, 10 percent of the 815 facilities in the Great Lakes states were not complying with standards, including 23 percent of the 56 facilities in Ohio.* Also, 9 percent of the major industrial facilities in the Great Lakes states failed to comply with final discharge standards.

## ENFORCEMENT

Enforcement of environmental laws and regulations is essential both to deal with recalcitrant polluters and to encourage high levels of voluntary compliance. A weak enforcement effort encourages noncompliance and may also put those who do comply at a competitive disadvantage.

---

*The statistics reported in this paragraph are for what EPA labels "significant noncompliance," a term that distinguishes major from minor violations. More recent statistics, for 421 major municipal plants in the Great Lakes targeted for special treatment under EPA's "National Municipal Policy," show a continuing compliance problem in the Great Lakes. As of the July 1, 1988, deadline for compliance with the policy, only 67 percent of the plants in the Great Lakes states were in compliance. Enforcement action had been launched or was contemplated against another 22 percent, while another 13 percent were en route to compliance under judicial or administrative order. The compliance rate for plants in the Great Lakes states was significantly below the 89 percent compliance rate for the entire United States.[40]

Enforcement takes a wide variety of forms, from informal notifications of dischargers to criminal actions in the courts. It includes technical assistance, cajolery, and punitive action. It appears that in Canada primary emphasis is placed on the first two of these three, whereas in the United States the emphasis is on the last two.

In evaluating the adequacy of environmental programs in the United States, with its adversarial legal system, much attention frequently focuses on the number of lawsuits that are filed against dischargers. Lawsuits are, however, just the tip of the enforcement iceberg. In some respects, a lawsuit reflects a failure of alternative efforts to bring about compliance.

During the early years of the Reagan administration in the United States, lawsuits filed by EPA (on a nationwide basis) showed a dramatic drop, reflecting both administrative changes within the agency and a more conciliatory attitude towards industry. Lawsuits referred to the U.S. Department of Justice by EPA between 1980 and 1982 dropped 50 percent.[41] They have more than tripled since that time.

Much enforcement activity in the United States occurs at the state rather than the federal level. Although correlating compliance rates and enforcement practices is difficult, it is reasonable to conclude that enhanced enforcement leads to enhanced compliance. Ohio's state Environmental Protection Agency claims that improvements in compliance with its air quality regulations were primarily the result of stepped-up enforcement activity.[42]

Under most major U.S. environmental laws, individual citizens and citizen groups can file lawsuits against individual dischargers for violation of discharge requirements. Such citizen suits are obvious indicators of shortfalls in federal and state enforcement activity. Indeed, a sharp rise in citizen lawsuits in 1982 was directly related to a perceived lack of federal EPA enforcement at the time. Within the Great Lakes states, one citizen group, the Atlantic States Legal Foundation, has filed an estimated 50 to 100 lawsuits against dischargers for violations of water discharge permits.[43]

Enforcement practices in Canada are strikingly different from those in the United States. Several federal environmental laws (for example, the Fisheries Act) contain provisions for enforceable regulations, but much of the federal effort is devoted to adopting nonenforceable guidelines. In some instances, provinces use these guidelines as the basis for establishing provincial requirements that are made legally binding on dischargers. In other instances, Environment Canada reaches agreements under which provinces are the primary enforcers of federal requirements.

Although much of the responsibility for environmental legislation and enforcement is in the hands of the provinces, it has been generally recognized that enforcement within federal jurisdiction has been inadequate. In parliamentary debate on CEPA in 1987, it was noted that few successful prosecutions had been brought under existing legislation and that the penalties had been relatively trivial (figure 9.5).[44]

That situation may be about to change. CEPA has significantly stronger enforcement provisions than earlier legislation, including unlimited fines and/or imprisonment for up to five years against anyone who "intentionally or recklessly causes a disaster that results in a loss of the use of the environment."[45] It remains to be seen how firmly this and similar provisions are enforced.

In Ontario, interest in enforcement by the courts has been on the rise in recent years.[46] Signs of this include statutory increases in the fines that can be levied for violating Ontario's environmental laws, establishment in 1985 of an Investigations and Enforcement branch in MOE, and rising numbers of prosecutions. Despite this, MOE has been criticized by Ontario's auditor general for insufficiently investigating and taking enforcement action against dischargers in the province.[47] The greater emphasis on prosecutions in Ontario is a marked departure from what in the past has often been regarded as a congenial relationship between government and industry. The Quebec government has also recently stepped up its enforcement efforts.

Obstacles to citizen lawsuits are higher in Canada than in the United

## Figure 9.5
## Prosecutions under Selected Canadian Environmental Statutes, 1985–1986

| Statute | Number of Charges | Successful Prosecutions | Total Fines |
|---|---|---|---|
| Fisheries Act (1985) | 18 | 9 | $33,800 |
| Fisheries Act (1986) | 18 | 12 | $93,950 |
| Arctic Waters Pollution Prevention Act | 1 | 1 | $14,000 |
| Ocean Dumping Control Act | 1 | — | — |

Source: Canadian House of Commons.

States. Only a few "private prosecutions" have been brought. Obstacles such as lack of standing to sue, the expense and time involved in litigation, informational demands, the uncertainty of results, and the risk of having to pay defendants' court costs if private prosecution is unsuccessful make private prosecution difficult.[48]

## BEYOND WATER QUALITY ISSUES

The broad purpose of the 1978 Water Quality Agreement makes it a useful approach to the problems involved in comprehensive environmental rehabilitation. But what about issues that extend well beyond the agreement—for example, acid deposition or water quantity issues such as lake levels, impoundments, diversions, and exports? And what about still broader questions such as the need to reconcile economic development with environmental improvement?

In principle, it would be relatively easy to transform the agreement into a broader Great Lakes basin ecosystem health agreement. The present agreement contains much that is relevant to the ecosystem as a whole, and the 1987 protocol extended the agreement's provisions into areas that until recently were regarded as marginal to surface water quality considerations. The protocol is a demonstration of the ecosystem principle that everything is related to everything else.

How desirable is it that the 1978 agreement should be broadened into such an overall commitment to ecosystem health in the Great Lakes basin? There can be little doubt that this would be a logical development. It has to be recognized that the principal element that would be added to the agreement would be the atmosphere. But because acid deposition and other long-range transport problems cannot be tackled effectively solely within the boundaries of the basin, a separate binational agreement on acid precipitation, involving the whole of the United States and Canada, would be even more useful.

The situation is more straightforward when it comes to water quantity. It may indeed seem rather perverse to develop a major international agreement on water quality with the implied assumption that water quantity can be regarded as some sort of independent variable or that alterations in flows and levels are of minor significance to water quality. Water quantity, unlike the atmosphere, is "basin-oriented": the basin is essentially a hydrological unit.

Various suggestions for an agreement on water quantity have been made from time to time,[49] and the Canadian government gave cautious approval in 1986 to the idea of a "water quantity management system for the Great Lakes basin" that would parallel the 1972 and 1978 water quality agreements.[50] Such a management system could emerge from the reference on Great Lakes levels that the IJC was given in 1986 (see chapter 4). Whether it would be more effective as a parallel agreement or as an element in a more comprehensive ecosystem health agreement is a matter for debate.[51]

One of the most persuasive factors arguing for a Great Lakes basin agreement on water quantity between Canada and the United States, and for its close integration with water quality issues, is the prospect of rapid climatic change during the next half-century, with consequent substantial declines in average lake levels. The effect on those uses of the Great Lakes that are primarily dependent on lake levels (navigation, power generation, shoreline property, recreation, etc.) are likely to be immense. However, falls in the average levels on the scale indicated by present computer models (2 to 6 feet [.6 to 1.8 meters] for Lake Erie, for example) would have effects on water quality of comparable magnitude. The effects might include mobilization of contaminants from sediments, changes in the impact of groundwater on the lakes, and lowered levels of dissolved oxygen in the system.[52] The changing shoreline character, expressed in major changes of wetland areas and spawning grounds, would have ecosystem health effects that are unknown but potentially of great significance.

It is therefore a reasonable possibility that, over the next 5 to 10 years, water quantity issues will become more closely integrated with the water quality considerations that are embodied in the current version of the Water Quality Agreement. It is also possible to discern the prospect of growing convergence between economic and social development and ecosystem objectives, although this is not likely to be expressed in the form of specific national or international agreements.

Until comparatively recently, economic and environmental considerations have come together primarily (indeed, almost exclusively) in terms of setting standards for discharges or assessing the "environmental impact" of projects. The emphasis has been on stopping, preventing, or cleaning up specific activities or behaviors that damage the natural environment. The adoption of an ecosystem approach, however, implies the need for a more complete integration of economic and environmental decision making. The Great Lakes basin ecosystem necessarily includes everything that happens within the basin.

The chief effect of this changed outlook is a gradual shift away from a focus on regulation and enforcement toward the concept of sustainable development. This recognizes that, as the Great Lakes basin clearly demonstrates, there are limits on the ability of the biosphere to absorb the effects of human activities.[53] Sustainable development is

> a process of change in which the exploitation of resources, the direction of investments, the orientation of technological development, and institutional change are made consistent with future as well as present needs.[54]

The concept of sustainable development has much in common with the broad vision of the ecosystem approach—both represent a major shift in society's values. In that sense, the implementation of the Water Quality Agreement in the Great Lakes basin may be regarded as an attempt to apply the principles of sustainable development in a major region of North America.[55]

## CONCLUSION

Numerous agreements have been created, laws enacted, and regulations promulgated for the purpose of protecting the Great Lakes ecosystem. Significant progress has been made in some areas; yet problems remain. Many environmental objectives have not been reached, deadlines for action have been missed, the full potential of existing programs has not been realized, and significant gaps exist in the framework of action.

Despite the shortfall, the many jurisdictions involved in governance—and the many individuals in the private sector who have dedicated their lives to understanding and protecting the lakes—deserve considerable credit both for advances produced in ecosystem science and for setting ambitious standards for protection and enhancement. Perhaps the most important contribution of this binational community has been to foster the ecosystem approach as a set of principles for guiding future development in the lakes. What remains is to translate these principles into practice. As the Great Lakes community looks towards the year 2000, much work lies ahead.

# Chapter 10

# Towards 2000, and Beyond

Changes in the Great Lakes basin ecosystem began with early 19th-century settlement and land clearance. Those who moved into the basin found so much land, so many trees, so many rivers and lakes, that it seemed inconceivable that human activity could ever threaten the bounty of nature. The environment represented a wilderness to tame, farmland to be cleared, fisheries to be harvested, shipping and railroad systems to be established, towns and cities to be built.

Within half a century, it became evident that the resource base was not inexhaustible. Fishery yields began to decline, forests were devastated, and pollution expressed itself in epidemics of cholera, typhus, and other diseases. Nevertheless, the early attitudes survived long after nature was not merely subdued, but beaten.

Over the last hundred years, human capacity to alter and destroy the environment increased rather than diminished. One of the world's great industrial areas emerged in the Great Lakes basin, while a population of a few tens of thousands of native people, scattered over a vast area, became the 35 million residents of today. With this growth came dramatic shifts in the economic base of Great Lakes society, from resource extraction through manufacturing to the scientific-industrial complex of today. A major element of this change, particularly since the middle of the 20th century, has been an extraordinary increase in the use of manufactured chemicals. Every facet of human life has been touched; every facet of the natural environment has been affected by the massive dumping of by-products and wastes from this manufacture—and by dumping the products themselves during and after use.

We are now entering the 1990s. For the last quarter-century there has been a sustained effort, and certainly sustained and increasing concern, to prevent further deterioration of the Great Lakes basin environment and ecosystem and to attempt a rehabilitation. Though much has been achieved, far more remains to be done, especially since the easiest problems were tackled first. The zero discharge goal for persistent toxic chemicals established in the 1978 Great Lakes Water Quality Agreement, for example, will not be achieved in the foreseeable future.

The present concern for the environment—a concern expressed in different ways by politicians, business leaders, scientists, action groups, and individuals—provides the best opportunity that has ever existed to tackle such momentous issues. Yet there is no doubt that progress has not matched expectations. For every bit of good news that emerges, there seems to be at least as many items of bad news.

The good news is that a general recovery of Great Lakes water quality from pollution by toxic metals, excess nutrients, and organic contaminants has been taking place since the early 1970s. But the bad news is that there are some major exceptions to this general decline, the rate of improvement has slowed in the present decade, and in some cases concentrations have stabilized above target levels.

The good news is that recent sediments deposited in the Great Lakes seem less contaminated than those of earlier decades. The bad news is that the legacy continues to affect the basin and its inhabitants, as contaminants from sediments are released back into the lake water by disturbance by dredging and new construction and by natural processes. The bad news is that few practical ways exist to decontaminate these sediments, and the costs are enormous.

The good news is that the problems of creating and disposing of wastes of all kinds (and especially hazardous wastes) are being recognized by practically everyone. The bad news is that effective systems to reduce waste are still in their infancy, and the legacy of the past will not easily be eliminated. Groundwater contaminated by leaks from hazardous waste sites is probably the single most important source of contaminants to the Niagara River and seems likely to continue for decades to come.

The good news is that new regulations, and new concern, have been effective in achieving major improvements at massive "point sources" of contamination: steel mills, chemical plants, sewage treatment plants, and so on. The bad news is that little has yet been achieved in controlling nonpoint pollution, whether from urban or rural areas.

The good news is that ambient levels of phosphorus in lake waters, the main cause of the crisis in Lake Erie in the 1960s, have been significantly reduced and recovery has been swift. The bad news is that target levels of phosphorus loading have not yet been achieved everywhere and that, meanwhile, levels of another nutrient, nitrogen, are steadily rising throughout the Great Lakes.

The good news is that, to achieve this improvement, the United States and Canada have committed about $10 billion to improved municipal sewage treatment. The bad news is that this is a tiny sum when compared to the estimated cost of eliminating toxic contamination of the waters around major population centers in the basin.

The good news is that, over the past two decades, both emissions and ambient concentrations of sulfur dioxide in the atmosphere—a major contributor to acid deposition—have been significantly reduced in the basin. The bad news is that virtually no progress has been made in reducing emissions of nitrogen oxides, another component of acid rain. In Ontario, for example, nitrogen oxide emissions were almost 30 percent higher in 1984 than in 1970.

The good news is that the major pollutants and contaminants in air and water appear to have been clearly defined and standards are being established. The bad news is that monitoring systems remain grossly inadequate and enforcement provisions underused.

The good news is that citizen concern has been maintained and expanded. Meetings take place, politicians are lobbied, bureaucrats are harassed, and scientists are enlisted to the cause of reform. The bad news is that there are far more brave statements than bold actions and that concern for deficit reduction or for avoiding tax increases may equal concern for the environment.

Overall, the good news is that the state of the Great Lakes basin ecosystem is better now than it was 30 years ago. The bad news is that most of the easiest and cheapest solutions have already been adopted. Society is moving in the right direction, but perhaps nowhere near quickly enough to avert future crises.

On a world scale, the good news is that the Great Lakes region is a leader in transnational comprehensive environmental management. The bad news is that this may say more about inadequacies elsewhere than about the health of the basin ecosystem.

Despite the abundance of bad news, there is reason for optimism. The growing recognition that a healthy, rich, and productive environment is fundamental for social, cultural, economic, and spiritual health justifies the continued hope that the environmental legacy to future generations will be far better than what has been inherited from the past. Many of the greatest tests of that hope will come during the 1990s.

As we enter that decade, two basic propositions seem fundamental to efforts to restore the health of the Great Lakes basin ecosystem and create sustainable development in the future. The propositions can be stated very simply, but achieving them is likely to be much more difficult.

The first proposition is that Americans and Canadians throughout the Great Lakes region must collectively develop a vision of what they are trying to achieve. This vision must be generally shared by the varied "stakeholders" in the region—politicians, business leaders, environmentalists, and others. Some outlines of such a vision are emerging, but there is a much better understanding of what must be eliminated or prevented than of what must be created. The vision that is needed is of a lifestyle in the Great Lakes that embraces human well-being, a healthy environment, and a prosperous economy. More must be done than simply respond to crises.

The second proposition is that policies and actions should work with and adapt to natural processes, rather than resist or avoid recognizing such processes. If anything has been learned from the history of the Great Lakes region, it is that attempts to force nature into submission are unworkable.[1] Along lake shores, for example, this proposition means an end to subsidies and incentives that encourage homes to be built in places where the natural fluctuation of lake levels ensures that water will rule eventually. It also means less emphasis on creating an artificially supported sport fishery, through fish ranching, and more emphasis on restoring the lakes to the point where self-reproducing native fish species can thrive and be consumed safely by humans and wildlife alike.

From these general propositions, and from the experience of the last two or three decades, six* broad directions for policy emerge, as well as a large number of actions needed to give effect to these policies.

**1. The environment and the economy must be put on an equal footing, to be weighed and measured together as the basis for**

---

*These are presented in different form and detail in the overview to this volume. More detailed recommendations developed by The Conservation Foundation for federal, state, and local officials in the United States are presented in *The Conservation Foundation Letter*, 1989, no. 5, available from The Conservation Foundation.

**development decisions. This will require governments, industry, and individuals alike to integrate environmental and economic decision making.**

No one can pretend that this is easy. Attempting to envisage all the implications of a proposal can easily lead to paralysis rather than sensible action. Nevertheless, the attempt must be made, and it should begin by eliminating the glaring conflicts and contradictions that now exist: for example, the current governmental support for wetland preservation that occurs simultaneously with financial assistance for yet more wetland drainage. Environmental issues and implications must be brought into the mainstream of policy making in all sectors of the economy and society. Despite a widespread and growing recognition of environmental imperatives in recent decades, the attention given to economic well-being still far outweighs the evaluation of environmental well-being.

How is this to be achieved? Two possible means are:

- developing and adopting mechanisms to ensure that prices for such services as energy supply, water supply, sewage treatment, and solid waste disposal reflect the costs of avoiding environmental damage; and
- launching an across-the-board review of tax and incentive policies to identify and eliminate those that encourage unwise use of resources and to encourage resource conservation.

**2. The operating perspective of governments, industry, and the public must be an ecosystem perspective that recognizes the essential unity of land, air, water, and all living organisms.**

This perspective is being increasingly adopted—or perhaps it is being increasingly forced on society—by evidence that many problems have been solved only by creating new ones. The vision for the future of the Great Lakes region will be inadequate if it is not founded on this ecosystem perspective. During the next decade, to build this vision, there is a need to:

- encourage and extend the efforts under way to develop a Great Lakes Ecosystem Charter as a set of principles and goals for sustainable development that will guide policies and actions throughout the region;
- develop a bilateral agreement between Canada and the United States on objectives and measures to tackle air quality problems

(including acid deposition, ozone smog, and airborne toxic contamination) as well as global atmospheric problems that affect the basin (such as CFCs and global warming);

- expand the existing Great Lakes Water Quality Agreement into an Ecosystem Agreement that recognizes broader issues of shared concern such as habitat protection, fisheries management, shoreline protection, and water quantity; and
- develop and adopt a binational strategy to integrate and extend efforts to protect areas of natural beauty, wildlife habitat, or ecological significance, especially wetland areas.

**3. At least as much effort must be given to prevention as to cure: to adopting policies and lifestyles that will avoid creating future legacies, as well as to dealing with the legacy that has been inherited.**

The problems of pollution and contamination that have been inherited are obvious, but the effects of continuing present patterns are potentially even more catastrophic. Prevention and restoration are inherently compatible: restoration requires money and time; prevention demands changes in attitude and behavior. This commitment to the future should be expressed in actions such as:

- reducing pollution and waste generation through changes in products, manufacturing processes, and packaging;
- setting and enforcing standards, based on the principle of zero discharge, for persistent toxic contaminants;
- preventing the introduction of exotic species that could have devastating effects on the Great Lakes ecosystem;
- adopting farming practices that do not create long-term ecosystem problems in order to maximize short-term revenue or output;
- recognizing the potential ecosystem effects of disastrous accidents in the Great Lakes basin by increasing emphasis on measures to avoid accidents and by developing response plans that recognize ecosystem needs as well as protection of human life and property;
- adopting effective Lakewide Management Plans, within the framework of the Great Lakes Water Quality Agreement, to protect beneficial uses in open lake waters; and
- setting ambitious new goals to cut per capita energy and water use and to cut per capita generation of waste.

**4. Commitments made over the past 15 years must be fulfilled.**

**Governments must set goals, establish a reliable system to monitor progress, and follow through on implementation.**

The purpose of the 1978 Great Lakes Water Quality Agreement—"to restore and maintain the chemical, physical and biological integrity of the waters of the Great Lakes Basin Ecosystem"[2]—is still a long way from being achieved. During the next decade, much more action will be required than was achieved during the 1980s. This includes:

- tackling the long-standing problems posed by nonpoint pollution, through the development of effective watershed management plans and, in urban areas, by preventing untreated discharges from combined sewer systems;
- completing the task of cleaning up hazardous waste sites, and providing mechanisms to ensure the safe disposal of wastes currently being generated;
- completing the identification, mapping, and assessment of contaminated groundwater required by annex 16 of the Water Quality Agreement and initiating effective control measures; and
- achieving substantial progress, based on adequate resources and strong governmental, industrial, and public support, in implementing the Remedial Action Plans for the 42 Areas of Concern throughout the Great Lakes basin.

**5. Governments must act now to increase understanding of human and ecosystem health conditions in the Great Lakes basin.**

This need for understanding is not an excuse to delay action: it is clear that many wildlife populations are suffering and that clear grounds exist for concern about human health. The studies that are needed can be defined clearly and are long overdue. Major tasks include:

- investigating the extent to which bioaccumulation and biomagnification of toxic contaminants in the food web may lead to developmental defects in children (this includes epidemiological studies of groups at risk as well as research on the mechanisms through which toxic substances affect physiological processes in wildlife and humans);
- amending warnings about Great Lakes basin food resources to further discourage consumption of contaminated fish and other predators by females planning to have children, in order to reduce potential risks to offspring from long-term consumption; and

- increasing the binational effort to monitor wildlife populations in the Great Lakes basin, both to restore and protect these populations and to use them as sentinels of hazards to human health.

**6. Efforts to restore and maintain ecosystem health, and to adopt sustainable development patterns, must use a broad-based process of decision making, involving as many interest groups and individuals as possible.**

The experience of the last decade—for example, in developing Remedial Action Plans and the Canadian Environmental Protection Act—has demonstrated that a broad-based approach is essential to achieving effective solutions, equitable treatment, and public support and commitment. Experience has also shown that a broad basis for decision making can save both time and money.

If it is accepted that preventing future legacies—achieving sustainable development—will require substantial changes in present patterns of behavior and lifestyles, then it seems obvious that such changes will not be achieved without broad public understanding and commitment. During the 1990s, three issues in particular in the Great Lakes basin seem likely to demand a new and more broad-based approach:

- fisheries management, including issues such as competition between sport fisheries and commercial fisheries, and the compatibility of stocking the lakes with exotic species while attempting to reestablish self-reproducing populations of native species;
- energy development, involving hard choices among different methods of electricity generation, production within the basin or purchase from other sources, and the environmental and economic implications of the various options; and
- shoreline use, for example in regard to protection of multiple use and in relation to variations in lake levels.


## SUMMING UP

If these policy directions can be followed during the 1990s, and a substantial number of the indicated actions achieved, then the prospects for a healthy and sustainable environment, ecosystem, and economy in the Great Lakes basin should be bright. More than this, the binational effort made in the Great Lakes during the last quarter of the 20th century might provide a model for similar problems throughout the world.

Much of what is valued today in the landscape and history of Canada and the United States can be traced back to the vision and initiative of a few determined individuals. What is being attempted in the Great Lakes basin at present stands comparison with any of these earlier achievements, but it is taking place as a collective effort in a densely populated and highly organized region, not on a blank part of the map. The effort in the Great Lakes represents a test of the belief that economic and social development is compatible with a rehabilitated environment and ecosystem. It will be several decades yet before the success of the experiment can be determined, but a start has been made and the prospects are encouraging.

# References

## 1. AN ECOSYSTEM APPROACH TO GREAT LAKES POLICY

1. The phrase probably comes from Samuel de Champlain, who reached Lake Huron in July or August 1615 and described it as "La Mer Douce."

2. See chapter 3, figure 3.13 for trends in basin population growth, and chapter 3, figure 3.2 for basin-by-basin population figures.

3. University of Wisconsin Sea Grant Institute, *The Fisheries of the Great Lakes, 1984-86 Biennial Report* (Madison, Wisc.: Sea Grant Institute, 1986), p. 9.

4. Phil Weller, "State of the Great Lakes Region Environment: Wetlands," prepared for Environment Canada, Environmental Interpretation Division, Conservation and Protection (Ottawa: Environment Canada, 1988), pp. 7-8.

5. International Joint Commission, Great Lakes Water Quality Board, *1987 Report on Great Lakes Quality* (Windsor, Ont.: International Joint Commission, 1987), p. 185.

6. International Joint Commission, "Revised Great Lakes Water Quality Agreement of 1978: Agreement with Annexes and Terms of Reference, between the United States and Canada, signed at Ottawa November 22, 1978, and Phosphorus Load Reduction Supplement, signed October 7, 1983, as amended by Protocol, signed November 18, 1987" (Windsor, Ont., 1988), article II. This agreement is cited hereafter as "1978 Water Quality Agreement"; except where noted, citations are to the version incorporating the 1987 protocol revisions and additions.

7. 1978 Water Quality Agreement, Article I(g).

8. 1978 Water Quality Agreement, Annexes 13 (Pollution from Non-Point Sources), 14 (Contaminated Sediment), 15 (Airborne Toxic Substances), and 16 (Pollution from Contaminated Groundwater).

9. 1978 Water Quality Agreement, Article III.

10. 1978 Water Quality Agreement, Article II.

11. National Research Council of the United States and The Royal Society of Canada, *The Great Lakes Water Quality Agreement: An Evolving Instrument for Ecosystem Management* (Washington, D.C.: National Academy Press, 1985), p. 109.

## Box: Canada, the United States, and the International Joint Commission

1. The text of the treaty has been reprinted in several sources, including Robert Spencer, John Kirton, and Kim R. Nossal, eds., *The International Joint Commission Seventy Years On* (Toronto: Centre for International Studies, University of Toronto, 1981).

## Figures

1.1. Map provided by Environment Canada.
1.2. This figure is an elaboration upon a table in Henry Regier, "Generic Guidelines for the Review of Ecosystemic Initiatives in the Great Lakes Basin" (unpublished manuscript, University of Toronto, Institute of Environmental Studies, 1988).
1.3. Michael J. Donahue, *Institutional Arrangements for Great Lakes Management* (Lansing, Mich.: Michigan Sea Grant College Program, 1987); and H. Regier, "Progress with Remediation, Rehabilitation and the Ecosystem Approach," *Alternatives* 13, no. 3 (1986):45-54.
1.4. National Research Council of the United States, and the Royal Society of Canada, *The Great Lakes Water Quality Agreement: An Evolving Instrument for Ecosystem Management* (Washington, D.C.: National Academy Press, 1985), p. 82.

## 2. DEFINING AND MEASURING ECOSYSTEM HEALTH

1. 1978 Water Quality Agreement, Article II.
2. *Webster's New World Dictionary of the American Language*, 2nd College Edition, s.v. "ecosystem."
3. Information provided by D. V. Weseloh (Environment Canada, Canada Centre for Inland Waters), 1988.
4. R. Norstrom, D. Hallett, and R. Sonstergard, "Coho Salmon (*Oncorhynchus kisutch*) and Herring Gulls (*Larus argenatus*) as Indicators of Organochlorine Contamination in Lake Ontario," *Journal of the Fisheries Research Board of Canada* 35, no. 22 (1978):1401-09.
5. 1978 Water Quality Agreement, Article I(v).
6. 1978 Water Quality Agreement, Annex 12, 1(a).
7. International Joint Commission, Great Lakes Water Quality Board, *1987 Report on Great Lakes Quality* (Windsor, Ont.: International Joint Commission, 1987), chapters 2 and 3.
8. Ibid., p. 15.
9. Ibid., chapter 3.
10. National Wildlife Federation, Great Lakes Natural Resource Center (in cooperation with 20 other organizations), *Promises to Keep: Making the Great Lakes Water*

*Quality Agreement Work through the Development of Uniform Water Quality Standards and U.S. Regulations* (Ann Arbor, Mich.: National Wildlife Federation, Great Lakes Natural Resource Center, 1989).

11. International Joint Commission, Great Lakes Science Advisory Board, *1987 Report* (Windsor, Ont.: International Joint Commission, 1987), p. 55.

12. 1978 Water Quality Agreement, Annex 11, 4(a).

13. Robert G. Wetzel, *Limnology*, 2d ed. (Ann Arbor, Mich.: Saunders College Publishing, 1983).

14. International Joint Commission, Great Lakes Science Advisory Board, *1989 Report* (Windsor, Ont.: International Joint Commission, 1989), sections 5.2 and 5.2.1.

15. 1978 Water Quality Agreement, Annex 11, 2.

16. International Joint Commission, *Fourth Biennial Report* (Windsor, Ont.: International Joint Commission, 1989), p. 29.

17. Letter from Peter Wise (U.S. Environmental Protection Agency, Great Lakes National Program Office) to E.T. Wagner (Environment Canada, Inland Waters Directorate), 25 March 1987.

18. Anne V. Whyte and Ian Burton, eds., *Environmental Risk Assessment*, SCOPE 15 (New York: John Wiley and Sons, 1980), p. 75.

19. R. Norstrom et al., "Mirex and Its Degradation Products in Great Lakes Herring Gulls," *Environmental Science and Technology* 14, no. 7 (1980):860-66.

20. R. Norstrom and M. Simon, "Preliminary Appraisal of Tetra- to Octachlorodibenzodioxin Contamination in Eggs of Various Species of Wildlife in Canada," undated and unpublished manuscript.

21. 1978 Water Quality Agreement, Annex 12, 5(e).

22. International Joint Commission, *Third Biennial Report* (Windsor, Ont.: International Joint Commission, 1986), Annex II.

23. Kirstin Dow and Lee Liebenstein, "Considerations for the Development of a Great Lakes Regional Tissue Banking Program," in Council of Great Lakes Governors, *First Annual Review of the Great Lakes Toxic Substances Control Agreement* (Chicago: Council of Great Lakes Governors, 1987), pp. 63-67.

24. David A. Ross, "Sea Grant—A National Investment for the Future," *Oceanus* 31, no. 3 (1988):6-11.

25. "The Great Lakes Protection Fund," fact sheet produced by the Center for the Great Lakes (Chicago and Toronto, 1989).

## Box: Is Zero Discharge Possible?

1. Ontario Ministry of the Environment, *Guide to Eating Ontario Sport Fish* (Toronto: Ontario Ministry of the Environment, 1988), pp. 28-29.

## Figures

2.1. Information provided by Michael Miller (University of Wisconsin, Madison), June 1989; information provided by Mary Baker (University of Wisconsin, Superior), June 1989; U.S. Army Corps of Engineers, *Proposed Diked Disposal Area on Dickinson Island, St. Clair Country, Michigan*, Final Environmental Assessment (Detroit: U.S. Army Corps of Engineers, 1974), cited in Charles E. Herdendorf, C. Nicholas

Raphael, and Walter G. Duffy, *The Ecology of Lake St. Clair Wetlands: A Community Profile*, U.S. Fish and Wildlife Service Biological Report 85(7.7) (Washington, D.C.: U.S. Government Printing Office, 1986), p. 74.

2.2. Information provided by D. V. Weseloh (Environment Canada, Canadian Wildlife Service, Canada Centre for Inland Waters), 1988.

2.3. The Conservation Foundation.

2.4. Marlene S. Evans, ed., *Toxic Contaminants and Ecosystem Health: A Great Lakes Focus* (New York: John Wiley and Sons, 1988), p. 495.

# 3. LEGACIES AND CHALLENGES: LAND

1. International Joint Commission, *First Biennial Report* (Windsor, Ont.: International Joint Commission, 1982), pp. 18-19.

2. R. Cole Harris, ed., *Historical Atlas of Canada*, vol. 1 (Toronto, Ont., and Buffalo, N.Y.: University of Toronto Press, 1987), plate 44.

3. *Canadian Encyclopedia* (Edmonton, Alta.: Hurtig, 1988), vol. 1, p. 258; vol. 2, p. 1106.

4. Samuel Eliot Morison, *The Oxford History of the American People* (New York: Oxford University Press, 1965), p. 301.

5. *Canadian Encyclopedia*, vol. 2, p. 1250.

6. M. C. Urquhart and K. A. H. Buckley, eds., *Historical Statistics of Canada*, series A2-A14 (Toronto: Macmillan, 1965).

7. Jerry Sullivan et al., *Decisions for the Great Lakes* (Hiram, Ohio: Great Lakes Tomorrow and the Purdue Foundation), p. 88.

8. Ibid., p. 88.

9. Ibid., p. 91.

10. These figures are for 1981 in Canada and 1982 in the United States. They refer to the amount of land classified as "area of farmland" (Canada) and "total land in farms" (U.S.). Farmland area: information provided by Statistics Canada, Structural Analysis Branch, *1981 Canadian Census of Agriculture*, August 1988, and by Jim Horsfield, U.S. Department of Agriculture, *1982 U.S. Census of Agriculture*, April 1988; total land area: Environment Canada and U.S. Environmental Protection Agency, *The Great Lakes: An Environmental Atlas and Resource Book* (Chicago: U.S. Environmental Protection Agency, Great Lakes National Program Office, and Toronto, Ont.: Environment Canada, Ontario Region, 1987), p. 4.

11. Ontario Ministry of Agriculture and Food, Economics and Policy Coordination Branch, *1986 Agricultural Statistics for Ontario* (Toronto: Queen's Printer for Ontario, 1987), pp. 6-7; "Michigan Futures Team Plans Long-Range Agriculture Strategy," *Great Lakes Commission Advisor* 1, no. 9 (1988):6.

12. The Conservation Foundation, *State of the Environment: A View toward the Nineties* (Washington, D.C.: The Conservation Foundation, 1987), pp. 347-54; Gordon K. Douglass, "The Meanings of Agricultural Sustainability," in Gordon K. Douglass, ed., *Agricultural Sustainability in a Changing World Order* (Boulder, Colo.: Westview Press, 1984), pp. 8-9.

13. Elizabeth G. Nielsen and Linda K. Lee, *The Magnitude and Costs of Groundwater Contamination from Agricultural Chemicals*, Agricultural Economic Report no. 576 (Washington, D.C.: U.S. Department of Agriculture, 1987), p. 2.

14. The Conservation Foundation, "A Guide to Groundwater Pollution: Problems, Causes, and Government Responses," in *Groundwater Protection* (Washington, D.C.: The Conservation Foundation, 1987), p. 148.

15. Bill McGee, *Survey of Pesticide Use in Ontario, 1983: Estimates of Pesticides Used on Field Crops, Fruits, Vegetables, and in Roadside Weed Control*, Economics Information Report no. 84-05 (Toronto: Ontario Ministry of Agriculture and Food, 1984), p. 26.

16. These pesticide use estimates are based on an assessment of the percentage of acres treated and the annual application rate for 21 active ingredients on 64 crops; they assume uniformity for all counties within states for the same pesticide/crop use. It is not known to what extent the actual use pattern varies within each state. Some uses of the selected pesticides in the Great Lakes region, such as livestock, rights-of-way, mosquito control, and aquatic weed control, are not accounted for in these estimates. Also, it is not known to what extent these estimates, which are for a year in the middle 1980s, reflect current use patterns. Unfortunately, it is not known what proportion of pesticide use these estimates represent, nor is it possible to determine whether pesticide use is increasing or decreasing. It is likely, though, that national trends, such as the rising proportion of pesticide use that is comprised by herbicides, also apply to the Great Lakes region. See Leonard P. Gianessi, Resources for the Future, "Use of Selected Pesticides in Agricultural Crop Production in the Great Lakes Region," report submitted to The Conservation Foundation, March 1988; McGee, *Survey of Pesticide Use in Ontario*, 1983, p. 28.

17. Thomas E. Waddell and Blair T. Bower with Kathy Cox, *Managing Agricultural Chemicals in the Environment: The Case for a Multimedia Approach* (Washington, D.C.: The Conservation Foundation, 1988), p. 42; Tamim M. Younos and Diana L. Weigmann, "Pesticides: A Continuing Dilemma," *Journal Water Pollution Control Federation* 60, no. 7 (1988):1,199.

18. Younos and Weigmann, p. 1,199; Keith S. Porter and Michael W. Stimmann, *Pesticides and Groundwater: A Guide for the Pesticide User* (Ithaca, N.Y.: U.S. Environmental Protection Agency and U.S. Department of Agriculture, 1988), p. 1, executive summary.

19. Waddell and Bower, p. 78.

20. The half-life of 57.5 years is in soils of orchards. See Barry K. Cooke and Austin Stringer, "Distribution and Breakdown of DDT in Orchard Soil," *Pesticide Science* 13 (1982):545-51, table 5; L. Blus et al., "Persistence of DDT and Metabolites in Wildlife from Washington State Orchards," *Archives of Environmental Contamination and Toxicology* 16 (1987):467-76.

21. The Conservation Foundation, *State of the Environment: A View Toward the Nineties*, p. 144; Younos and Weigmann, p. 1,202.

22. The Conservation Foundation, *State of the Environment: A View Toward the Nineties*, pp. 350-51.

23. The 19-million-acre figure is based on 14.3 million acres in the U.S. portion of the basin as of 1982 and 5.3 million acres in the Ontario portion as of 1980. Information provided by Jim Horsfield, U.S. Department of Agriculture, *1982 U.S. Census of Agriculture*; see also Statistics Canada, *Human Activity and the Environment: A Statistical Compendium* (Ottawa: Minister of Supply and Services, 1986), p. 99.

24. Ibid.

25. G. J. Wall, E. A. Pringle, and W. T. Dickinson, "Assessment of Agricultural Nonpoint Source Pollution Potential in the Canadian Great Lakes Basin," Technical Publication Series 88-3 (American Water Resources Association, 1988), p. 182. For more information, see Sharon Green, *Agriculture and the Environment in the Great Lakes Basin* (Washington, D.C.: The Conservation Foundation, forthcoming).

26. International Joint Commission, *Environmental Strategy for the Great Lakes System*, report from the International Reference Group on Great Lakes Pollution from Land Use Activities (Windsor, Ont.: International Joint Commission, 1978), p. 23; International Joint Commission, *Nonpoint Source Pollution Abatement in the Great Lakes Basin: An Overview of Post-PLUARG Developments* (Windsor, Ont.: International Joint Commission, 1983), pp. 66-67; Great Lakes Commission, *Soil Erosion and Sedimentation in the Great Lakes Region*, final report of the Soil Erosion and Sedimentation Task Force (Ann Arbor, Mich.: Great Lakes Commission, 1987), p. 16.

27. International Joint Commission, Great Lakes Water Quality Board, *1987 Report on Great Lakes Quality* (Windsor, Ont.: International Joint Commission, 1987), pp. 84-87.

28. Great Lakes Commission, *Soil Erosion and Sedimentation in the Great Lakes Region*, p. 2.

29. Leonard C. Johnson, "Soil Loss Tolerance: Fact or Myth?" *Journal of Soil and Water Conservation* 42, no. 3 (1987):159.

30. Development Consulting House and Land Resource Research Institute, *A Preliminary Economic Assessment of Agricultural Land Degradation in Atlantic and Central Canada and Southern British Columbia*, prepared for Regional Development Branch, Agriculture Canada, January 1986, p. 160.

31. Dell Coleman and Peter Roberts, *Cropping, Tillage and Land Management Practices in Southwestern Ontario 1986* (Soil and Water Environmental Enhancement Program, 1987), pp. 1, 12; International Joint Commission, *1987 Report on Great Lakes Quality*, pp. 63-64; information provided by Greg Wall, Agriculture Canada, February 1989; Environment Canada, "First Report of Canada under the 1987 Protocol to the 1978 Great Lakes Water Quality Agreement, December 1988," Appendix 1.

32. International Joint Commission, *1987 Report on Great Lakes Quality*, pp. 59, 63.

33. Vladimir Novotny, "Diffuse (Nonpoint) Pollution: A Political, Institutional, and Fiscal Problem," *Journal of the Water Pollution Control Federation* 60, no. 8 (August 1988):1,406.

34. The Conservation Foundation, *State of the Environment: A View Toward the Nineties*, pp. 380-382.

35. See, for instance, David R. Cressman, "The Promise of Low-Input Agriculture," *Journal of Soil and Water Conservation* 44, no. 2 (1989):98; Charles M. Benbrook, "The Environment and the 1990 Farm Bill," *Journal of Soil and Water Conservation* 43, no. 6 (1988):440-43; and "Fowler Sponsors Legislation to Reduce Farm Chemical Use," *Chemical Regulation Reporter*, May 5, 1989, p. 159.

36. Benjamin R. Stinner and Garfield J. House, "The Search for Sustainable Agroecosystems," *Journal of Soil and Water Conservation* 44, no. 2 (1989):111-16.

37. Personal communication, Dr. Richard Frank, Ontario Ministry of Agriculture and Food, January 1989.

38. "EPA Proposes Dramatic Streamlining of FIFRA'S Cancellation, Suspension Process," *Inside EPA* 10, no. 31 (1989):1, 7-11.

39. U.S. Department of Agriculture, Cooperative State Research Service and Extension Service, "Low-Input/Sustainable Agriculture: Research and Education Program," brochure, 1989.

40. Richard Frank and Peter Boyer, "State of Integrated Pest Management Programs in the Great Lakes Basin and on a Global Basis," prepared for the Science Advisory Board, International Joint Commission, April 1988.

41. Sullivan et al., *Decisions for the Great Lakes*, p. 90; and *Canadian Encyclopedia*, vol. 4, p. 2,160.

42. Sullivan et al., *Decisions for the Great Lakes*, p. 90.

43. Ibid., p. 90. See also Susan L. Flader, ed., *The Great Lakes Forest: An Environmental and Social History* (Minneapolis: University of Minnesota and Forest History Society, 1983).

44. *Canadian Encyclopedia*, vol. 3, p. 1,789.

45. Rebecca Hanmer, acting assistant administrator for water, U.S. Environmental Protection Agency, "Interim Strategy for the Regulation of Pulp and Paper Mill Dioxin Discharges to the Waters of the United States," memo, August 9, 1988. See also "Excessive Discharges of Dioxin Confirmed in EPA/Industry Pulp and Paper Mill Study," *BNA Environment Reporter*, July 7, 1989, p. 507.

46. Expert Committee on Kraft Mill Toxicity, "Kraft Mill Effluents in Ontario" (Toronto, Ont.: Ministry of the Environment, 1988), pp. 1-17 to 1-19.

47. International Joint Commission, *1987 Report on Great Lakes Quality*, appendix A, pp. 5-21.

48. See, for example, I. McBeath, *Status Report on Compliance with the Chlor-Alkali Mercury Regulations, 1984-1985* (Ottawa: Environment Canada, 1987).

49. Larry Pedersen and Daniel E. Chappelle, "The Economic Importance of the Upper Lake States' Forest Resources: Modeling Lake States Forest Products and Services," in William E. Shands, ed., *The Lake States Forests: A Resources Renaissance* (St. Paul: Lake States Forestry Alliance, 1988), pp. 168-94.

50. Ontario Ministry of Natural Resources, *Statistics 1987* (Toronto: Queen's Printer for Ontario, 1987), pp. 33-34.

51. William E. Shands, "Conference Overview," in Shands, *The Lake States Forests*, p. 1.

52. F. Dale Robertson, "The Importance of the Lake States Forest: A National Perspective," in Shands, *The Lake States Forests*, p. 62.

53. See, for instance, Forest Stearns, "The Changing Forests of the Lake States," in Shands, *The Lake States Forests*, pp. 25-35; and Clifford E. Ahlgren and Isabel F. Ahlgren, "The Human Impact on Northern Forest Ecosystems," in Susan L. Flader, ed., *The Great Lakes Forest: An Environmental and Social History* (Minneapolis: University of Minnesota Press, in association with the Forest History Society, 1983), pp. 33-51.

54. William S. Alverson, Donald M. Waller, and Stephen L. Solheim, "Forests Too Deer: Edge Effects in Northern Wisconsin," *Conservation Biology* 2, no. 4 (1988):350.

55. Ibid., pp. 348-58.

56. Quotation supplied by J. S. Maini, Canadian Forestry Service.

57. Sullivan et al., *Decisions for the Great Lakes*, p. 90.

58. International Joint Commission, *1987 Report on Great Lakes Water Quality*, appendix A, pp. 57-61; William E. Schmidt, "Poisonous Sediments Clog Harbor, But Where Else Can Sludge Go?" *New York Times*, August 8, 1989.

59. International Joint Commission, *1987 Report on Great Lakes Quality*, appendix A, p. 27.

60. William E. Lautenbach, "The Greening of Sudbury," *Journal of Soil and Water Conservation* 44, no. 4 (1989):228-31.

61. Mark Girouard, *Cities and People: A Social and Architectural History* (New Haven: Yale University Press, 1985), pp. 303-304; see also Morison, *The Oxford History of the American People*, p. 775.

62. Sullivan et al., *Decisions for the Great Lakes*, p. 93. Sullivan et al. do not indicate which Sandusky.

63. Ibid., p. 93.

64. Ibid., p. 94.

65. Personal communication, James McLaren.

66. *Report of the International Joint Commission, United States and Canada, on the Pollution of Boundary Waters* (Washington, D.C., and Ottawa: International Joint Commission, 1951), p. 172.

67. Information provided by David Allardice, vice president and assistant director of research, Federal Reserve Bank of Chicago, April 1989; U.S. Department of Commerce, Bureau of the Census, *Statistical Abstract of the United States 1988* (Washington, D.C.: U.S. Government Printing Office, 1988), p. 387.

68. Diane C. Swonk, *The Great Lakes Economy*, background report prepared by The First National Bank of Chicago, September 1988, p. 2.

69. Eileen O'Connor and Steven T. Hulett, "Charting the Great Lakes Economy: Employment Changes Since 1980," Center for Regional Economic Issues, *REI Review*, Fall 1988, p. 34.

70. Robert H. Schnorbus and Philip R. Israilevich, "Midwest Manufacturing: Shining Up the Rustbelt," *Chicago Fed Letter*, no. 20, April 1989, p. 1.

71. Conservation Foundation calculations. Based on U.S. Department of Energy, Energy Information Administration, *State Energy Data Report, 1960-1986* (Washington, D.C.: U.S. Government Printing Office, 1988).

72. Ibid.

73. Ibid.

74. Information supplied by Waclaw Dajnowiec, Ontario Ministry of Energy, based on Statistics Canada data, January 1989.

75. "Even After 10 Years, Victims of Love Canal Can't Quite Escape It," *Wall Street Journal*, March 9, 1989.

76. Adeline Gordon Levine, *Love Canal: Science, Politics, and People* (Lexington, Mass.: Lexington Books, 1982), pp. 9-15.

77. Levine, *Love Canal*, pp. 15-26.

78. Dennis Hevesi, "The History of a Toxic-Waste Nightmare," *New York Times*, September 28, 1988.

79. Eric Schmitt, "Health Chief Says 250 Love Canal Families Can Return," *New York Times*, September 28, 1988.

80. "Habitability of Love Canal Questioned After New Discoveries," *Pesticide and Toxic Chemical News*, March 15, 1989, pp. 1, 4-6.

81. John F. Burns, "Fire and Toxic Cloud in Canada Cause Alarm and Recrimination," *New York Times*, September 2, 1988.

82. U.S. Environmental Protection Agency, Region V, Superfund Program, *CER-CLIS List-8: Site/Event Listing* (Washington, D.C.: U.S. Environmental Protection Agency, 1989); U.S. Environmental Protection Agency, Office of Emergency and Remedial Response, *National Priorities List, Supplementary Lists and Supporting Materials, March 1989* (Washington, D.C.: U.S. Environmental Protection Agency, 1989); U.S. Environmental Protection Agency, Office of Emergency and Remedial Response, *Descriptions of 272 Sites Placed on the Final Priorities List, 1985-1987* (Washington, D.C.: U.S. Environmental Protection Agency, 1987); U.S. Environmental Protection Agency, Office of Emergency and Remedial Response, *Descriptions of 273 Sites Proposed for the Final Priorities List as of March 1989* (Washington, D.C.: U.S. Environmental Protection Agency, 1989); information provided by Lori Acker, U.S. Environmental Protection Agency, Region III, Superfund Office, April 1989.

83. Wisconsin Department of Natural Resources, "Inventory of Sites or Facilities Which May Cause or Threaten to Cause Environmental Pollution," July 1987; Wisconsin Department of Natural Resources, "Active and Abandoned Landfills in Wisconsin," April 1988 update.

84. Information provided by Ulo Sibul, Ontario Ministry of the Environment, May 1988.

85. "Canadian Provincial, Federal Ministers Agree on Policy for Cleanup of Waste Sites," *BNA International Environment Reporter*, May 1989, p. 246.

86. Ontario Ministry of the Environment, "Environment Ministry Releases Updated List of Ontario Landfills," news release, May 5, 1988.

87. Ontario Ministry of the Environment, *Waste Disposal Site Inventory* (Toronto: Queen's Printer for Ontario, 1988).

88. See, for instance, U.S. Congress, Office of Technology Assessment, *Are We Cleaning Up?* (Washington, D.C: U.S. Government Printing Office, 1988); Environmental Defense Fund et al., *Right Train, Wrong Track: Failed Leadership in the Superfund Cleanup Program* (New York: Environmental Defense Fund, 1988).

89. Comprehensive Environmental Response, Compensation, and Liability Act, as amended by Superfund Amendments and Reauthorization Act, 42 U.S.C. 9605 (a)(8)(a).

90. 53 Fed. Reg. 51977 (1988).

91. Ontario's manifest tracking system is under the authority of Regulation 309 under the Ontario Environmental Protection Act, while in the United States such a system was mandated by the Resource Conservation and Recovery Act. See also Environment Canada, *From Cradle to Grave: A Management Approach to Chemicals*, report of a Task Force (Ottawa: Environment Canada, 1986).

92. R.S.C. 35-36-37 Eliz.II 1988, c.22.

93. Canadian Environmental Protection Act, 13, 33-37 and Schedule I. The items already included in Schedule I, "List of Toxic Substances," are some chlorobiphenyls, polybrominated biphenyls and polychlorinated terphenyls, dodecachloropentacyclo $[5.3.0.0^2.6.0^3.9.0^4.8]$ decane, chlorofluorocarbon, asbestos, lead, mercury, and vinyl chloride.

94. "Priority List for Toxic Substances Released by Canadian Environmental Agency," *BNA International Environment Reporter*, March 1989, p. 125.

95. Environment Canada, "Assessing and Controlling Toxic Substances," Canadian Environmental Protection Act fact sheet (Ottawa: Environment Canada, 1988).

96. Ontario Waste Management Corporation, *Environmental Assessment for a Waste Management System*, vol. 1, *The OWMC Undertaking* (Toronto: Ontario Waste Management Corporation, 1988), pp. 3-9; "Hitting the Road: Hazardous Waste Hauling on the Rise," *The Great Lakes Reporter* 6, no. 2 (1989):3.

97. The estimates by the states and national estimates are not necessarily comparable (see figure 3.17 for an explanation of what is included in state estimates and for sources of state estimates). See, for example, Development Planning and Research Associates, Inc., *1985 National Biennial Report of Hazardous Waste Generators and Treatment, Storage and Disposal Facilities Regulated under RCRA*, prepared for U.S. Environmental Protection Agency, Office of Solid Waste (Washington, D.C.: U.S. Environmental Protection Agency, 1989).

98. "Hitting the Road," p. 3.

99. International Joint Commission, Great Lakes Science Advisory Board, *Spills: The Human-Machine Interface, Proceedings of the Workshops on Human Machine Interface* (Windsor, Ont.: International Joint Commission, 1988), p. 2.

100. The Conservation Foundation, *State of the Environment: A View toward the Nineties*, chapter 7.

101. Estimates from data supplied by state and provincial agencies. Conversion to number of football fields based on: National Solid Waste Management Association, "Disposal Costs Continue to Climb," *Facts on File*, April 1989, p. 1.

102. Joseph R. Visalli, "The Similarity of Environmental Impacts from All Methods of Managing Solid Wastes," paper presented at the Conference on Hazardous and Municipal Solid Waste Minimization, February 7-8, 1989, p. 5.

103. Illinois Environmental Protection Agency, Division of Land Pollution Control, *Available Disposal Capacity for Solid Waste in Illinois, Second Annual Report* (Springfield, Ill.: Illinois Environmental Protection Agency, 1988), p. 41.

104. National Solid Wastes Management Association, *Landfill Capacity in the U.S.: How Much Do We Really Have?* (Washington, D.C.: National Solid Wastes Management Association, 1989).

105. New York State Department of Environmental Conservation, *New York State Solid Waste Management Plan 1987-1988 Update* (Albany, N.Y.: New York State Department of Environmental Conservation, 1987), p. S-8; Wisconsin Department of Natural Resources, Bureau of Solid Waste Management, *Wisconsin Waste Reduction and Recovery Plan* (Madison, Wis.: Wisconsin Department of Natural Resources, 1986), p. 1.

106. Kathleen S. Meade, "Ontario Is Running Out of Landfills," *Waste Age*, September 1988, p. 107.

107. "Rates Up in Ohio," *Waste Age*, August 1988, p. 30.

108. U.S. Environmental Protection Agency, Office of Solid Waste, *Proposed Revisions to Criteria for Municipal Solid Waste Disposal Landfills: A Summary* (Washington, D.C.: U.S. Environmental Protection Agency, 1988).

109. National Solid Wastes Management Association, *Landfill Capacity in the U.S.*, appendix 2; "Ontario Regulation 309 under the Environmental Protection Act O. Reg.

309/80, as amended by O. Reg. 175/83, 574/84, 322/85, and 464/85,'' Sec. 8, *BNA International Environmental Reporter*, September 10, 1986, p. 17; "State Solid Waste Management Programs Vary Widely but Face Similar Problems Such as Capacity, Siting Limits," *BNA Environment Reporter*, October 3, 1986, p. 845.

110. National Solid Wastes Management Association, *Landfill Capacity in the U.S.*, appendix 1.

111. See, for instance, U.S. Environmental Protection Agency, *The Solid Waste Dilemma: An Agenda for Action* (Washington, D.C.: U.S. Environmental Protection Agency, 1989), pp. 10, 16; National Solid Wastes Management Association, "Disposal Costs Continue to Climb," p. 3.

112. The hierarchy was embodied in a national policy statement issued by the U.S. Environmental Protection Agency in 1976. See 41 *Fed. Reg.* no. 161 (1976). See also sources cited ibid.

113. Fred Clinton, "Michigan Perspectives," paper prepared for the Workshop on State and Local Municipal Solid Waste Programs, U.S. Congress, Office of Technology Assessment, Washington, D.C., March 17-18, 1988, p. 1; Michigan Department of Natural Resources, Waste Management Division, *Michigan Solid Waste Policy* (Lansing, Mich.: Michigan Department of Natural Resources, 1988), pp. 4-6.

114. Bill Richards, "Energy from Garbage Loses Some of Promise as Wave of the Future," *Wall Street Journal*, June 16, 1988; Robert Hanley, "Lacking Garbage, A Jersey Incinerator Is Losing Money," *New York Times*, January 25, 1989.

115. "Ontario's Bradley Vows to Continue Fight for Pollution Controls on Detroit Incinerator," *BNA Environment Reporter*, June 10, 1988, p. 210; "Federal Court Gives Detroit Go-Ahead to Build Municipal Solid Waste Incinerator," *BNA Environment Reporter*, March 4, 1988, p. 2,265; "Ash from Detroit Trash Incinerator May Be Hazardous, State Agency Says," *BNA Environment Reporter*, March 24, 1989, p. 2,523; "Detroit Incinerator Case Remanded for State Court Review of Challenges," *BNA Environment Reporter*, May 12, 1989, p. 114; and information provided by Mike Brinker, Greater Detroit Resource Recovery Authority, October 1989.

116. Letter from Robert O. Homme, acting deputy assistant secretary of state, European and Canadian Affairs, to David LaRoche, secretary, U.S. Section, International Joint Commission, September 30, 1988.

117. "Some Recent Initiatives on Solid Waste Management: Assembly Bill 10652 (Hinchey)/Senate Bill 8107(Bruno)," Legislative Commission on Solid Waste Management, Albany, New York, n.d; New York Solid Waste Management Act of 1988.

118. Richard Sahli, "Nowhere to Go: State Efforts Will Be Overwhelmed without a National Response to Solid Waste," *Northeast-Midwest Economic Review*, August 7, 1989, pp. 9-11.

119. "Statewatch: Ontario," *Resource Recycling*, January-February 1989, p. 7; Ontario Ministry of the Environment, "Provincial Plan Targets of 25 Per Cent Recycling by 1992, 50 Per Cent by 2000," news release, March 10, 1989; William Steggles, Ontario Ministry of the Environment, personal communication.

120. See, for instance, U.S. Congress, Office of Technology Assessment, *Facing America's Trash: What Next for Municipal Solid Waste?*, interim summary (Washington, D.C.: U.S. Government Printing Office, 1989).

121. Paul G. R. Smith, *Towards the Protection of Great Lakes Natural Heritage*

*Areas*, Technical Paper no. 2 (Waterloo, Ont.: University of Waterloo, Heritage Resources Centre, 1987), pp. 33-35.

122. Great Lakes Commission, *Travel, Tourism and Outdoor Recreation in the Great Lakes States* (Ann Arbor, Mich.: Great Lakes Commission, 1989), p. 33.

123. George McKibbon, Cecil Louis, and Frank Shaw, "Protecting the Niagara Escarpment," *Journal of Soil and Water Conservation* 42, no.2 (1987):78-82; Paul G. R. Smith, *Towards the Protection of Great Lakes Natural Heritage Areas*, p. 27.

124. "Carolinian Canada Zone to Be Preserved," *Journal of Soil and Water Conservation* 42, no. 4 (1987):19, 25; World Wildlife Fund Canada, *Annual Report 1986* (Toronto: World Wildlife Fund Canada, 1986), pp. 16-17.

## Box: Accidents in the Great Lakes Ecosystem

1. Denis Amyot, Emergency Planning Commission, "Report on Mississauga Train Derailment and Evacuation," undated, unpublished typescript.

2. Memorandum from the secretary of the Great Lakes Science Advisory Board to the International Joint Commission, March 2, 1989. The resolution had been adopted at a meeting on February 15-17, 1989.

3. International Joint Commission, Great Lakes Science Advisory Board, *Spills: The Human-Machine Interface, Proceedings of the Workshops on Human Machine Interface* (Windsor, Ont.: International Joint Commission, 1988), p. 101. See also, International Joint Commission, Great Lakes Water Quality Board, "1987 Report on Great Lakes Water Quality," p. 121.

## Figures

3.1. Environment Canada and U.S. Environmental Protection Agency, *The Great Lakes: An Environmental Atlas and Resource Book* (Chicago: U.S. Environmental Protection Agency, Great Lakes National Program Office, and Toronto: Environment Canada, Ontario Region, 1988), p. 19

3.2. U.S. Department of Commerce, Bureau of the Census, "Local Population Estimates," *Current Population Reports*, Series P-26, no. 86-A (Washington, D.C.: U.S. Government Printing Office, 1987), table 1 (1986 estimates are as of July 1, 1986); Statistics Canada, *Human Activity and the Environment: A Statistical Compendium* (Ottawa: Minister of Supply and Services, 1986), p. 46; Environment Canada and U.S. Environmental Protection Agency, *The Great Lakes*, p. 4.

3.3. International Joint Commission, Great Lakes Water Quality Board, *1987 Report of Great Lakes Water Quality* (Windsor, Ont.: International Joint Commission, 1987), p. 38.

3.4. National Geographic Society, *Historical Atlas of the United States*, centennial ed. (Washington, D.C.: National Geographic Society, 1988), pp. 188, 196; Thomas F. McIlwraith, "British North America, 1763-1867," in Robert D. Mitchell and Paul A. Groves, *North America: The Historical Geography of a Changing Continent* (Totowa, N.J.: Rowman and Littlefield, 1987), pp. 246-47; Madeline Sadler Waggoner, *The Long Haul West: The Great Canal Era, 1817-1850* (New York: Putnam's, 1958), inside jacket; Donald Creighton, *The Empire of the St. Lawrence* (Boston: Houghton Mifflin, 1958).

3.5. U.S. Bureau of the Census, Census of Agriculture.

3.6. Ibid.

3.7. Ibid.

3.8. Ibid.

3.9. Leonard P. Gianessi, "Use of Selected Pesticides in Agricultural Crop Production in the Great Lakes Region," Resources for the Future, report submitted to The Conservation Foundation, March 1988; Bill McGee, *Survey of Pesticide Use in Ontario, 1983: Estimates of Pesticides Used on Field Crops, Fruits, Vegetables, and in Roadside Weed Control*, Economics Information Report no. 84-05 (Toronto: Ontario Ministry of Agriculture and Food, 1984), p. 28. U.S. pesticide use estimates are based on an assessment of the percentage of acres treated and the annual application rate for 21 active ingredients on 64 crops; they assume uniformity for all counties within states for the same pesticide/crop use. It is not known to what extent the actual use pattern varies within each state. Some uses of the selected pesticides in the Great Lakes region, such as livestock, rights-of-way, mosquito control, and aquatic weed control, are not accounted for in these estimates. Also, it is not known to what extent these estimates, which are for a year in the middle 1980s, reflect current use patterns. Unfortunately, it is not known what proportion of pesticide use these estimates represent, nor is it possible to determine whether pesticide use is increasing or decreasing. It is likely, though, that national trends, such as the rising proportion of pesticide use that is comprised by herbicides, also apply to the Great Lakes region.

3.10. I. J. Shelton, G. J. Wall, and W. T. Dickinson, *Phosphorus Fertilizer Management in the Canadian Great Lakes Basin*, summary report, O.I.P. pubn. no. 88-2 (Guelph, Ont.: Institute of Pedology, 1988).

3.11. Information provided by Jeff Goebel, U.S. Soil Conservation Service, 1982 National Resources Inventory computer tape, March 1988.

3.12. Vernon Renshaw, Edward A. Trott, Jr., and Howard L. Friedenberg, "Gross State Product by Industry, 1963-1986," *Survey of Current Business* 68, no. 5 (1988):39.

3.13. Environment Canada, Canada Centre for Inland Waters, *Population Estimates for the Great Lakes Basins and Their Major Tributaries*, Social Science Series no. 1 (Ottawa: Information Canada, 1973), pp. 5, 43; Great Lakes Basin Commission, Economic and Demographic Studies Work Group, *Great Lakes Basin Framework Study*, appendix 19: "Economic and Demographic Studies" (Ann Arbor, Mich.: Great Lakes Basin Commission, 1975), pp. 15, 18, 21, 25, 27, 30, 33, 36, 39, 42, 45, 48, 51, 54, 57; U.S. Department of Commerce, "Local Population Estimates," table 1 (1986 estimates are as of July 1, 1986); Statistics Canada, *Human Activity and the Environment: A Statistical Compendium*, p. 46.

3.14. U.S. Department of Energy, Energy Information Administration, *State Energy Data Report: Consumption Estimates 1960-1986* (Washington, D.C.: U.S. Government Printing Office, 1988), pp. 105, 111, 159, 165, 219, 237, 255, 321.

3.15. Personal communication from Waclaw Dajnowiec, Ontario Ministry of Energy, 1989, based on Statistics Canada publications.

3.16. U.S. Environmental Protection Agency, Region V, Superfund Program, *CERCLIS List-8: Site/Event Listing* (Washington, D.C.: U.S. Environmental Protection Agency, 1989); U.S. Environmental Protection Agency, Office of Emergency and Remedial Response, *National Priorities List, Supplementary Lists and Supporting Materials, March 1989* (Washington, D.C.: U.S. Government Printing Office, 1989);

U.S. Environmental Protection Agency, Office of Emergency and Remedial Response, *Descriptions of 272 Sites Placed on the Final Priorities List, 1985-1987* (Washington, D.C.: U.S. Government Printing Office, 1987); U.S. Environmental Protection Agency, Office of Emergency and Remedial Response, *Descriptions of 273 Sites Proposed for the Final Priorities List as of March 1989* (Washington, D.C.: U.S. Government Printing Office, 1989); U.S. Environmental Protection Agency, Office of Emergency and Remedial Response, *Descriptions of 101 Sites Placed on the Final Priorities List in March 1989* (Washington, D.C.: U.S. Government Printing Office, 1989); New York information provided by Donna Vizian and Diane Cox, EPA Region II, Superfund Office, April 1989; Pennsylvania information provided by Lori Acker, EPA Region III, Superfund Office, April 1989.

3.17. Illinois Environmental Protection Agency, Division of Land Pollution Control, *Summary of Annual Reports on Hazardous Waste for 1983 through 1985* (Springfield, Ill.: Illinois Environmental Protection Agency, 1986); Illinois Environmental Protection Agency, Division of Land Pollution Control, *Summary of Annual Reports on Hazardous Waste for 1983 through 1986* (Springfield, Ill.: Illinois Environmental Protection Agency, 1987); personal communication, Hope A. Wright, Illinois Environmental Protection Agency; Indiana Department of Environmental Management, Office of Solid and Hazardous Waste Management, *Hazardous Waste Activity Biennial Report 1985* (Indianapolis, Ind.: Indiana Department of Environmental Management, 1985); Michigan Department of Natural Resources, Waste Management Division, *Hazardous Waste Management Capacity Needs Study* (Lansing, Mich.: Michigan Department of Natural Resources, 1985); personal communication, Lois DeBacker, Michigan Department of Natural Resources; Minnesota Waste Management Board, *Manifested Shipments of Hazardous Waste by Generators 1983-1987: Commercial and Major Captive Facilities* (St. Paul, Minn.: Minnesota Waste Management Board, 1988); personal communication, Ed Meyer, Hazardous Waste Division, Minnesota Pollution Control Agency, May 1988; New York Department of Environmental Conservation, Division of Hazardous Substances Regulation, *1986 Report on the Generation of Hazardous Waste in New York* (Albany, N.Y.: New York State Department of Environmental Conservation, 1987); Ohio Environmental Protection Agency, Division of Solid and Hazardous Waste Management, *Technical Statistics on Ohio's Generation, Treatment, Storage and Disposal of Hazardous Wastes during 1982, 1983, and 1984* (Columbus, Ohio: Ohio Environmental Protection Agency); Ohio Environmental Protection Agency, Division of Solid and Hazardous Waste Management, *General Statistics on Ohio's Generation, Treatment, Storage and Disposal of Hazardous Wastes during 1982, 1983, 1984, 1985 and 1986* (Columbus, Ohio: Ohio Environmental Protection Agency); Ohio Environmental Protection Agency, Division of Solid and Hazardous Waste Management, *1986 Facility Annual Report* (Columbus, Ohio: Ohio Environmental Protection Agency); Ontario Waste Management Corporation, *Draft Environmental Assessment: Waste Treatment Facility (Vol. I)* (Toronto: Ontario Waste Management Corporation, 1988), p. 4-12; Pennsylvania Department of Environmental Resources, *Hazardous Waste Facilities Plan* (Harrisburg, Pa.: Pennsylvania Department of Environmental Resources, 1986); Wisconsin Department of Natural Resources, Bureau of Solid and Hazardous Waste Management, *Biennial Report* (Madison, Wis.: Wisconsin Department of Natural Resources, 1985); U.S. Environmental Protection Agency, Office of Solid Waste, *National Summary Biennial*

*Report on 1985 Hazardous Waste Generation, Treatment, Storage and Disposal Activities* (Washington, D.C.: U.S. Environmental Protection Agency, 1989).

3.18. Michigan Department of Natural Resources, Waste Management Division, *Michigan Solid Waste Policy* (Lansing, Mich.: Michigan Department of Natural Resources, 1988).

# 4. LEGACIES AND CHALLENGES: WATER

1. Estimate for the U.S. portion of the basin based on current population estimates and Great Lakes Basin Commission, *Great Lakes Basin Framework Study* (Ann Arbor, Mich.: Great Lakes Basin Commission, 1975), appendix 6; 1988 estimate for the Canadian side of the basin provided by T. Yakutchik, Ontario Ministry of the Environment, Water Resources Branch.

2. C. J. Haefeli, *Regional Groundwater Flow Between Lake Simcoe and Lake Ontario*, Technical Bulletin no. 23 (Ottawa: Canada Department of Energy, Mines and Resources, Inland Waters Branch, 1970); C. J. Haefeli, *Groundwater Inflow into Lake Ontario from the Canadian Side*, Scientific Series no. 9 (Ottawa: Canada Department of the Environment, Inland Waters Branch, 1972), p. 63.

3. International Joint Commission, Great Lakes Science Advisory Board, Groundwater Contamination Task Force, *A Study Proposal for Assessing Potential for Great Lakes Contamination via Groundwater* (Windsor, Ont.: International Joint Commission, 1985), p. 28.

4. Great Lakes Basin Commission, *Great Lakes Basin Framework Study*, appendix 3, p. 8.

5. Ontario Ministry of Natural Resources, *Water Quantity Resources of Ontario* (Toronto: Ontario Ministry of Natural Resources, 1984), p. 46.

6. Michigan Department of Natural Resources, *Water Quality and Pollution Control in Michigan*, 1988 305(b) Report (Lansing, Mich.: Michigan Department of Natural Resources, 1988), pp. 95-98.

7. A. P. Visocky, M. G. Sherrill, and K. Cartwright, *Geology, Hydrology, and Water Quality of the Cambrian and Ordovician Systems in Northern Illinois*, Cooperative Groundwater Report no. 10 (Champaign-Urbana, Ill.: Illinois State Geological Survey, Illinois State Water Survey, and U.S. Geological Survey, 1985), pp. 73, 105.

8. H. L. Young et al., "Northern Midwest Regional Aquifer-System Study," in R. J. Sun, ed., *Regional Aquifer-System Analysis Program of the U.S. Geological Survey, Summary of Projects, 1978-84*, USGS Circular 1002 (Washington, D.C.: U.S. Government Printing Office, 1986), p. 75.

9. Great Lakes Basin Commission, *Great Lakes Basin Framework Study*, appendix 3, p. 29.

10. Ibid., pp. 25-26.

11. Christian Pupp and G. Grove, "Groundwater Quality in Ontario: Hydrogeology, Quality Concerns, and Management," unpublished draft (Ottawa: Environment Canada, State of Environment Reporting Branch, 1989).

12. Wisconsin Department of Natural Resources, *Wisconsin Water Quality Report to Congress, 1988*, 305(b) Report (Madison, Wis.: State of Wisconsin, 1988), p. 44.

13. K. S. Novakowski and P. A. Lapcevic, "Regional Hydrogeology of the Silurian

and Ordovician Sedimentary Rock Underlying Niagara Falls, Ontario, Canada," *Journal of Hydrology* 104 (1988):211-36.

14. E. Ford and J. Quarles, *Groundwater Contamination in the United States* (Philadelphia: University of Pennsylvania Press, 1987), p. 4.

15. J. A. Cherry, "Groundwater Occurrence and Contamination in Canada," *Canadian Bulletin of Fisheries and Aquatic Sciences* 215 (1987):387-426.

16. U.S. Environmental Protection Agency, Environment Canada, Michigan Department of Natural Resources, and Ontario Ministry of the Environment, *Upper Great Lakes Connecting Channels Study* (1988), vol. 2, p. 277.

17. Ibid., p. 279.

18. Intera Technologies Ltd., *Hydrogeologic Study of the Fresh Water Aquifer and Deep Geologic Formations, Sarnia, Ontario,* prepared for Ontario Ministry of the Environment, Detroit/St.Clair/St. Marys Rivers Project (Sarnia, Ont.: Intera Technologies Ltd., 1989); U.S. Environmental Protection Agency et al., *Upper Great Lakes Connecting Channels Study*, vol. 2, pp. 282-83.

19. Michigan Department of Natural Resources, *Water Quality and Pollution Control in Michigan*, pp. 99-106.

20. Environment Canada, U.S. Environmental Protection Agency, Ontario Ministry of the Environment, and New York State Department of Environmental Conservation, *Final Report of the Niagara River Toxics Committee* (1984).

21. Gradient Corporation and GeoTrans, Inc., *Potential Contaminant Loadings to the Niagara River from U.S. Hazardous Waste Sites*, prepared for the Niagara River Toxics Committee (Washington, D.C.: U.S. Geological Survey and U.S. Environmental Protection Agency, 1988).

22. M. G. Brooksbank, "Control and Management of Hazardous Waste Sites in the Niagara River Area," paper presented at the Hazardous Materials Management Conference and Exhibition of Canada, Toronto, September 9-11, 1987.

23. Ibid., p. 7.

24. Ibid.

25. Cherry, "Groundwater Occurrence and Contamination in Canada," pp. 399-401.

26. Geolog Testing Consultants, Ltd., *Hydrogeologic Evaluation of the Hooker Niagara Plant Site*, report to the Niagara River Steering Committee (Toronto: Ontario Ministry of the Environment, 1984).

27. International Joint Commission, "Revised Great Lakes Water Quality Agreement of 1978: Agreement with Annexes and Terms of Reference, between the United States and Canada, signed at Ottawa, November 22, 1978, and Phosphorus Load Reduction Supplement, signed October 7, 1983, as amended by Protocol, signed November 18, 1987" (Windsor, Ont., 1988), annex 16. This agreement is cited hereafter as "1978 Water Quality Agreement."

28. Bob Campbell, "Warning Signs: 'Mercury Levels in Inland Game Fish May Pose Health Threat,' Experts Say," *Detroit Free Press*, December 4, 1988.

29. Minnesota Department of Public Health, "Minnesota Fish Consumption Advisory," Minneapolis, Minn., 1985 and 1987.

30. Michigan Department of Natural Resources, "Michigan's 1988 Nonpoint Pollution Assessment Report," draft, Lansing, Mich., 1988.

31. The percentages quoted for Wisconsin and Ohio are for the entire state, not

just the Great Lakes basin. Wisconsin Department of Natural Resources, *Wisconsin Water Quality Report to Congress, 1988* (Madison, Wis.: Wisconsin Department of Natural Resources, 1988).

32. Ohio Environmental Protection Agency, *Ohio Water Quality Inventory*, 1988 305(b) Report (Columbus, Ohio: Ohio Environmental Protection Agency, 1988).

33. Ohio Environmental Protection Agency, *Ohio Nonpoint Source Assessment* (Columbus, Ohio: Ohio Environmental Protection Agency, 1988).

34. This conclusion is based on a review of all the 305(b) reports from the eight Great Lakes states.

35. International Joint Commission, Great Lakes Water Quality Board, *1987 Report on Great Lakes Quality* (Windsor, Ont.: International Joint Commission, 1987), p. 148.

36. Ibid., pp. 78-80.

37. E. B. Bennett, "The Nitrifying of Lake Superior," *Ambio* 15, no. 5 (1986):272-75.

38. J. Barica, "Increases of Nitrate in the Great Lakes," *Symposium Document, 5th International Symposium of CIEC* (Balatonfured, Hungary, 1987), vol. 2, sect. I, pp. 300-12.

39. W. Swain, "Chlorinated Organic Residues in Fish, Water, and Precipitation from the Vicinity of Isle Royale, Lake Superior," *Journal of Great Lakes Research* 4 (1978):398-407.

40. S. J. Eisenreich, B. B. Looney, and G. J. Hollod, "PCBs in the Lake Superior Atmosphere, 1978-1980," in D. MacKay et al., eds., *Physical Behavior of PCBs in The Great Lakes* (Ann Arbor, Mich.: Ann Arbor Science Publishers, 1983), pp. 115-25.

41. William J. Strachan and Steven J. Eisenreich, "Mass Balancing of Toxic Chemicals in the Great Lakes: The Role of Atmospheric Deposition," appendix I from International Joint Commission, International Air Quality Advisory Board, Workshop on the Estimation of Atmospheric Loadings of Toxic Chemicals to the Great Lakes Basin, October 29-31, 1986 (Windsor, Ont.: International Joint Commission, 1988).

42. International Joint Commission, Great Lakes Water Quality Board, *1987 Report on Great Lakes Quality, Appendix A* (Windsor, Ont.: International Joint Commission, 1987).

43. International Joint Commission, *1987 Report on Great Lakes Quality*, pp. 78-80.

44. Ibid., p. 86.

45. International Joint Commission, *1987 Report on Great Lakes Quality, Appendix A*.

46. D. Scavia et al., "Influence of Salmonid Predation and Weather on Long-term Water Quality Trends in Lake Michigan," *Canadian Journal of Fisheries and Aquatic Science* 43 (1986):435-43.

47. U.S. Environmental Protection Agency, Great Lakes National Program Office, *Lake Michigan Intensive Survey 1976-1977, Management Report*, EPA-905/4-80-003-B (Chicago: U.S. Environmental Protection Agency, 1980), pp. 10, 11; W. C. Ackerman, R. H. Harmeson, and T. A. Sinclair, "Some Long Trends in Water Quality of Lakes and Rivers," *American Geophysical Union* 15 (1970):515-22; A. M. Beeton,

"Changes in the Environment and Biota of the Great Lakes," in *Eutrophication: Causes, Consequences, Correctives* (Washington, D.C.: National Academy of Sciences, 1969), pp. 150-87; D. C. Rockwell et al., "Environmental Trends in Lake Michigan," in R. C. Loehr, C. S. Martin, and W. Rast, eds., *Phosphorus Management Strategies for Lakes* (Ann Arbor, Mich.: Ann Arbor Science Publishers, 1980), pp. 91-132; D. C. Rockwell et al., *Lake Michigan Intensive Survey 1976-1977*, EPA-905/4-80-003-/A (Chicago: U.S. Environmental Protection Agency, 1980); M. S. Torrey, *Environmental Status of the Lake Michigan Region*, vol. 3, *Chemistry of Lake Michigan* (Argonne, Ill.: Argonne National Laboratory, 1976); B. M. Lesht and D. C. Rockwell, *The State of the Middle Great Lakes: Results of the 1984 Water Quality Survey of Lakes Erie, Huron, and Michigan*, ANL/ER-87-1 (Argonne, Ill.: Argonne National Laboratory, 1987); International Joint Commission, *1987 Report on Great Lakes Quality*, p. 82.

48. C. L. Schelske, "Silica Depletion in Lake Michigan: Verification Using Lake Superior as an Environmental Reference Standard," *Journal of Great Lakes Research* 11, no. 4 (1985):492-500; Illinois Environmental Protection Agency, *Illinois Water Quality Report, 1984-1985* (Springfield, Ill.: Illinois Environmental Protection Agency, 1986), p. 106.

49. Michigan Department of Natural Resources, *Water Quality and Pollution Control in Michigan*, pp. 53-54.

50. Ibid.

51. R. A. Cahill, *Geochemistry of Recent Lake Michigan Sediments* (Champaign-Urbana, Ill.: Illinois Geological Survey, 1981); P. W. Rodgers and W. R. Swain, "Analysis of Polychlorinated Biphenyl (PCB) Loading Trends in Lake Michigan," *Journal of Great Lakes Research* 9, no. 4 (1983):548-58.

52. International Joint Commission, Great Lakes Science Advisory Board, Aquatic Ecosystem Objectives Committee, *1981 Report* (Windsor, Ont.: International Joint Commission, 1981).

53. A. H. Berst and G. R. Spangler, *Lake Huron: The Ecology of the Fish Community and Man's Effects on It*, Technical Report no. 21 (Ann Arbor, Mich.: Great Lakes Fishery Commission, 1973), p. 1; D. M. Dolan et al., eds., *Lake Huron 1980 Intensive Survey, Summary Report to the Surveillance Work Group* (Windsor, Ont.: International Joint Commission, 1986); International Joint Commission, *1987 Report on Great Lakes Quality*.

54. Berst and Spangler, *Lake Huron*, p. 9.

55. International Joint Commission, *1987 Report on Great Lakes Quality*, p. 81.

56. Dolan et al., *Lake Huron 1980 Intensive Survey, Summary Report*, p. 41.

57. International Joint Commission, *1987 Report on Great Lakes Quality*, p. 87.

58. Ibid., p. 80.

59. International Joint Commission, *1987 Report on Great Lakes Quality*, Appendix A.

60. International Joint Commission, *1987 Report on Great Lakes Quality*, p. 88.

61. Dolan et al., *Lake Huron 1980 Intensive Survey, Summary Report*, p. 42.

62. W. L. Hartman, *Effects of Exploitation, Environmental Changes, and New Species on the Fish Habitat and Resources of Lake Erie*, Technical Report no. 22 (Ann Arbor, Mich.: Great Lakes Fishery Commission, 1973).

63. International Joint Commission, *1989 Report on Great Lakes Water Quality*, p. 84.

64. International Joint Commission, *Fourth Biennial Report* (Windsor, Ont.: International Joint Commission, 1989), p. 11.

65. International Joint Commission, *1987 Report on Great Lakes Quality*, p. 80.

66. A. M. Beeton, "Eutrophication of the St. Lawrence Great Lakes," *Limnology and Oceanography* 10 (1965):240-54; International Joint Commission, *1987 Report on Great Lakes Quality*, p. 83.

67. R. P. Apman, *Historical Trends in Pollutant Loadings to Lake Erie* (Buffalo, N.Y.: U.S. Army Corps of Engineers, 1975).

68. N. M. Burns, *Erie: The Lake That Survived* (Totowa, N.J.: Rowman and Allanheld, 1985), p. 93.

69. D. E. Rathke and C. J. Edwards, *A Review of Trends in Lake Erie Water Quality with Emphasis on the 1978-1979 Intensive Survey* (Windsor, Ont.: International Joint Commission, 1985), p. 98.

70. International Joint Commission, *1987 Report on Great Lakes Quality*, table 17, p. 89.

71. International Reference Group on Great Lakes Pollution from Land Use Activites (PLUARG), *Environmental Management Strategy for the Great Lakes System* (Windsor, Ont.: International Joint Commission, 1978), quoted in Burns, *Erie*, p. 129.

72. Burns, *Erie*, pp. 130-31.

73. U.S. Environmental Protection Agency, Environment Canada, New York State Department of Environmental Conservation and Ontario Ministry of the Environment, Lake Ontario Toxics Committee, *Lake Ontario Toxics Management Plan*, 1989, appendix I, p. 2.

74. Ibid.

75. Ibid., p. 3; International Joint Commission, Great Lakes Water Quality Board, Task Force on Chemical Loadings, *Report on Modeling the Loading-Concentration Relationship for Critical Pollutants in the Great Lakes* (Windsor, Ont.: International Joint Commission, 1988).

76. H. F. H. Dobson, "Principal Ions and Dissolved Oxygen in Lake Ontario," *Proceedings of the 10th Conference on Great Lakes Research* (International Association of Great Lakes Research, 1967), pp. 337-56; Beeton, "Changes in the Environment and Biota of the Great Lakes."

77. R. J. J. Stevens, *A Review of Lake Ontario Water Quality with Emphasis on the 1981-1982 Intensive Years, Report to the Surveillance Work Group* (Windsor, Ont.: International Joint Commission, 1988), table 3, p. 44.

78. International Joint Commission, *1987 Report on Great Lakes Quality*, p. 84.

79. J. Barica, *Increases of Nitrate in the Great Lakes*, Contribution no. 87-77, (Burlington, Ont.: Environment Canada, National Water Research Institute, Lakes Research Branch, 1987).

80. M. A. Neilson, *Trace Metals in Lake Ontario, 1979*, Scientific Series no. 133 (Burlington, Ont.: Environment Canada, Inland Waters Directorate, 1983).

81. International Joint Commission, Great Lakes Water Quality Board, *1983 Report on Great Lakes Quality* (Windsor, Ont.: International Joint Commission, 1983); also 1985 and 1987 reports; U.S. Environmental Protection Agency et al., *Lake Ontario Toxics Management Plan*, p. 4.

82. R. J. Allen and A. J. Ball, "An Overview of Chemical Concentrations and Trends in Waters, Suspended Solids and Bottom Sediments of the Laurentian Great Lakes and Their Connecting Channels," unpublished draft report (Burlington, Ont.: Environment Canada, National Water Research Institute, 1989), p. 292.

83. U.S. Environmental Protection Agency et al., *Lake Ontario Toxics Management Plan*, appendix I, p. 5.

84. Ibid.

85. International Joint Commission, *Report of the International Joint Commission, United States and Canada, on the Pollution of Boundary Waters* (Washington, D.C. and Ottawa: International Joint Commission, 1950); U.S. Environmental Protection Agency et al., *Upper Great Lakes Connecting Channels Study*; Environment Canada et al., *Final Report of the Niagara River Toxics Committee.*

86. International Joint Commission, *1987 Report on Great Lakes Quality, Appendix A.*

87. Eco Logic, "Great Lakes St. Lawrence Linkage," unpublished report (Ottawa: Institute for Research on Public Policy, 1989), p. v.

88. Environment Canada, Lands Directorate, *Wetlands of the St. Lawrence River Region, 1950-1978*, Environment Conservation Service Working Paper no. 45 (Ottawa: Environment Canada, 1985).

89. U.S. Environmental Protection Agency et al., *Lake Ontario Toxics Management Plan*, appendix II, p. 13.

90. International Joint Commission, *1987 Report on Great Lakes Quality, Appendix A*, p. 55.

91. B. G. Oliver, M. N. Charlton, and R. W. Durham, *Distribution, Redistribution and Geochronology of PCB Congeners and Other Chlorinated Hydrocarbons in Lake Ontario Sediments*, Control no. ECD132 (Burlington, Ont.: Environment Canada, National Water Research Institute, 1987), p. 5.

92. Allen and Ball, "An Overview of Chemical Concentrations and Trends in Waters, Suspended Solids and Bottom Sediments of the Laurentian Great Lakes and Their Connecting Channels," p. 190.

93. U.S. Environmental Protection Agency et al., *Upper Great Lakes Connecting Channels Study.*

94. International Joint Commission, Great Lakes Water Quality Board, Dredging Subcommittee, *Guidelines and Register for Evaluation of Great Lakes Dredging Projects* (Windsor, Ont.: International Joint Commission, 1982).

95. International Joint Commission, *1987 Report on Great Lakes Quality, Appendix A.*

96. Environment Canada et al., *Final Report of the Niagara River Toxics Committee.*

97. U.S. Environmental Protection Agency et al., *Upper Great Lakes Connecting Channels Study.*

98. U.S. Environmental Protection Agency et al., *Lake Ontario Toxics Management Plan.*

99. 1978 Water Quality Agreement, Annex 2, 6(a).

100. International Joint Commission, *1989 Report on Great Lakes Water Quality*, p. 73.

101. Ibid., p. 68.

102. Ibid., p. 66.

103. Environment Canada and U.S. Environmental Protection Agency, *The Great Lakes: An Environmental Atlas and Resource Book* (Chicago: U.S. Environmental Protection Agency, Great Lakes National Program Office, and Toronto: Environment Canada, Ontario Region, 1988), p. 4.

104. Great Lakes Commission, *Water Level Changes: Factors Influencing the Great Lakes* (Ann Arbor, Mich.: The Great Lakes Commission, 1986), p. 1.

105. Paul MacClennan and Mike Vogel, "The Rise and Fall of the Great Lakes," *Buffalo Evening News*, April 28, 1987.

106. Great Lakes Commission, *Water Level Changes*, p. 3.

107. International Joint Commission, Levels Reference Project Management Team, *Living with the Lakes: Challenges and Opportunities* (Windsor, Ont.: International Joint Commission, 1989), p. 2.

108. This difference is for Lake St. Clair. See U.S. Army Corps of Engineers, *Monthly Bulletin of Lake Levels for the Great Lakes*, July 1989.

109. Great Lakes Commission, *Water Level Changes*.

110. Environment Canada, *Living with the Great Lakes*, brochure, 1986.

111. U.S. Army Corps of Engineers, *Monthly Bulletin of Lake Levels for the Great Lakes*, July 1989.

112. Great Lakes Commission, *Water Level Changes*, p. 5.

113. Ibid., p. 8.

114. Ibid.

115. International Joint Commission, *Living with the Lakes*, p. 1.

116. These are summarized in International Joint Commission, *Great Lakes Diversions and Consumptive Uses: Report to the Governments of the United States and Canada under the 1977 Reference* (Washington, D.C., and Ottawa: International Joint Commission, 1985). See Appendix G.

117. The description of the Grand Canal in the text is based on Great Lakes Commission, *Water Level Changes*, p. 8.

118. For details on legal aspects of diversion, see The Center for the Great Lakes, *The Law and the Lakes* (Chicago, Illinois, and Toronto, Ont.: Center for the Great Lakes, 1985), and "Seminar Papers, Great Lakes Legal Seminar: Diversion and Consumptive Use," *Case Western Reserve Journal of International Law* 18, no. 1 (1986). A broad review of data and issues pertaining both to diversion and to consumptive uses of Great Lakes water is provided in a 1985 report of the International Joint Commission, responding to a 1977 reference to the IJC by the United States and Canada. See International Joint Commission, *Great Lakes Diversions and Consumptive Uses*. See also "Guarding the Lakes: Diversion Ideas Arise Closer to Home," *The Great Lakes Reporter*, June/July 1988.

119. International Joint Commission, *Great Lakes Diversions and Consumptive Uses*, p. 39.

120. The text of the reference is reprinted in International Joint Commission, *Living With the Lakes*, p. 3.

121. Ibid., p. 12.

122. Ibid., p. 3.

123. Ibid., p. 2.

124. U.S. Department of Commerce, Coastal Zone Information Center, *CZM Information Exchange* (Washington, D.C.: U.S. Department of Commerce, 1984), pp. 53-63.

125. "Ohio Enacts Law to Protect Shore of Lake Erie," *Land Use Planning Report*, January 4, 1989, p. 4.

126. Beth Millemann, *And Two If By Sea* (Washington, D.C.: Coast Alliance, 1986), p. 13.

127. Great Lakes Coastal Barriers Act of 1988, codified at 16 U.S.C. 3501 et seq. (1988).

128. Reid D. Kreutzwiser, "Managing the Great Lakes Shoreline Hazard," *Journal of Soil and Water Conservation* 42, no. 3 (1987):153.

129. Ibid. For a review of recent developments in Great Lakes shoreline management, see Center for the Great Lakes, *A Look at the Land Side* (Chicago and Toronto: Center for the Great Lakes, 1988).

## Niagara Falls—From Sublimity to Toxicity

1. Elizabeth McKinsey, *Niagara Falls, Icon of the American Sublime* (New York: Cambridge University Press, 1985), p. 31.

2. Ibid., pp. 32-33.

3. Ibid.

4. "Niagara Falls Mist Contains Toxics, Canadian Environmental Group Reports," *BNA Environment Reporter Current Developments*, May 29, 1987, p. 482; "Niagara Falls under a Cloud of Chemicals," *Philadelphia Inquirer*, May 10, 1987; Zenon Environmental, *Analysis of Tenax Traps by GL/MS*, report to Pollution Probe (Toronto, Ont.: Pollution Probe, 1986); See also R. M. Hoff et al., *Vapour Phase Air Concentrations of PCBs and Chloroform at Niagara Falls*, Report ARD 87-4 (Downsview, Ont.: Environment Canada, Atmospheric Environment Service, 1987).

## Figures

4.1. Tony Hodge, Institute for Research on Public Policy, and Aartvark Creative Design and Photography.

4.2. Robert Makomson and J. A. Kraulis, "Niagara in Crisis," *Canadian Geographic*, October-November 1987, p. 14; Gradient Corporation and GeoTrans, Inc., *Potential Contaminant Loadings to the Niagara River from U.S. Hazardous Waste Sites*, prepared for the Niagara River Toxics Committee (Washington, D.C.: U.S. Geological Survey and U.S. Environmental Protection Agency, 1988), p. 12.

4.3. Department of Environmental Conservation, "Comparisons of 1981-82 and 1985-86 Toxic Substance Discharges to the Niagara River" (Albany: New York State Department of Environmental Conservation, 1987); Ontario Ministry of the Environment, "Chemical Loadings from Ontario Point Sources Discharging to the Niagara River, 1981-1987" (Toronto: Ontario Ministry of the Environment, 1987); and Gradient and Geotrans, Inc., *Potential Contaminant Loadings to the Niagara River*.

4.4. Environment Canada and U.S. Environmental Protection Agency, *The Great Lakes: An Environmental Atlas and Resource Book* (Chicago: U.S. Environmental

Protection Agency, Great Lakes National Program Office, and Toronto: Environment Canada, Ontario Region, 1987), p. 4; G. K. Rodgers, "Temperature and Currents in the Great Lakes," in D. V. Anderson, ed., *The Great Lakes as an Environment*, Great Lakes Institute Report PR 39 (Toronto: University of Toronto, 1969), pp. 36-50, reprinted in A. Donald Misener and Glenda Daniels, eds., *Decisions for the Great Lakes*, a project of Great Lakes Tomorrow (Hiram, Ohio: Great Lakes Tomorrow and the Purdue Foundation, 1982), p. 53.

4.5. Data provided by David Dolan, Windsor Regional Office, International Joint Commission, August 1989.

4.6. Ibid.

4.7. Ibid.

4.8. International Joint Commission, Great Lakes Water Quality Board, *1987 Report on Great Lakes Water Quality* (Windsor, Ont.: International Joint Commission, 1987), p. 92.

4.9. S. J. Eisenreich, B. B. Looney, and G. J. Hollod, "PCBs in the Lake Superior Atmosphere, 1978-1980," in D. MacKay et al., eds., *Physical Behavior of PCBs in The Great Lakes* (Ann Arbor, Mich.: Ann Arbor Science Publishers, 1983), pp. 115-25.

4.10. Adapted from R. L. Thomas et al., "Sources, Fate, and Controls of Toxic Contaminants," in Norbert W. Schmidtke, ed., *Toxic Contamination in Large Lakes, Volume III* (Chelsea, Mich.: Lewis Publishers, Inc., 1988).

4.11. Information provided by Roger Gauthier, U.S. Army Corps of Engineers, Detroit District, June 1989.

4.12. Data provided by Dr. Frank H. Quinn, National Oceanic and Atmospheric Administration, and by U.S. Army Corps of Engineers, Detroit District.

4.13. C. Southam and S. Dumont, "$CO_2$-Induced Climate Change and its Potential Impact on Great Lakes Levels and Outflows," Summary of Atmospheric Environment Service work, presented at the 31st Conference on Great Lakes Research, McMaster University, Hamilton, Ontario, May 17-20, 1988; T. E. Croley and H. Hartman, "Great Lakes Levels Response to Climate Change," Summary of Great Lakes Environmental Research Laboratory work, presented at the 31st Conference on Great Lakes Research; and L. T. Wong et al., "Future Great Lakes Levels: Environmental and Political Impacts" (Windsor, Ont.: University of Windsor, Great Lakes Institute, 1988), pp. 185-204.

# 5. LEGACIES AND CHALLENGES: AIR AND CLIMATE

1. International Joint Commission, *Third Biennial Report* (Windsor, Ont.: International Joint Commission, 1986), pp. 11, 19.

2. See International Air Quality Board, *Progress Report #5 to the International Joint Commission* (Downsview, Ont.: International Air Quality Board, 1988). See also Peter W. Summers and James W. S. Young, " 'The Airshed,' or 'Atmospheric Region of Influence' for the Great Lakes Basin," paper presented at the International Joint Commission Symposium, "Towards Integrated Monitoring—A Great Lakes Perspective," Toledo, Ohio, November 18, 1987.

3. National Acid Precipitation Assessment Program, *Interim Assessment: The Causes

*and Effects of Acidic Deposition*, vol. 2, *Emissions and Controls* (Washington, D.C.: U.S. Government Printing Office, 1987), pp. I-35, I-52.

4. Environment Canada, *Emissions and Trends of Common Air Contaminants in Canada: 1970 to 1980* (Ottawa: Minister of Supply and Services Canada, 1986), pp. 26, 91.

5. National Acid Precipitation Assessment Program, *Interim Assessment*, pp. I-33, I-61.

6. Ibid., p. I-35; Environment Canada, *Emissions and Trends of Common Air Contaminants in Canada*, pp. 26, 91.

7. National Acid Precipitation Assessment Program, *Interim Assessment*, p. I-52.

8. Environment Canada, *Emissions and Trends of Common Air Contaminants in Canada*, pp. 26, 91; ICF, Inc., "Final Report—Canada's Air Quality Program," prepared for U.S. Environmental Protection Agency, Office of Program Development, Office of Air and Radiation, September 1987, table A-2c.

9. Conservation Foundation calculations from U.S. Environmental Protection Agency, *Maps Depicting Nonattainment Areas Pursuant to Section 107 of the Clean Air Act—1985* (Research Triangle Park, N.C.: U.S. Environmental Protection Agency, Office of Air Quality Planning and Standards, 1985); from U.S. Environmental Protection Agency rule-making notices in the Federal Register, 1978, and from computer data provided by the U.S. Environmental Protection Agency, Office of Air Quality Planning and Standards, Research Triangle Park, N.C., 1989.

10. Environment Ontario, *Air Quality in Ontario—1986 Report* (Toronto: Queen's Printer for Ontario, 1988), pp. 2-7, 12.

11. Ibid.

12. Thomas Dann, *Canadian Urban Monitoring Programs for $O_3$, $NO_x$, and VOC* (Downsview, Ont.: Environment Canada, Conservation and Protection, Pollution Measurement Division, 1989), figure 5.

13. D. Yap et al., *An Assessment of Source Contributions to the Ozone Concentrations in Southern Ontario* (Rexdale, Ont.: Ontario Ministry of the Environment, Air Resources Branch, 1987).

14. Environment Canada, *The Clean Air Act Report 1985-1986* (Ottawa: Environment Canada, 1987), p. 24.

15. See figures 5 and 6 in International Air Quality Board, *Progress Report #6 to the International Joint Commission* (Windsor, Ont.: International Air Quality Board, 1988).

16. Ibid.

17. Ibid.

18. Letter dated March 25, 1987, from Great Lakes National Program Office Director Peter Wise to E. T. Wagner, Inland Waters Directorate, Environment Canada, describing Great Lakes National Program Office's response to the Great Lakes International Surveillance Plan (GLISP).

19. E. C. Voldner et al., "Production, Usage and Atmospheric Emissions of 14 Priority Toxic Chemicals," appendix 2 from International Joint Commission, International Air Quality Advisory Board Workshop on the Estimation of Atmospheric Loadings of Toxic Chemicals to the Great Lakes Basin, October 29-31, 1986 (December 1, 1987, typescript, p. 92).

20. The initial responses of the United States and Canada to the annex are described

in Environment Canada, *First Report of Canada under the 1987 Protocol to the 1978 Great Lakes Water Quality Agreement* (Toronto: Environment Canada, 1988), pp. 61-64; and U.S. Environmental Protection Agency, Great Lakes National Program Office, *U.S. Progress in Implementing the Great Lakes Water Quality Agreement* (Chicago, Ill.: U.S. Environmental Protection Agency, 1988).

21. E. R. Haemisegger et al., "EPA's Experience with Assessments of Site-Specific Environmental Problems: A Review of IEMD's Geographic Study of Philadelphia," *Journal of the Air Pollution Control Association* 35 (1985):809-15; and U.S. Environmental Protection Agency memorandum cited in The Conservation Foundation, "Examples of Cross-Media Pollution Problems and Control Approaches in North America," report prepared for the Organisation for Economic Cooperation and Development, Environment Directorate, Paris (Washington, D.C.: The Conservation Foundation, 1987).

22. John Summerhays, "Estimation and Evaluation of Cancer Risks Attributed to Air Pollution in Southeast Chicago" (Chicago, Ill.: U.S. Environmental Protection Agency, 1989).

23. U.S. Environmental Protection Agency, Science Advisory Board, *Evaluation of Scientific Issues Related to Municipal Waste Combustion* (Washington, D.C.: U.S. Environmental Protection Agency, 1988), pp. 31-35.

24. Ibid., p. 7; See also Environment Canada, *The National Incinerator Testing and Evaluation Program: Air Pollution Control Technology* (Ottawa: Environment Canada, 1986), and *The National Incinerator Testing and Evaluation Program: Two-Stage Combustion (Prince Edward Island)* (Ottawa: Environment Canada, 1985).

25. Michigan Department of Natural Resources, *Air Quality Report—1986* (Lansing, Mich.: Michigan Department of Natural Resources, 1987), p. 33; Julian Chazin, *Measurement, Assessment, and Control of Hazardous (Toxic) Air Contaminants in Landfill Gas Emissions in Wisconsin* (Madison, Wis.: Wisconsin Department of Natural Resources, 1987), p. 1.

26. William J. Strachan and Steven J. Eisenreich, "Mass Balancing of Toxic Chemicals in the Great Lakes: The Role of Atmospheric Deposition," appendix I from International Joint Commission, International Air Quality Advisory Board, Workshop on the Estimation of Atmospheric Loadings of Toxic Chemicals to the Great Lakes Basin, October 29-31, 1986 (Windsor, Ont.: International Joint Commission, 1988), p. 9.

27. The descriptions of toxaphene and DDT in this paragraph are based primarily on John R. Sullivan and David E. Armstrong, *Toxaphene: Status in the Great Lakes* (Madison, Wis.: University of Wisconsin, Sea Grant Institute, 1985); and R. A. Rapaport et al., " 'New' DDT Inputs to North America: Atmospheric Deposition," *Chemosphere* 14 (1985):1167-73.

28. See, generally, Canadian Federal-Provincial Research and Monitoring Coordinating Committee, *Assessment of the State of Knowledge on the Long-Range Transport of Pollutants and Acid Deposition* (Downsview, Ont.: Environment Canada, Atmospheric Environment Service, 1987); and National Acid Precipitation Assessment Program, *Interim Assessment*.

29. See, for example, D. S. Jeffries et al., "Regional Chemical Characteristics of Lakes in North America, Part 1: Eastern Canada," *Water, Air and Soil Pollution* 31 (1986):551-67; and Environment Canada, Inland Waters and Lands Directorate, *Acid*

*Rain: A National Sensitivity Assessment*, Environmental Fact Sheet 88-1 (Ottawa: Environment Canada, 1988).

30. National Acid Precipitation Assessment Program, *Interim Report*, vol. 4, pp. 8-21.

31. Ibid.

32. International Joint Commission, Great Lakes Water Quality Board, *1987 Report on Great Lakes Quality* (Windsor, Ont.: International Joint Commission, 1987), pp. 84, 86.

33. John H. Hartig and John E. Gannon, "Opposing Phosphorus and Nitrogen Trends in the Great Lakes," *Alternatives* 13, no. 2 (1986):19-23.

34. U.S National Acid Precipitation Assessment Program and Canadian Federal/Provincial Research and Monitoring Coordinating Committee, *Joint Report to Bilateral Advisory and Consultative Group* (Washington, D.C., and Downsview, Ont., 1987), p. 3.

35. See, generally, Canadian Federal/Provincial Research and Monitoring Coordinating Committee, *Assessment of the State of Knowledge of Acid Deposition—Part 5—Human Health Effects* (1986).

36. National Acid Precipitation Assessment Program, *Interim Report*, vol. 2, pp. 1-26.

37. Ibid., pp. 1-27.

38. Sheila Machado and Rick Piltz, *Reducing the Rate of Global Warming: The States' Role* (Washington, D.C.: Renew America, 1988), p. 6.

39. "Conference Statement," *Conference on the Changing Atmosphere–Proceedings* (Geneva, Switzerland: World Meteorological Organization, 1988), p. 293.

40. C. Southam and S. Dumont, "$CO_2$-Induced Climate Change and Its Potential Impact on Great Lakes Levels and Outflows," paper presented at the 31st Conference on Great Lakes Research, McMaster University, Hamilton, Ontario, May 17-20, 1988; T. E. Croley and Holly Hartman, "Great Lakes Levels Response to Climate Change," paper presented at the 31st Conference on Great Lakes Research, McMaster University, Hamilton, Ontario, May 17-20, 1988; L. T. Wong, J. A. McCorquodale, and M. E. Sanderson, "Future Great Lakes Levels: Environmental and Political Impacts," report to the Donner Canadian Foundation from the Great Lakes Institute (Windsor, Ont.: University of Windsor, 1988), pp. 185-204.

41. Barry Smit, *Implications of Climatic Change for Agriculture in Ontario*, Climate Change Digest CCD 87-02 (Downsview, Ont.: Environment Canada, 1987). See also, U.S. National Climate Office, National Oceanic and Atmospheric Administration, and Canadian Climate Centre, *Report of the First U.S.-Canada Symposium on Impacts of Climate Change on the Great Lakes Basin*, Oak Brook, Illinois, September 1988.

42. R. S. Bartz, "Great Lakes Water Quantity Management and the State of Ohio," paper presented at the 31st Conference on Great Lakes Research, McMaster University, Hamilton, Ontario, May 17-20, 1988.

## Southeast Chicago's Toxic Soup

1. John Summerhays and Harriet Croke, *Air Toxics Emission Inventory for the Southeast Chicago Area* (Chicago, Ill.: U.S. Environmental Protection Agency, Region V, Air and Radiation Branch, 1987), p. 1.

2. John Summerhays, *Updates to an Air Toxics Emission Inventory for the Southeast Chicago Area* (Chicago, Ill.: U.S. Environmental Protection Agency, Region V, Air and Radiation Branch, 1989), p. 1.

3. Ibid., p. 38.

4. Ibid., table 16.

5. Ibid.

6. Ibid., table 12.

7. Ibid., table 16; Summerhays and Croke, *Air Toxics Emission Inventory for the Southeast Chicago Area*, table 6.

8. Summerhays, *Updates to an Air Toxic Emission Inventory for the Southeast Chicago Area*, table 16.

## Enhanced Information on Chemical Discharges to Air, Land, and Water Required by U.S. Superfund Legislation

1. U.S. Environmental Protection Agency, "EPA Releases Toxic Inventory Data," Press Release R-72, April 12, 1989, and attached briefing materials.

### Figures

5.1. International Air Quality Advisory Board, *Progress Report #5 to the International Joint Commission* (Downsview, Ont.: International Air Quality Board, 1988), p. 16.

5.2. National Acid Precipitation Assessment Program, *Interim Assessment: The Causes and Effects of Acid Deposition*, vol. 2, *Emissions and Controls* (Washington, D.C.: U.S. Government Printing Office, 1987), p. 1-33.

5.3. Ibid., p. 1-61.

5.4. Conservation Foundation calculations from U.S. Environmental Protection Agency rule-making notices in the *Federal Register*, 1978; U.S. Environmental Protection Agency, Office of Air Quality Planning and Standards, *Maps Depicting Nonattainment Areas pursuant to Section 107 of the Clean Air Act—1985* (Research Triangle Park, N.C.: U.S. Environmental Protection Agency, 1985); and from computer data provided by the Office of Air Quality Planning and Standards, Research Triangle Park, N.C., 1989.

5.5. Michigan Department of Natural Resources and Ohio Environmental Protection Agency, data reproduced in Public Interest Research Groups, *Exhausting Our Future: An Eighty-Two City Study of Smog in the '80s* (Washington, D.C.: Public Interest Research Groups, 1989).

5.6. T. Dann, *Canadian Urban Monitoring Programs for $O_3$, $NO_x$, and VOC* (Toronto: Environment Canada, Pollution Measurement Division, 1989).

5.7. John Summerhays, *Updates to an Air Toxics Emission Inventory for the Southeast Chicago Area* (Chicago, Ill: U.S. Environmental Protection Agency, Region V, Air and Radiation Branch, 1989).

5.8. William M. J. Strachan and Steven J. Eisenreich, "Mass Balancing of Toxic Chemicals in the Great Lakes: The Role of Atmospheric Deposition," appendix I from International Joint Commission, International Air Quality Advisory Board, Workshop on the Estimation of Atmospheric Loadings of Toxic Chemicals to the Great Lakes Basin, October 29-31, 1986 (Windsor, Ont.: International Joint Commission, 1988), p. 9.

5.9. Effects compiled by the Institute for Research on Public Policy from the following sources: S. J. Cohen, "Impacts of $CO_2$-Induced Climatic Change on Water Resources in the Great Lakes Basin," *Climate Change* 8 (1986):135-53; C. Southam and S. Dumont, "$CO_2$-Induced Climate Change and its Potential Impact on Great Lakes Levels and Outflows," Summary of Atmospheric Environment Service work, presented at the 31st Conference on Great Lakes Research, McMaster University, Hamilton, Ontario, May 17-20, 1988; T. E. Croley and H. Hartman, "Great Lakes Levels Response to Climate Change," Summary of Great Lakes Environmental Research Laboratory work, presented at the 31st Conference on Great Lakes Research; and S. J. Cohen, "How Climate Change in the Great Lakes Region May Affect Energy, Hydrology, Shipping, and Recreation," in *Preparing for Climate Change*, Proceedings of the First North American Conference on Preparing for Climate Change: A Cooperative Approach, October 27-29, 1987, Washington, D.C.

## 6. FISH, WILDLIFE, AND HABITAT

1. L. Sicko-Goad and E. Stoermer, "Effects of Toxicants on Phytoplankton with Special Reference to the Laurentian Great Lakes," in Marlene S. Evans, ed., *Toxic Contaminants and Ecosystem Health: A Great Lakes Focus* (New York: John Wiley and Sons, 1988), p. 20.

2. M. Evans and D. MacNaught, "The Effects of Toxic Substances on Zooplankton Populations: A Great Lakes Perspective," in Evans, *Toxic Contaminants and Ecosystem Health*, pp. 53-76.

3. B. Eadie, T. Nalepa, and P. Landrum, "Toxic Contaminants and Benthic Organisms in the Great Lakes: Cycling, Fate, and Effects," *Toxic Contaminants in Large Lakes* 1 (1988):161-78.

4. International Joint Commission, *Fourth Biennial Report* (Windsor, Ont.: International Joint Commission, 1989), pp. 11-12.

5. R. Frank, M. Holdrinet, and P. Suda, "Organochlorine and Mercury Residues in Wild Mammals in Southern Ontario, Canada, 1973-1974," *Bulletin of Environmental Contamination and Toxicology* 22 (1979):500-507; M. Gilbertson and G. Fox, "Pollutant-Associated Embryonic Mortality of Great Lakes Herring Gulls," *Environmental Pollution* 12 (1977):211-16; A. Gilman et al., "Herring Gulls (*Larus argentatus*) as Monitors of Contamination in the Great Lakes," in *Animals as Monitors of Environmental Pollution* (Washington, D.C.: National Academy Press, 1977), pp. 280-89; D. Hallett et al., "Incidence of Chlorinated Benzenes and Chlorinated Ethylenes in Lake Ontario Herring Gulls," *Chemosphere* 11, no. 3 (1982):277-85; S. Haseltine et al., "Organochlorine and Metal Residues in Eggs of Waterfowl Nesting on Islands in Lake Michigan off Door County, Wisconsin, 1977-78," *Pesticide Monitoring Journal* 15, no. 2 (1981):90-97; J. Ludwig and C. Tomoff, "Reproductive Success and Insecticide Residues in Lake Michigan Herring Gulls," *The Jack-Pine Warbler* 44, no. 2 (1966):77-84; T. Kubiak et al., "Microcontaminants and Reproductive Impairment of the Forster's Tern on Green Bay, Lake Michigan 1983," *Archives of Environmental Contamination and Toxicology* 18 (1989):706-17; Inter-

national Joint Commission, Great Lakes Water Quality Board, *Emerging Issues: On-going and Emerging* (Windsor, Ont.: International Joint Commission, 1989), appendix B; D. Stalling et al., "Patterns of PCDD, PCDF, and PCB Contamination in Great Lakes Fish and Birds and Their Characterization by Principal Components Analysis," *Chemosphere* 14, no. 6/7 (1985):627-43; M. Gilbertson, R. Morris, and R. Hunter, "Abnormal Chicks and PCB Residue Levels in Eggs of Colonial Birds on the Lower Great Lakes (1971-73)," *The Auk* 93 (1976):434-42; J. Black, "Epidermal Hyperplasia and Neoplasia in Brown Bullheads (*Ictalurus nebulosus*) in Response to Repeated Applications of a PAH Containing Extract of Polluted River Sediment," in M. Cooke and A. Dennis, eds., *Polynuclear Aromatic Hydrocarbons: Seventh International Symposium on Formation, Metabolism and Measurement* (Batelle Press, 1982), pp. 99-111; J. Black, P. Dymerski, and W. Zapisek, "Environmental Carcinogenesis Studies in the Western New York Great Lakes Aquatic Environment," in D. Branson and K. Dickson, eds., *Aquatic Toxicology and Hazard Assessment: Fourth Conference*, ASTM STP 377 (Philadelphia: American Society for Testing and Materials, 1981), pp. 215-225; R. Masse et al., "Concentrations and Chromatographic Profile of DDT Metabolites and Polychlorobiphenyl (PCB) Residues in Stranded Beluga Whales (*Delphinapterus leucas*) from the St. Lawrence Estuary, Canada," *Archives of Environmental Contamination and Toxicology* 15 (1986):567-79; D. Martineau et al., "Levels of Organochlorine Chemicals in Tissues of Beluga Whales (*Delphinapterus leucas*) from the St. Lawrence Estuary, Quebec, Canada," *Archives of Environmental Contamination and Toxicology* 16 (1987):137-47; H. Kurita, J. Ludwig, and M. Ludwig, *Results of the 1987 Michigan Colonial Waterbird Monitoring Project on Caspian Terns and Double-crested Cormorants: Egg Incubation and Field Studies of Colony Productivity, Embryologic Mortality and Deformities* (Bay City, Mich.: Ecological Research Services, 1987).

6. International Joint Commission, *Emerging Issues*; R. Foley et al., "Wild Mink and Otter Organochlorine and Mercury Residues: Comparison with Fish Environmental Toxicology and Chemistry," *Environmental Toxicology and Chemistry* 7 (1988):363-74; and T. Colborn, "Cause-Effect Linkages: Bald Eagles in the Great Lakes Basin," paper presented at symposium on cause-effect linkages, sponsored by Council of Great Lakes Research Managers, International Joint Commission, Great Lakes Science Advisory Board, Chicago, March 1989.

7. R. Faber and J. Hickey., "Eggshell Thinning, Chlorinated Hydrocarbons, and Mercury in Inland Aquatic Bird Eggs, 1969 and 1970," *Pesticides Monitoring Journal* 7, no. 1 (1973):27-36; G. Heinz et al., "Contaminant Levels in Colonial Waterbirds from Green Bay and Lake Michigan, 1975-80," *Environmental Monitoring and Assessment* 5 (1985):233-236; S. Wiemeyer et al., "Residues of Organochlorine Pesticides, Polychlorinated Biphenyls, and Mercury in Bald Eagle Eggs and Changes in Shell Thickness—1969 and 1970," *Pesticides Monitoring Journal* 6 (1972):50-55; S. Wiemeyer et al., "Organochlorine Pesticide, Polychlorobiphenyl, and Mercury Residues in Bald Eagle Eggs—1969-79—and Their Relationships to Shell Thinning and Reproduction," *Archives of Environmental Contamination Toxicolology* 13 (1984):529-49; A. Gilman et al., "Reproductive Parameters and Egg Contaminant Levels of Great Lakes Herring Gulls," *Journal of Wildlife Management* 41, no. 3 (1977):450-68; International Joint Commission, *Emerging Issues*, appendix B; S. Postupalsky, "Toxic Chemicals and Cormorant Populations in the Great Lakes,"

paper presented at the Fish-Eating Birds Conference, December 2-3, 1976; and D. Weseloh, S. Teeple, and M. Gilbertson, "Double-Crested Cormorants of the Great Lakes: Egg-Laying Parameters, Reproductive Failure, and Contaminant Residues in Eggs, Lake Huron, 1972-1973," *Canadian Journal of Zoology* 61 (1983):427-36.

8. T. Kubiak et al., "Microcontaminants and Reproductive Impairment of the Forster's Tern on Green Bay, Lake Michigan 1983."

9. Ibid.

10. For an additional perspective on the difficulty of establishing cause-effect relationships, see Martin Holdgate, *A Perspective of Environmental Pollution* (New York: Cambridge University Press, 1979).

11. International Joint Commission, *Emerging Issues*, appendix B; and S. Postupalsky, *Toxic Chemicals and Declining Bald Eagles and Cormorants in Ontario*, Report no. 20 (Hull, Ont.: Canadian Wildlife Service, 1971).

12. M. Gilbertson, personal communication, 1988.

13. Kurita, Ludwig, and Ludwig, "Results of the 1987 Michigan Colonial Waterbird Monitoring Project on Caspian Terns and Double-Crested Cormorants."

14. P. Conners et al., "Investigations of Heavy Metals in Common Tern Populations," *Canadian Field-Naturalist* 89 (1975):157-62; D. V. Weseloh, T. W. Custer, and B. M. Braune, "Organochlorine Contaminants in Eggs of Common Terns from the Canadian Great Lakes," *Environmental Pollution* 59 (1989):141-60; M. Gilbertson, "Seasonal Changes in Organochlorine Compounds and Mercury in Common Terns of Hamilton Harbour, Ontario," *Bulletin of Environmental Contamination and Toxicology* 12, no. 6 (1974):726-32.

15. J. Ludwig, "Decline, Resurgence and Population Dynamics of Michigan and Great Lakes Double-Crested Cormorants," *Jack-Pine Warbler* 62, no. 4 (1984):91-102; S. Postupalsky, "Toxic Chemicals and Cormorant Populations in the Great Lakes"; D. Weseloh, Teeple, and Gilbertson, "Double-Crested Cormorants of the Great Lakes."

16. Kubiak et al., "Microcontaminants and Reproductive Impairment of the Forster's Tern on Green Bay, Lake Michigan, 1983"; T. Kubiak and H. Harris, "Microcontaminants and Reproductive Impairment of the Forster's Tern on Green Bay, Lake Michigan," final report to U.S. Fish and Wildlife Service, September 1985.

17. M. Gilbertson, "Pollutants in Breeding Herring Gulls," *The Canadian Field-Naturalist* 88, no. 3 (1974):273-80; J. Keith, "Reproduction in a Population of Herring Gulls (*Larus argentatus*) Contaminated by DDT," *Journal of Applied Ecology* 3 (1966):57-70; Ludwig and Tomoff, "Reproductive Success and Insecticide Residues in Lake Michigan Herring Gulls"; P. Mineau and D. Weseloh, "Low-Disturbance Monitoring of Herring Gull Reproductive Success on the Great Lakes," *Colonial Waterbirds* 4 (1981):138-42; and P. Mineau et al., "Using the Herring Gull to Monitor Levels and Effects of Organochlorine Contamination in the Canadian Great Lakes," in J. Nriagu and M. Simmons, eds., *Toxic Contaminants in the Great Lakes* (New York: John Wiley and Sons, 1984), pp. 426-52.

18. D. Berger and J. Mueller, "Ospreys in Northern Wisconsin," in J. Hickey, ed., *Peregrine Falcon Populations: Their Biology and Decline* (Madison: University of Wisconsin Press, 1969), pp. 340-41; S. Postupalsky, "1980 Bald Eagle and Osprey Nesting Surveys in Michigan," report to Michigan Department of Natural Resources, 1980; S. Postupalsky, *1983 Bald Eagle and Osprey Nesting Surveys in Michigan*,

Report no. 2964 (Ann Arbor: Michigan Department of Natural Resources, Wildlife Division, 1983); S. Postupalsky, "1985 Bald Eagle and Osprey Nesting Surveys in Michigan," report to Michigan Department of Natural Resources, 1985; and S. Postupalsky, "The Status of the Osprey in Michigan in 1965," in J. Hickey, ed., *Peregrine Falcon Populations: Their Biology and Decline* (Madison: University of Wisconsin Press, 1969), pp. 338-40.

19. L. Sileo et al., "Organochlorine Poisoning of Ring-Billed Gulls in Southern Ontario," *Journal of Wildlife Diseases* 13(July 1977):313-22.

20. P. Beland, A. Vezina, and D. Martineau, "Potential for Growth of the St. Lawrence (Quebec, Canada) Beluga Whale (*Delphinapterus leucas*) Population Based on Modelling," *Journal du Conseil international pour Exploration de la mer* 45 (1988):22-32; L. Pippard, "Status of the St. Lawrence River Population of Beluga, *Delphinapterus leucas*," *Canadian Field-Naturalist* 99, no. 3 (1985):438-50; R. Reeves, and E. Mitchell, "Catch History and Initial Population of White Whales (*Delphinapterus leucas*) in the River and Gulf of St. Lawrence, Eastern Canada," *Naturaliste Canada* 111 (1984):63-121; and D. Sergeant, "Present Status of White Whales *Delphinapterus leucas* in the St. Lawrence Estuary," *Naturaliste Canada* 113 (1986):61-81.

21. C. Pils, *The 1986-87 Otter Tagging Report* (Madison: Wisconsin Department of Natural Resources, Bureau of Wildlife Management, 1987).

22. M. Mac, C. Edsall, and J. Seelye, "Survival of Lake Trout Eggs and Fry Reared in Water from the Upper Great Lakes," *Journal of Great Lakes Research* 11, no. 4 (1985):520-29; and M. Mac, T. Schwartz, and C. Edsall, "Correlating PCB Effects on Fish Reproduction Using Dioxin Equivalents," 1988 paper presented at the Ninth Annual SETAC Meeting, U.S. Fish and Wildlife Service, Arlington, Virginia.

23. C. Bishop, "The Case Concerning a Cause-Effect Linkage between Organochlorine Contamination and Reproductive Effects in Snapping Turtle Eggs from Great Lakes Shoreline Wetlands," paper presented at symposium on cause-effect linkages, sponsored by Council of Great Lakes Research Managers, International Joint Commission, Great Lakes Science Advisory Board, Chicago, March 1989.

24. International Joint Commission, *Emerging Issues*, appendix B; Kubiak et al., "Microcontaminants and Reproductive Impairment of the Forster's Tern on Green Bay, Lake Michigan, 1983"; Kurita, Ludwig, and Ludwig, "Results of the 1987 Michigan Colonial Waterbird Monitoring Project on Caspian Terns and Double-Crested Cormorants"; M. Gilbertson, "Etiology of Chick Edema Disease in Herring Gulls in the Lower Great Lakes," *Chemosphere* 12, no. 3 (1983):357-70; M. Gilbertson, R. Morris, and R. Hunter, "Abnormal Chicks and PCB Residue Levels in Eggs of Colonial Birds on the Lower Great Lakes (1971-73)," *The Auk* 93 (1976):434-42; M. Mac and W. Willford, "Bioaccumulation of PCBs and Mercury from Toronto and Toledo Harbor Sediments," in International Joint Commission, *Evaluation of Sediment Bio-assessment Techniques, Report of the Dredging Subcommittee to the Great Lakes Water Quality Board* (Windsor, Ont.: International Joint Commission, 1986), pp. 81-90; C. Bishop, "The Case Concerning a Cause-Effect Linkage Between Organochlorine Contamination and Reproductive Effects in Snapping Turtle Eggs from Great Lakes Shoreline Wetlands"; T. Erdman, report to USFWS on common and Forster's tern productivity on Kidney Island CDF, Green Bay, 1987 with supplemental necropsy

pathology reports (Green Bay: University of Wisconsin, April 1, 1988); Sileo et al., "Organochlorine Poisioning of Ring-Billed Gulls in Southern Ontario."

25. Ibid; D. Weseloh, *Eggshell Thickness and Chemical Contaminants in Eggs of Double-Crested Cormorants in Ontario in 1979 and 1981: A Report of Results Obtained under Collection Permits 0729 (1979) and 0871 (1981)* (Hull: Canadian Wildlife Service, 1982).

26. Statement of Timothy Kubiak, Environmental Contaminant Specialist, before the Michigan Natural Resources Commission, April 6, 1988.

27. Gilbertson and Fox, "Pollutant-Associated Embryonic Mortality of Great Lakes Herring Gulls"; Gilbertson, Morris, and Hunter, "Abnormal Chicks and PCB Residue Levels in Eggs of Colonial Birds on the Lower Great Lakes (1971-73)"; Weseloh, *Eggshell Thickness and Chemical Contaminants in Eggs of Double-Crested Cormorants in Ontario in 1979 and 1981.*

28. G. Fox and D. Weseloh, "Colonial Waterbirds as Bio-Indicators of Environmental Contamination in the Great Lakes," in A. Diamond and F. Filion, eds., *The Use of Birds*, ICBP Technical Publication (Cambridge, England: International Council of Bird Preservation, 1988).

29. D. Fry and C. Toone, "DDT-Induced Feminization of Gull Embryos," *Science* 213 (1981):922-24.

30. D. Martineau et al., "Rupture of a Dissecting Aneurysm of the Pulmonary Trunk in a Beluga Whale *(Delphinapterus leucas)*," *Journal of Wildlife Disease* 22, no. 2 (1986):289-94; D. Martineau et al., "Pathology of Stranded Beluga Whales *(Delphinapterus leucas)* from the St. Lawrence Estuary, Quebec, Canada," *Journal of Comparative Pathology* 98 (1988):287-311; D. Martineau et al., "Transitional Cell Carcinoma of the Urinary Bladder in Beluga Whale *(Delphinapterus leucas),*" *Canadian Veterinary Journal* 26 (1985):297-302; D. Martineau et al., "Levels of Organochlorine Chemicals in Tissues of Beluga Whales *(Delphinapterus leucas)* from the St. Lawrence Estuary, Quebec, Canada."

31. P. Baumann, "Cancer in Wild Freshwater Fish Populations with Emphasis on the Great Lakes," *Journal of the Great Lakes Resources* 10, no. 3 (1984):251-53; V. Cairns and J. Fitzsimmons, "The Occurrence of Epidermal Papillomas and Liver Neoplasia in White Suckers *(Catostomus commersoni)* from Lake Ontario," abstract and presentation at 14th Annual Aquatic Toxicity Workshop, Toronto, November 1-4, 1987; J. Harshbarger and J. Black, "A Strategy for Using Fish Bioassays and Surveys to Identify and Eliminate Point Source Environmental Carcinogens," in B. Bandurski et al., eds., *Toward a Transboundary Monitoring Network: A Continuing Binational Exporation*, proceedings of International Joint Commission Convention, vol. 2 (1986):510-17.

32. John Black et al., "Carcinogenic Effects of River Sediment Extracts in Fish and Mice," chapter 33 in R. Jolley et al., eds., *Water Chlorination: Chemistry, Environmental Impact and Health Effects*, vol. 5, proceedings of the Fifth Conference on Water Chlorination, Williamsburg, Va., June 3-8, 1984 (Chelsea, Mich.: Lewis Publishers, 1985), pp. 415-27; and A. Maccubbin et al., "Evidence for Polynuclear Aromatic Hydrocarbons in the Diet of Bottom-Beeding Fish," *Bulletin of Environmental Contaminants and Toxicology* 34 (1985):876-82.

33. Colborn, "Cause-Effects Linkages: Bald Eagles in the Great Lakes Basin"; Bishop, "The Case Concerning a Cause-Effect Linkage between Organochlorine Con-

tamination and Reproductive Effects in Snapping Turtle Eggs from Great Lakes Shore-
line Wetlands''; M. Mac, ''Mortality of Lake Trout Swim-Up Fry from Southeastern
Lake Michigan: Documentation and Hepatic Structural Analysis,'' thesis, Department
of Zoology and Physiology, University of Wyoming, 1986; Mac, Edsall, and Seelye,
''Survival of Lake Trout Eggs and Fry Reared in Water from the Upper Great Lakes'';
A. Gilman et al., ''Effects of Injected Organochlorines on Naturally Incubated Herring
Gull Eggs,'' *Journal of Wildlife Management* 42, no. 3 (1978):484-93; Kubiak et al.,
''Microcontaminants and Reproductive Impairment of the Forster's Tern on Green
Way, Lake Michigan, 1983''; Kurita, Ludwig, and Ludwig, ''Results of the 1987
Michigan Colonial Waterbird Monitoring Project on Caspian Terns and Double-Crested
Cormorants.''

   34. R. Moccia, G. Fox, and A. Britton, ''A Quantitative Assessment of Thyroid
Histopathology of Herring Gulls (*Larus argentatus*) from the Great Lakes and a
Hypothesis on the Causal Role of Environmental Contaminants,'' *Journal of Wildlife
Diseases* 22, no. 1 (1986):60-70.

   35. Gilbertson and Fox, ''Pollutant-Associated Embryonic Mortality of Great Lakes
Herring Gulls''; D. Peakall and G. Fox, ''Toxicological Investigations of Pollutant-
Related Effects in Great Lakes Gulls,'' *Environmental Health Perspectives* 71 (1987):187-
93; and G. Fox et al., ''Porphyria in Herring Gulls: A Biochemical Response to
Chemical Contamination of Great Lakes Food Chains,'' *Environmental Toxicology
and Chemistry* 7 (1988):831-39.

   36. Kubiak et al., ''Microcontaminants and Reproductive Impairment of the Fors-
ter's Tern on Green Way, Lake Michigan, 1983''; Kurita, Ludwig, and Ludwig,
''Results of the 1987 Michigan Colonial Waterbird Monitoring Project on Caspian
Terns and Double-Crested Cormorants.''

   37. G. Shugart, ''Frequency and Distribution of Polygyny in Great Lakes Herring
Gulls in 1978,'' *Condor* 82 (1980):426-29; M. Fitch and G. Shugart, ''Comparative
Biology and Behavior of Monogamous Pairs and One Male-Two Female Trios of
Herring Gulls,'' *Behavior Ecology and Sociobiology* 14 (1983):1-7.

   38. G. Hunt and M. Hunt, ''Female-Female Pairing in Western Gulls (*Larus oc-
cidentalis*) in Southern California,'' *Science* 196 (1977):1466-67. See also J. Diamond,
''Goslings of Gay Geese,'' *Nature* 340 (July 13, 1989):101.

   39. S. Safe, ''Polychlorinated Biphenyls (PCBs) and Polybrominated Biphenyls
(PBB): Biochemistry, Toxicology and Mechanism of Action,'' *CRC Critical Reviews
in Toxicology* 13, no. 4 (1984):319-95; S. Safe, ''Comparative Toxicology and Mechanism of Action of Polychlorinated Dibenzo-p-dioxins and Dibenzofurans,'' *Annals
of Revised Pharmacology Toxicology* 26 (1986):371-99; G. Mason et al., ''The Dioxin
Receptor: Characterization of its DNA-Binding Properties,'' *Journal of Steroid Biochemistry* 30, nos. 1-6 (1988):307-10; G. Mason et al., ''Polybrominated Dibenzo-
p-dioxins and Related Compounds: Quantitative in vivo and in vitro Structure Activity
Relationships,'' *Toxicology* 44 (1987):245-55; G. Mason et al., ''Polychlorinated
Dibenzo-p-dioxins: Quantitative in vitro and in vivo Structure Activity Relationships,''
*Toxicology* 41 (1986):21-31.

   40. G. Kimmel, *Reproduction and Developmental Toxicity of 2,3,7,8-TCDD: A
Cancer Risk-Specific Dose Estimate for 2,3,7,8-TCDD* (Washington, D.C.: U.S.
Environmental Protection Agency, 1988), appendices A-F; T. Helder, ''Effects of
2,3,7,8-Tetrachlorodibenzo-p-dioxin (TCDD) on Early Life Stages of the Pike (*Esox*

*lucius* L.), *The Science of the Total Environment* 14 (1980:255-64; D. Mattison et al., "Oocyte Destruction by Polycyclic Aromatic Hydrocarbons," *American Journal of Industrial Medicine* 4 (1983):191-202; U.S. Public Health Service, Agency for Toxic Substances and Disease Registry (ATSDR), "Toxicological Profile for Benzo[a]pyrene," draft (Atlanta, Ga.: Oak Ridge National Laboratory, 1987); U.S. Public Health Service, ATSDR, "Toxicological Profile for Cadmium," draft (1987); J. Cranmer, M. Cranmer, and P. Goad, "Prenatal Chlordane Exposure: Effects on Plasma Corticosterone Concentrations Over the Lifespan of Mice," *Environmental Research* 35, no. 1 (1984):204-10; U.S. Public Health Service, ATSDR, "Toxicological Profile for Chlordane," draft (1988); C. Lundberg, "Effects of Long-Term Exposure to DDT on the Oestrus Cycle and the Frequency of Implanted Ova in the Mouse," *Environ. Physiol. Biochem.* 3 (1973):127-31; Fry and Toone, "DDT-Induced Feminization of Gull Embryos"; U.S. Public Health Service, ATSDR, "Toxicological Profile for Aldrin/Dieldrin," draft (1987); D. Arnold et al., "Long-Term Toxicity of Hexachlorobenzene in the Rat and the Effect of Dietary Vitamin A," *Food Chemistry and Toxicology* 23, no. 9 (1985):779-93; U.S. Public Health Service, ATSDR, "Toxicological Profile for Lead," draft (1988); W. Sloof and A. Matthijsen, *Integrated Criteria Document Hexachlorocyclohexanes*, Report no. 758473011 (Bilthoven, The Netherlands: National Institute of Public Health and Environmental Protection, 1988); World Health Organization, *Environmental Health Criteria 1: Mercury* (Geneva: World Health Organization, 1976); U.S. Public Health Service, ATSDR, "Toxicological Profile for Mercury," draft (1988); World Health Organization, *Environmental Health Criteria 44: Mirex* (Geneva: World Health Organization, 1984); U.S. Public Health Service, ATSDR, "Toxicological Profile for Selected PCBs (Aroclor-1260, -1254, -1248, -1242, -1232, -1221, and -1016)," draft (1987).

41. B. Sonawane, R. Smialowicz, and R. Luebke, "Immunotoxicity of 2,3,7,8-TCDD: Review, Issues, and Uncertainties," appendix E in U.S. Environmental Protection Agency, *A Cancer Risk-Specific Dose Estimate for 2,3,7,8-TCDD*, review draft, EPA/600/6-88/007Ab (Washington, D.C.: U.S. Environmental Protection Agency, Office of Health and Environmental Assessment, 1988), appendixes A-4; M. Myers, R. Blanton, and P. Bick, "Inhibition of IL-2 Responsiveness Following Exposure to Benzo[a]pyrene Is Due to Alterations in Accessory Cell Function," *International Journal of Immunopharmacology* 10, no. 2 (1988):177-86; J. Spyker-Cranmer et al., "Immunoteratology of Chlordane: Cell-Mediated and Humoral Responses in Adult Mice Exposed in Utero," *Toxicology of Applied Pharmacology* 62 (1982):402-8; M. Beggs, J. Menna, and J. Barnett, "Effect of Chlordane on Influenza Type A Virus and Herpes Simplex Type 1 Virus Replication in Vitro," *Journal of Toxicology and Environmental Health* 16, no. 2 (1985):173-88; J. Barnett et al., "The Effect of Prenatal Chlordane Exposure on Specific Anti-Influenza Cell-Mediated Immunity," *Toxicology Letters* 25, no. 3 (1985):229-38; B. Banerjee, "Effects of Sub-Chronic DDT Exposure on Humoral and Cell-Mediated Immune Responses in Albino Rats, *Bulletin of Environmental Contamination and Toxicology* 39 (1987):827-34; B. Banerjee, "Sub-Chronic Effect of DDT on Humoral Immune Response to a Thymus-Independent Antigen (Bacterial Lipopolysaccharide) in Mice," *Bulletin of Environmental Contamination and Toxicology* 39 (1987):822-26; B. Banerjee, M. Ramachandran, and Q. Hussain, "Sub-Chronic Effect of DDT on Humoral Immune Response in Mice," *Bulletin of Environmental Contamination and Toxicology* 37 (1986):433-

40; J. Bernier et al., "Suppression of Humoral Immunity in Inbred Mice by Dieldrin," *Toxicology Letters* 35, nos. 2-3 (1987):231-40; U.S. Public Health Service, "Toxicological Profile for Aldrin/Dieldrin"; J. Barnett et al., "The Effect of in Utero Exposure to Hexachlorobenzene on the Developing Immune Response of BALB/c Mice," *Toxicology Letters* 39, nos. 2-3 (1987):263-74; U.S. Public Health Service, "Toxicological Profile for Lead"; F. Van Velsen et al., "The Subchronic Oral Toxicity of the B-isomer of Hexachlorocyclohexane in Rats," *Fundamental and Applied Toxicology* 6 (1986):697-712; J. Contrino et al., "Effects of Mercury on Human Polymorphonuclear Leukocyte Function in Vitro," *American Journal of Pathology* 132, no. 1 (1988)):110-18; C. Reardon and D. Lucas, "Heavy-Metal Mitogenesis: Zn+ + and Hg+ + Induce Cellular Cytotoxicity and Interferon Production in Murine T Lymphocytes," *Immunobiology* 175, no. 5 (1987):455-69; World Health Organization, *Environmental Health Criteria 44: Mirex*; S. Safe, "Polychlorinated Biphenyls (PCBs) and Polybrominated Biphenyls (PBBs): Biochemistry, Toxicology and Mechanism of Action," *CRC Critical Reviews in Toxicology* 13, no. 4 (1984):319-95; E. Nikolaidis, B. Brunstrom, and L. Dencker, "Effects of the Congeners 3,3',4,4'-Tetrachlorobiphenyl and 3,3',4,4'-Tetrachloroazobenzene on Lymphoid Development in the Bursa of Fabricus of the Chick Embryo, *Toxicology and Applied Pharmacology* 92 (1988):315-23.

42. P. Mehrle et al., "Toxicity and Bioconcentration of 2,3,7,8-Tetrachlorodibenzodioxin and 2,3,7,8-Tetrachlorodibenzofuran in Rainbow Trout," *Environmental Toxicology and Chemistry* 7, no. 1 (1988):47-62; B. Fishman and G. Gianutsos, "Inhibition of 4-aminobutyric Acid (GABA) Turnover by Chlordane," *Toxicology Letters* 26 (1985):219-23; T. Narahashi, "Mode of Action of Chlorinated Hydrocarbon Pesticides on the Nervous System," in Khan and Stanton, eds., *Toxicology of Halogenated Hydrocarbons: Health and Ecological Effects* (Great Britain: Pergamon Press, 1981), pp. 222-42; World Health Organization, *Environmental Health Criteria 9: DDT and its Derivatives* (Geneva: World Health Organization, 1979); J. Carlson and R. Rosellini, "Exposure to Low Doses of the Environmental Chemical Dieldrin Causes Behavioral Deficits in Animals Prevented from Coping with Stress," *Psychopharmacology* 91, no. 1 (1987):122-26; W. Albrecht, "Central Nervous System Toxicity of Some Common Environmental Residues in the Mouse," *Journal of Toxicology and Environmental Health* 21 (1988):405-21; S. Kennedy and D. Wigfield, "The Delay in Polyhalogenated Aromatic Hydrocarbon-Induced Porphyria: The Effect of Diet Preparation," *Toxicology Letters* 32, no. 3 (1986):195-202; D. Rice, "Chronic Low-Level Lead Exposure in Monkeys Does Not Affect Simple Reaction Time," *NeuroToxicology* 9, no. 1 (1988):105-8; D. Rice, "Schedule-Controlled Behavior in Infant and Juvenile Monkeys Exposed to Lead from Birth," *NeuroToxicology* 9, no. 1 (1988):75-88; U.S. Public Health Service, "Toxicological Profile for Lead"; J. Cordoba et al., "Alterations in Acetylcholinesterase Activity in Plasma and Synaptosomal Fractions from C.N.S. of Rats Acutely Intoxicated with Lindane: Effect of Succinylcholine," *Bulletin of Environmental Contamination and Toxicology* 39, no. 4 (1987):647-55; B. Fishman and G. Gianutsos, "CNS Biochemical and Pharmacological Effects of the Isomers of Hexachlorocyclohexane (Lindane) in the Mouse," *Toxicology and Applied Pharmacology* 93, no. 1 (1988):146-53; L. Stark, R. Joy, and M. Hollinger, "Effects of Two Isomers of Hexachlorocyclohexane (HCH) on Cortical B-adrenoceptors in Rat Brain," *Experimental Neurology* 98, no. 2 (1987):276-

84; World Health Organization, *Environmental Health Criteria for Lead* (Geneva: World Health Organization, 1976); World Health Organization, *Environmental Health Criteria 44: Mirex*; and U.S. Public Health Service, "Toxicological Profile for Selected PCBs (Aroclor-1260, -1254, -1248, -1242, -1232, -1221, and -1016)."

43. Kimmel, *Reproduction and Developmental Toxicity of 2,3,7,8-TCDD*; U.S. Public Health Service, Agency for Toxic Substances and Disease Registry (ATSDR), "Toxicological Profile for 2,3,7,8-Tetrachlorodibenzo-p-dioxin," draft (Atlanta, Ga.: Oak Ridge National Laboratory, 1987); U.S. Public Health Service, "Toxicological Profile for Cadmium"; U.S. Public Health Service, "Toxicological Profile for Benzo[a]pyrene"; U.S. Public Health Service, Toxicological Profile for Chlordane"; Spyker-Cranmer et al., "Immunoteratology of Chlordane"; Barnett et al., "The Effect of in Utero Exposure to Hexachlorobenzene on the Developing Immune Response of BALB/c Mice"; and U.S. Public Health Service, "Toxicological Profile for Lead."

44. F. Bellrose and R. Heister, "The Wood Duck," in Roger DiSilvestro, ed., *Audubon Wildlife Report 1987* (New York: Academic Press, 1987).

45. Great Lakes/Northern Great Plains Piping Plover Recovery Team, *Recovery Plan for Piping Plovers of the Great Lakes and Northern Great Plains* (Washington, D.C.: U.S. Fish and Wildlife Service, 1988), p. 20.

46. Ibid., pp. 10, 14-15.

47. Ibid., p. 27.

48. Ibid., p. 34.

49. Ibid., p. 55.

50. Ibid.

51. S. DeStefano, "The Lynx," in DiSilvestro, *Audubon Wildlife Report 1987*.

52. International Joint Commission, *Protecting Great Lakes Nearshore and Coastal Diversity*, report from a consultation meeting (Windsor, Ont.: International Joint Commission, 1988), annex 1.

53. Ibid., p. 10.

54. The two paragraphs in the text on protection efforts are based upon International Joint Commission, Great Lakes Science Advisory Board, *1989 Report* (Windsor, Ont.: International Joint Commission, 1989), sections 4.3, 4.4; Rob Alvo, "Canada Joins the Heritage Network," *The Nature Conservancy Magazine*, July/August 1989, pp. 24-25.

55. "The Tragedy of the Commons," *Science*, December 13, 1968, pp. 1243-48. For a critique of the commons example used by Hardin, see Susan J. B. Cox, "No Tragedy on the Commons," *Environmental Ethics* 7, no. 1 (1985):49-61.

56. See University of Wisconsin, Sea Grant Institute, *The Fisheries of the Great Lakes*, 1984-86 Biennial Report (Madison, Wis.: Sea Grant Institute, 1986), p. 9; Wilbur L. Hartman, *Effects of Exploitation, Environmental Changes and New Species on the Fish Habitats and Resources of Lake Erie*, Technical Report no. 22 (Ann Arbor, Mich.: Great Lakes Fishery Commission, 1973). The latter places more emphasis on the lack of adequate spawning areas for the lamprey in Lake Erie tributaries.

57. W. Christie, *A Review of the Changes in the Fish Species Composition of Lake Ontario*, Technical Report no. 23 (Ann Arbor, Mich.: Great Lakes Fishery Commission, 1973).

58. H. Lickers, "Native Peoples Share in Great Lakes' Treasures, Tragedies," *The Great Lakes United* 4, no. 2 (1989):8.

59. Robert J. Morris, "State of the Great Lakes Region Environment—Fisheries," prepared for Environment Canada, Environmental Interpretation Division, Conservation and Protection (Ottawa, Ont.: Environment Canada, 1988), p. 210.

60. F. J. Berkes et al., *Ontario's Great Lakes Fisheries: Managing the User Groups* (St. Catherines, Ont.: Brock University, Institute of Urban and Environmental Studies, 1983).

61. Daniel R. Talhelm, *Economics of Great Lakes Fisheries: A 1985 Assessment*, Technical Report no. 54 (Ann Arbor, Mich.: Great Lakes Fishery Commission, 1988), p. 11.

62. Ibid., p. 25.

63. For the United States, see University of Wisconsin, *The Fisheries of the Great Lakes*, p. 13.

64. See, for example, Kevin Kasowski, "A North Woods Saga: Tension Mounts over Treaty Rights," *Outdoor America*, Fall 1986, pp. 6-9, 32-33; Great Lakes Indian Fish and Wildlife Commission, *Chippewa Treaty Rights: Hunting . . . Fishing . . . Gathering on Ceded Territory* (Odanah, Wis.: Great Lakes Indian Fish and Wildlife Commission, n.d.).

65. Ibid.

66. This and the following paragraphs are based mainly on University of Wisconsin, *The Fisheries of the United States*, pp. 2-10.

67. Ibid., p. 9.

68. Carlos Fetterolf, Jr., *A Sketch of the Great Lakes Fishery Commission: Interagency, Interstate, International Programs* (Ann Arbor, Mich.: Great Lakes Fishery Commission, 1986). See also Great Lakes Fishery Commission, "Great Lakes Fishery Commission Annual Meeting, 1987—Minutes" (Ann Arbor, Mich.: Great Lakes Fishery Commission, 1987).

69. Center for the Great Lakes et al., *Funding for Federal Great Lakes Environmental Programs: A White Paper* (Chicago: Center for the Great Lakes, 1989), p. 15.

70. The fishing up model was applied in H. A. Regier and K. H. Loftus, "Effects of Fisheries Exploitation on Salmonid Communities in Oligotrophic Lakes," *Journal of the Fisheries Resources Board of Canada* 29, no. 6 (1972):959-68. See also H. A. Regier et al., "Rehabilitative Redevelopment of the Fish and Fisheries of the Baltic Sea and the Great Lakes," *Ambio* 17, no. 2 (1988):121-30; T. H. Whillans and F. Berkes, "Use and Abuse, Conflict and Harmony: The Great Lakes Fishery in Transition," *Alternatives* 13, no. 3 (1986):10-18.

71. However, some have argued that the dwindling catch was the result of environmental degradation. The contending arguments are reported in Wilbur L. Hartman, "Historical Changes in the Major Fish Resources of the Great Lakes," in Evans, *Toxic Contaminants and Ecosystem Health*, pp. 103-31.

72. Ibid., p. 121.

73. Ibid.

74. *Sport Fishing Institute Bulletin*, no. 403, April 1989, excerpted in *Great Lakes Program* 3, no. 2 (1989):6, published by the Great Lakes Program, State University of New York-Buffalo.

75. International Joint Commission, *1989 Report*, section 5.4. This document is the basis for the discussion in the succeeding three paragraphs of the text.

76. Personal communication, Dr. Henry Regier, Department of Zoology, University of Toronto, and goal statements for individual lakes provided by Great Lakes Fishery Commission.

77. Ontario Ministry of Natural Resources, *A Proposed Strategic Plan for Ontario Fisheries—SPOF II—Explanatory Booklet* (Toronto: Queen's Printer for Ontario, 1989), p. 8. See also W. J. Christie et al., "A Perspective on Great Lakes Fish Community Rehabilitation," *Canadian Journal of Fisheries and Aquatic Sciences* 44, supp. II (1987):496.

78. Cameron Davis and Glenda Daniel, "Return of the Natives," *Lake Michigan Monitor*, April-June 1988, p. 1; published by the Lake Michigan Federation, Chicago, Illinois.

79. Personal communication, Randy Eshenroder, Great Lakes Fishery Commission, August 1989; Randy Eshenroder, "A Perspective on Artificial Fishery Systems for the Great Lakes," paper presented at Wild Trout IV, Yellowstone National Park, September 18-19, 1989.

80. Ibid.

81. The discussion in this paragraph is based on International Joint Commission, Great Lakes Science Advisory Board, *1987 Report* (Windsor, Ont.: International Joint Commission, 1987), p. 47. For more detailed discussion of the impact of changes at the top of the food web, in nearshore and offshore waters of Lake Michigan, and on the composition of the algal community, see Donald Scavia and Gary L. Fahnenstiel, "From Picoplankton to Fish: Complex Interactions in the Great Lakes," in Stephen R. Carpenter, ed., *Complex Interactions in Lake Communities* (New York: Springer-Verlag, 1988), pp. 85-97.

82. This paragraph is based on International Joint Commission, Great Lakes Regional Office, *Rehabilitation of Lake Ontario: The Role of Nutrient Reduction and Food Web Dynamics* (Windsor, Ont.: International Joint Commission, 1988).

## The Bald Eagle

1. Mark Stalmaster, *The Bald Eagle* (New York: Universe Books, 1987).

2. F. Weekes, "Bald Eagle Nesting Attempts in Southern Ontario in 1974," *Canadian Field-Naturalist* 89 (1975):438-444; F. Weekes, "A Survey of Bald Eagle Nesting Attempts in Southern Ontario, 1969-1973," *Canadian Field-Naturalist* 88, no. 4 (1974):415-19.

3. International Joint Commission, Great Lakes Water Quality Board, *Emerging Issues—Ongoing and Emerging* (Windsor, Ont.: International Joint Commission, 1989), appendix B.

4. These paragraphs are based on T. Colborn, "Cause-Effect Linkages: Bald Eagles in the Great Lakes Basin," paper presented at symposium on Cause-Effect Linkages, sponsored by Council of Great Lakes Research Managers, International Joint Commission, Great Lakes Science Advisory Board, March 1989.

5. International Joint Commission, Great Lakes Science Advisory Board, *1989 Report* (Windsor, Ont.: International Joint Commission, 1989), section 5.2.1.

## Toxic Substances and Health Effects in Wildlife: The Challenge of Linking Cause and Effect

1. This box is an abridged version of Michael Gilbertson, "Linkages between Toxics and Health Effects," paper presented at International Joint Commission Workshop, *Focus on International Joint Commission Activities*, July/August 1989, pp. 7, 8.

## Troubled Beluga Whale Population in the St. Lawrence Estuary

1. Canadian geneticist Dr. Joseph Cummings, quoted in Andre Carothers, "Cry of the Beluga," *Greenpeace* 12, no. 2 (1987):15.
2. P. Beland and D. Martineau, "The Beluga Whale (*Delphinapterus leucas*) as Integrator of the St. Lawrence Basin Contamination History," paper presented at International Conference on Bio-indicators: Exposure and Effects, Oak Ridge National Laboratory, Knoxville, Tenn., March 20-23, 1988.
3. D. Martineau et al., "Levels of Organochlorine Chemicals in Tissues of Beluga Whales (*Delphinapterus leucas*) from the St. Lawrence Estuary, Quebec, Canada," *Archives of Environmental Contamination and Toxicology* 16 (1987):137-47.
4. L. Pippard, "Status of the St. Lawrence River Population of Beluga, *Delphinapterus leucas*," *Canadian Field-Naturalist* 99, no. 3 (1985):438-50; R. Reeves and E. Mitchell, "Catch History and Initial Population of White Whales (*Delphinapterus leucas*) in the River and Gulf of St. Lawrence, Eastern Canada," *Naturaliste Canada* 111 (1984):63-121; and D. Sergeant, "Present Status of White Whales *Delphinapterus leucas* in the St. Lawrence Estuary," *Naturaliste Canada* 113 (1986):61-81.

## Chemical Action at the Cellular and Sub-Cellular Level

1. S. Safe, "Polychlorinated Biphenyls (PCBs) and Polybrominated Biphenyls (PBBs): Biochemistry, Toxicology and Mechanism of Action," *CRC Critical Reviews in Toxicology* 13, no. 4 (1984):319-95; and S. Safe, "Comparative Toxicology and Mechanism of Action of Polychlorinated Dibenzo-p-dioxins and Dibenzofurans," *Annals of Revised Pharmacology Toxicology* 26 (1986):371-99.
2. L. Zhong-Xiang et al., "Inhibition of Gap Junctional Intercellular Communication in Human Teratocarcinoma Cells by Organochlorine Pesticides," *Toxicology of Applied Pharmacology* 83 (1986):10-19; L. Warngard et al., "Calmodulin Involvement in TPA and DDT Induced Inhibition of Intercellular Communication, *Chemistry and Biology Interactions* 65 (1988):41-9; J. Trosko and C. Chang, "Non-Genotoxic Mechanisms in Carcinogenesis: Role of Inhibited Intercellular Communication," *Banbury Report*, in press; J. Klaunig and R. Ruch, "Strain and Species Effects on the Inhibition of Hepatocyte Intercellular Communication by Liver Tumor Promoters," *Cancer Letters* 36 (1987):161-68; J. Klaunig and R. Ruch, "Role of Cyclic AMP in the Inhibition of Mouse Hepatocyte Intercellular Communication by Liver Tumor Promoters," *Toxicology and Applied Pharmacology* 91 (1987):159-70; R. Ruch, J. Klaunig, and M. Pereira, "Inhibition of Intercellular Communication Between Mouse Hepatocytes by Tumor Promoters," *Toxicology and Applied Pharmacology* 87

(1987):111-20; M. Zeilmaker and H. Yamasaki, "Inhibition of Functional Intercellular Communication as a Possible Short-Term Test to Detect Tumor-Promoting Agents: Results With Nine Chemicals Tested by Dye Transfer Assay in Chinese Hamster V79 Cells," *Cancer Research* 46, no. 121 (1986):6, 180-86; J. Carlson and R. Abraham, "Nuclear Ploidy of Neonatal Rat Livers: Effects of Two Hepatic Carcinogens (Mirex and Dimethylnitrosamine)," *Journal of Toxicology and Environmental Health* 15, no. 5 (1985):551-59; D. Rosenbaum and A. Charles, "In Vitro Binding of Mirex by Mouse Hepatocytes," *Journal of Toxicology and Environmental Health* 17, no. 4 (1986):385-93; G. Tsushimoto et al., "Inhibition of Intercellular Communication by Various Congeners of Polybrominated Biphenyl and Polychlorinated Biphenyl," chapter 18 in F. M. D'Itri and M. A. Kamrin, eds., *PCBs: Human and Environmental Hazards* (Ann Arbor, Mich.: Ann Arbor Science Publishers, 1983), pp. 241-51.

3. E. Silbergeld and D. Mattison, "Experimental and Clinical Studies on the Reproductive Toxicology of 2,3,7,8-Tetrachlorodibenzo-p-dioxin," *American Journal of Industrial Medicine* 11, no. 2 (1987):131-44; J. Bradlaw and J. Casterline, "Induction of Enzyme Activity in Cell Culture: A Rapid Screen for Detection of Planar Polychlorinated Organic Compounds," *Journal of the Association of Analytical Chemists* 62, no. 4 (1979):904-16; P. Traber et al., "Expression of Cytochrome P450b and P450e Genes in Small Intestinal Mucosa of Rats Following Treatment with Phenobarbital, Polyhalogenated Biphenyls, and Organochlorine Pesticides," *Journal of Biology and Chemistry* 263, no. 19 (1988):9449-55; J. Haake et al., "Aroclor 1254 as an Antagonist of the Teratogenicity of 2,3,7,8-tetrachlorodibenzo-p-dioxin," *Toxicology Letters* 38 (1987):299-306; J. Haake et al., "The Effects of Organochlorine Pesticides as Inducers of Testosterone and Benzo[a]pyrene Gydroxylases," *General Pharmacology* 18, no. 2 (1987):165-69; W. Bulger and D. Kupfer, "Effect of Xenobiotic Estrogens and Structurally Related Compounds on 2-hydroxylation of Estradiol and on Other Monooxygenase Activities in Rat Liver," *Biochemical Pharmacology* 32, no. 6 (1983):1005-10; N. Gutkina and V. Mishin, "Immunochemical Evidences that Hexachlorobenzene Induces Two Forms of Cytochrome p-450 in the Rat Liver Microsomes," *Chemical Biology Interactions* 58, no. 1 (1986):57-68; F. Stewart and A. Smith, "Metabolism of Hexachlorobenzene by Rat-Liver Microsomes," in Morris and Cabral, eds., *Hexachlorobenzene: Proceedings of an International Symposium* (Lyon, France: IARC, 1986), pp. 325-327; C. Schroter et al., "Dose-Response Studies on the Effects of a-, b-, and g-Hexachlorocyclohexane on Putative Preneoplastic Foci, Mooxygenases, and Growth in Rat Liver," *Cancer Research* 47, no. 1 (1987):80-8; F. Van Velsen et al., "The Subchronic Oral Toxicity of the b-isomer of Hexachlorocyclohexane in Rats," *Fundamentals of Applied Toxicology* 6 (1986):697-712; World Health Organization, *Environmental Health Criteria 44: Mirex* (Geneva: World Health Organization, 1984); S. Safe, "Comparative Toxicology and Mechanisms of Action of Polychlorinated Dibenzo-p-dioxins and Dibenzofurans," *Annals of Revised Pharmacology Toxicology* 26 (1984):371-99; S. Safe, "Polychlorinated Biphenyls (PCBs) and Polybrominated Biphenyls (PBBs): Biochemistry, Toxicology, and Mechanism of Action," *CRC Critical Reviews in Toxicology* 13, no. 4 (1984):319-95; G. Mason et al., "Polychlorinated Dibenzo-p-dioxins: Quantitative *In Vitro* and *In Vivo* Structure Activity Relationships," *Toxicity* 41 (1986):21-31; G. Mason et al., "Polybrominated Dibenzo-p-dioxins and Related Compounds: Quantitive *In Vitro* and *In Vivo* Structure Activity Relationships," *Toxicity* 44 (1987):245-55; G. Mason et al.,

"The Dioxin Receptor: Characterization of its DNA-Binding Properties," *Journal of Steroid Biochemistry* 30, nos. 1-6 (1988):307-10; World Health Organization, *Environmental Health Criteria 44: Campheclor* (Geneva: World Health Organization, 1984); I. Chu et al., "Reproduction Study of Toxaphene in the Rat," *Journal of Environmental Science and Health* B23, no. 2 (1988):101-26.

    4. E. Silbergeld and D. Mattison, "Experimental and Clinical Studies on the Reproductive Toxicology of 2,3,7,8-Tetrachlorodibenzo-p-dioxin," *American Journal of Industrial Medicine* 11, no. 2 (1987):131-44; J. Haake et al., "The Effects of Organochlorine Pesticides as Inducers of Testosterone and Benzo[a]pyrene Hydroxylases," *General Pharmacology* 18, no. 2 (1987):165-69; World Health Organization, *Environmental Health Criteria 44: Campheclor;* T. Umbreit and M. Gallo, "Physiological Implications of Estrogen Receptor Modulation by 2,3,7,8,-Tetrachlorodibenzo-p-dioxin," *Toxicology Letters* 42, no. 1 (1988):5-14; M. Gallo, "Rationale for Hormone-Like Mechanisms of 2,3,7,8-TCDD for use in Risk Assessment," appendix F, in U.S. Environmental Protection Agency, Office of Health and Environmental Assessment, *A Cancer Risk-Specific Dose Estimate for 2,3,7,8-TCDD*, review draft, EPA/600/6-88/007Ab (Washington, D.C.: U.S. Environmental Protection Agency, 1988), appendices A through F; M. Romkes and S. Safe, "Comparative Activities of 2,3,7,8-Tetrachlorodibenzo-p-dioxin and Progesterone as Antiestrogens in the Female Rat Uterus," *Toxicology and Applied Pharmacology* 92, no. 3 (1988):368-80; J. Cranmer, M. Cranmer, and P. Goad, "Prenatal Chlordane Exposure: Effects on Plasma Corticosterone Concentrations Over the Lifespan of Mice, *Environmental Research* 35, no. 1 (1984):204-10; R. Welch, W. Levine, and R. Kuntzman, "Effect of Halogenated Hydrocarbon Insecticides on the Metabolism and Uterotrophic Action of Estrogens in Rats and Mice," *Toxicology of Applied Pharmacology* 19 (1971):234-46; D. Fry et al., "Sex Ratio Skew and Breeding Patterns of Gulls: Demographic and Toxicological Considerations," *Studies in Avian Biology* 10 (1987):26-43; B. Rattner et al., "Avian Endocrine Responses to Environmental Pollutants," *Journal of Experimental Zoology* 232 (1984):683-89; W. Bulger and D. Kupfer, "Effect of Xenobiotic Estrogens and Structurally Related Compounds on 2-hydroxylation of Estradiol and on Other Monooxygenase Activities in Rat Liver," *Biochemical Pharmacology* 32, no. 6 (1983):1005-10; D. Fry and C. Toone, "DDT-Induced Feminization of Gull Embryos," *Science* 213 (1981):922-24; G. Lundberg, "Effects of Long-Term Exposure to DDT on the Oestrus Cycle and the Frequency of Implants Ova in the Mouse," *Environmental Physiology and Biochemistry* 3 (1973):127-31; M. Elissalde and D. Clark, "Testosterone Metabolism by Hexachlorobenzene-Induced Hepatic Microsomal Enzymes," *American Journal of Veterinary Research* 40, no. 12 (1979):1762-66; M. Rodamilans et al., "Lead Toxicity on Endocrine Testicular Function in an Occupationally Exposed Population," *Human Toxicology* 7, no. 2 (1988):125-8; U.S. Public Health Service, Agency for Toxic Substances and Disease Registry (ATSDR), "Toxicological Profile for Lead," draft (Atlanta, Ga.: Oak Ridge National Laboratory, 1988); U.S. Public Health Service, Agency for Toxic Substances and Disease Registry (ATSDR), "Toxicological Profile for Mercury," draft (Atlanta, Ga.: Oak Ridge National Laboratory, 1988); L. Uphouse, "Decreased Rodent Sexual Receptivity After Lindane," *Toxicology Letters* 39, no. 1 (1987):7-14; F. Van Velsen et al., "The Subchronic Oral Toxicity of the B-Isomer of Hexachlorocyclohexane in Rats," *Fundamental and Applied Toxicology* 6 (1986):697-712; P. Van Giersbergen et al., "Does

b-HCH Exert an Oestrogenic Effect?" *Med. Fac. Landouww. Rijksuniv. Gent.* 49, no. 3b (1984):1195-1202; J. Veltman and M. Maines, "Alterations of Heme, Cytochrome p-450, and Steroid Metabolism by Mercury in Rat Adrenal," *Archives of Biochemistry and Biophysiology* 248, no. 2 (1986):476-8; C. Dieringer et al., "Short Communications: Altered Ontogeny of Hepatic Steroid-Metabolizing Enzymes by Pure Polychlorinated Biphenyl Congeners," *Biochemical Pharmacology* 28 (1979):1511-14; A. Biessman, "Effects of PCBs on Gonads, Sex Hormone Balance and Reproduction Processes of Japanese Quail *Coturnix coturnix japonica* After Ingestion During Sexual Maturation," *Environmental Pollution* (Series A) 27 (1982):15-30; A. Mohammed et al., "Toxaphene: Accumulation in the Adrenal Cortex and Effect on ACTH-Stimulated Corticosteroid Synthesis in the Rat," *Toxicology Letters* 24, nos. 2-3 (1985):137-43.

## Wetlands Drainage and Protection

1. Charles E. Herdendorf et al., *The Ecology of Lake St. Clair Wetlands: A Community Profile*, Biological Report 85(7.7) (Washington, D.C.: U.S. Fish and Wildlife Service, 1986), p. iii.

2. Ibid., pp. 101-103.

3. Phil Weller, "State of the Great Lakes Region Environment: Wetlands," prepared for Environment Canada, Environmental Interpretation Division, Conservation and Protection (Ottawa, Ont.: Environment Canada, 1988), p. 14.

4. Calculated from ibid, table 13.

5. Charles Herdendorf, *The Ecology of the Coastal Marshes of Western Lake Erie: A Community Profile*, Biological Report 85(7.9) (Washington, D.C.: U.S. Fish and Wildlife Service, 1987), p. 141.

6. Connie L. Gaudet, "The Agricultural Drainage Subsidy Program in Ontario: Impact on the Great Lakes Environment," unpublished report to the Institute for Research on Public Policy, May 1988, p. 8.

7. Ibid., p. 11.

8. See, for example, National Wetlands Policy Forum, *Protecting America's Wetlands: An Action Agenda* (Washington, D.C.: The Conservation Foundation, 1988).

## Sport Versus Commerce: The Alewife in Lake Michigan

1. This section is based mainly on University of Wisconsin Sea Grant Institute, *The Fisheries of the Great Lakes*, 1984-86 Biennial Report (Madison, Wis.: Sea Grant Institute, 1986).

2. D. Scavia et al., "Influence of Salmonine Predation and Weather on Long-Term Water Quality Trends in Lake Michigan," *Canadian Journal of Fisheries and Aquatic Sciences* 43 (1986):435-43.

3. Richard Bishop, University of Wisconsin, Sea Grant Institute, quoted in *Littoral Drift*, November-December 1987.

4. Scavia, "Influence of Salmonine Predation and Weather on Long-Term Water Quality Trends in Lake Michigan."

## The Great Lakes Fishery Commission

1. This box is based on Carlos Fetterolf, Jr., *A Sketch of the Great Lakes Fishery Commission: Interagency, Interstate, International Programs* (Ann Arbor, Mich.: Great Lakes Fishery Commission, 1986).

## Figures

6.1. The Conservation Foundation.
6.2. Phil Weller, "State of the Great Lakes Region Environment: Wetlands," prepared for Environment Canada, Environmental Interpretation Division, Conservation and Protection (Ottawa: Environment Canada, 1988).
6.3. Jane L. Forsyth, *The Black Swamp*, Ohio Department of Natural Resources, Division of the Geological Survey, 1960; in Charles E. Herdendorf, *The Ecology of the Coastal Marshes of Lake Erie: A Community Profile*, Biological Report 85(7.9) (Washington, D.C.: U.S. Fish and Wildlife Service, 1987), p. 140.
6.4. Bernhard Grzimek, ed., *Grzimek's Animal Life Encyclopedia*, vol. 4, *Fishes I*, and vol. 5, *Fishes II and Amphibians* (New York: Van Nostrand Reinhold, 1974); Tom Kuchenberg and Jim Legault, *Reflections in a Tarnished Mirror: The Use and Abuse of the Great Lakes* (Sturgeon Bay, Wis.: Golden Glow Publishing, 1978); W. B. Scott and E. J. Crossman, *Freshwater Fishes of Canada*, Bulletin 184 (Ottawa: Fisheries Research Board of Canada, 1973).
6.5. Great Lakes Fishery Commission (GLFC), *Commercial Fish Production in the Great Lakes, 1867-1977*, Technical Report no. 3 (Ann Arbor, Mich.: GLFC, 1979), p. 126; GLFC, *1978 Report* (Ann Arbor, Mich.: GLFC, 1978), p. 25-32; GLFC, *1979 Report* (Ann Arbor, Mich.: GLFC, 1979), errata insert, pp. 33a-33c; GLFC, *1980 Report* (Ann Arbor, Mich.: GLFC, 1980), pp. 24-28; GLFC, *1981 Report* (Ann Arbor, Mich.: GLFC, 1981), pp. 26-32; GLFC, *1982 Report* (Ann Arbor, Mich.: GLFC, 1982), pp. 26-31; GLFC, *1983 Report* (Ann Arbor, Mich.: GLFC, 1983), pp. 32-37; National Oceanic and Atmospheric Administration (NOAA), "Commercial Fish Production—Pounds and Value ($), 1985," data sheet; NOAA, "Commercial Fish Production—Pounds and Value, 1986," data sheet; NOAA, "Commercial Fish Production—Pounds and Value, 1987," data sheet.
6.6. See reference 6.5.
6.7. See reference 6.5.
6.8. International Joint Commission, Great Lakes Science Advisory Board, *Rehabilitation of Lake Ontario: The Role of Nutrient Reduction and Food Web Dynamics* (Windsor, Ont.: International Joint Commission, 1988); International Joint Commission, Great Lakes Science Advisory Board, *1987 Report* (Windsor, Ont.: International Joint Commission, 1987), p. 47; and Donald Scavia and Gary L. Fahnenstiel, "From Picoplankton to Fish: Complex Interactions in the Great Lakes," in Stephen R. Carpenter, ed., *Complex Interactions in Lake Communities* (New York: Springer-Verlag, 1988), pp. 85-97.

## 7. HUMAN HEALTH

1. R. Faber and J. Hickey, "Eggshell Thinning, Chlorinated Hydrocarbons, and Mercury in Inland Aquatic Bird Eggs, 1969 and 1970," *Pesticides Monitoring Journal*

7, no. 1 (1973):27-36 1973; M. Gilbertson, "Need for Development of Epidemiology for Chemically Induced Diseases in Fish in Canada," *Canadian Journal of Fish and Aquatic Science* 41 (1984):1534-40; G. Heinz et al., "Contaminant Levels in Colonial Waterbirds from Green Bay and Lake Michigan, 1975-80," *Environmental Monitoring and Assessment* 5 (1985):233-36; S. Wiemeyer et al., "Residues of Organochlorine Pesticides, Polychlorinated Biphenyls, and Mercury in Bald Eagle Eggs and Changes in Shell Thickness—1969 and 1970," *Pesticides Monitoring Journal* 6 (1972):50-55; S. Wiemeyer et al., "Organochlorine Pesticide, Polychlorobiphenyl, and Mercury Residues in Bald Eagle Eggs—1969-79—and Their Relationships to Shell Thinning and Reproduction," *Archives of Environmental Contamination Toxicolology* 13 (1984):529-49.

2. G. Szmcynski and S. Waliszewski, "Chlorinated Pesticide Residues in Testicular Tissue Samples," *Andrologia* 15, no. 6 (1983):696-98; R. Dougherty et al., "Sperm Density and Toxic Substances: A Potential Key to Environmental Health Hazards," chapter 13 in J. McKinney, ed., *Environmental Health Chemistry* (Ann Arbor, Mich.: Ann Arbor Science Publishers, 1980), pp. 263-78; and B. Bush, A. Bennett, and J. Snow, "Polychlorobiphenyl Congeners, p,p'-DDE, and Sperm Function in Humans," *Archives of Environmental Contaminants and Toxicology* 15 (1986):333-41.

3. V. Baukloh et al., "Biocides in Human Follicular Fluid," *Annals of the New York Academy of Sciences* 442 (1985):240-50; M. Trapp et al., "Pollutants in Human Follicular Fluid," *Fertility and Sterility* 42, no. 1 (1984):146-48.

4. H. Korpela et al., "Lead and Cadmium Concentrations in Maternal and Umbilical Cord Blood, Amniotic Fluid, Placenta, and Amniotic Membranes," *American Journal of Obstetrics and Gynecology* 155, no. 5 (1986):1086-9; B. Kuhnert and P. Kuhnert, "Lead and Cadmium Concentrations in Mother and Fetus," letter, *American Journal of Obstetrics and Gynecology* 158, no. 1 (1988):220; U.S. Public Health Service, Agency for Toxic Substances and Disease Registry, "Toxicological Profile for Aldrin/ Dieldrin," draft (Atlanta, Ga.: Oak Ridge National Laboratory, 1987); M. Ando, S. Hirano, and Y. Itoh, "Transfer of Hexachlorobenzene (HCB) from Mother to New-Born Baby through Placenta and Milk," *Archives of Toxicology* 56, no. 3 (1985):195-200; K. Courtney and J. Andrews, "Neonatal and Maternal Blood Burdens of Hexachlorobenzene (HCB) in Mice: Gestational Exposure and Lactational Transfer," *Fundamental and Applied Toxicology* 5, no. 2 (1985):265-77; R. Capelli et al., "The Presence of Mercury (Total and Organic) and Selenium in Human Placentae," *The Science of the Total Environment* 48, nos. 1-2 (1986):69-79.

5. D. Williams, G. LeBel, and E. Junkins, "Organohalogen Residues in Human Adipose Autopsy Samples from Six Ontario Municipalities," *Journal of the Association of Analytical Chemists* 71, no. 2 (1988):410-14; J. Holleman. and A. Hammons, "Levels of Chemical Contaminants in Nonoccupationally Exposed U.S. Residents," prepared for U.S. Environmental Protection Agency, Health Effects Research Laboratory, Office of Research and Development, Research Triangle Park, N.C., 1980; J. Ryan, R. Lizotte, and B. Lau, "Chlorinated Dibenzo-p-dioxins and Chlorinated Dibenzofurans in Canadian Human Adipose Tissue," *Chemosphere* 67, no. 7 (1985):697-706; and J. Ryan et al., "Tissue Distribution of Dioxins and Furans in Humans from the General Population," *Chemosphere* 14, nos. 6/7 (1985):929-32.

6. G. Mason et al., "Polychlorinated Dibenzofurans (PCDFs): Correlation Between *In Vivo* and *In Vitro* Structure Activity Relationships," *Toxicity* 37 (1985):1-12; G.

Mason et al., "Polychlorinated Dibenzo-p-dioxins: Quantitative *In Vitro* and *In Vivo* Structure Activity Relationships," *Toxicity* 41 (1986):21-31; G. Mason, et al., "Polybrominated Dibenzo-p-dioxins and Related Compounds: Quantitive *In Vitro* and *In Vivo* Structure Activity Relationships," *Toxicity* 44 (1987):245-55.

7. P. Beland and P. Martineau, "About Carcinogens and Tumors," letter, *Canadian Journal of Fisheries and Aquatic Sciences*, 1988.

8. P. Baumann, "Cancer in Wildlife Freshwater Fish Populations with Emphasis on the Great Lakes," *Journal of Great Lakes Research* 10, no. 3 (1984):251-53.

9. R. Bannister et al., "Arochlor 1254 as a 2,3,7,88-tetrachlorodibenzo-p-dioxin Antagonist: Effects on Enzyme Induction and Immunotoxicity," *Toxicology* 46 (1987):29-42; S. Safe, "Polychlorinated Biphenyls (PCBs) and Polybrominated Biphenyls (PBBs): Biochemistry, Toxicology, and Mechanism of Action," *CRC Critical Reviews in Toxicology* 13, no. 4 (1984):319-95; K. Tomaszewski, C. Montgomery, and R. Melnick, "Modulation of 2,3,7,8-tetrachlorodibenzo-p-dioxin Toxicity in F344 Rats by Di(2-ethylhexyl)phthalate," *Chemical Biology Interactions* 65, no. 3 (1988):205-22.

10. D. Janerich et al., "Cancer Incidence in the Love Canal Area," *Science* 212 (1981):1404-7.

11. U.S. National Institutes of Health, Public Health Service, no. (NIH) 87-2900, *Atlas of Cancer Mortality among Whites: 1950-1980* (Washington, D.C.: U.S. Government Printing Office, 1987).

12. Health and Welfare Canada, "Cancer Mortality in Niagara County, Ontario, 1951-1981," Special Report no. 5, *Chronic Diseases in Canada*, July 1, 1984.

13. Ontario Ministry of Health, "Variations in Clefting, Ontario: 1973-1981," *Ontario Disease Surveillance Report* 5, no. 41 (1984):429-30.

14. Ontario Ministry of Health, Disease Control and Epidemiology Service, Public Health Branch, "Selected Reproductive Outcomes among Residents of the Niagara Region and a Comparison Region, Ontario," May 1986.

15. U.S. Public Health Service, ATSDR, "Toxicological Profile for 2,3,7,8-Tetrachlorodibenzo-p-dioxin," draft (Atlanta, Ga.: Oak Ridge National Laboratory, 1987); U.S. Environmental Protection Agency, Office of Water Regulations and Standards, *The National Dioxin Study: Tiers 3,4,6, and 7*, EPA/440/4-87-003 (Washington, D.C.: U.S. Environmental Protection Agency, 1987).

16. U.S. Environmental Protection Agency, Office of Water Regulations and Standards, *Work/Quality Assurance Project Plan for the Bioaccumulation Study* (Washington, D.C., U.S. Environmental Protection Agency, 1986).

17. R. Murphy and C. Harvey, "Residues and Metabolites of Selected Persistent Halogenated Hydrocarbons in Blood Specimens from a General Population Survey," *Environmental Health Perspectives* 60 (1985):115-20.

18. D. Williams, G. LeBel, and E. Junkins, "Organohalogen Residues in Human Adipose Autopsy Samples from Two Ontario Municipalities," *Journal of the Association of Analytical Chemists* 71, no. 2 (1988):410–14.

19. D. Davies and J. Mes, "Comparison of the Residue Levels of Some Organochlorine Compounds in Breast Milk of the General and Indigenous Canadian Populations," *Bulletin of Environmental Contamination and Toxicology* 39 (1987):743-49.

20. J. Mes et al., "Polychlorinated Biphenyl and Organochlorine Pesticide Residues in Adipose Tissue of Canadians," *Bulletin of Environmental Contamination*

*and Toxicology* 17, no. 2 (1977):196-203; Williams, LeBel, and Junkins, "Organochlorine Residues in Human Adipose Autopsy Samples from Six Ontario Municipalities."

21. J. Mes et al., "Levels and Trends of Chlorinated Hydrocarbon Contaminants in the Breast Milk of Canadian Women," *Food Additives and Contaminants* 3, no. 4 (1986):313-22; J. Mes, D. Davies, and D. Turton, "Polychlorinated Biphenyl and Other Chlorinated Hydrocarbon Residues in Adipose Tissue of Canadians," *Bulletin of Environmental Contamination and Toxicology* 28 (1982):97-104; U.S. Environmental Protection Agency, *Work/Quality Assurance Project Plan for the Bioaccumulation Study.*

22. E. Calabrese, "Human Breast Milk Contamination in the United States and Canada by Chlorinated Hydrocarbon Insecticides and Industrial Pollutants: Current Status," *Journal of the American College of Toxicology* 1, no. 3 (1982):91–98.

23. Ibid.; Davies and Mes, "Comparison of the Residue Levels of Some Organochlorine Compounds in Breast Milk of the General and Indigenous Canadian Populations."

24. A. Astrup-Jensen, "Environmental and Occupational Chemicals," chapter 10 in P.N. Bennett, ed., *Drugs and Human Lactation* (New York: Elsevier Science Publishers, 1988), pp. 551-73.

25. G. Fein et al., "Prenatal Exposure to Polychlorinated Biphenyls: Effects on Birth Size and Gestational Age," *The Journal of Pediatrics* 105, no. 2 (1984):315-20; S. Jacobson et al., "Intrauterine Exposure of Human Newborns to PCBs: Measures of Exposure," chapter 22 in F. M. D'Tri and M. A. Kamrin, eds., *PCBs: Human and Environmental Hazards* (Ann Arbor, Mich.: Ann Arbor Science Publishers, 1983), pp. 311-43; J. Jacobson et al., "Prenatal Exposure to Environmental Toxin: A Test of the Multiple Effects Model," *Developmental Psychology* 20, no. 4 (1984):523-32; P. Schwartz et al., "Lake Michigan Fish Consumption as a Source of Polychlorinated Biphenyls in Human Cord Serum, Maternal Serum, and Milk," *American Journal of Public Health* 73, no. 3 (1983):293-96.

26. Fein et al., "Prenatal Exposure to Polychlorinated Biphenyls."

27. Jacobson, "Intrauterine Exposure of Human Newborns to PCBs"; Schwartz et al., "Lake Michigan Fish Consumption as a Source of Polychlorinated Biphenyls in Human Cord Serum, Maternal Serum, and Milk."

28. Jacobson et al., "Prenatal Exposure to Environmental Toxin."

29. H. Kodawa and H. Ota, "Studies on the Transfer of PCB to Infants from Their Mothers," *Japan Journal of Hygiene* 32 (1977):567; Y. Masuda et al., "Transfer of Various Polychlorinated Biphenyls to the Fetuses and Offspring of Mice," *Food and Cosmetic Toxicology* 17 (1979):623-27.

30. S. Jacobson et al., "The Effect of Intrauterine PCB Exposure on Visual Recognition Memory," *Child Development* 56 (1985):853-60.

31. M. Meaburn, "Consumption of Fishery Products in the United States," remarks at symposium on "Chemically Contaminated Aquatic Food Resources and Human Cancer Risk," sponsored by National Institute of Environmental Health Sciences, Research Triangle Park, North Carolina, September 29-30, 1988.

32. The model is being developed by a Canadian federal-provincial *ad hoc* work group on multimedia standards.

33. M. Wariishi, Y. Suzuki, and K. Nishiyama, "Chlordane Residues in Normal

Human Blood," *Bulletin of Environmental Contaminants and Toxicology* 36, no. 5 (1986):635-43.

34. Wisconsin Division of Health and State Laboratory of Hygiene, *Study of Sport Fishing and Fish Consumption Habits and Body Burden Levels of PCBs, DDE, and Mercury of Wisconsin Anglers*" (Madison, Wis.: Wisconsin Division of Health, 1987); W. Rogan et al., "Polychlorinated Biphenyls (PCBs) and Dichloridiphenyl Dichloroethene (DDE) in Human Milk: Effects of Maternal Factors and Previous Lactation," *American Journal of Public Health* 76, no. 2 (1986):172-77; L. Kanja et al., "Organochlorine Pesticides in Human Milk from Different Areas of Kenya 1983-1985," *Journal of Toxicology and Environmental Health* 19, no. 4 (1986):449-64; and K. Noren, "Levels of Organochlorine Contaminants in Human Milk in Relation to the Dietary Habitats of the Mothers," *Acta Paediatr Scandinavia* 72, no. 6 (1983):811-16.

35. Noren, "Levels of Organochlorine Contaminants in Human Milk in Relation to the Dietary Habits of the Mothers."

36. W. Sloof and A. Matthijsen, *Integrated Criteria Document Hexachlorocyclohexanes*, Report no. 758473011 (Bilthoven, The Netherlands: National Institute of Public Health and Environmental Protection, 1988).

37. S. Langworth, C. Elinder, and A. Akesson, "Mercury Exposure from Dental Fillings," *Swedish Dental Journal* 12 (1988):69-70; Wisconsin Division of Health and State Laboratory of Hygiene, *Study of Sport Fishing and Fish Consumption Habits and Body Burden Levels of PCBs, DDE, and Mercury of Wisconsin Anglers*; H. Mykkanen et al., "Dietary Intakes of Mercury, Lead, Cadmium, and Arsenic by Finnish Children," *Human Nutrition: Applied Nutrition* 40A (1986):32-9; A. Lommel, H. Kruse, and O. Wassermann, "Organochlorines and Mercury in Blood of a Fish-Eating Population at the River Elbe in Schleswig-Holstein, FRG," *Archives of Toxicology Supplement* 8 (1985):264-68.

38. World Health Organization, *Environmental Health Criteria 44: Mirex* (Geneva: World Health Organization, 1984).

39. J. Jacobson and S. Jacobson, "New Methodologies for Assessing the Effects of Prenatal Toxic Exposure on Cognitive Functioning in Humans," chapter 18 in Marlene S. Evans, ed., *Toxic Contaminants and Ecosystem Health: A Great Lakes Focus* (New York: John Wiley and Sons, 1988); Wisconsin Division of Health and State Laboratory of Hygiene, *Study of Sport Fishing and Fish Consumption Habits and Body Burden Levels of PCBs, DDE, and Mercury of Wisconsin Anglers*; H. Humphrey "Chemical Contaminants in the Great Lakes: The Human Health Aspect," chapter 7 in Evans, *Toxic Contaminants and Human Health*; Schwartz et al., "Lake Michigan Fish Consumption as a Source of Polychlorinated Biphenyls in Human Cord Serum, Maternal Serum, and Milk."

40. Schwartz et al., "Lake Michigan Fish Consumption as a Source of Polychlorinated Biphenyls in Human Cord Serum, Maternal Serum, and Milk''; B. Smith, *PCB Levels in Human Fluids: Sheboygan Case Study*, Technical Report no. 83-240 (Madison, Wis.: University of Wisconsin, Sea Grant Institute, 1984).

41. A. Jensen, "Polychlorobiphenyls (PCBs), Polychlorodibenzo-p-dioxins (PCDDs), and Polychlorodibenzofurans (PCDFs) in Human Milk, Blood, and Adipose Tissue," *The Science of the Total Environment* 64 (1987):259-93.

42. Jacobson et al., "Intrauterine Exposure of Human Newborns to PCBs."

43. W. Swain, "Human Health Consequences of Consumption of Fish Contaminated with Organochlorine Compounds," *Aquatic Toxicology* 11 (1988):357-77.

44. Astrup-Jensen, "Environmental and Occupational Chemicals"; Jensen, "Polychlorobiphenyls (PCBs), Polychlorodibenzo-p-dioxins (PCDDs), and Polychlorodibenzofurans (PCDFs) in Human Milk, Blood, and Adipose Tissue"; A. Schecter, J. Ryan, and J. Constable, "Polychlorinated Dibenzo-p-dioxin and Polychlorinated Dibenzofuran Levels in Human Breast Milk from Vietnam Compared with Cow's Milk and Human Breast Milk from the North American Continent," *Chemosphere* 16, nos. 8/9 (1987):2003-16; and A. Schecter and T. Gasiewicz, "Health Hazard Assessment of Chlorinated Dioxins and Dibenzofurans Contained in Human Milk," *Chemosphere* 16, nos. 8/9 (1987):2147-54.

45. A. Poland and E. Glover, "Studies on the Mechanism of Toxicity of the Chlorinated Dibenzo-p-dioxins," *Environmental Health Perspectives* 5 (1973):245-51; Wisconsin Division of Health and State Laboratory of Hygiene, *Study of Sport Fishing and Fish Consumption Habits and Body Burden Levels of PCBs, DDE, and Mercury of Wisconsin Anglers.*

46. Wayland R. Swain, "Toxic Substances in the Ecosystem," in A. D. Misener and G. Daniel, eds., *Decisions for the Great Lakes* (Hiram, Ohio: Great Lakes Tomorrow, and Hammond, Ind.: Purdue University Calumet, 1982).

47. 54 Fed. Reg. 27505 (1989).

48. See, for example, U.S. Geological Survey, *National Water Summary, 1986: Groundwater Quality* (Reston, Va.: U.S. Geological Survey, 1988); N. L. Dean, *Danger on Tap: The Government's Failure to Enforce the Federal Safe Drinking Water Act* (Washington, D.C.: National Wildlife Federation, 1988); J. A. Cherry, "Groundwater Occurrence and Contamination in Canada," *Canadian Bulletin of Fisheries and Aquatic Sciences* 215 (1987):387-426.

49. U.S. Public Health Service, Agency for Toxic Substances and Disease Registry, "Toxicological Profile for Lead," draft (Atlanta, Ga.: Oak Ridge National Laboratory, 1988).

50. R. Maguire et al., "Occurrence of Organotin Compounds in Ontario Lakes and Rivers," *Environmental and Science Technology* 16, no. 10 (1982):698-702; H. Gucinski, "The Aerial Transport and Deposition of Toxic Substances: Implications from the Study of the Air-Water Interface," testimony before the U.S. House of Representatives, Committee on Public Works and Transportation, Subcommittee on Investigations and Oversight, April 14, 1988; R. Arimoto, *The Atmospheric Deposition of Chemical Contaminants to the Great Lakes*, report for U.S. Environmental Protection Agency as AAAS/EPA Environmental Science and Engineering Fellow, 1987.

51. U.S. Public Health Service, "Toxicological Profile for Cadmium"; H. Sternowsky and R. Wessolowski, "Lead and Cadmium in Breast Milk: Higher Levels in Urban vs. Rural Mothers during the First 3 Months of Lactation," *Archives of Toxicology* 57 (1985):41-45; A. Brockhaus et al., "Exposure to Lead and Cadmium of Children Living in Different Areas of North-West Germany: Results of Biological Monitoring Studies 1982-1986," *International Archives of Occupational Environmental Health* 60, no. 3 (1988):211-22.

52. U.S. Public Health Service, "Toxicological Profile for Lead"; Sternowsky and Wessolowski, "Lead and Cadmium in Breast Milk"; Brockhaus et al., "Exposure to Lead and Cadmium of Children Living in Different Areas of North-West Germany."

53. W. Ernst, V. Weigelt, and K. Weber, "Octachlorostyrene a Permanent Micropollutant in the North Sea," *Chemosphere* 13, no. 1 (1984):161-68; Health and Welfare Canada, *Polychlorinated Styrenes: An Environmental Health Perspective*, 85-EHC-128 (Ottawa, Ont.: Health and Welfare Canada, 1985).

54. S. Slorach and R. Vaz, "PCB Levels in Breast Milk: Data from the UNEP/WHO Pilot Project on Biological Monitoring and Some Other Recent Studies," *Environmental Health Perspectives* 60 (1985):121-26.

55. B. Smith, *PCB Levels in Human Fluids: Sheboygan Case Study*, Technical Report no. 83-240 (Madison: University of Wisconsin, Sea Grant, 1984); J. Mes, "Polychlorobiphenyl in Children's Blood," *Environmental Research* 44 (1987):213-220.

56. Williams, LeBel, and Junkins, "Organohalogen Residues in Human Adipose Autopsy Samples from Six Ontario Municipalities"; Williams, LeBel, and Junkins, "A Comparison of Organochlorine Residues in Human Adipose Tissue Autopsy Samples from Two Ontario Municipalities."

57. S. Barbieri et al., "Long-term Effects of 2,3,7,8-tetrachlorodibenzo-p-dioxin on the Peripheral Nervous System," *Neuroepidemiology* 7 (1988):29-37; C. Levy, "Agent Orange Exposure and Posttraumatic Stress Disorder," *Journal of Nervous and Mental Disease* 176, no. 4 (1988):242-45; U.S. Environmental Protection Agency, Environmental Criteria and Assessment Office, *Research and Development: Drinking Water Criteria Document for Heptachlor, Heptachlor Epoxide and Chlordane* (Cincinnati, Ohio: U.S. Environmental Protection Agency, Office of Drinking Water, 1985); U.S. Public Health Service, Agency for Toxic Substances and Disease Registry (ATSDR), "Toxicological Profile for Chlordane," draft (Atlanta, Ga.: Oak Ridge National Laboratory, 1988); Rogan et al., "Polychlorinated Biphenyls (PCBs) and Dichlorodiphenyl Dichloroethene (DDE) in Human Milk"; U.S. Public Health Service, ATSDR, "Toxicological Profile for DDT, DDE, and DDD," draft (Atlanta, Ga.: Oak Ridge National Laboratory, 1988); U.S. Public Health Service, ATSDR, "Toxicological Profile for Aldrin/Dieldrin," draft; U.S. Environmental Protection Agency, Office of Drinking Water, "Hexachlorobenzene: Health Advisory Draft," March 1987; U.S. Public Health Service, ATSDR, "Toxicological Profile for Lead; H. Needleman et al., "The Relationship between Prenatal Exposure to Lead and Congenital Anomalies," *Journal of American Medical Association* 251 (1984):2956-59; World Health Organization, *Environmental Health Criteria 1: Mercury* (Geneva: World Health Organization, 1976); G. Nordberg, "Current Concepts in the Assessment of Effects of Metals in Chronic Low-Level Exposures: Considerations of Experimental and Epidemiological Evidence," *The Science of the Total Environment* 71 (1988):243-52; B. Grubb, S. Driscoll, and P. Bentley, "Mercury Exchanges and Toxicity in the Crystalline Lens *In Vitro*," *Ophthalmic Research* 19, no. 2 (1987):101-6; Jacobson and Jacobson, "New Methodologies for Assessing the Effects of Prenatal Toxic Exposure on Cognitive Functioning in Humans"; W. Rogan et al., "Congenital Poisoning by Polychlorinated Biphenyls and Their Contaminants in Taiwan," *Science* 241 (1988):334-36; Smith, "PCB Levels in Human Fluids"; World Health Organization, *Environmental Health Criteria: Toxaphene* (Geneva: World Health Organization, 1984).

58. P. Silva et al., "Blood Level, Intelligence, Reading Attainment, and Behaviour in Eleven Year Old Children in Dunedin, New Zealand," *Journal of Child Psychology*

286     GREAT LAKES, GREAT LEGACY?

*and Psychiatry* 29, no. 1 (1988):43-51; G. Winneke, W. Collet, and H. Lilienthal, "The Effects of Lead in Laboratory Animals and Environmentally-Exposed Children," *Toxicology* 49, nos. 2-3 (1988):291-98; Needleman et al., "The Relationship between Prenatal Exposure to Lead and Congenital Anomalies."

59. International Joint Commission, Great Lakes Science Advisory Board, Health Committee, workshop on "Research Strategies to Appraise Adverse Health Effects from Hazardous Substances or Agents in the Great Lakes System," March 1989.

60. F. Sullivan and S. Barlow, "The Relevance for Man of Animal Data on Reproductive Toxicity of Industrial Chemicals," *Prevention of Physical and Mental Congenital Defects, part B, Epidemiology, Early Detection and Therapy, and Environmental Factors* (1985), pp. 301-5.

61. See, for example, U.S. Environmental Protection Agency, Region 10, Office of Puget Sound, *Guidance Manual for Health Risk Assessment of Chemically Contaminated Seafood*, Report no. TC-399-07 (U.S. Environmental Protection Agency, 1986).

62. International Joint Commission, Great Lakes Science Advisory Board, *1989 Report* (Windsor, Ont.: International Joint Commission, 1989), section 6.5.

## Fish Advisories

1. Ontario Ministry of the Environment, *Guide to Eating Ontario Sport Fish* (Toronto: Ontario Ministry of the Environment and Ministry of Natural Resources, 1988).

2. Louis F. Schneider, "FDA Regulation of Chemical Contaminants in Fish," report delivered at the Annual Meeting of the International Association of Great Lakes Researchers, Hamilton, Ontario, May 1988, p. 10.

3. Jeffery A. Foran et al., "Sport Fish Consumption Advisories and Projected Cancer Risks in the Great Lakes Basin," *American Journal of Public Health* 79, no. 3 (1989):322-25; National Wildlife Federation, *Lake Michigan Sport Fish: Should You Eat Your Catch?* (Ann Arbor, Mich.: National Wildlife Federation, 1989).

4. S. Tanabe et al., "Highly Toxic Coplanar PCBs: Occurrence, Source, Persistency, and Toxic Implications to Wildlife and Humans," *Environmental Pollution* 47 (1987):147-63.

5. T. Colborn, "The Use of Toxicity Equivalency as a Complement to Biomonitoring and Wildlife Research in the Great Lakes," unpublished, August 1988.

## Figures

7.1. Adapted from Wayland R. Swain, "Toxic Substances in the Ecosystem," in A. D. Misener and G. Daniel, eds., *Decisions for the Great Lakes* (Hiram, Ohio: Great Lakes Tomorrow, and Hammond, Ind.: Purdue University Calumet, 1982), p. 355.

7.2. Ontario Ministry of Health, "Variations in Clefting, Ontario: 1973-1981," *Ontario Disease Surveillance Report* 5, no. 41 (1984):429-30.

7.3. K. Davies, "Human Exposure Routes to Selected Persistent Toxic Chemicals in the Great Lakes Basin: A Case Study of Toronto and Southern Ontario Region" (Toronto, Ont.: Toronto Department of Public Health, December, 1986).

7.4. The Conservation Foundation.

7.5. Adapted from H. E. Humphrey, "Population Studies of PCBs in Michigan Residents," in F. M. D'Itri and M. A. Kamrin, eds., *PCBs: Human and Environmental Hazards* (Ann Arbor, Mich.: Ann Arbor Science Publishers, 1983).

## 9. FROM AGREEMENT TO ACTION: IMPLEMENTING PROGRAMS

1. Boundary Waters Treaty of 1909, Article IV. The text of the treaty has been reprinted in several sources, including Robert Spencer, John Kirton, and Kim R. Nossal, eds., *The International Joint Commission Seventy Years On* (Toronto: Centre for International Studies, University of Toronto, 1981).

2. Gordon Robertson, "The United States and Problems of Canadian Federalism," in Charles Doran and John H. Sigler, eds., *Canada and the United States: Enduring Friendship, Persistent Stress* (Englewood Cliffs, N.J.: Prentice-Hall, 1985), p. 34.

3. See Michael J. Donahue, *Institutional Arrangements for Great Lakes Management: Past Practices and Future Alternatives* (Lansing: Michigan Sea Grant College Program, 1987) for a comprehensive review of the present structure and other options.

4. International Joint Commission, "Revised Great Lakes Water Quality Agreement of 1978: Agreement with Annexes and Terms of Reference, between the United States and Canada, signed at Ottawa November 22, 1978, and Phosphorus Load Reduction Supplement, signed October 7, 1983, as amended by Protocol, signed November 18, 1987" (Windsor, Ont., 1988). This agreement is cited hereafter as "1978 Water Quality Agreement." The purpose and general objectives are defined in Article II; specific objectives and similar detail in Articles IV-VI; the role of the International Joint Commission and its subsidiary boards in Articles VII-IX; financial and legislative commitments and state/provincial cooperation in Article XII.

5. Barry G. Rabe, "Overcoming Fragmentation in Canadian Environmental Management," in Nigel Haigh and Frances Irwin, eds., *Integrated Pollution Control in Europe and North America* (Washington, D.C.: The Conservation Foundation, forthcoming).

6. Donahue, *Institutional Arrangements for Great Lakes Management*, p. 432.

7. Greenpeace, *Water for Life: The Greenpeace Report on the State of the Great Lakes* (Toronto: Greenpeace, 1989), p. 4.

8. International Joint Commission, *Second Biennial Report* (Windsor, Ont.: International Joint Commission, 1984), p. 15.

9. International Joint Commission, *Fourth Biennial Report* (Windsor, Ont.: International Joint Commission, 1989), p. 59.

10. Ibid.

11. See, for example, Don Munton, "Paradoxes and Prospects," and Marcel Cadieux, "The View from the Pearson Building," both in Robert Spencer, John Kirten, and Kim R. Nossal, eds., *The International Joint Commission Seventy Years On*, (Toronto: University of Toronto, Centre for International Studies, 1981), pp. 60-105.

12. See, for example, U.S. General Accounting Office, *Need to Reassess U.S. Participation in the International Joint Commission* (Washington, D.C.: U.S. General Accounting Office, 1989); Clayton Edwards, *Review of the Research Advisory Board/ Science Advisory Board Recommendations and Supporting Reports with IJC and*

*Government Responses, 1973 through 1985* (Windsor, Ont.: International Joint Commission, 1988).

13. 1978 Water Quality Agreement, Article VII (3).

14. 1978 Water Quality Agreement, Terms of Reference for the Joint Institutions and the Great Lakes Regional Office, 3(b)(ii).

15. Open letter dated March 1, 1989, concerning events at the time of the October 1989 International Joint Commission meeting, signed by representatives of the Canadian Environmental Law Association, Great Lakes United, Greenpeace, Pollution Probe, and the Programme for Zero Discharge.

16. International Joint Commission, Great Lakes Water Quality Board Report, *1985 Report on Great Lakes Quality*, (Windsor, Ont.: International Joint Commission, 1985), pp. 29-33.

17. The Great Lakes Water Quality Board has recommended the designation of a 43rd Area of Concern: Presque Isle/Erie Harbor, on the south shore of Lake Erie. See International Joint Commission, Great Lakes Water Quality Board, *1989 Report on Great Lakes Quality* (Windsor, Ont.: International Joint Commission, 1989).

18. John Hartig, "Commission Finalizes Its RAP Review Process," *Focus on International Joint Commission Activities* 14, no. 1 (1989).

19. International Joint Commission, *1989 Report on Great Lakes Quality*, pp. 79-81 and table 16.

20. Ibid., pp. 80-81.

21. International Joint Commission, Great Lakes Water Quality Board, *1987 Report on Great Lakes Quality* (Windsor, Ont.: International Joint Commission, 1987), appendix A, which describes problems but includes no costs; U.S. General Accounting Office, *Water Pollution: Efforts to Clean Up Michigan's Rouge River* (Washington, D.C.: U.S. General Accounting Office, 1988), appendix VIII; David J. Rapport, "Review of the Great Lakes Remedial Action Programs: What Might the RAPs Accomplish and What Might It Cost?" report prepared for Statistics Canada and the Institute for Research on Public Policy, May 1989.

22. Most of what follows is taken from the "discussion document," *Remedial Action Plan for Hamilton Harbour: Goals, Problems and Options*, March 1988. This is *not* the RAP itself, but a stage in the RAP's development.

23. Ibid., p. 1.

24. Ibid., p. 22.

25. International Joint Commission, *1989 Report on Great Lakes Quality*, p. 81.

26. *Remedial Action Plan for Hamilton Harbour: Goals, Problems and Options*, p. x.

27. Peyton L. Smith et al., "Estuary Rehabilitation: The Green Bay Story," *Oceanus* 31, no. 3 (1988):12-20.

28. Wisconsin Department of Natural Resources, *Lower Green Bay Remedial Action Plan*, public review draft (Madison, Wis.: Wisconsin Department of Natural Resources, 1987).

29. John Hartig, "IJC Completes Review of Two RAP's," *Focus on International Joint Commission Activities* 14, no. 1 (1989):17.

30. See, generally, Susan H. MacKenzie, "The Council of Great Lakes Governors: Analysis of Major Environmental Initiatives and Implementation Progress to Date," unpublished report to The Conservation Foundation, November 1988.

31. Great Lakes Charter, Principle III, published in *The Great Lakes Reporter*, March/April 1985, p. 4.

32. David Estrin and John Swaigen, eds., *Environment on Trial* (Toronto: Canadian Environmental Law Research Foundation, 1978), p. 466.

33. Kernaghan Webb, "Taking Matters into Their Own Hands: The Increasing Role of the Public in Canadian Pollution Control," paper delivered to meeting of the Law and Society Association, Learned Societies Conference, Windsor, Ontario, June 7, 1988, p. 12.

34. Great Lakes United, Water Quality Task Force, *Unfulfilled Promises: A Citizen's Review of the International Great Lakes Water Quality Agreement* (Buffalo, N.Y.: Great Lakes United, 1987), p. 2.

35. Donahue, *Institutional Arrangements for Great Lakes Management*, p. 324.

36. Environment Canada, *From Cradle to Grave: A Management Approach to Chemicals* (Ottawa: Environment Canada, 1986).

37. Ontario Ministry of the Environment, *Report on the 1986 Industrial Direct Discharges in Ontario* (Toronto: Queen's Printer for Ontario, 1987), p. 11.

38. Conservation Foundation calculation from ibid., pp. 17-20.

39. The U.S. statistics in these paragraphs were provided by U.S. Environmental Protection Agency, Office of Enforcement and Compliance Monitoring, to The Conservation Foundation, June 1988.

40. Chuck Evans, U.S. Environmental Protection Agency, Office of Water Enforcement, personal communication, August 5, 1988.

41. U.S. Environmental Protection Agency, "EPA Releases Enforcement Statistics," January 28, 1988.

42. *Air and Water Pollution Report*, May 16, 1988, p. 189.

43. Sam Sage, Atlantic States Legal Foundation, personal communication, June 14, 1988.

44. Canada, House of Commons Debates (Hansard), September 16, 1987, p. 9018.

45. Canadian Environmental Protection Act (CEPA), 35-36-37 Eliz.II, 1988, c.22, para 115.

46. Although dated in some particulars, an excellent review of provincial policies is provided in Robert Gibson, *Control Orders and Industrial Pollution Abatement in Ontario* (Toronto: Canadian Environmental Law Research Foundation, 1983).

47. Office of the Provincial Auditor, *Annual Report of the Provincial Auditor of Ontario* (Toronto: Office of the Provincial Auditor, 1987), p. 64.

48. Webb, "Taking Matters into Their Own Hands," p. 13. See also Paul Muldoon, "The Fight for an Environmental Bill of Rights," *Alternatives* 15, no. 2 (1988):33-39.

49. Andrew Hamilton, "Towards a Framework Agreement on Water Quantity in the Great Lakes-St. Lawrence River Basin," paper prepared for International Joint Commission, Great Lakes-St. Lawrence Level Study, Functional Group 5, workshop on alternative policies and governance approaches for lake-related issues, Indianapolis, February 8-10, 1989.

50. Ibid., p. 2.

51. See Michael J. Donahue and Holly Hartman, "Toward an Institutional and Policy Framework for Addressing Great Lakes Water Level Fluctuations: A Case

Study Approach,'' paper prepared for International Joint Commission Reference Study on Fluctuating Water Levels, Functional Group 3, 1989.

52. C. Southam and S. Dumont, "CO$_2$-induced Climate Change and Its Potential Impact on Great Lakes Levels and Outflows," paper presented at the 31st Conference on Great Lakes Research, McMaster University, Hamilton, Ontario, May 17-20, 1988; T. E. Croley and Holly Hartman, "Great Lakes Levels' Response to Climate Change," paper presented at the 31st Conference on Great Lakes Research, McMaster University, Hamilton, Ontario, May 17-20, 1988; L. T. Wong, J. A. McCorquodale, and M. E. Sanderson, *Future Great Lakes Levels: Environmental and Political Impacts*, report to the Donner Canadian Foundation from the Great Lakes Institute (GLI) (Windsor, Ont.: University of Windsor, 1988); and *Impacts of Climate Change on the Great Lakes Basin*, report of the First U.S.–Canada Symposium on Impacts of Climate Change on the Great Lakes Basin (Rockville, Md.: National Climate Program Office, 1989).

53. World Commission on Environment and Development, *Our Common Future* (Oxford: Oxford University Press, 1987) p. 8.

54. Ibid., p. 9.

55. The Water Quality Board urges that "the principle of sustainable development should be applied within the basin": International Joint Commission, *1989 Report on Great Lakes Quality*, pp. xii, 133-34.

## What Will It Cost to Clean Up Areas of Concern?

1. David J. Rapport, "Review of the Great Lakes Remedial Action Programs: What Might the RAPs Accomplish and What Might It Cost?" report prepared for Statistics Canada and the Institute for Research on Public Policy, May 1989. For his work, Rapport drew on Cate Leger, "Cleaning Up Great Lakes Toxic Hotspots: How Much Will It Cost: How Can It Be Paid For?" (Washington, D.C.: Northeast-Midwest Institute, 1989), working draft.

2. Rapport, "Review of the Great Lakes Remedial Action Programs," pp. 11, 13.

## Federal Funding for U.S. Great Lakes Programs

1. Conservation Foundation calculations from U.S. Environmental Protection Agency annual budget submissions to U.S. Congress, using deflator for federal nondefense purchases.

2. Center for the Great Lakes et al., *Funding for Federal Great Lakes Environmental Programs: A White Paper* (Chicago: Center for the Great Lakes, May 1989).

## Michigan's Environmental Budget

1. The percentage change represents "full-time equivalent" personnel. Michigan Department of Natural Resources Office of Budget and Federal Aid, "Budget Trends and Problems FY75-76 through FY86-87; Budget Opportunities FY87-88 and Beyond," report to to Michigan Natural Resources Commission, October 1986; and conversation with Dennis Adams, chief of Office of Budget and Federal Aid, Michigan Department of Natural Resources.

2. Michigan Department of Natural Resources, Office of Budget and Federal Aid, "Opportunities for a Better Michigan: Budget Initiatives Fiscal Year 1987-88," undated, p. 2.

3. Ibid., p. 3; and Michigan Department of Natural Resources, "Budget Trends and Problems FY75-76 through FY86-87," p. 57.

4. Michigan Department of Natural Resources, Office of the Great Lakes, "Great Lakes Initiative," report prepared for U.S. Congress, House and Senate Budget Subcommittee hearings, spring 1988, p. 1.

5. David Hales, director, Michigan Department of Natural Resources, memo to "Supporters of Michigan's Environment," "$800 Million Bond Proposal," September 16, 1988.

## Figures

9.1. International Joint Commission, Great Lakes Water Quality Board, *1987 Report on Great Lakes Quality* (Windsor, Ont.: International Joint Commission, 1987).

9.2. Canadian Hydrographic Navigation Map (1984); T. N. Watson, Hamilton, Ontario, cartographer.

9.3. Illustrations courtesy of Jim McEvoy, Wisconsin Department of Natural Resources.

9.4. Center for the Great Lakes et al., *Funding for Federal Great Lakes Environmental Programs: A White Paper* (Chicago: Center for the Great Lakes, 1989), p. 19; Terry Grindstaff, U.S. Environmental Protection Agency, Office of the Comptroller, Budget Division, personal communication, June 15, 1989; U.S. Department of Commerce, Bureau of the Census, *Statistical Abstract of the United States—1989* (Washington, D.C.: U.S. Government Printing Office, 1989), p. 464; Jim Dobbs, U.S. Bureau of Economic Analysis, personal communication, June 19, 1989.

9.5. Canada, House of Commons Debates (Hansard), September 16, 1987, p. 9018.

## 10. TOWARDS 2000, AND BEYOND

1. This theme, using other examples in North America, has recently been developed by John McPhee, *The Control of Nature* (New York: Strauss, Farrar & Giroux, 1989).

2. 1978 Water Quality Agreement, Article II.

# Index

effects of Love Canal on, 59*b*
exposure pathways, 174-81
mirex and, 172, 181
potential effects of toxic substances
    on, 181-82
public health data, 169-70
wildlife as indicators for, 168-69
Health and Welfare Canada, 170
Herring gulls, 27-28, 132, 139
Hormonal changes in wildlife, 139
Human impact, 2-3, 13, 141-47

**I**

IJC. *See* International Joint Commission
Illinois, shoreline management and,
    111-12
Implementing programs, 193-226, 233
Incineration, 70, 125
Indicators of health, 26, 168-69, 188*f*-
    91*f*
Industrial development, 51-56
Industrial dischargers, compliance and,
    220-21
Industry
    in Hamilton Harbour, 206-9
    toxic substances and, 12
Injection wells, 80
Institutions in the Great Lakes Basin, 8*f*
Integrated Atmospheric Deposition
    Network, 114
Integrated pest management (IPM), 47
International Association for Great
    Lakes Research, 216
International Joint Commission (IJC), 9,
    10*f*, 195, 198-201
    Great Lakes Water Quality Board, 9,
        20-21, 22*f*-23*f*, 85, 199
    implementation of programs and, 194
    International Air Quality Advisory
        Board, 121
    Levels Reference Project
        Management Team, 110
    Love Canal and, 57
    Science Advisory Board, 9, 147, 199
        accidental spills and, 61, 66

Ecosystem Objectives Committee,
    25-26
    measuring ecosystem health and,
        25
    sewage treatment and, 53
International Reference Group on Great
    Lakes Pollution from Land Use
    Activities (PLUARG), 9, 195
IPM. *See* Integrated pest management

**J**

Joint Strategic Plan for Great Lakes
    Fisheries, 160

**L**

Laboratory studies, wildlife and, 141,
    142*b*
Lac Saint-François, 102
Lac Saint-Louis, 102
Lac Saint-Pierre, 102
Lachine Canal, effect of on settlement,
    36
Lake Erie
    Areas of Concern in, 201-4
    bald eagles and, 135*b*
    contaminated sediments in, 103
    dredging in, 104
    eutrophication in, 95
    fertilizers and, 42, 43*f*
    fish in, 148-49, 157-58
    global warming and, 130
    International Joint Commission and,
        9
    nitrate levels in, 90-91, 95
    pesticides and, 39
    population in drainage basin of, 32-
        33
    sea lamprey and, 155
    sewage treatment and, 53
    silting in, 36
    water level of, 106
    water quality of, 94-96
Lake Huron
    Areas of Concern in, 201-4
    bald eagles and, 135*b*
    contaminated sediments in, 102-3

International Joint Commission and,
9
lake trout as an indicator of
ecosystem health for, 160
population in drainage basin of, 32,
33f
sea lamprey and, 155
sewage treatment and, 53
silica in, 94
water levels of, 107
water quality of, 93-94
Lake levels, 106-10, 130, 225
Lake Michigan
Areas of Concern in, 201-4
birds and, 28, 135b
contaminated sediments in, 103
diatom growth and, 132
dredging in, 104
eutrophication in, 92
fish in, 155, 160, 172-74
Green Bay, 209-12
groundwater contribution to, 77
industrial development and, 51
International Joint Commission and,
9
population in drainage basin of, 32-
33
sedimentation in, 51
silica in, 92-93
water levels of, 107
water quality of, 92-93
Lake Ontario
Areas of Concern in, 201-4
atmospheric interaction with, 97
biomagnification in, 19f
birds and, 28, 135b
contaminated sediments in, 103
fish in, 98, 149-50, 160
groundwater contribution to, 77
Hamilton Harbour, 206-9
International Joint Commission and,
9
Love Canal and, 57
mirex and, 181
nitrate levels in, 90-91
population in drainage basin of, 32-
33

St. Lawrence River and, 102
sea lamprey and, 155
water quality of, 97-99
Lake St. Clair, 39, 42, 43, 53, 107
Lake Superior
Areas of Concern in, 201-4
bald eagles and, 135b
contaminated sediments in, 102-3
ecosystem indicator for, 25
fish in, 148-49, 157-58, 159
forage shortage in, 160-61
industrial development and, 51
International Joint Commission and,
9
paper mills and, 49
PCBs in, 28-29
population in drainage basin of, 32,
33f
water quality of, 88-92
Lake trout, 25, 150, 154, 159, 177
Lake Winnebago, 79
Land, 31-74
agricultural activities, 38-47
colonial settlement of, 35-38
forest activities, 47-51
hazardous wastes, 56-66
industrial development, 51-56
parks and protected areas, 72-74
solid wastes, 66-72
-water ratio, 1
Landfills, 67-68, 69-70, 125
Lawsuits, 222, 223-24
Logging, 47-48, 50
Love Canal, 56-57, 59-60, 169
Lynx, 146-47

## M

Mass-balance model, 126
Maumee River, silting and, 36
Mayfly, as indicator of ecosystem
health, 26
Mercury
acidity and, 86
fish and, 3, 98, 157, 158
paper mills and, 49
St. Louis Bay and, 124-25